THE DAY IT RAINED MILITIA

THE DAY IT RAINED MILITIA

Huck's Defeat and the Revolution
in the South Carolina Backcountry
May–July 1780

MICHAEL C. SCOGGINS
Foreword by Dr. Walter Edgar

THE
History
PRESS

Published by The History Press
Charleston, SC 29403
www.historypress.net

Front Cover: Whig militia open fire on the loyalists at Williamson's Plantation on the morning of 12 July 1780. *Photograph by the author, from a reenactment at Historic Brattonsville, McConnels, South Carolina.*

Back Cover: New York Volunteers mount a bayonet charge against the rebel lines as smoke fills the air from the Whit volleys. *Photograph by the author, from a reenactment at Historic Brattonsville.*

First published 2005
Second printing 2011

Manufactured in the United States

ISBN 978-1-59629-015-0

Library of Congress Cataloging-in-Publication Data

Scoggins, Michael C.
The day it rained militia : Huck's defeat and the revolution in the South Carolina backcountry, May-July, 1780 / Michael C. Scoggins ; with a foreword by Walter Edgar.
p. cm.
Includes bibliographical references and index.
ISBN 1-59629-015-3 (alk. paper)
1. South Carolina--History--Revolution, 1775-1783--Campaigns. 2. United States--History--Revolution, 1775-1783--Campaigns. I. Title.
E.263.S7S23 2005
973.3'36'09757--dc22
2005011675

To my family

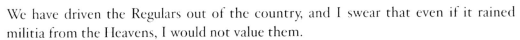

We have driven the Regulars out of the country, and I swear that even if it rained militia from the Heavens, I would not value them.

Captain Christian Huck to the James Williamson family on the morning of 12 July 1780.

Captain Huck was attacked this morning about sunrise by a large body of rebels and has been totally defeated. Captain Huck they inform me is killed.

Lieutenant Colonel George Turnbull to Lieutenant Colonel Francis, Lord Rawdon, on the afternoon of 12 July 1780.

Contents

Foreword by Dr. Walter Edgar   9
Acknowledgements   11
Introduction   13

Chapter I. "I turned my course into the new acquisition"   19
Chapter II. "A vindictive asperity not easily restrained"   41
Chapter III. "God Almighty had become a Rebel"   57
Chapter IV. "English Sanity is thrown away"   93
Chapter V. "A good dressing before day light"   109
Chapter VI. "Their success will no doubt Encourage them"   143
Epilogue. Some observations on the South Carolina Backcountry militia   155

Appendix A. Accounts of Huck's Defeat in pension applications   161
Appendix B. British Army correspondence, June–July 1780   185
Appendix C. How many men were in the battle?   205
Appendix D. The Huck's Defeat battlefield   209
Appendix E. A biography of Christian Huck   215
Appendix F. Roster of soldiers at the Battle of Huck's Defeat   229

Notes   243
Bibliography   279
Index   305
About the Author   317

Foreword

The Battle of Huck's Defeat (or the Battle of Williamson's Plantation as it is sometimes known) was one of the more significant battles of the American Revolution. Alas, today, it—like many other battles of the Southern Campaign in the American Revolution—has been forgotten. American history, especially the history of the war that won us our independence, has taken a shorter, less historical route from Lexington and Concord, Massachusetts, to Yorktown, Virginia. In many American history textbooks, there is little or nothing about the Revolutionary War in the South. But, as the British know (just read their accounts from the eighteenth century to the present), they lost the war in the backwoods of South Carolina.

On 12 July 1780, the South Carolina militia defeated a detachment of Banastre Tarleton's feared British Legion. That in itself was a significant accomplishment, but the psychological effect of this victory in what was then the New Acquisition District of South Carolina reverberated far beyond the immediate vicinity. The victory bolstered the hopes of patriots all across the northern districts. Men flocked to join the various partisan bands under Thomas Sumter, William Bratton, William Hill, Edward Lacey, William Davie and others. Conversely, those men who might have been inclined to join Tory militia units had second thoughts—especially hearing reports of this battle and its aftermath: "[M]any of the wounded Tories escaped into the woods," noted Lacey's biographer, "and were afterwards found dead."[1]

Just two weeks after Lord Cornwallis had confidently reported to his superiors that he had South Carolina well under control, he received word of the Battle at Williamson's Plantation in the New Acquisition District. He was not a happy man: "The unlucky affair that happened to the detachment of Captain Huck of the Legion has given me great uneasiness."

Cornwallis had every reason to be concerned. For, from this date onward, he faced mounting opposition to the British occupation of South Carolina. Especially in the northern districts along the South Carolina–North Carolina border, partisan warfare erupted violently—and with a vengeance.

---

1. Maurice A. Moore, *The Life of Gen. Edward Lacey* (Spartanburg, SC: Douglas, Evins & Co., 1859), 10.

In this wonderfully detailed account of the Battle of Huck's Defeat, Michael Scoggins provides twenty-first-century readers with an opportunity to learn more about the battle, the events leading up to it and its place in American history. The Battle of Huck's Defeat was just the first of nearly two dozen defeats that the partisans of South Carolina would inflict on the British Army of occupation over the course of two months of 1780. And, only twenty miles and eighty-five days separated the defeat of Captain Christian Huck of the British Legion and the magnificent partisan triumph at the Battle of Kings Mountain.

Walter Edgar
Columbia, South Carolina
6 February 2005

Acknowledgements

The cooperation and assistance of a great many individuals and institutions went into the research and production of this book. I would like to express my appreciation and indebtedness first of all to Dr. Bobby G. Moss of Blacksburg, South Carolina, whose pioneering research on the Revolutionary War soldiers of this state—both patriot and Loyalist—made it possible to track down the names and service records of many of the soldiers who fought in the Battle of Huck's Defeat. Reading the firsthand accounts of the men from what are now York and Chester Counties who fought in the American Revolution is an incredible experience for a military historian, and Dr. Moss's dedication and hard work made tracking those accounts down a much easier task. The work of two other historians also inspired me on this project. Allan W. Eckert's amazing series of books on the settlement of the Ohio frontier demonstrates how primary source records can be turned into fascinating historical narratives that outclass any work of fiction. Dr. Lawrence E. Babit's painstaking study of the Battle of Cowpens, *A Devil of a Whipping*, shows how a modern historian can reconstruct a Revolutionary War battle by bringing together information from Federal pension applications and other fragmentary first-person accounts. Honorable mention should also go to Brent H. Holcomb and Elmer O. Parker, whose transcription and publication of the early court records of North and South Carolina provided much needed background on the eighteenth-century settlers of the Carolina Upcountry.

I would like to extend my lasting gratitude to the interlibrary loan staff of the Dacus Library at Winthrop University in Rock Hill, South Carolina. Jackie McFadden, Camille Livingston, Ann Thomas and Doug Short tirelessly worked to track down "many a curious and quaint volume of forgotten lore," no matter how obscure or hard to find, and I owe them a great debt. Likewise Gina Price-White of the Winthrop University Archives was of great help in my research. Robert McIntosh and the rest of the staff at the South Carolina Department of Archives and History rendered tremendous assistance during the many hours I spent there. Other institutions whose resources I utilized include the York County Public Library, the Chester County Public Library, the Spartanburg County Library, South Caroliniana Library and the Spartanburg County Regional Museum of History.

For permission to reproduce drawings, photographs and period documents, I would like to acknowledge the Sumter County Museum, the South Caroliniana Library, the University of South

Carolina Press, the Library of Congress, the National Archives (Public Record Office) of Great Britain, the Wisconsin Historical Society, the Company of Military Historians, the South Carolina Historical Society, the New-York Historical Society and two of South Carolina's excellent military artists, Mr. Robert Windsor Wilson of Woodruff and Mr. Darby Erd of Columbia.

I would also like to extend my warmest thanks to the following individuals and groups for their support and assistance in putting this book together: the historical reenactors of the New Acquisition Regiment (NAM), for sharing their expertise on eighteenth-century camp life, militia drill, weapons and tactics, and for the opportunity to "serve" with them during a reenactment of the Battle of Huck's Defeat; to John Misskelley of the NAM, for pointing out the numerous references to Huck's Defeat and Sumter's men in the Lyman C. Draper Manuscript Collection and for sharing his research on the battle and soldiers in the battle; to Bob McCann, Kip Carter and Joe Hinson of the NAM for their support on this project and for sharing their knowledge of the Revolution in the Backcountry; to Patrick O'Kelley of the Second North Carolina Regiment, for sharing his research on the Revolutionary War in the Carolinas; to Todd Braisted, for answering my endless questions about the Royal Provincial soldiers of the British Legion and the New York Volunteers, and for his excellent Web site The On-Line Institute for Advanced Loyalist Studies (www.royalprovincials.com), which he and Nan Cole maintain; to Marge Baskin, for providing me with copies of Christian Huck's service records in Emmerick's Chasseurs, and for sharing her research on Huck, Banastre Tarleton, Lord Rawdon, and other British and Provincial officers via e-mails and on her Web site Oatmeal for the Foxhounds: Banastre Tarleton and the British Legion (www.banastretarleton.org); to my coworkers at the Historical Center of York County, Nancy Sambets and Heather South, for all of their help on this project; to interns Les Arkin and Jennifer Brown, who assisted me in my research on the soldiers at Huck's Defeat; to Sam Thomas and Chuck LeCount of the Culture & Heritage Museums, for sharing their knowledge on the Revolution and for proofreading the manuscript; to Pat Veasey and Sarah LeCount, for providing input on Backcountry domestic life during the Revolution; to the rest of the staff, management and volunteers of the Culture & Heritage Museums, for their support and encouragement; and last but not least, to Kirsten Sutton, Amanda Lidderdale, Julie Hiester and all the other talented folks at The History Press in Charleston, South Carolina, for their support and assistance in bringing this project to publication.

Introduction

In the early summer of 1780, when the Revolutionary War in the Southern states seemed doomed to failure, a small but important battle took place on the plantation of James Williamson in what is now York County, South Carolina. This battle, fought between local Carolina militiamen on one side and Provincial and Loyalist soldiers on the other, proved to be a harbinger of things to come for the British campaign to reclaim the Southern colonies. Early on the morning of 12 July 1780, several companies of men from General Thomas Sumter's partisan brigade ambushed a combined force of British Legion cavalry, New York Volunteers and local Loyalist militia, all operating under the command of Captain Christian Huck. In a few short minutes of fighting, Sumter's men completely routed the Loyalists in a battle that became an archetype for the partisan war in the South Carolina Backcountry. In later years, the Whig veterans referred to this engagement by a variety of names—including the Battle of Williamson's Plantation, the Battle of Williamson's Lane and the Battle of Bratton's Plantation—but since that time, it has become more commonly known simply as Huck's Defeat. In the struggle for control of the Carolinas, Huck's Defeat was a precursor to the larger-scale defeats the British suffered at Kings Mountain and Cowpens, also in the South Carolina Backcountry. This engagement demonstrated for the first time that local militiamen could fight and win against better-equipped Provincial forces of the British Army. It boosted the morale of a people who had almost given up on the cause of American independence and demonstrated to the British that South Carolina was not a conquered state, as was frequently boasted after the surrender of Charleston in May 1780.

The story of Huck's Defeat begins with an examination of the experiences of the South Carolina Backcountry settlers during the late colonial period and the first five years of the Revolution. These experiences heavily influenced the behavior of these settlers after the British captured Charleston in May 1780. The story continues with a day-by-day chronology of happenings in the Backcountry during the critical months of May, June and July 1780, when the British occupation created a cause-and-effect sequence of events that unfolded like a game of dominoes. Geographically, the primary focus is the area between the Broad and Catawba Rivers encompassed by the modern South Carolina counties of York, Chester and Fairfield, but the wider scope of interrelated events in the North and South Carolina Backcountry is also analyzed. And finally, examination of the battle's aftermath helps demonstrate how this small patriot victory dramatically influenced subsequent events and helped pave the way for the larger American victories at Kings Mountain and Cowpens. The ultimate goal is to restore Huck's Defeat to its proper place within the greater context of the Southern Campaign of the Revolutionary War and thus present a truer picture of the battle's overall significance in the struggle for American independence.

In order to piece together an accurate picture of exactly what happened that day at Williamson's Plantation, the modern historian must rely heavily on accounts written by the victorious South Carolina militiamen who ambushed Huck's detachment as well as the descendants of those militiamen. Most of these veterans were Scotch-Irish Presbyterians[2] from the Broad and Catawba River Valleys, and their common background and their shared experiences on the South Carolina frontier clearly shaped their reminiscences. Very few of these written accounts predate the year 1800, and the vast majority was only written down when the participants were applying for Revolutionary War pensions in the 1830s and 1840s. In the minds of many of these aging veterans and their descendants, the battle had taken on a magnitude out of proportion to its original scale. The numerous accounts that have survived are filled with inconsistencies, exaggerations and contradictions, and thus it is necessary to evaluate the reliability of each witness and attempt to reconcile the conflicting information contained in his or her account with that found in similar accounts from other sources. This problem in not unique to the American Revolution; historians encounter such problems when evaluating eyewitness accounts of battles in any war. For instance, Stephen Ambrose faced a similar situation when he interviewed American and British World War II veterans for his books *Pegasus Bridge* and *Band of Brothers*. Ambrose noted that the men's statements were sometimes "inaccurate and exaggerated," and that they "frequently contradicted each other on small points, and very occasionally on big ones." Thus he found it necessary to use his "best judgment [in determining] what was true, what had been misremembered, what had been exaggerated by the soldiers telling their war stories, [and] what acts of heroism had been played down by a man too modest to brag on himself."[3]

As is the case for most of the small skirmishes and battles in the Carolina Backcountry, there are no firsthand accounts from the British soldiers at Huck's Defeat—or at least, none has yet been found. In fact, most of the so-called "British soldiers" in the battle were actually Americans who were still loyal to Great Britain. Some of these Loyalists were Provincial soldiers from New York and Pennsylvania who were transferred to the South in 1779 and 1780, while others were militiamen from upper South Carolina who supported the British cause. The only accounts that tell their side are a few short notices in the letters and diaries of British and Loyalist officers who were not present at the battle, and they give only the barest of details.

In the nineteenth century, both popular writers and historians took up the story of the Revolution in South Carolina and gave the story of Huck's Defeat new life as a glamorized and romanticized example of the heroic struggle between "noble Patriots," "bloodthirsty Tories" and "inhuman British monsters." The books and articles penned by these writers and historians varied greatly as to accuracy, detail and documentation, but they were widely read and continue to influence historians and writers today. While these nineteenth-century histories record legitimate local and family traditions that were not documented elsewhere, they also contain many errors and distortions, and must be evaluated with great caution.

In attempting to reconstruct the events covered in this book, it is necessary to evaluate the evidence from all the sources available and make value judgments on what is reliable and accurate, and what is unreliable and inaccurate. No source can be accepted as completely reliable, but no source should be rejected as completely unreliable. By comparing and analyzing all of the firsthand, secondhand and thirdhand accounts, it is possible to come up with a general consensus of what actually happened. Such techniques are frequently utilized by military historians when reconstructing ancient battles in detail. To cite one of the better examples, Dr. Lawrence E. Babits of Eastern Carolina University studied hundreds of pension applications and other firsthand accounts while researching another famous Revolutionary War battle in the South Carolina Backcountry. The result was his book *A Devil of a Whipping*, a detailed examination of the Battle of Cowpens.[4]

As often as practical, the actual words of the men and women who lived through the Revolution are used to describe the events in this book. Provided in the appendices are extensive transcriptions of many of these primary source documents; detailed discussions of some of the more problematic aspects of the Battle of Huck's Defeat, such as the number of men involved and the precise location of the battlefield; a biography of Captain Christian Huck; and a listing of all known participants in the battle. An overview of the sources used in this book accompanies the bibliography.

A Note on Terminology

The Americans who fought for independence from Great Britain between 1775 and 1783 almost universally described themselves as "Whigs." They referred to their countrymen who remained loyal to Great Britain as "Tories" or, less frequently, as "Loyalists" or "Royalists." The terms "Whig" and "Tory" were then (and still are) the names of British political parties, but during the Revolution they became synonymous with "rebel" and "loyalist." The British soldiers and American Loyalists generally referred to the Whigs simply as "rebels" (often capitalized), and to themselves as "the King's troops" or "the Crown forces." By the early nineteenth century, most Americans had adopted the term "patriot" to denote their Whig ancestors.

Both the American and British armies consisted of full-time soldiers of the "regular" service and part-time soldiers of the militia. During the Revolution, the American regulars were the Continental Army; the British regulars were well-trained professional soldiers of the British Army. While the regular soldiers were important in all phases of the Revolution, much of the military action in the Southern Campaign, especially after May 1780, was fought by militia. Technically, the militia consisted of all free males between the ages of sixteen and sixty, and could include individuals of European, Native American and African American ancestry. Every colony or state in America was required to raise, equip and train its own militia, but in actual practice the training and equipment varied from minimal to excellent, usually falling somewhere in between. In the Carolina Backcountry after the fall of Charleston, the Whig militia generally outperformed the Tory militia in battle, due partly to greater resolve and partly to more military experience and better leaders. By the summer of 1780, many Whig militiamen were veterans of five years or more of Continental and/or militia service, and they performed functions that the regular American Army, or Continental Army, never could.

When describing military actions in the South, the Whig militiamen generally did not distinguish between the professional soldiers of the British Army and the soldiers serving in the British Provincial regiments that were raised in North America. The Whigs referred to both Provincials and British regulars as "British soldiers," without differentiating between the two, and they almost always referred to Loyalist militiamen simply as "Tories." The term "Provincials" was the official British designation for Loyalist units recruited and trained in North America during the colonial wars and the Revolution, as opposed to the units of the "Regular Establishment" of the British Army who were natives of Great Britain and Ireland. While the Provincials did not rank as high in the British military establishment as the professional soldiers of the Regular Army, they were better equipped and better trained than the Loyalist militia, and Provincial officers always outranked militia officers in the field, even when they were technically of a lower rating. Provincial units were often commanded by experienced British soldiers transferred from the regular service; well-known examples in the Southern Campaign were the British Legion, commanded by Lieutenant Colonel Banastre Tarleton; the New York Volunteers, commanded by Lieutenant Colonel George Turnbull; and the American Volunteers, commanded by Major Patrick Ferguson. All three officers were veterans of the British Army, while their units were composed chiefly of American Loyalists.

In the Southern Campaign, the most effective soldiers on both sides were frequently the cavalry, that is, soldiers mounted on horseback. Their horses afforded them great mobility, and the shock value of charging cavalry was unparalleled in battle. In both the Continental and British Army, the mounted soldiers or cavalry were usually referred to as "dragoons." When the Revolution began, the terms technically meant two different types of soldier. Cavalry were trained to fight from horseback with sabers and firearms, while dragoons rode their horses to battle but then dismounted and fought on foot like infantry soldiers. In actual practice, the term dragoon quickly came to be synonymous with cavalryman, and during most of the Revolution the terms were used interchangeably. Tarleton's British Legion was a mixed corps composed of both cavalry and infantry, but his horsemen were almost always referred to as dragoons. Turnbull's New York Volunteers included several companies of mounted infantry, who were also usually referred to as dragoons, at least by their enemies in the Whig militia. The Whig militiamen in the Carolina Backcountry were also for the most part mounted, and used their horses to great advantage in moving quickly from place to place. Both Whig and Tory mounted militia often called themselves "rangers," a term originally used to refer to the mounted South Carolina state troops and Continentals who patrolled the frontier and the Backcountry during the colonial wars and the early years of the Revolution. The mounted militia sometimes also referred to themselves as cavalry and did occasionally fight from horseback like actual cavalry, although technically they were really dragoons because they usually rode to battle and fought dismounted. But as noted earlier, the difference between dragoon and cavalryman in common usage was practically nonexistent by the summer of 1780.

Finally, a note on spelling and punctuation of quoted material is in order. This book contains a great many quotations and literal transcriptions of Revolutionary War-period documents, including letters, memoirs, reminiscences, pension applications and so on. I have made every effort to reproduce this quoted material exactly as it appeared in the original sources, which presents many problems for the modern reader. Spelling and punctuation in eighteenth- and nineteenth-century documents were far from standardized, and varied greatly from individual to individual and document to document. In some cases, I have added letters to words to make them more recognizable, while in other cases I have left them as they originally appeared. Periods and commas have occasionally be added where none existed originally, again to make the meaning of the quoted passage more clear to the modern reader. In most cases, however, the passages appear in the text exactly as they appeared in the original documents, with all peculiarities of spelling, punctuation and obsolete usage intact.

Portion of a 1787 map drawn by William Faden, geographer to King George III, showing the Carolina Backcountry during the American Revolution. *From an original copy of* A History of the Campaigns of 1780 and 1781 in the Southern Provinces of North America *by Banastre Tarleton (Second Edition, 1796). Courtesy of the South Caroliniana Library, University of South Carolina, Columbia, South Carolina.*

Chapter I

"I turned my course into the new acquisition"

South Carolina can be divided geographically into three sections: the swampy coastal plain or "Lowcountry"; the sandy midlands; and the hilly "Upcountry," which transitions into the mountains of the northwest. During the eighteenth century, the middle and upper portions of the state were both considered to be part of the "Backcountry." To most modern readers the term "Backcountry" might be regarded as synonymous with "Upcountry," but during the early history of the state the South Carolina Backcountry was considered to extend from well below the fall line of the rivers, through the foothills of the Piedmont region and into the Appalachian and Blue Ridge Mountains. In South Carolina, the Lowcountry was settled first, in the seventeenth century, and rapidly developed an economy based on large plantations and mercantile enterprises centered in the provincial capital of Charleston.

The Backcountry remained solely inhabited by American Indian tribes, such as the Catawbas and Cherokees, until about 1750, when settlers began filtering into the region from the Lowcountry and from Pennsylvania, Maryland, Virginia and North Carolina. During the French and Indian War, the South Carolina Backcountry became a refuge for families fleeing the bloody conflict on the Appalachian frontiers of Pennsylvania and Virginia. Many of these refugees were Protestants from the north of Ireland who called themselves "Scotch-Irish." The Scotch-Irish were for the most part Presbyterians whose ancestors moved from Lowland Scotland and northern England to the Ulster Province in northern Ireland in the sixteenth century. The descendants of these "Scotch colonists in Ulster" launched a second great migration from Ulster to North America, where—along with large numbers of German settlers—they thickly settled the western frontiers of Pennsylvania and Virginia in the early seventeenth century. In July 1755, the disastrous defeat of General Edward Braddock's British Army by French and Indian forces on the Ohio frontier prompted thousands of Scotch-Irish and German families to move down the Great Philadelphia Wagon Road from Pennsylvania and Virginia into the fertile valleys of the upper Catawba and Yadkin Valleys of western North Carolina. After populating the colonial North Carolina counties of Orange, Anson, Rowan, Mecklenburg and Tryon, they spread south down the Great Wagon Road and made their homes along the Saluda, Broad, Catawba and Lynches River systems in upper South Carolina.[5]

In order to issue land grants to these new settlers, and collect taxes from them, the South Carolina Colonial Assembly needed to create counties and parishes in the Backcountry. In 1750, the assembly extended the boundaries of its original three coastal counties—named after the Lords Proprietors Colleton, Berkeley and Craven—to the north and west to encompass the Upcountry. The assembly also created a new county, named Granville, to include the growing settlements along the Savannah River. Craven County was by far the largest of these early divisions and included all of the Backcountry above the Saluda-Congaree-Santee River system. Between 1757 and 1768, the South Carolina Colonial Assembly further divided the Backcountry into three parishes: St. Matthew's Parish, which extended from the Savannah River to the Congaree and Santee Rivers; St. Mark's Parish, from the Congaree and Santee Rivers to Lynches River; and St. David's Parish, from Lynches River to the easternmost boundary of the state.[6]

In spite of their impressive titles, however, these counties and parishes were nothing more than lines on a map for the convenience of issuing land grants and collecting taxes, and the inhabitants of the South Carolina Backcountry still did not have any local government, courts of law or representation in Charleston.[7] To make matters worse for the early settlers, before 1764 the border between North and South Carolina had been surveyed from the Atlantic coast only as far west as the Peedee River, and the governments of the two colonies could not agree on the boundary west of the Peedee. Throughout the period of the border dispute, North Carolina also claimed much of what is now upper South Carolina and assigned the territory to the early North Carolina counties of Anson (1750–1762), Mecklenburg (1762–1768) and Tryon (1768–1772). Between 1750 and 1772, both states issued hundreds of land grants in the area north of the 34th parallel between the Peedee River and the Cherokee territory. While South Carolina was handing out grants in the counties of Granville and Craven, as well as in the parishes of St. Mark, St. David and St. Matthew, North Carolina was granting land within the same territory as part of its counties of Anson, Mecklenburg and Tryon.[8] Unlike South Carolina, North Carolina actually established courts in these frontier counties, and many of the inhabitants along the border looked to the north, rather than to the south, for protection and legal jurisdiction. Other settlers preferred to play the two colonies against each other, claiming citizenship in one colony to avoid paying taxes to the other, and the area became a haven for debtors, runaways, squatters and outlaws.[9] The two colonies also disagreed over which province would claim the Catawba Indian Nation, a situation that was not settled until the final resolution of the border dispute placed the Catawba Nation within the territory of South Carolina.[10]

In late 1759, the Cherokees went to war in an effort to drive the newcomers out of their territory, and in 1761, Lieutenant Colonel James Grant of the British Army led a large military expedition of British regulars and colonial militia into the Indian lands to quell the uprising. Many of the South Carolina officers who later were to distinguish themselves during the American Revolution received their first taste of battle during the Cherokee War of 1760–1761.[11] The peace treaty that ended that conflict established the Indian Line of 1767—a boundary located along the present-day Greenville-Spartanburg and Anderson-Abbeville county lines—and the territory west of that line came to be known as "Indian Land" or "Cherokee Land." This treaty quieted the Cherokees for a time and officially opened the Backcountry east of the Indian Line to settlement.[12]

In 1764, the two Carolinas received a royal commission to extend the provincial boundary line along the 35th parallel to run from the Peedee River to the old Salisbury-Charlotte road in

North Carolina just east of the Catawba territory. However, the surveyors mistakenly ran the line about eleven miles south of the actual 35th parallel, causing South Carolina to lose some 422,000 acres to North Carolina.[13] Although the 1764 commission forbade the extension of the boundary line west of the Catawba lands, the population of the western settlements continued to grow and the North Carolina government aggressively lobbied for a boundary extension. In 1767, North Carolina Governor Arthur Dobbs ordered the 1764 line to be extended to the Saluda River. South Carolina rejected this survey and the establishment of Tryon County in the disputed area without the consent of the British government. A portion of the 1767 province line west of the Catawba River still exists as the modern border between York and Chester Counties.[14]

By the late 1760s, almost three-fourths of South Carolina's white population resided in the Backcountry, but the area was still too far removed from the government in Charleston for the effective enforcement of law and order. Following the end of the Cherokee War, the region became a refuge for criminals; bands of outlaws called *banditti* roamed the area, plundering homes and travelers, stealing horses and rustling livestock.[15] The colonial governments of both Carolinas complained to the British government about the difficulties of collecting taxes in the disputed areas, the general contempt for courts and officers, the confusion through duplication of land grants and the virtual anarchy that prevailed in some regions of the Backcountry. The continuing controversy over the provincial boundary hampered militia organization, Indian affairs, imperial relations and the most basic functions of government and commerce in the disputed areas.[16] Meanwhile the residents of the South Carolina Backcountry repeatedly petitioned the colonial government to establish courts, appoint sheriffs and allow them to send representatives to the legislature. The pleas of the Backcountry for assistance, and for proper representation in the colonial government, met with little action in Charleston; the settlers were forced to take the law into their own hands by forming vigilante groups called Regulators.[17]

During the winter of 1767–1768, the Regulators effectively eliminated the gangs of outlaws roaming the South Carolina Backcountry. Unfortunately, many of the Regulators then used their authority to settle personal grudges and enforce their own ideas of law and order. Alarmed by this trend, some of the more influential residents of the Backcountry organized a counter-Regulator, or Moderator, movement to curb the Regulators' excesses and became guilty of equal excesses themselves. With the support of the South Carolina government, a Backcountry leader of ill repute named Joseph Coffell raised his own vigilante band and began taking revenge on the Regulators.[18] The Regulators considered Coffell to be nothing more than a criminal and the leader of a gang of "rogues." Coffell's followers soon became known as Coffellites, and in a derogatory corruption of Coffell's name, the Regulators in both Carolinas referred to them as Scoffelites, Scopholites or Scovelites. Confrontations between the two parties frequently erupted into armed conflict, and the civilian populace suffered depredations from both sides. Although the government eventually brought the conflict between the Regulators and the Scoffelites under control, the war left a lasting mark on the Backcountry. Within a few short years, leaders of both parties once again took sides in an even more divisive conflict.[19]

In an effort to address these and other problems, in 1769 the South Carolina Colonial Assembly passed the Circuit Court Act, which created three legal districts in the Backcountry

In 1769, the South Carolina Colonial Assembly divided the province into seven legal districts. Following the border survey of 1772, the newly acquired territory taken from North Carolina was incorporated into the Ninety Six District and the Camden District. *South Carolina Circuit Court District Map compiled by Historical Records Survey, Works Progress Administration, 1938. Courtesy of the South Carolina Department of Archives and History, Columbia, South Carolina.*

with a courthouse and jail in each: the Ninety Six District, stretching from the Savannah River to the Broad River; the Camden District, from the Broad River to Lynches River, territory that included the Catawba River Valley; and the Cheraw District, extending eastward from the Lynches River to the Peedee River.[20] Meanwhile, the mistakes in the 1764 survey became painfully obvious, and South Carolina commissioned a new survey of the western boundary line running from the Catawba River to the Cherokee Indian Line. After completion of the survey in 1772, North Carolina reluctantly relinquished its claims to a considerable amount of territory located between the Catawba River and the Indian Line.[21] This territory was both prosperous and populous, and North Carolina bitterly resented its loss. The soil was very fertile, and it produced indigo, hemp, tobacco, Indian corn, wheat and all other English grains in abundance. At the time of the survey, the population of the area exceeded five thousand.[22] The South Carolina Colonial Assembly dubbed this territory "the New Acquisition," and in 1772, it included all of the present-day South Carolina counties of York and Cherokee, most of Spartanburg County and the northernmost section of Union County.[23] With this territory finally under the official control of South Carolina, in 1773, the assembly formed a militia regiment called the New District Regiment to patrol the New Acquisition.[24]

By the time the 1772 survey was completed, the inhabitants of the South Carolina Backcountry had suffered more than twenty years of Indian wars, border disputes, governmental apathy, banditti raids, Regulator-Moderator conflicts and economic difficulties. Throughout all these troubles, the Backcountry settlers persevered and flourished. They grew accustomed to self-governance and self-reliance, and learned to depend on neither colonial nor royal authority for protection and justice. They worshipped as they pleased without interference from the Church of England and educated their children as they saw fit. They practiced subsistence farming, traded and bartered for what they needed and protected themselves by force of arms when necessary. They developed a well-deserved reputation for independence and frontier justice that owed little to the mercantile interests and elitist government of the Lowcountry.

The Cherokee War and the Regulator-Moderator conflicts also had a profound influence on the development of the militia in the South Carolina Backcountry. The years of frontier warfare against Indians and banditti left South Carolina with a well-organized militia force as well as a large corps of trained officers and enlisted men. However, the unconventional and often brutal nature of this warfare forced the Backcountry militia to learn different tactics than those practiced by the conventional military forces of Europe. Large ranks of slow-moving foot soldiers gave way to small troops of mobile rangers capable of moving quickly on horseback. Backwoods ambushes, surprise attacks and small skirmishes—accompanied by the burning of homes, destruction of crops and looting of property—replaced the large-scale, organized battles of the British and French Armies. The deliberate targeting of officers and noncombatants, abhorred on the European battlefield, also became commonplace on the frontier. This irregular or "guerilla" warfare also required the militia to adopt the same type of weapons used by their enemies. Smoothbore muskets with bayonets, while standard issue for European armies, proved ineffective in Backcountry skirmishes and were replaced by the long rifle, tomahawk and scalping knife.[25]

Meanwhile the growing discord between Great Britain and the thirteen colonies resulted in South Carolina's first steps toward independence. In January 1775, the Colonial Assembly dissolved itself and a convention of elected delegates from across South Carolina convened the First Provincial Congress, which became the first independent governing body of the province.[26] The Backcountry was poorly represented in the first congress, and the New Acquisition was not represented at all. In order to rectify this situation, the congress created several new electoral districts in the Backcountry in June 1775. The First Provincial Congress divided the central part of the Upcountry between the Broad and Catawba Rivers into "the District in the Upper Part of the New Acquisition, extending from the old to the new boundary line" and "the District between Broad & Catawba Rivers adjoining the New Acquisition." The upper portion of the Ninety Six District, including the newly acquired territory west of the Broad River, became "the District between the Broad and Saludy Rivers." The section of the New Acquisition located between the Broad and Catawba Rivers continued to be known simply as "the New Acquisition" and was identical to York County as it was originally established in 1785. "The District between the Broad & Catawba Rivers adjoining the New Acquisition" was identical in area to modern Chester, Fairfield and Richland Counties.[27] In February 1776, the Second Provincial Congress further subdivided the District between the Broad and Saluda Rivers into

In 1775, the First Provincial Congress divided the Cheraw, Camden and Ninety Six Legal Districts into nine electoral districts, with representatives from each electoral district serving in the legislature. Each electoral district raised at least one militia regiment, and the larger districts raised two or three such regiments. *South Carolina Election District Map, 1775–1776, from* Biographical Directory of the South Carolina House of Representatives, Volume I, Session Lists 1692–1973, *edited by Walter Edgar and Inez Watson (1974). Courtesy of the University of South Carolina Press, Columbia, South Carolina.*

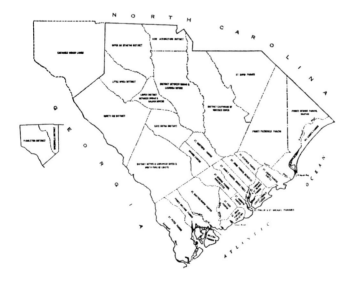

In order to provide for more equitable representation, the South Carolina government created additional electoral districts between 1776 and 1778. Both patriot and Loyalist militia regiments were organized along electoral district lines throughout the years of the American Revolution. *South Carolina Election District Map, 1778, from* Biographical Directory of the South Carolina House of Representatives, Volume I, Session Lists 1692–1973, *edited by Walter Edgar and Inez Watson (1974). Courtesy of the University of South Carolina Press, Columbia, South Carolina.*

the Lower, or Dutch Fork, District; the Middle, or Little River, District; and the Upper, or Spartan, District, which encompassed that section of the original New Acquisition located west of the Broad River.[28] Each of these districts had its own regiment of militia, and in turn these regiments fell under the overall command of Colonel Richard Richardson, the senior militia officer in the Backcountry.[29]

Some historians have adopted the stance that the majority of the inhabitants of the South Carolina Backcountry, especially the Scotch-Irish settlers in the upper valleys of the Broad and Catawba Rivers, were "largely indifferent" to the American Revolution and refrained from becoming involved in the conflict until it arrived on their doorsteps in the summer of 1780.[30] Since virtually none of the early battles of the Revolution took place in the districts along the Broad and Catawba Rivers, these historians have assumed that the residents of these districts were not involved in the Revolution and remained aloof to events happening elsewhere in the state. However, the historical record tells quite a different tale. The journals of the South Carolina provincial government as well as the memoirs, pension applications and audited accounts of South Carolina's Revolutionary War veterans clearly demonstrate that the settlers of the upper districts, especially those of the Broad and Catawba Valleys, were involved in the Revolution from the beginning. In fact, by the time armed conflict broke out in the Northern colonies in April 1775, most of the inhabitants of the South Carolina Backcountry had already decided where their allegiances lay. As a general rule, the former Regulators became Whigs and aligned themselves with the Revolutionary party, while the former Moderators or Scoffelites became Tories and remained loyal to England. Furthermore, much of the early military action in South Carolina during the Revolution took place in the Backcountry, although it was confined to the territory west of the Broad River: the Ninety Six District, the Cherokee territory and the Savannah River Valley between Georgia and South Carolina.[31]

On 3 June 1775, the First Provincial Congress, acknowledging the "actual commencement of hostilities against this continent, by the British troops, in the bloody scene on the 19th of April last, near Boston" (a reference to the battles at Lexington and Concord in Massachusetts), unanimously passed an association, with which the representatives vowed to:

> UNITE ourselves, under every tie of religion and of honour, and associate, as a band in her defence, against every foe: Hereby solemnly engaging that, whenever our Continental or Provincial Councils shall decree it necessary, we will go forth, and be ready to sacrifice our lives and fortunes to secure her freedom and safety. This obligation to continue in full force until a reconciliation shall take place between Great-Britain and America, upon constitutional principles—an Event which we most ardently desire. And we will hold all those persons inimical to the liberty of the colonies, who shall refuse to subscribe this association.[32]

The passage of this association, and the demand for all male citizens to sign it or be considered enemies of the state, drove an even greater wedge between those residents who supported armed revolution against England and those who opposed it. Many of the Backcountry settlers who favored greater freedom for the colonies drew the line at signing their name to a document they considered treasonous to their lawful sovereign, a decision that pushed them into the ranks of the hard-line Loyalists.[33]

South Carolina then began to prepare itself for armed conflict. On 6 June 1775, the Congress authorized two permanent regiments of foot soldiers, consisting of 750 rank and file each, and a regiment of mounted troops or rangers, consisting of 450 privates. The assembly further ordered that the regiments be "put under the direction of the Congress."[34] The legislators elected Christopher Gadsden and William Moultrie from the Lowcountry to command the First and Second Regiments of Foot. Since it would be the rangers' job to patrol the Backcountry, the congress appointed William Thomson from the upper Congaree to serve as lieutenant colonel commandant of the rangers, with James Mayson from the Dutch Fork District as major and second-in-command.[35] Other officers in the Third South Carolina Regiment included Captain Ezekiel Polk and First Lieutenant Samuel Watson, commanding the ranger company from the New Acquisition, as well as Captain Eli Kershaw and First Lieutenant Richard Winn, who commanded the ranger company from the District between the Broad and Catawba Rivers.[36] Comprised primarily of frontiersmen and militia veterans from the Backcountry, the Third Regiment soon became known throughout the state as Thomson's Rangers.[37]

On 14 June, the Provincial Congress formed a Council of Safety from its members and gave the Council the authority to direct, regulate, maintain and order new state regiments and the militia. The Council's specific duties included arranging military operations, issuing commissions to officers and confirming or reversing sentences of general courts-martial in capital cases.[38] Other resolutions quickly followed. If the Council of Safety found it necessary to call out the militia, then the officers and men of the militia would be allowed "a daily pay and rations, equal to the pay allowed in the new-raised regiments of foot."[39] The Council granted the inhabitants of the colony the liberty to form "volunteer troops of horse and companies of foot, not to exceed one hundred men in each troop or company...for the purpose of training and holding themselves in readiness, to turn out upon all occasions of emergency...subject to the orders of the field-officers of the district in which they shall associate and form."[40] (Field officers in both the British and American Armies were commissioned officers holding the rank of major, lieutenant colonel or colonel.) Throughout the summer and fall of 1775, many men from the New Acquisition and the District between the Broad and Catawba Rivers enlisted in the rangers under Lieutenant Colonel Thomson and Major Mayson, or formed volunteer companies of militia under the command of local officers.[41] In order to keep these volunteer companies in a condition of readiness, the Council of Safety ordered that "every Captain or other commanding Officer of a company, shall assemble, muster, train and exercise his company once in every fortnight, under a penalty of twenty-five pounds currency for every default."[42]

Unlike the militia regiments in the more densely populated coastal regions, the Backcountry militia in the Carolinas were primarily mounted militia. While they were not trained to fight on horseback like the European cavalry, they relied on their horses for speed and mobility in traveling between the widely separated, sparsely populated settlements of the Backcountry. South Carolina's lieutenant governor, William Bull, commented on this fact when he toured the Backcountry in 1770. "In the country almost every militia man marches on Horseback," he noted.[43] The use of horses proved to be a great tactical advantage for the militia in the Backcountry, but it also created a logistical burden because the soldiers had to feed and care for the horses as well as themselves. On several occasions in the early phase of the conflict, the Provincial Congress ordered field officers "not to allow any of the militia companies, or militia Volunteers, to take the field on horseback—militia horses being, by experience, found to be an incumbrance to the men, on a military expedition."[44] The state government found it almost impossible to enforce these orders, however, and throughout the war in the South, the Backcountry militia generally rode rather than walked.[45]

Faced with what appeared to be substantial resistance to the association in the Backcountry, the Council of Safety resolved to do something about it. In late July 1775, the Council of Safety dispatched William Henry Drayton, one of Charleston's most vocal proponents of American independence, into the back settlements to explain the congress's point of view. Accompanying Drayton were two ministers who also supported independence: Reverend Oliver Hart, a Baptist, and Reverend William Tennent, a Presbyterian. The Council hoped the eloquence of these individuals would help sway the large numbers of recent immigrants from the British Isles and German states, who so far had remained neutral or pro-British. Over the course of the summer, Drayton debated several prominent Backcountry Loyalists—including Robert Cunningham, Patrick Cunningham, Moses Kirkland, Thomas Browne, Joseph Robinson and Thomas Fletchall—but in spite of his best efforts, the mission was less than successful, especially in the Ninety Six District and the predominantly German Saxe-Gotha and Orangeburg Districts.[46] However, among the Scotch-Irish Presbyterians in the upper districts east of the Saluda, Drayton's party found more sympathetic ears. In the Spartan District, Drayton convinced the men to organize a new militia regiment under Colonel John Thomas Sr., in defiance of their old colonel, Thomas Fletchall. Although Drayton did not cross to the east side of the Broad River, he did send Reverend Tennent into that district. Tennent arrived in the New Acquisition in late August, where he met with Colonel Thomas Neal Sr. and the New Acquisition Militia Regiment. Colonel Neal—whose name is variously spelled Neel, Neil or Neill—lived near Crowder's Creek on the west side of the Catawba River and was one of the most prominent and respected men in the area. He had served as a justice of the peace and magistrate under the Tryon County (North Carolina) and Camden District (South Carolina) governments, and was also a Presbyterian elder. As were many of the older officers on the frontier, he was a veteran of the Regulator War and had served as colonel of the Tryon County Militia Regiment at the Battle of Alamance in 1771. Following the border survey of 1772, he was elected commander of the New Acquisition Militia Regiment. Neal had twin sons, Andrew and Thomas Jr., who served as junior officers under their father.[47]

From Bullock's Creek in the New Acquisition, Tennent wrote to Henry Laurens on 20 August praising the residents of the district: "I turned my course into the new acquisition, where I am to have a meeting, from day to day, in Col. Neal's regiment...I have formed one, and am forming in this District another troop of Volunteer Horse Rangers, who are as good as sworn to the Council of Safety when they enlist. We are hemming in the diffidents on all sides as much as possible...I have forsook my chaise and ride on horse back, from day to day, meeting people."[48]

Encouraged by Tennent's success in the New Acquisition, the next day Drayton sent a letter from Lawson's Fork in the Spartan District to the Council of Safety, in which he stated: "Mr. Tennent and Col. Richardson, were successful in their journey, beyond Broad River. Mr. Tennent, is now in Neel's quarters; where, they are very hearty in our cause."[49] On 30 August, Drayton

This close-up of William Faden's 1787 map shows the Carolina Backcountry during the American Revolution. *From an original copy of* A History of the Campaigns of 1780 and 1781 in the Southern Provinces of North America *by Banastre Tarleton (Second Edition, 1796). Courtesy of the South Caroliniana Library, University of South Carolina, Columbia, South Carolina.*

sent another letter to the Council of Safety in order to guarantee that Colonel Neal's regiment was supplied with powder and ammunition. "I beg leave to recommend," Drayton wrote, "that a proper quantity of powder and ball, be sent to Colonel Richardson, so that he may be enabled to supply Colonel Neal's regiment."[50] Duly energized by Tennent's visit, the residents of the New Acquisition complied with the Council of Safety's instructions and organized several new volunteer companies under the command of Colonel Neal. Other officers elected to the New Acquisition Militia Regiment included Major Francis "Frank" Ross as well as Captains William Byers, Alexander Love, Thomas Fitzpatrick, Robert McAfee and William Bratton. All of these officers served in the colonial militia before 1775, and most of them (including Ross, Neal, Byers, Love and McAfee) also served in the Provincial Congress and the South Carolina General Assembly.[51] While Bratton did not serve in the Provincial Congress or the General Assembly, he was a justice of the peace and magistrate for Camden District and a tax collector for the New Acquisition during the same period.[52] The qualifications for serving in the Provincial Congress and General Assembly were the same as they had been in the colonial period: "white males, aged twenty-one, owning a 'settled' plantation and ten slaves or property valued at £100 currency in the province, 'construed to mean clear of debt,' which was to guarantee that independence of thought and action legislators were supposed to possess."[53]

Almost all of these men were Scotch-Irish Presbyterians drawn from the congregations of the "four B's": Bethel, Beersheba, Bullock's Creek and Bethesda Churches in what is now York County. The ministers for these Presbyterian "meeting houses" were all ardent Whigs, and they constantly reminded their congregations of the troubles with the English church and state that they had left Ireland to escape. Reverend Joseph Alexander, who presided over Bullock's Creek Church and supplied at Beersheba Church, was a prominent Whig from the influential Alexander family of Mecklenburg County, North Carolina. He grew up under the ministry of Reverend Alexander Craighead, a third-generation Presbyterian minister who preached sermons against British authority in Mecklenburg County years before the Revolution began and whose influence continued to dominate the region long after his death in 1766.[54] Bethel Church, where Thomas Neal and his family worshipped, was ministered by Reverend Hezekiah Balch until shortly after the beginning of the Revolution, after which it was supplied by various pastors, including Reverend James McRee of Mecklenburg County and Francis Cummins, both of whom were also staunch Whigs. The Bethesda congregation, located on the South Fork of Fishing Creek in the New Acquisition, did not have a permanent minister during the period of the Revolution but was supplied by Reverend John Simpson of Fishing Creek. These frontier preachers wielded great influence over their congregations and were one of the reasons why antagonism toward the British was so strong in this part of the Backcountry.[55]

In the area just south of the New Acquisition, corresponding to modern Chester County, the predominantly Scotch-Irish residents also raised several independent mounted militia companies during the summer and fall of 1775. One of the earliest of these units was the Turkey Creek Volunteer Militia Company raised by Captain Edward Lacey Jr. The Turkey Creek Volunteers consisted of men living on upper Turkey Creek and upper Sandy River on both sides of the old provisional boundary line, corresponding to the modern border between York and Chester Counties. After selecting Lacey to be their captain, the volunteers elected Charles Miles as their first lieutenant and Patrick "Paddy" McGriff as second lieutenant.[56]

At thirty-three years of age, Lacey stood five feet and eleven inches tall, was a veteran of the French and Indian War and was a natural choice for a militia captain. In 1755, at the age of thirteen, Lacey ran away from his home in Pennsylvania and joined British General Edward Braddock's disastrous expedition. For the next two years, he served as a pack-horse driver in the British Army until his father found him and brought him home. At the age of sixteen, Lacey ran away again and came to South Carolina with the family of William Adair Sr., to whom he apprenticed himself as a bricklayer. In the 1760s, Lacey obtained several large land grants on the waters of Turkey Creek and Fishing Creek, and established a residence on the south fork of Susy Bole's Branch, lying along the ridge between Turkey Creek and the headwaters of Sandy River. When the Revolution began, he was a staunch Whig, which put him in continuous conflict with his father Edward Lacey Sr., an uncompromising Tory who had followed his son to the Carolinas along with the rest of his family. Captain Lacey quickly established himself as one of the preeminent Whig militia commanders in the upper part of the District between the Broad and Catawba Rivers.[57]

Further downstream, in the area where Susy Bole's Branch enters Turkey Creek in what is now western Chester County, the local Whigs organized another "volunteer company of horse-men" with William Gaston as their captain, Thomas Robins as first lieutenant and James Kirkpatrick as second lieutenant.[58] Most of the Scotch-Irish Presbyterians in these two companies worshipped at Bullock's Creek Presbyterian Church, located a few miles to the north in the New Acquisition. Others attended services at Sandy River Baptist Church, a small Baptist meeting house located on upper Turkey Creek near Susy Bole's Branch. Reverend James Fowler pastored at this church, originally known as Flat Rock Meeting House. Although Fowler was born and raised as a Scotch-Irish Presbyterian, he was ordained as a Baptist minister in

December 1776 by the Sandy River Baptist Church. Like the nearby congregation at Bullock's Creek, most of Fowler's flock were Whigs.[59]

Others families in the area belonged to the congregation at Upper Fishing Creek Presbyterian Church, also known as Simpson's Meeting House, founded in 1755 and located just south of the 1767 province line. A large community of Scotch-Irish settlers lived in the area around this church, most of whom migrated to the area from Pennsylvania. Throughout the years of the Revolution, Reverend John Simpson led this congregation and encouraged his constituents to support the cause of independence. Of Scotch-Irish ancestry himself, Simpson was a native of New Jersey, was a graduate of the College of New Jersey (now Princeton University) and moved to South Carolina in 1773. Simpson also supplied the congregations at Bethesda Presbyterian Church, located on the South Fork of Fishing Creek in the New Acquisition, and at Lower Fishing Creek Presbyterian Church, located near the modern town of Lewisville in what is now Chester County. The two Fishing Creek congregations included members of the interrelated Gaston, McClure and Strong families, all staunch Whigs.[60] Among the early militia captains in the upper Fishing Creek community were Joseph Brown, Michael Dickson, Alexander Pagan and Philip Walker, who owned Walker's Mill, later known as White's Mill, where the town of Lando is now situated.[61] Brown and Dickson (or Dixon) were Camden District justices of the peace and served in the Provincial Congress; Brown also served in the General Assembly.[62]

Simpson also supplied Catholic Presbyterian Church, located further to the south on Rocky Creek. This congregation was comprised primarily of Scotch-Irish settlers who migrated to the area from Pennsylvania and Virginia in the early 1750s.[63] About two miles southeast of Catholic Presbyterian, a fiery minister named William Martin ministered a small congregation of Covenanters at Rocky Creek Presbyterian Church. Martin led five shiploads of immigrants from northern Ireland to South Carolina in 1772, and after debarking, these new arrivals fanned out into the Backcountry and settled along the tributaries of the Broad and Catawba Rivers. These Covenanters were descendants of Scottish Presbyterians who swore blood oaths or "covenants" during the sixteenth and seventeenth centuries to oppose what they perceived as Church of England heresies, which included accepting the king of England as the head of the church. Of all the Protestant immigrants from the north of Ireland, they were the most averse to English dominance of church and state. Like Simpson, Martin also occasionally supplied at Catholic Presbyterian.[64]

Most of the members of the Catholic and Rocky Creek congregations were resolute Whigs; many of them, like the large Knox family, were related by blood or marriage to the Gastons and McClures on Fishing Creek.[65] The Rocky Creek Whigs served in a militia company commanded by Captain John Nixon, a Camden District justice of the peace who also served in the Provincial Congress and the General Assembly.[66] These volunteer militia companies located in the northern section of the District between the Broad and Catawba generally operated in close conjunction with Colonel Neal and the New Acquisition Militia Regiment throughout the early campaigns of the Revolution. The men from these upper militia companies, along with their neighbors and relatives who served in the Continental regiments, later formed the battle-tested core of Thomas Sumter's partisan brigade during the summer and fall of 1780.

The influence of the Presbyterian ministers in this part of the Backcountry was commented on frequently by the Whig veterans of the war. One of them, John Craig, lived in the New

Acquisition during the Revolution and later moved to Pickens District. His memoirs, originally published in 1839, mentioned this influence:

> *The above named men who fought and suffered with me from the Districts of York and Chester were composed of the Presbyterian denomination of Christians. Rev. Mr. Martin from the north of Ireland, who emigrated with my father, a Presbyterian minister or Covenanter with many hearers who came over to America to get rid of British laws and their tyrannical government, settled in the lower edge of Chester District, S. C., and there formed a congregation. When the British attempted to enforce the duties on tea and other oppressions, he with his band of heroes stood true to the cause of liberty. It was fortunate they had such a patriotic pastor, who was calculated to direct them in the way to contend against that tyranny from which he had so lately fled. When Charleston fell this same patriot was taken prisoner by the Tories and put in close confinement as a rebel. Rev. Mr. Simpson, and Rev. Mr. Alexander, had to flee from their District or they would have shared the same fate. Both were Presbyterian clergymen and were equally expert in encouraging the men of their acquaintance to resist oppression.*[67]

The armed conflict of the Revolution descended on the South Carolina Backcountry in the fall of 1775. In late October, the South Carolina Provincial Congress received intelligence that the pro-British Cherokee Indians might go to war again "unless the Indians were furnished with some small supplies of ammunition, to enable them to procure deer skins for their support and maintenance." In order to head off trouble, the Provincial Congress dispatched a wagon train with one thousand pounds of gunpowder and ammunition to the Cherokees as a peace offering. On 3 November, a group of Loyalists from the Ninety Six District under Captain Patrick Cunningham ambushed the convoy and made off with the powder and ammunition.[68] Four days later, the Provincial Congress ordered Colonel Richard Richardson, the senior militia colonel in the Upcountry, to assemble drafts of militia from his own regiment and the militia regiments of Colonels William Thomson, John Savage, Thomas Neal Sr. and John Thomas Sr., along with six companies of Rangers from the Third South Carolina Regiment and Captain Polk's company of volunteers, who had previously withdrawn from Thomson's Rangers. These men received orders to march toward Fort Ninety Six, recover the stolen munitions and arrest Cunningham and his party. On 19 November, Cunningham drove the Ninety Six District Militia Regiment under Major Andrew Williamson into Fort Ninety Six and completely surrounded the fort. After a siege lasting for two days, Williamson and Cunningham negotiated a truce and the Tories lifted the siege. Soon afterward, a force of militia and regulars under Colonels Richardson and Thomson moved into the region between the Broad and Saluda Rivers to quell the growing Loyalist uprising there. [69]

On 22 December, a detachment of Richardson's army—including Thomson's Rangers, the New Acquisition Militia Regiment and Lacey's company—surprised and captured most of Cunningham's Loyalist force at Great Canebrake on the Reedy River in what became known as the Battle of Great Canebrake. The next day a heavy snow began to fall and continued unabated for thirty hours. The snow eventually reached a depth of two feet and, after three days, changed to sleet and freezing rain. Richardson's men, ill clad and unprepared for such weather, were forced to march for eight days under the most nightmarish of conditions, and many of the men suffered severely from frostbite. Because of the heavy snowfall, the Carolinians came to refer to this expedition as "the Snow Campaign" or the "Snowy Camps," and all the veterans who experienced it remembered it vividly for the rest of their lives.[70]

Meanwhile the South Carolina legislature, anticipating a British attack on Charleston, authorized the formation of a regiment of artillery "to manage and fire the artillery in Fort Johnson, and the other fortifications now erected, and such batteries as it may hereafter be thought necessary to erect."[71] This new artillery regiment entered service as the Fourth South Carolina Regiment. In early February 1776, the congress saw the need for additional regular troops to defend the colony and authorized a fifth regiment of seven hundred men to be raised. Unlike the original two foot regiments, whose soldiers were armed with smoothbore muskets, the Provincial Congress decreed that the new regiment was to consist of "*expert* Rifle-men," with emphasis on the "expert." Generous enlistment bonuses and pay made service in the new rifle regiment an attractive option for men in the rural settlements. The congress also authorized an increase in the size of the regiment of Rangers, and further declared that the Ranger regiment "shall be composed of *expert* Rifle-men, who shall act on horseback, or on foot, as the service may require; each man, at his own expence, to be constantly provided with a good horse, rifle, shot-pouch and powder-horn, together with a tomahawk or hatchet." But congress was adamant that the new recruits enlisting in the regiments of Rangers and Riflemen "be approved of by the commanding officer of each regiment respectively,—as *expert Rifle-men*."[72] To command the First Rifle Regiment, the legislature elected Isaac Huger of Charleston as colonel, Alexander McIntosh as lieutenant colonel and Isaac's brother Benjamin Huger as major.

Such was the state of alarm over the threat of imminent invasion—by Indians, British or both—that before the month was out, the congress approved a proposal to raise a second regiment of riflemen to rank as the sixth regiment in the colony service and consist of five hundred men, "upon the same terms and establishment as the first regiment of Rifle-men." The legislators decided that the Second Rifle Regiment did not need a full colonel to command it, and elected Thomas Sumter from the upper Santee River to serve as lieutenant colonel commandant and William Henderson of the Pacolet River as major.[73] While relatively few men from the Backcountry served in the artillery regiment, the rifle regiments were stocked with experienced sharpshooters from the area. Most of Sumter's recruits for the Second Rifle Regiment came from the upper districts along the Broad and Catawba Rivers, and this regiment was to prove a valuable training ground for many of the men who later served in Sumter's Brigade.[74]

Active militia duty in the Southern states during the Revolution was arranged around a combination volunteer and draft system. When the militia was needed, the company and regiment commanders would usually call for volunteers first. If enough volunteers were not forthcoming, the officers would then hold a draft. Because Backcountry militia companies were raised from small rural communities, drafts were conducted so that militia duty was rotated among the eligible men. This ensured that all the men from a given area would not be forced to serve at the same time and guaranteed that communities would not be left defenseless. Draftees were also allowed to hire substitutes, who could be an unmarried or unemployed kinsman, a slave or an indentured servant. Former Continental soldiers who had served out their tour of duty were also frequently drafted into the militia. The draft generally applied to rank-and-file privates only. Company commanders and field officers were fewer in number and less easily replaced, and they usually accompanied their units whenever the units were called out.[75]

In April 1776, the Provincial Congress passed a resolution requiring that drafts from each of the "country militia" march to Charleston and assist in the defense of that city. Each draft was to remain on duty for one month and then be relieved by a new draft. Some men from Colonel Neal's regiment, along with Thomson's Rangers and a company of Catawba Indians, helped man the fortifications at Sullivan's Island in June 1776. Under the command of Colonel William Moultrie, the Continentals and militia at Sullivan's Island repulsed an invasion by British Army and Navy forces under the command of Sir Henry Clinton and Sir Peter Parker on 28 June. Sumter's riflemen were stationed on the mainland but were not involved in the battle. The Backcountry militia was again called into action in early July 1776 when the Cherokee, encouraged by the Shawnee Indians and Backcountry Loyalists, began attacking frontier settlements in western South Carolina. Along with a company of Catawba Indian scouts, the New Acquisition Militia Regiment marched west to the Reedy River, where the men joined the other Upcountry militia units under Colonel Andrew Williamson. Williamson, who lived about six miles west of Fort Ninety Six, was a veteran of James Grant's Cherokee expedition of 1761 as well as the Regulator Wars in 1768. He had also been recently promoted to colonel of the Ninety Six District Militia Regiment.[76]

On the evening of 31 July 1776, Williamson's men began marching toward the Lower Cherokee Towns. As his men crossed the Seneca River near the Indian village of Essenecca (or Seneca Old Town) in the early morning hours of 1 August, a combined force of Cherokees and Loyalists ambushed Williamson's party. A sharp engagement ensued during which Major Frank Ross of the New Acquisition Militia Regiment was wounded in the head by a Cherokee tomahawk. Williamson's men were thrown into confusion until Colonel Le Roy Hammond rallied his men from the Lower Ninety Six District and put the Indians and Tories to flight. After destroying Seneca Old Town, Williamson's troops moved into what is now Oconee County, South Carolina, destroying Cherokee towns and skirmishing with their warriors along the way. During this march Captain Andrew Pickens, commanding a company of militia from Long Cane Creek, distinguished himself in several hard-fought engagements with the Cherokees, including a skirmish at Tugaloo River on 10 August and the famous "Ring Fight" two days later.[77]

During August, a detachment of one hundred men from the Third Regiment arrived from Charleston to reinforce Williamson's expedition. In early September, the Second South Carolina Regiment of Riflemen under Lieutenant Colonel Thomas Sumter joined as well.[78] It was during this campaign that many of the Backcountry militiamen from the area first became acquainted with their future commander, Sumter. On 13 September, Williamson's army, now numbering between fifteen hundred and eighteen hundred men, moved into southwestern North Carolina and began attacking the Cherokees' Lower or Valley Towns. In conjunction with Williamson's expedition, Colonel William Christian started down the Holston River with militia from Augusta and Botetourt Counties in western Virginia to attack the Upper or Overhill Towns, while Brigadier General Griffith Rutherford led some twenty-four hundred North Carolina militiamen into the Cherokee Middle Towns.[79] On 19 September, a force of about six hundred Cherokee warriors ambushed Williamson's army in the mountains of what is now Macon County, North Carolina. Colonel Neal's regiment succeeded in driving off the Cherokees after a fierce two-hour fight that came to be known as the Battle of Black Hole. Veterans of the battle later recalled that Colonel Neal, although in his fifties, rushed up the mountain at the head of his men "as one invincible, throwing his regiment headlong among the Indians, routing and defeating them with great slaughter."[80]

The day after the Battle of Black Hole, there was a change in the status of the South Carolina state regiments. On 20 September, the General Assembly passed a resolution accepting a request from the Continental Congress to place all six of the state regiments on the Continental Establishment. Sumter's Second Regiment of Riflemen thus became the Sixth Regiment of the South Carolina Continental Line. It would be some time, however, before the men learned of their new status.[81] Meanwhile, General Williamson had linked up with General Rutherford's North Carolinians, and for the next two weeks, the troops destroyed the Cherokee towns and burned their fields throughout the mountains of southwestern North Carolina. The South Carolinians went as far as the village of Chotee on the headwaters of the Chattahoochee River before stopping. After conferring with Colonels Neal, Hammond and Sumter, Williamson decided his men had gone far enough and turned back toward South Carolina. On 7 October, the men reentered Essenecca. During their campaign, they burned thirty-two Cherokee villages, destroyed hundreds of acres of corn and defeated the Indians in five separate battles. On 11 October, Williamson dismissed the troops and sent them home.[82]

By February 1777, the Cherokees were starving and were ready to sue for peace. The Indians ceded their remaining South Carolina land, consisting of the modern counties of Greenville, Oconee, Pickens and Anderson, at the Treaty of Dewitt's Corner on 20 May 1777.[83] In spite of the peace treaty, however, Indians continued to harass the Backcountry settlers. In November 1777, Colonel Neal led the New Acquisition Militia Regiment against the Creek Indians on the south side of the Okmulgee River in Georgia. The regiment marched through Ninety Six District and camped on the Savannah River about twenty miles above Augusta, but never encountered the Creeks. The regiment was in the field for two months on this campaign before returning home.[84]

By early 1778, the logistical burden of coordinating the large number of militia regiments in the state prompted the South Carolina government to organize the militia into brigades, each commanded by a brigadier general. On 28 March, the General Assembly created three militia brigades, commanded by Generals Stephen Bull, Richard Richardson and Andrew Williamson. Bull commanded the Lowcountry, while Richardson's brigade included the upper districts east of the Broad-Congaree-Santee River system. Williamson commanded the brigade to the west of the Santee that included the Ninety Six District.[85]

The Backcountry militia went out again in the summer of 1778 on the Florida Expedition, an ill-fated attempt to take St. Augustine from the British. Major General Robert Howe, recently appointed commander of the Continental Army in the South, decided to invade East Florida, where Major General Augustine Prevost was raising a combined British-Loyalist army and raiding Whig plantations in southern Georgia. In early May, Howe set off from Charleston with some 550 Continentals, including Sumter's Sixth South Carolina Regiment of Riflemen. The New Acquisition Militia Regiment and the regiment from the upper District between the Broad and Catawba Rivers, now commanded by Colonel Edward Lacey Jr., joined the militia from the western districts under General Williamson and marched toward Georgia to assist the Continentals. The South Carolina militia and a contingent of Georgia militia under Georgia Governor John Houston caught up with Howe's Continentals in early July at Fort Tonyn in northern East Florida. However, both Williamson and Houston refused to put their men under Howe's command, and the expedition fell apart without engaging Prevost's army. The Backcountry militia served about four months on this expedition.[86]

November 1778 saw the beginning of a new British campaign against Georgia and South Carolina that began with Prevost landing on the southern coast of Georgia. Emboldened by these events, Loyalist officers in the Carolina Backcountry began recruiting volunteers and raiding Whig settlements. One of these Tories was Captain Christopher Coleman, who organized a Loyalist company from the Thicketty Creek area of the Spartan District. Major Frank Ross, Captain Andrew Love and Captain Thomas Kirkpatrick held an enlistment and draft in the New Acquisition during December 1778 and raised about three hundred men to put down the Tories. The Whigs crossed the Broad River and fanned out into the Thicketty Creek and Fair Forest settlements, only to discover that Coleman's Tories were on their way to Georgia to join the British and had too much of a head start to be easily overtaken. In retaliation for the Tory attacks on Whig settlements, the New Acquisition Militia Regiment burned several prominent Loyalist plantations and then returned home.[87]

After capturing Savannah, Georgia, on 29 December 1778, the British began consolidating their hold on that state and advancing up the Savannah River toward Augusta, Georgia. Major General Benjamin Lincoln, who replaced Howe as commander of the Continental Army in the South, made preparations at his base in Purysburg, South Carolina, to rescue Georgia from the British. As part of this operation, Lincoln ordered out the South Carolina militia in force and directed them to report to General Williamson. In early January 1779, Colonel Neal called for volunteers from the New Acquisition to go to the relief of Georgia. Two hundred mounted troops were raised, as well as a complement of foot soldiers to escort the supply and baggage wagons. Meanwhile, Augusta fell to a force of British regulars and Provincial troops under Lieutenant Colonel Archibald Campbell on 29 January. In February 1779, the New Acquisition Militia Regiment crossed the Broad River under Lieutenant Colonel Samuel Watson and Major Ross, and began the march to Augusta under miserable conditions of heavy rainfall. Williamson had established a position on the South Carolina side of the Savannah River across from Augusta with some twelve hundred South Carolina militia. On 13 February, Brigadier General John Ashe joined Williamson with a force of about fourteen hundred North Carolina militia and one hundred Georgia Continentals under Lieutenant Colonel Samuel Elbert. Lieutenant Colonel Campbell, now substantially outnumbered, abandoned Augusta that night and retreated south along the Savannah River. Ashe crossed the river the next day and followed the British down the west bank of the Savannah.[88] A detachment of Williamson's troops, under Colonel Andrew Pickens, engaged a group of Loyalists under Lieutenant Colonel James Boyd at Kettle Creek, Georgia on 14 February. Pickens's troops, including Captain John Nixon's men from what is now Chester County, South Carolina, won a significant victory over the Loyalists thanks to Pickens's tactical skills.[89]

Shortly after Ashe left in pursuit of Campbell, the New Acquisition troops arrived in Augusta and reported to Williamson, who ordered them south to join Ashe's North Carolinians. Ashe arrived at Briar Creek, in present-day Screven County, Georgia, on 27 February and found that the retreating British had destroyed the only bridge across the rain-swollen creek. He posted his men between the creek and the deep swamp that formed where the creek entered the river; he then ordered his men to begin repairing the bridge. A day or so after Ashe reached Briar Creek, the troops from the New Acquisition joined him there. General Ashe was unaware that General Prevost had sent a detachment of British soldiers under his younger brother, Lieutenant Colonel Mark Prevost, to outflank the Americans and take them by surprise from the rear. While on scouting duty, some of Ross's men received intelligence that the British were coming up the opposite side of the creek from Ebenezer, and they reported the news to Ashe. On the morning of 3 March, Ashe sent Ross and 160 of his men to reconnoiter the area and verify the intelligence, but the general made no effort to prepare his men for an attack. This allowed Lieutenant Colonel Prevost to complete his maneuver and attack the Americans without warning. The attack quickly became a rout, and Ashe fled the scene on horseback. About forty of Ross's men were still in camp, and they made a brief stand with Elbert's Continentals before the British drove them into the river. Most of the South Carolinians escaped by swimming across the Savannah, and they eventually joined the remnants of the North Carolina militia on the other side. The rest of Ross's detachment returned to camp that night with several Tory prisoners, unaware of the defeat; the British opened fire on them and drove them back over the creek. The next day Ross's divided command reunited and moved up the river to Williamson's camp. The survivors of the battle at Briar Creek blamed Ashe for the debacle and recalled the fiasco bitterly for the rest of their lives. Years later, a veteran of the battle, James Fergus of the New Acquisition Militia Regiment, met Elbert in Virginia, and Elbert swore that if he ever saw Ashe again, "one of them should die before they parted."[90]

Following the Battle of Briar Creek, the New Acquisition Regiment retreated north toward Augusta and fell in with Colonel LeRoy Hammond's militia regiment from the Lower Ninety Six District, which was pursuing a party of Cherokee and Tory raiders. On 29 March 1779, Ross and Hammond overtook and attacked the raiders five miles east of Rocky Comfort Creek, in modern Richmond County, Georgia.[91] A fierce hand-to-hand battle ensued between the militia and the Indians, and Ross received a tomahawk wound in the abdomen. John Linn, who was in Captain William Gaston's company during the battle, wrote home to his wife from Camp Augusta on 1 April:

> *There was a scout went into Georgia—all horsemen, about 600; Capt.* [William] *Gaston, with his company, was along. They killed and scalped eight Indians & two white men, and took three Indians & three white men prisoners, & brought the eight Indian scalps along to camp. We had only one man wounded, Maj. Ross, who got a slight wound below his short rib, and is hoped he will live.*[92]

Ross did not recover from his wound; he died on 1 April and was buried with full military honors, across from Augusta on the South Carolina side of the Savannah River. Captain William Bratton moved up in rank to major and assumed Ross's command. Shortly afterward, Williamson discharged the men and they returned to the New Acquisition under Lieutenant Colonel Watson. The men reached their homes in late April and discovered that Neal had raised the rest of the regiment, about 150 men, and headed to Orangeburg to reinforce Lincoln's army. The Briar Creek veterans who were still able and willing to fight grabbed their summer gear and headed south to join their comrades.[93]

While General Lincoln led a force of some four thousand men north in an effort to retake Augusta, the British Army under General Prevost prepared to move into South Carolina in order to divert Lincoln's attention from Georgia.[94] Colonels Neal and Lacey led their regiments down the North Fork of the Edisto River to Orangeburg, where they received orders to join Brigadier General William Moultrie, the hero of Sullivan's Island, at Black Swamp in what is now Hampton County.[95] On 29 May, Prevost crossed the Savannah River into South Carolina with some two thousand British and Loyalist troops. About 130 Whigs, including veterans from Neal's and Lacey's commands, took up positions at the Coosawhatchie Bridge in what is now Jasper County to cover Moultrie's withdrawal, and a sharp skirmish followed.[96] Moultrie fell back toward Charleston with Prevost in pursuit, while Lincoln aborted his attempt to recover Augusta and went to the rescue of Charleston. Prevost advanced as far as Charleston before breaking off and withdrawing to Savannah, but he left a nine-hundred-man rear guard under Lieutenant Colonel John Maitland posted on James Island and Johns Island. Lincoln attacked Prevost's outpost on 20 June, and a fierce battle ensued near Stono Ferry. Neal and Lacey, along with the other Carolina militia units, made up the right wing of Lincoln's advance. The men from the Upcountry fought hard in the battle, and during the action, Neal and several other members of the New Acquisition Regiment were killed.[97] The battle accomplished little for the Americans, since Maitland had already decided to withdraw to Port Royal Island (now Beaufort) and was only waiting for ships to transport his troops. Maitland abandoned his position on 23 June and slowly retreated to Port Royal.[98] Following the death of Neal, Samuel Watson advanced in rank to senior colonel and assumed command of the regiment, while William Bratton became lieutenant colonel and second-in-command. The regiment returned to the New Acquisition with Neal's body and his family buried him at Bethel Presbyterian Church.[99] The disastrous Georgia Campaign of 1779 failed in all of its goals to recover Savannah and Augusta, and cost the New Acquisition two of its most experienced and revered officers.

In October 1779, several companies of men set out from the New Acquisition for guard duty in the "over-mountain" settlements of eastern and middle Tennessee. One of these men, William Fleming, later recalled this service in his pension application:

> [I] volunteered as a private militiaman under Capt. [Robert] Leeper and marched to Cumberland in the State of Tennessee to guard the settlements against the Indians and was stationed at a place called the French Lick (the place where Nashville now stands). Shortly after getting there Capt. Leeper was wounded in a skirmish with the Indians and was succeeded by Capt. Drake. We had several skirmishes with the Indians during this campaign in which I served eight months.[100]

Throughout late 1779 and early 1780, the militia from the Upcountry continued to serve three-month tours of duty at Charleston and the Georgia border. Captain Joseph McJunkin and a company of men from the Fair Forest Regiment went to Charleston in November 1779 and returned home in February 1780, after which another militia group took their place.[101] Militia drafts were held in the New Acquisition during February and March 1780 for three months' service on the Georgia frontier against a group of East Florida Loyalists under Daniel McGirt.[102]

Meanwhile Charleston remained in American hands, but the British were only biding their time. In December 1779, the commander-in-chief of the British Army in North America, Lieutenant General Sir Henry Clinton, set out from New York with some 8,700 soldiers aboard a fleet of ships commanded by Vice Admiral Marriot Arbuthnot. Clinton launched his new offensive against Charleston with a landing on Simmons (now Seabrook) Island on 11 February 1780 and gradually deployed his forces about the city.[103] At the same time, the South Carolina government drafted the Fifth and Sixth Regiments of Riflemen into the First and Second Regiments of Foot in order to bolster the state's complement of infantrymen.[104] The Third South Carolina Regiment of Rangers had already undergone such a conversion; the state dismounted the Rangers and equipped them with muskets and bayonets in two phases during August 1777 and July 1778.[105] South Carolina Governor John Rutledge called for more of the "country militia" to reinforce Lincoln's garrison at the capital, but rumors of an outbreak of smallpox in the city and the ever-present danger of Indian attacks and Tory uprisings made many in the Backcountry unwilling to leave home for very long.[106] Nonetheless, a few companies from the Upcountry did respond. One of those was Captain John McClure's company of mounted rangers from the Upper Fishing Creek congregation, who rode south in early April to help defend the city against Clinton's new invasion.[107]

In the spring of 1780, John McClure was about twenty-five years old and was a seasoned veteran of the Revolution in South Carolina. McClure was the nephew of John Gaston, a deputy surveyor and justice of the peace for Camden District who was one of the most influential men in the District between the Broad and Catawba Rivers. Gaston's large extended family included the McClures, Knoxes, Walkers, Strongs, Gills and most of the other Fishing Creek families, almost all Scotch-Irish Presbyterians who embraced the patriot cause.[108] Since the early days of the war, McClure had commanded a small group of dedicated Whigs from Fishing Creek that included his brother Hugh McClure, his friend John Steele (or Steel) and his cousins, the Gaston brothers: William, John Jr., James, Robert, Hugh, Alexander, David, Ebenezer and Joseph. The McClure brothers, along with Steele and seven of the Gastons, had served together in Captain Eli Kershaw's company of the Third South Carolina Regiment under Colonel William Thomson, from 1775 until 1778. All of them were veterans of the Snow Campaign, the Battle of Sullivan's Island, the Georgia Campaign, the fights at Coosawhatchie Bridge and Stono Ferry, as well as other engagements. In 1778, after serving three years in the Rangers, they formed a volunteer company of militia from the Fishing Creek area that became known as "McClure's Rangers." Under Captain John McClure, First Lieutenant Hugh McClure and Second Lieutenant John Steele, this volunteer ranger company generally operated as part of Colonel Edward Lacey's Militia Regiment, along with similar companies commanded by Captain John Nixon from the Catholic Presbyterian congregation and Captain Alexander Pagan from the Upper Fishing Creek congregation.[109]

McClure's Rangers arrived in the vicinity of Charleston in early April 1780. Brigadier General Isaac Huger, commanding the American defenses outside the city, stationed them with the Continental dragoons under Colonel William Washington near Monck's Corner.[110] At three o'clock in the morning on 14 April 1780, elements of the British Legion under Lieutenant Colonel Banastre Tarleton, supported by infantry of the American Volunteers under Major Patrick Ferguson, launched a surprise attack on Huger's position.

Tarleton and Ferguson were both experienced officers in the British Army who had received important commands during the Northern campaigns, and both were to become famous and notorious during the Southern Campaign. Born the son of a wealthy merchant and slave trader in Liverpool, England, the twenty-six-year-old Tarleton had studied at the University of Liverpool and Oxford University before accepting a commission in the King's Dragoon Guards in April 1775. Later that year, he volunteered for service in America and took part in the early campaigns in the North. In 1778, Tarleton was commissioned lieutenant colonel commandant of the British Legion—a combined Provincial corps of cavalry and infantry organized by Sir William Cathcart in New York—and came south with Clinton's expedition in early 1780.[111]

Thirty-six-year-old Patrick Ferguson was a native of Aberdeen, Scotland; his father was a senator in the College of Justice and one of the lords commissioners of the Scottish justiciary, while his mother was the daughter of the fourth Lord of Elibank. Ferguson studied artillery and fortifications in London and by the time he was fifteen he had been commissioned a cornet in the Royal Northern British Dragoons. In 1768 he received command of a company in the Seventieth Regiment of Foot, and in 1776 he designed and patented a breech loading rifle for the British Army that was one of the most advanced firearms of its day, although the army never adopted it for service. Ferguson was allowed to form a volunteer rifle corps in America for service in the Northern campaigns, but the corps was disbanded after Ferguson was wounded at Brandywine. In October 1779 he was promoted to major and assigned to the Seventy-first Highland Regiment of Foot, but by the time the army moved south Ferguson had been given command of a Provincial corps known as the American Volunteers.[112]

Tarleton found the Continental cavalry posted along the road to Biggin's Bridge on the west branch of the Cooper River, with the "country militia" guarding provisions at a meeting house across the bridge on the opposite side of the river. The Americans had received marching orders and were preparing to break camp, which prevented them from being taken completely by surprise. Nonetheless, the British dragoons quickly routed the Continental cavalry, and the British Legion infantry under Major Charles Cochrane crossed the bridge and drove the Whig militia from the meeting house with only minimal resistance. Most of Huger's men escaped on foot, but they left their horses, wagons and supplies behind. The American losses totaled about twenty men killed or wounded in the engagement and another sixty-seven taken prisoner. Tarleton captured 42 fully loaded supply wagons, 102 draft horses, 83 dragoon horses and a large number of officers' and militia mounts. The rebels' thoroughbred cavalry horses were a godsend for Tarleton, who had lost almost all of his mounts at sea on the journey south from New York, and the animals were quickly put to use by the British Legion.[113] McClure's company retreated up the Santee River and fell in with a company of North Carolina militia coming down to reinforce Charleston.[114]

Around the beginning of May, Lieutenant Colonel Joseph Brown raised a battalion of volunteers from Lacey's militia regiment—including companies commanded by Captain William Jones and Captain James Frost—to go to the aid of Charleston. After passing through Camden, they headed down the road toward Charleston, fully expecting to take part in the defense of their capital.[115]

Chapter II

"A vindictive asperity not easily restrained"

Friday, 12 May 1780

At 11:00 a.m., Major General Benjamin Lincoln surrendered the entire Southern Continental Army in Charleston to the British expeditionary force under Sir Henry Clinton. Lincoln's army included all four of South Carolina's remaining Continental regiments, two North Carolina Continental regiments and six Virginia Continental regiments, as well as a large number of North and South Carolina militia—a total of some five thousand men.[116] Under the terms of the surrender, the Continentals were to remain as prisoners of war until exchanged, but the patriot militiamen "were to be permitted to return to their respective homes, as prisoners on parole; and while they adhered to their parole, were not to be molested by the British troops in person or property."[117]

The surrender of Charleston sent a shock wave that reverberated across the Carolinas into Virginia and the northern states. Charleston was the largest and most important city in the South, and its loss was a serious blow to the morale of the rebellious Americans. For the Loyalists in the country, however, the surrender of Lincoln's army was cause for celebration, and large numbers of them began coming to Charleston and renewing their allegiance to the king. Clinton had great faith in these Loyalists, fully expecting that they would swell the ranks of the royal militia and help his troops restore control to the region. The Backcountry Loyalists assured the British commander that the few diehard rebels who were still in arms were no match for the king's troops and would be easily defeated or driven out of the province.[118]

There were still some rebel troops outside the city under the command of General Isaac Huger who had not surrendered with the rest of Lincoln's army. These troops included the remnants of William Washington's Continental dragoons and a few companies of militia, such as John McClure's company, which had rejoined Huger with the men from North Carolina. Having no further use for the militia, Huger dismissed them. Devastated by the capitulation of their capital city and angered by the loss of their horses, McClure's company broke camp and began the long walk home.[119] The remnants of Washington's cavalry removed to Lenud's Ferry on the Santee River, where they joined forces with a group of about 350 Continentals under Colonel Abraham Buford. Buford's regiment had come from Virginia to join Lincoln's army and learned of Charleston's surrender upon reaching Lenud's Ferry. Huger ordered the Virginians to

Lieutenant General Charles, Lord Cornwallis (1738–1805) was the second Earl of Cornwallis and later the first Marquis of Cornwallis. He commanded the British Army in the Southern Department under Sir Henry Clinton during 1780 and 1781. *Engraving from a portrait painted by American artist John Singleton Copley in 1793. Courtesy of the Culture & Heritage Museums, York County, South Carolina.*

withdraw to Hillsborough, North Carolina, along with South Carolina Governor John Rutledge. Rutledge, who escaped Charleston before the surrender, intended to set up a government in exile in North Carolina and continue the fight against the British from there.[120]

Monday, 15 May

Having received intelligence that Buford was retreating back to North Carolina along with fugitive Governor Rutledge, Clinton dispatched his second-in-command, Lieutenant General Charles, Earl Cornwallis, with a corps of some twenty-five hundred infantry, cavalry and artillery, to follow Buford and neutralize his force. Clinton and Cornwallis were in agreement that the pacification of the Backcountry was of major importance in the success of their campaign, and Clinton hoped Cornwallis would "meet, arm and protect our friends there." Sir Henry also appointed Major Patrick Ferguson of the Seventy-First Highland Regiment of Foot to be "Inspector of Militia in the Southern Provinces." He sent Ferguson toward Fort Ninety Six with a battalion of the American Volunteers and orders to recruit and train Loyalist militia on the way.[121]

Members of Lieutenant Colonel Joseph Brown's battalion from Lacey's Regiment were on the road to Charleston when they were met by Governor Rutledge on his way north. Rutledge gave the men the bad news that Charleston had fallen and advised them to return with him to Camden. After reaching Camden, Brown discharged his men and they set out for their homes in the District between the Broad and Catawba Rivers, disheartened by the news of Lincoln's surrender.[122]

Monday, 22 May

From his headquarters in Charleston, Clinton issued a proclamation promising protection to faithful supporters of the crown and threatening severe penalties for anyone who took up arms against British authority in the future. The proclamation stated, in part,

> that if any person shall hereafter appear in arms, in order to prevent the establishment of His Majesty's government in this country, or shall, under any pretence or authority whatsoever, attempt to compel any other person or persons to do so, or who shall hinder or intimidate, or attempt to hinder or intimidate, the King's faithful and loyal subjects from joining his forces, or otherwise performing those duties their allegiance requires, such person or persons so offending shall be treated with that severity so criminal and hardened an obstinacy will deserve, and his or their estates will be immediately seized, in order to be confiscated. And for the encouragement of the King's faithful and peaceable subjects, I do again assure them, that they shall meet with effectual countenance, protection, and support; and whenever the situation of the country will permit of the restoration of civil government and peace, they will, by the commissioners appointed by His Majesty for that purpose, be restored to the full possession of that liberty in their persons and property which they had before experienced under the British government.[123]

Ten days after Lincoln's surrender, Clinton had every reason to expect that the small numbers of scattered rebels would soon be captured or defeated, and that the loyal inhabitants of South Carolina would quickly assist in the restoration of the royal government.[124]

Saturday, 27 May

Realizing that his main army was advancing too slowly to catch Buford, Cornwallis detached Lieutenant Colonel Banastre Tarleton with 130 British Legion cavalry, 100 British Legion infantry and 40 troopers of the Seventeenth Light Dragoons. By riding hard and stopping only when absolutely necessary, Tarleton hoped to overtake the rebels and bring on an attack before Buford reached North Carolina and rendezvoused with the Continental forces mustering there. With many of his horses carrying both a dragoon and an infantryman, Tarleton moved north up the Santee.[125]

Sunday, 28 May

At about 10:00 a.m., young Tom Sumter, the son of Colonel Thomas Sumter, was riding his horse through the Hill Hills of the Santee River. He was surprised when a neighbor rode past at full gallop, crying that the British cavalry was on its way. Tom put spurs to his horse and made for home. Arriving breathlessly, he informed his father what he had heard. Sumter called to Soldier Tom, his African-born manservant, and ordered him to saddle their horses. After donning his old uniform from the Sixth South Carolina Regiment, Sumter bade farewell to Tom and his wife, Mary, and headed for North Carolina with Soldier Tom, only a few hours ahead of the British Legion.

Although Sumter had retired from active military service in September 1778, he was well known to the British as a prominent Whig officer. Tarleton dispatched Captain Charles Campbell of the British Legion to bring in the former Continental colonel. Campbell's detachment arrived at the Sumter plantation later that day. Finding Sumter gone, they plundered his plantation and put his house to the torch, leaving Sumter's family homeless. Tarleton proceeded on toward Camden.[126]

Arriving in Camden later that evening, Tarleton wasted no time in setting off after Buford. At about midnight, he departed the town with his dragoons and infantry.[127]

Monday, 29 May

In the early afternoon, Tarleton's troops finally caught up with the rear of Buford's column in what is now Lancaster County, South Carolina, in a region known as the Waxhaws. Named after an Indian tribe that once lived in the area, the Waxhaw settlement was a predominantly Scotch-Irish Presbyterian community that sprawled across both sides of the state line, with its focal point some thirteen miles to the west at Waxhaw Presbyterian Meeting House on the Catawba River.[128] As Buford's column advanced into the Waxhaws, Governor Rutledge left his escort and rode on toward Charlotte to avoid possible capture. Buford continued to march due north on the Camden-Salisbury road, with his supply train and field artillery well in front of his infantry. When Tarleton drew near, he sent up a rider with a flag of truce and offered Buford the opportunity to surrender; Buford sharply declined and continued on his march.

At 3:00 p.m., Tarleton's lead elements attacked Buford's rear guard and easily routed them. Buford then halted his advance and the Continentals turned to face the British, forming into a single line near an open wood. Tarleton deployed his men into three elements of combined cavalry and infantry, and attacked from about three hundred yards. As the British troops charged toward the Continentals, Tarleton was surprised to hear the American officers order their men not to fire until the dragoons were within ten paces of their line. By that time, the dragoons could not be stopped; the Continentals got off one volley but had no time to reload. Tarleton's horse was shot out from under him, and the battle quickly turned into a rout.[129] As Tarleton reported in his memoirs: "[T]he slaughter was commenced before Lieutenant-colonel Tarleton could remount another horse, the one with which he led his dragoons being overturned by the volley....The loss of officers and men was great on the part of the Americans, owing to the dragoons so effectually breaking the infantry, and to a report amongst the [British] cavalry, that they had lost their commanding officer, which stimulated the soldiers to a vindictive asperity not easily restrained."[130]

Buford did not wait to see the final outcome of the battle; as defeat seemed inevitable, he galloped away on horseback, leaving the infantry to their fate.[131] Some of the Virginians tried to surrender while others continued to fight, and a few dropped their weapons only to pick them up again and resume the battle. The British dragoons and infantry attacked relentlessly with sabers and bayonets, and the battle became a bloody mêlée.[132] When the hand-to-hand fighting finally subsided and the British officers regained control of their men, 113 Continentals were dead and 203 were captured. Of the prisoners, 150 were too badly wounded to be moved any great distance; only 53 could be transported to Camden. Tarleton reported his losses were five men killed, fourteen wounded and thirty-one horses dead or injured.[133] He then added: "The wounded of both parties were collected with all possible dispatch, and treated with equal humanity. The American officers and soldiers who were unable to travel, were paroled the next morning, and placed at the neighbouring plantations and in a meeting house, not far distant from the field of battle: Surgeons were sent for from Camden and Charlotte town to assist them, and ever possible convenience was provided by the British."[134]

Tarleton's humane treatment of the wounded prisoners was lost on the local Scotch-Irish families. Throughout all the years of Indian wars and the Regulator conflict, and throughout the first five years of the Revolution, the people of the Backcountry had never seen such carnage. The one hundred wounded Continentals brought to the Waxhaw Meeting House on the evening of 29 May had suffered few, if any, gunshot wounds; these men had been stabbed with British infantry bayonets and slashed with British cavalry sabers. In the words of the North Carolina historian Walter Clark, "perhaps a more complicated scene of misery in proportion to their number was never exhibited in the whole war."[135] As people came in from the surrounding community to help treat the wounded and bury the dead, word spread quickly that the Virginians had surrendered and then been mercilessly cut down after grounding their arms. Coming so soon after the shock of Charleston's surrender, the total defeat of Buford's command at the Waxhaws stunned the

Backcountry. Even worse for the British cause, the belief that Buford's men had been cut down after they asked for quarter soon resulted in the battle becoming known as "Buford's Massacre," and Whigs throughout the Carolinas began referring to Tarleton as "Bloody Ban" and "Butcher Tarleton." Within a short period of time, the catch phrase "Tarleton's Quarter," meaning "no quarter at all," become the battle cry of the Backcountry.[136]

Recently several military historians have questioned just how much of a "massacre" the Battle of the Waxhaws was. Several studies have suggested that the chaotic and confused nature of the engagement, and the tactical mistakes of the American commanders, contributed more to the "slaughter" of Buford's men than any bloodthirsty desire on the part of the British soldiers to kill Americans who had already surrendered.[137] As Dr. Anthony Scotti Jr. points out, "Under the rules of eighteenth-century warfare, an enemy force called upon to surrender which fails to do so forfeits its right to quarter in any upcoming combat."[138] Thomas Rider concludes, "The dynamics of the battlefield contributed as much and probably more to the carnage on 29 May 1780 than any predisposition to cruelty on the part of Banastre Tarleton or his men."[139] And Mark Boatner III puts the matter more bluntly, asserting that "a successful cavalry charge exploited by a bayonet attack is bound to be messy, and the dividing line between military success and slaughter depends on which side you're on."[140]

Tarleton placed most of the blame for the debacle on the poor tactical decisions made by the Continental officers and on the fact that the British soldiers could not be "easily restrained" after they saw their commander go down in battle.[141] Nonetheless, Tarleton did not attempt to sugarcoat the bloody nature of the incident; in a brief letter written to Lord Cornwallis immediately after the engagement, he reported that he had "cut 170 Off'rs and Men to pieces," and in his memoirs, he did not hesitate to call the affair a "slaughter."[142] Tarleton's own statements notwithstanding, some modern historians contend that the battle should not be referred to as a massacre.[143] The distinction boils down to whether most of Buford's men had surrendered before they were killed or wounded. The statistics tell their own story: Tarleton attacked with 270 men and suffered 5 killed and 14 wounded. Buford defended with more than 300 men and suffered 113 killed and 150 badly wounded. Faced with such a disproportionate number of casualties, it is easy to see why the Backcountry residents called the battle a massacre.

In the final analysis, the residents of the Carolina Backcountry were not interested in what Tarleton or Cornwallis thought about the battle, and they did not waste time worrying about how future historians might later justify it. Important to them were the mangled bodies lying in the Waxhaw Meeting House and the fact that British soldiers had wrought this destruction on men who had reportedly tried to surrender. Although Clinton, Cornwallis and Tarleton did not know it at the time, the Battle of the Waxhaws was a prelude to almost three more years of bloody partisan warfare in the Carolina Backcountry. "The compassion stirred in the inhabitants who nursed the wounded and the cry of anguished rage that greeted the crime throughout the State turned Tarleton's victory into a British disaster," Dr. David Wallace stated in *The History of South Carolina*, "for it planted in the hearts of thousands who had accepted a renewed British rule as inevitable the invincible determination to expel a power which could be guilty of such cruelty."[144]

Wednesday, 31 May

After a hot and exhausting journey of over two weeks, John McClure and his men finally reached their homes in what is now upper Chester County. One of McClure's cousins, Joseph Gaston, described the incident years later:

> *Captain John McClure, a young man, perhaps twenty-five years old, had taken a part of his militia company on towards Charleston, and was at or near Monk's corner when the town surrendered. His men then returned home; and he, on his way, called at the house of John Gaston, Esq., in the then Chester county. When there, he and his friends received intelligence of the shocking massacre of Colonel Bradford's [Buford's] men by Tarleton two days previous, about twenty miles from the place where he had stopped....On the reception of this news, he (Captain McClure), and three of said Gaston's sons, and Captain John Steel, I think, arose upon their feet and made this united and solemn declaration, "that they would never submit nor surrender to the enemies of their country; that liberty or death, from that time forth, should be their motto."! Each of these young men had served three years in the company of Captain Eli Kershaw, of the Third Regiment of South Carolina Militia, commanded by Col. Wm. Thompson, with the above motto inscribed on the front of their military caps.[145]*

This small group vowed that night to continue the fight against the British forces in the Upcountry at the cost of their lives if necessary. The Whigs were about to go on the offensive.

Thursday, 1 June

On the first day of June 1780, Lord Cornwallis set up a temporary headquarters in Camden and began organizing the British occupation of the Upcountry. Cornwallis had no intentions of remaining in the rough frontier town any longer than necessary; he delegated the command of

Lieutenant Colonel Francis, Lord Rawdon (1754-1826) commanded the Volunteers of Ireland, a Provincial corps comprising Irish deserters from the Continental Army. He was also the commander of British and Loyalist troops in the Camden and Cheraw Districts after the fall of Charleston. *Engraving by Benson J. Lossing from a British print, originally published in* Pictorial Field-Book of the American Revolution, *Volume II (1854). Courtesy of the Culture & Heritage Museums, York County, South Carolina.*

the region to one of his subordinates, Lieutenant Colonel Francis, Lord Rawdon, and detached about seven hundred men to help Rawdon control the area.[140] Lord Rawdon was the twenty-six-year-old son of the Earl of Moira in County Derry, Ireland, and was one of Cornwallis's most able field officers. He was Oxford-educated and a former classmate of Tarleton. Rawdon came to North America with the British Army in July 1774 and distinguished himself in the battles of Bunker Hill, Massachusetts; Long Island, New York; and White Plains, New York. In June 1778, Clinton gave him the command of the Volunteers of Ireland, a Provincial regiment comprised almost entirely of Irish deserters from the American Army, and by the spring of 1780, he and his volunteers were experienced veterans of the campaigns in New York, New Jersey and Pennsylvania.[141]

Cornwallis's first priority was to establish a series of outposts along the northern frontier of South Carolina, and to garrison these posts with a combination of experienced Provincial troops from the north and local Loyalist militia. The locations he picked—undoubtedly with the advice of Loyalists from the area—were natural elevations situated at Rocky Mount and Hanging Rock in the Camden District and Cheraw Hill in the Cheraw District. The Rocky Mount outpost was a cluster of reinforced buildings on a high hill overlooking the confluence of Rocky Creek and the Catawba River. The Hanging Rock outpost was an encampment on the important road between Camden and Salisbury, located near Hanging Rock Creek, a

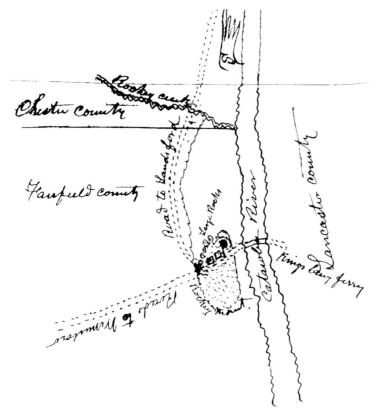

Map of the British fort at Rocky Mount, drawn by Daniel G. Stinson for Lyman C. Draper, 8 December 1871. *Thomas Sumter Papers, 5VV42, Draper Manuscript Collection. Image Number WHi-27319. Courtesy of the Wisconsin Historical Society, Madison, Wisconsin.*

tributary of Lynches River. The Cheraw outpost was located on a hill near Long Bluff, the seat of the Cheraw District. With the defense of the Backcountry thus defined, at least on paper, Cornwallis made plans to return to Charleston.[148]

That same day, Clinton and Admiral Marriot Arbuthnot, commander of the British naval fleet, issued a second proclamation that promised clemency to all those rebellious subjects who were willing to reaffirm their allegiance to the king, but granted no concessions to those who remained in arms against British authority:

> His Majesty having been pleased by his letters patent, under the great seal of Great Britain, to appoint us to be his commissioners, to restore the blessings of peace and liberty to the several colonies in rebellion in America, we do hereby make public his most gracious intentions, and in obedience to his commands, do declare to such of his deluded subjects as have been perverted from their duty by the factious arts of self-interested and ambitious men, that they will be received with mercy and forgiveness, if they immediately return to their allegiance, and a due obedience to those laws and that government which they formerly boasted was their best birthright and noblest inheritance; and upon a due experience of the sincerity of their professions, a full and free pardon will be granted for the treasonable offences which they have heretofore committed, in such manner and form as His Majesty's commission doth direct.
>
> Nevertheless it is only to those, who, convinced of their errors, are firmly resolved to return to and support that government under which they were formerly so happy and free, that these gracious offers are once more renewed; and therefore those persons are excepted, who, notwithstanding their present hopeless situation, and regardless of the accumulating pressure of the miseries of the people, which their infatuated conduct must contribute to increase, are nevertheless still so hardened in their guilt, as to endeavour to keep alive the flame of rebellion in this province, which will otherwise soon be reinstated in its former prosperity, security, and peace.[149]

In spite of these seemingly generous terms, Clinton and Arbuthnot refused to "extend the royal clemency" to any South Carolinians who had shed the blood of their Loyalist neighbors. The proclamation further assured the loyal subjects of the province that they had the full protection and support of the British forces, and promised that, "as soon as the situation of the province will admit, the inhabitants will be re-instated in the possession of all those rights and immunities which they heretofore enjoyed under a free British government." The general and the admiral called upon "all His Majesty's faithful subjects" to aid in their endeavors, in order that "the welfare and prosperity of the province, may be the more speedily and easily attained." They sincerely hoped this new proclamation would do much to restore order to the troubled province of South Carolina.[150]

Saturday, 3 June

Two days after his last proclamation, Clinton issued a new pronouncement that was destined to undermine much of what he had already accomplished toward pacifying South Carolina. The terms under which Lincoln surrendered on 12 May stated that, while the soldiers of the

Continental Line were to remain prisoners until exchanged, the militia would be released on parole. Clinton's new proclamation voided this earlier agreement and established new conditions for the parolees to remain free:

> *Whereas after the arrival of His Majesty's forces under my command in this province, in February last, numbers of persons were made prisoners by the army, or voluntarily surrendered themselves as such, and such persons were afterwards dismissed on their respective paroles; and whereas since the surrender of Charles town, and the defeats and dispersion of the rebel forces, it is become unnecessary that such paroles should be any longer observed; and proper that all persons should take an active part in settling and securing His Majesty's government, and delivering the country from that anarchy which for some time past hath prevailed; I do hereby issue this my proclamation, to declare, that all the inhabitants of this province, who are now prisoners upon parole, and were not in the military line, (those who were in fort Moultrie and Charles town at the times of their capitulation and surrender, or were then in actual confinement excepted) that from and after the twentieth day of June instant, they are freed and exempted from all such paroles, and may hold themselves as restored to all the rights and duties belonging to citizens and inhabitants.*
>
> *And all persons under the description before mentioned, who shall afterwards neglect to return to their allegiance, and to His Majesty's government, will be considered as enemies and rebels to the same, and treated accordingly.*[151]

In this one short document, Clinton not only revoked the paroles of the militia who were stationed at Charleston, but also required that they renew their allegiance to the crown and take an active part in restoring British control to the province, or be considered enemies. These men had hoped to return home and remain neutral; now they were expected to fight against their friends and family members who were still in arms against the British. Furthermore, those militiamen in the Backcountry who were not paroled at Charleston were now faced with the same choice: either support the crown or suffer the consequences. Clinton's proclamation left no middle ground.[152]

James P. Collins of the New Acquisition, who was sixteen years old when Charleston surrendered, recalled Clinton's proclamations and the effect they had in South Carolina:

> *So soon as Charleston fell, there was a proclamation for all to come forward, submit, and take protection; peace and pardon should be granted. In order to expedite the business, there were officers sent out in various directions, with guards or companies of men, to receive the submission of the people. Vast numbers flocked in and submitted; some through fear, some through willingness, and others, perhaps, through a hope that all things would settle down and war cease. But not so; there was some conditions annexed, that some of the patriots of the day could not submit to and therefore determined to hold out a little longer.*[153]

On or about the same day Clinton issued his last proclamation, Cornwallis appointed Lieutenant Colonel George Turnbull, a fifty-year-old Scottish officer, to command the important post at Rocky Mount. Turnbull's garrison at Rocky Mount would eventually include some 150 men of his own New York Volunteers Provincial regiment and a troop of some 35 or 40 British Legion dragoons under Captain Christian Huck; but Turnbull had to wait until mounts could be found for all of these men before they could be moved from Camden. He was also tasked with recruiting and training the local Loyalist militia, which would prove to be a more difficult chore. The exact date that he assumed his post at Rocky Mount is unknown, but it most likely happened during the first week of June.[154]

Turnbull was born to a wealthy family in Roxburghshire in the Borders area of southeastern Scotland in 1729 or 1730. He joined the army at the age of sixteen and served two years with the Scottish Brigade stationed in Holland in what was referred to as the "Dutch service." In 1757, he purchased a lieutenant's commission in the Fourth Battalion of the Sixtieth Regiment of Foot, or Royal American Regiment, which was raised in North America during the French and Indian War. Turnbull served with considerable distinction throughout that conflict and was involved in the Ticonderoga Campaign in 1758, the Niagara Expedition in 1759 and the capture of Montreal, Quebec, in 1760. Following Montreal, the Sixtieth transferred to the West Indies and helped capture the island of Martinique and Havana, Cuba, from the French and Spanish. The regiment returned to American in 1763 and played a major role in putting down Pontiac's Rebellion. In 1765, Turnbull was promoted to captain and given the command of a company in the Sixtieth. Following another tour of duty in the West Indies, Turnbull commanded the troops at Fort Detroit in what is now the state of Michigan, from 1766 until 1769. Following his service at Detroit, Turnbull sold his company in the Sixtieth, retired from the military and settled in New York. In early 1777, Turnbull returned to active duty as an officer in Colonel Beverly Robinson's Loyal American Regiment and received a lieutenant colonel's commission in that regiment in April. At the Battle of Fort Montgomery in New York on 6 October 1777, Turnbull took command of Major Alexander Grant's company of the New York Volunteers after Grant was killed in battle. As a reward for his bravery, Sir Henry Clinton granted Turnbull a commission as lieutenant colonel commandant of the New York Volunteers the following day. Over the next year, Turnbull commanded the Volunteers in New York and New Jersey, and in 1778, he married Miss Catherine Clopper, the daughter of an influential Loyalist family in New York. In October 1778, the New York Volunteers, with Turnbull in command, sailed south to participate in the capture of Savannah. Following this campaign, the Volunteers assisted in the siege of Charleston; part of the regiment then went to Camden with Lord Cornwallis.[155]

Turnbull's cavalry commander at Rocky Mount was Captain Christian Huck, whose name has been spelled variously as Hauk, Houck, Huik, Huyck and (most frequently) Hook. Christian Huck was born in one of the German principalities of Europe about 1748 and immigrated to Pennsylvania sometime before the outbreak of the Revolution. By 1775, he was a successful lawyer living in Philadelphia, and when the war began, he remained loyal to the crown. In 1778, the state legislature of Pennsylvania branded Huck a traitor and confiscated his property, and in July of that year, Huck raised a company of Loyalist volunteers and went to New York to join the British Army. In New York, he received a captain's commission in Emmerick's Chasseurs, a newly formed Provincial corps of light dragoons and infantry commanded by another German officer, Lieutenant Colonel Andreas Emmerick.[156]

In the summer of 1779, Clinton disbanded the Chasseurs because of morale and discipline problems, and reassigned most of the men. Clinton created several independent companies from the ranks of Emmerick's unit, including a troop of dragoons commanded by Huck. On 31 August 1779, Clinton attached Huck's troops to the command of Tarleton, with specific instructions that they were to serve under Tarleton but were not to be drafted into the legion. At that time, Huck's troop consisted of himself, Lieutenant Benjamin Hunt, Cornet Nathaniel Swaine, two sergeants, a quartermaster, a trumpeter and forty privates.[157]

In spite of Clinton's orders, by late 1779 or early 1780, Huck's troop was incorporated into the British Legion, and after that date British officers routinely referred to Huck and his troop as "of the Legion."[158] Huck and his dragoons participated in the siege and capture of Charleston and the various military actions around that city, and were also with Tarleton at Buford's Defeat on 29 May.[159] But unlike the Oxford-educated Tarleton, who could be quite debonair and charming when he wished to be, Huck was cut from a coarser cloth. He was arrogant, short-tempered, profane and blasphemous, and his colorful language earned him the nickname "the Swearing Captain." Not surprisingly, Huck had little patience with the Backcountry settlers in South Carolina, especially the Scottish and Irish Presbyterians, for whom he (like many other British officers) displayed an especially low regard.[160] Joseph Gaston of Fishing Creek, a first cousin of Captain John McClure, recalled that Huck "never failed, on convenient occasions, to curse Bibles and Presbyterians."[161] Major Joseph McJunkin, a Whig militia officer from the Fair Forest Regiment, quoted Huck as saying that "even if the rebels were as thick as the trees, and Jesus Christ would come down and lead them, he could defeat them."[162] Such sentiments were not destined to make Huck very popular in the Protestant settlements of the Backcountry, and his name soon became anathema to the Whigs between the Broad and Catawba Rivers.

Sunday, 4 June

At a secret location in what is now Union County, South Carolina, three Whig militia commanders from the west side of the Broad River held a meeting to decide their course of action. Colonel John Thomas Sr. commanded the Spartan Regiment, from the upper Spartan District; Colonel Thomas Brandon commanded the Fair Forest Regiment, from the lower Spartan District; and Colonel James Lisle (or Lyle) commanded the Dutch Fork Regiment, from the forks of the Enoree and Tyger Rivers, what is now Newberry County. These men had been active in the Revolution since the early days of the war. All three had served in the Snow Campaign, the Cherokee Expedition, the Florida and Georgia Campaigns and the defense of Charleston in 1779. In addition, Thomas had sat in the Provincial Congress, and Thomas and Brandon were members of the General Assembly.[163] By now word had reached them concerning Lincoln's surrender, Buford's Defeat, and Clinton's first proclamation. Would they continue the fight, or take the oath of allegiance and subject themselves to British authority? Unanimously they decided to fight and to combine their small bands at a camp on Fair Forest Creek, about four miles from where the city of Union now stands.[164]

That same day, some Loyalist soldiers set up camp at an old militia muster ground known as Alexander's Old Field, where the modern community of Beckhamville in

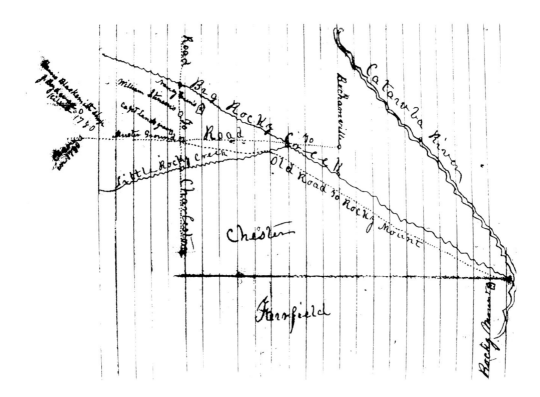

Map of the lower Rocky Creek area, showing William Martin's Covenanter church, George Harris's blacksmith shop, Ben Land's muster ground, Beckhamville and Rocky Mount. Drawn by Daniel G. Stinson for Lyman C. Draper, 28 January 1873. *Thomas Sumter Papers, 5VV48, Draper Manuscript Collection. Image Number WHi-27321, Wisconsin Historical Society, Madison, Wisconsin.*

Chester County now stands. Samuel McCalla, whose father David was a Whig militiaman from the area, remembered, "The Tories collected at Beckhamville and began to plunder everybody suspected of disloyalty, taking horses & cattle and household goods also all the grain & forage as it was needed to supply the British cavalry."[105] The Loyalists then began posting notices in the Scotch-Irish settlements along Rocky Creek and Fishing Creek on the west side of the Catawba. These notices summoned the local inhabitants to an assembly at Alexander's Old Field on 6 June. At this assembly, the notices stated, the people would be able to "give in their names as loyal subjects of King George, and receive British protection."[106]

Monday, 5 June

Confident that his work in the South was done, Sir Henry Clinton departed Charleston for New York with Admiral Arbuthnot aboard the British warship HMS *Romulus*, taking about a third of his troops with him. Before his departure, Clinton turned over command of the British Army in the South to Earl Cornwallis.[107]

In the Ninety Six District, Brigadier General Andrew Williamson had been planning a campaign to relieve Savannah when he learned of Charleston's surrender and Clinton's proclamation of 22 May. On 5 June, Williamson assembled his officers and men, including Colonel Andrew Pickens, read them Clinton's capitulation terms and offered to lead them into the mountains from where they could continue their operations against the British. Very few of the men showed any interest in pursuing the war. This included Colonel Pickens, who seemed to have lost his will to fight after the fall of Charleston. Williamson then sent word to Captain Richard Pearis, a Loyalist officer who was operating in the area, that he and his men were ready to accept parole and surrender their arms.[108]

That same day, a Loyalist officer named Captain Houseman came up from Rocky Mount with about fifty Tory militiamen to visit Justice John Gaston on Fishing Creek. Houseman knew that the old justice wielded a great deal of influence in the area, and he strongly desired Gaston's help in persuading the local rebel leaders—most of whom were Gaston's sons and nephews—to turn in their arms and sign the oath of allegiance at Alexander's Old Field the next day. Houseman employed a great deal of logic and eloquence attempting to convince Gaston of the futility of further resistance to the crown and of the wisdom of accepting British protection. Gaston refused his offers.

As soon as Houseman left, Gaston sent word to his older sons, his nephews John and Hugh McClure and their comrade John Steele, notifying them of Houseman's request and suggesting that they round up the militia and pay Houseman a "surprise visit" the next day at the old field. Steele and the McClures agreed to the plan, and for the rest of that day and night, they rode throughout the district recruiting volunteers from the Fishing Creek, Rocky Creek and upper Sandy River communities who were willing to take arms against the Loyalists.[109] Joseph Gaston, the youngest of Justice Gaston's nine sons, later remembered that over the course of the day and night, "they collected together, in all thirty-two volunteers: they were principally of the Knoxes, Walkers, Morrows, McClures and Johnsons."[170] Among them were two brothers, Samuel and Alexander McKeown, who had already scouted the Loyalist camp at Alexander's Old Field and were able to provide an exact description of its layout. As the Whigs prepared to depart, the old justice led them all in a solemn prayer, then gave each man a hearty handshake and a stiff drink from a gallon jug of peach brandy. The members of McClure's band then mounted their horses and set out for Houseman's camp.[171]

None of these early accounts gives any additional information on the identity of Captain Houseman. The Revolutionary War historian Dr. Lyman C. Draper thought that he was "perhaps a New York Tory" and "the first commandant at Rocky Mount," but his name does not appear on any of the existing muster rolls or payrolls for the northern Provincial regiments transferred to South Carolina in 1779 and 1780.[172] It is much more likely that he was a Tory militiaman from the upper Catawba region. In a letter to Lord Cornwallis dated 15 June, Turnbull stated: "I have appointed one Cap⁺. of Militia at Cedar Creek until your Lordships Pleasure is further known. Indeed He was the Choice of the People and I thought him Deserving."[173] Although Turnbull never mentioned the militia captain's name, the fact that he lived on Cedar Creek is an important clue. Cedar Creek empties into the east side of the Catawba River directly across from Rocky Mount and is shown on the map of Lancaster District in Robert Mills' 1825

South Carolina atlas.[174] During the Revolutionary War, a prominent landowner named Henry Houseman lived in this same area. Houseman had apparently been an attorney in Charleston in the early 1770s, but by 1780, he had moved to the Camden District and lived on the east bank of the Catawba opposite Rocky Mount.[175] Henry Houseman, then, was almost certainly the officer who commanded the Loyalist militia at Alexander's Old Field. Although Joseph Gaston referred to him as "Colonel Housman," most of the other accounts give his rank as captain. Gaston's statement that Houseman was accompanied by fifty militiamen tends to confirm that he was in fact a captain commanding a company of Tory militia.[176]

While Captain Houseman was paying a visit to Justice Gaston, some of the other Loyalists in his company were engaged in a different task. One of the more important duties assigned to the militiamen at Rocky Mount was rounding up suitable horses for the British troops stationed there, especially the dragoons, who were still having difficulty finding adequate cavalry mounts. On the same day that Houseman visited Gaston, two brothers named John and Richard Featherstone (also spelled Featherston, Fetherston or Fetherstone), members of a Loyalist family who lived on lower Rocky Creek, led a party of armed Tories to the plantations of several of their Whig neighbors, including David Leonard, George Wade and Thomas McDaniels. The Loyalists requisitioned all the horses that were deemed fit for military service "in the name of the King," which the Whigs saw as simply another version of horse stealing.[177] The Featherstone family included at least one additional brother, William, and a sister, Sarah ("Sally"), who were also Loyalists and assisted the king's troops during the British occupation of the Upcountry.[178]

Chapter III

"God Almighty had become a Rebel"

Tuesday, 6 June 1780

As the sun began to rise that morning, Captain John McClure's volunteers rode quietly along an old Indian trail running from upper Fishing Creek to lower Rocky Creek. When they neared Alexander's Old Field, they dismounted and spread out through the woods around the Loyalist camp. Captain Houseman and a group of armed Tory militiamen were present to administer the oath of allegiance and sign up volunteers for the king's service. Altogether, some two hundred people had assembled at the old field that morning. Many of them had no real desire to take British protection but believed they had no choice. The Whigs, seeing their neighbors and friends present on the field, aimed with care, concentrating their fire on the armed Tories. A number of locals had already taken the oath of allegiance when McClure's company opened fire, and two young men named Joe Wade and William Stroud Jr. fell to the ground and "played dead" while the Whigs picked their targets. The attack was a complete surprise and "a general stampede took place"; the assembly quickly scattered in all directions. John Featherstone, who sported a large bushy shock of hair, ran off bareheaded, and a Whig named James Wylie took aim at Featherstone's head, determined to shoot him as he ran. Wylie was in such a hurry that he missed his shot, and Featherstone escaped unharmed. However, some of the Tory militiamen stood their ground and returned the Whigs' fire before withdrawing from the field. In all, four Loyalists were killed and several more were wounded. Two of the Whigs were also wounded: William McGarity was slightly injured in one arm, and Hugh McClure took a musket ball in his right arm above the elbow, which left the arm crippled for the rest of his life. The Whigs took nine prisoners, and several men who had signed the oath of allegiance, including Wade and Stroud, renounced the declaration and immediately joined McClure's company. Wade and Stroud paid dearly for their decision later that summer when they fell into British hands: Stroud was hanged, and Wade was whipped almost to the point of death.[179]

At about the same time as these events were transpiring (the exact date is uncertain), Colonel Samuel Watson and Lieutenant Colonel William Bratton called a meeting of the New Acquisition Militia Regiment at Bullock's Creek Meeting House on the east side of the Broad River. The news of General Benjamin Lincoln's surrender, the capture of Charleston and Colonel Abraham Buford's defeat had already reached the New Acquisition; now the officers had learned that General Andrew Williamson, Colonel Andrew Pickens and other important Whig leaders in the Backcountry were going to take parole and turn in their arms. As one of the officers from the New Acquisition, Colonel William Hill, later described the incident, Watson and Bratton stated their belief that any further opposition to the British was useless:

> At this meeting, they did not encourage the men, but much the reverse, by telling them that they had hitherto done their duty. But it appeared to them that any further opposition to the British would not avail & as for their parts could have nothing more to say to them as officers but to advise each of them to do the best they could for themselves—Upon this the meeting broke up, but it was generally rumored about that a commissioner was sent to Lord Rawdon then in the Waxaw, so it was that a man of respectable character that had represented the District in the Gen' Assembly (did go) but whether employed by the officers or not, the author cannot say.[180]

Hill's subsequent statements make it clear that Watson and Bratton resigned their commands as colonels of the New Acquisition Militia Regiment, and he implies that the two men had lost their will to continue fighting against the British. This viewpoint is difficult to reconcile with other evidence, from both British and American sources, showing that Watson and Bratton were still active in the field during and immediately after this time.[181] Hill's account leaves a great deal unspoken, and in fact, there is no evidence to indicate that he was even present at the Bullock's Creek assembly. Fortunately, other accounts of this meeting exist that shed more light on the incident. In a sworn deposition attached to the Federal pension application of his friend James Clinton, Samuel Gordon of the New Acquisition Regiment stated that after the fall of Charleston, "Col. Watson despaired, and told his men to seek better service, & attach themselves to the American army."[182] Gordon's testimony indicates that the two colonels lacked confidence in the militia's ability to successfully resist the British occupation alone and that their services would be more effective if they cooperated with the Continental Army.

Other evidence points to a political rivalry between Hill and Bratton, and possibly even a personality clash that probably had much to do with Hill's unflattering portrait of Bratton's services during this period. There may have been a rivalry between the two even before the events of May and June 1780. Both men were influential leaders in their neighborhoods, and both held political ambitions that brought them into conflict. Bratton was a tax collector for the New Acquisition, and Hill owned thousands of acres of land, numerous slaves and a lucrative factory, making him subject to significant taxes. After the war, both men served as justices of the peace for York County and as state legislators, and frequently competed with each other for political offices.[183] Hill's grandson, Lieutenant General Daniel Harvey (D.H.) Hill of the Confederate Army, attested to the fact that when his grandfather served as a state senator, "his constant competitor was Mr. Wm. Bratton. The [York County] Court House was the scene of many battles, hundreds on each side, between the Bratton and Hill factions." Regarding Colonel William Hill's memoir, General D.H. Hill had this to say: "My father tried to prevent him from writing it. [My grandfather] was in his dotage at the time & my father thought that the egotism of the book was enormous."[184] It is probably no coincidence that Hill's memoirs were written in February 1815, the same month that Bratton died and was no longer around to defend himself.

William Hill was born about 1741, probably in County Antrim in the north of Ireland. His family was originally of English ancestry, but they moved to northern Ireland in the seventeenth century and were a part of the Scotch-Irish migration to Pennsylvania in the eighteenth century.[185] Around 1768, Hill relocated to Craven County, South Carolina, and obtained numerous land grants totaling several hundred acres in what is now York County.[186] When the Revolution began, Hill was a prominent leader of the Bethel congregation in the northeastern part of the New Acquisition, where he operated an ironworks on Allison Creek. By then he owned a large plantation with abundant timber and a substantial iron mine on Nanny's Mountain (named for his wife, Jane "Nanny" McCall) where he procured his ore. Initially lacking the capital to construct a furnace, Hill's early manufacturing was confined to forging plows, farm tools, smith's tools, kitchen ware and other implements. With financial assistance from Isaac Hayne of Charleston and a loan of £1,000 from the South Carolina treasury in 1776, Hill constructed sawmills, a gristmill and a blast furnace. Employing labor from some ninety slaves, Hill began casting swivel guns, cannons and cannonballs for the defensive works at Charleston, and Hill's Ironworks became the largest operation of its type in the South Carolina Upcountry.[187]

Although Hill was an adamant Whig, before the summer of 1780 he had not served in either the militia or the Continental regiments.[188] Undoubtedly his industrial and agricultural operations kept him quite busy and demanded his constant attention, and it would have been difficult for him to leave his business for months at a time to serve in the lengthy campaigns of the early Revolution. However, the fact that he owned the oldest and most productive ironworks in the state not only made his services invaluable to the rebellion but also gave him a great deal of political clout in his district, and from 1778 until 1780, he represented the New Acquisition in the South Carolina General Assembly and the Senate.[189]

William Bratton, like Hill, came from a family of Scotch-Irish immigrants and, like Hill, he was probably born about 1741 in northern Ireland. His family lived in both Pennsylvania and western Virginia before migrating to Rowan County, North Carolina, in the late 1750s or early 1760s.[190] Around 1765, several members of the Bratton family, including William and at least four siblings, moved to the Fishing Creek area, which at the time was part of southeastern Mecklenburg County, North Carolina. In August 1766, Bratton and his young wife Martha Robertson (or Robinson) purchased two hundred acres of land on the South Fork of Fishing Creek from Thomas Rainey, a wealthy land speculator who lived nearby. Other members of Bratton's family obtained adjoining land grants or purchased land nearby, and by 1771, the Bratton settlement in York County included Bratton's four brothers, Robert, Thomas, Hugh and John, as well as his older sister Jean Bratton Guy and her husband Samuel Guy.[191] Bratton's home was located at the junction of the Armstrong Ford Road and the Rocky Mount Road, and in July 1769, he received an appointment as a Tryon County road overseer.[192] Thus began a long career of public and military service for Bratton; by the beginning of the Revolution, he was a prominent local planter, an elder in the Bethesda congregation and a justice of the peace for Camden District. In 1775, he was commissioned a captain in the New Acquisition Militia Regiment with his brothers Hugh and John serving as lieutenants in his company. By June 1780,

Richard Winn (1750–1818) was a captain in the Third South Carolina Regiment of Rangers early in the Revolution and later commanded a militia regiment in General Thomas Sumter's Brigade. Winn was instrumental in organizing the Whig resistance in the Backcountry after the fall of Charleston in May 1780. *Courtesy of the Richard Winn Academy, Winnsboro, South Carolina.*

Bratton had served as a captain, major and lieutenant colonel in the New Acquisition Regiment, and had participated in virtually every campaign and battle since 1775; he was one of the most experienced field officers in the Upcountry.[193]

In spite of their many military and political accomplishments, neither Hill nor Bratton was very impressive physically. According to Dr. Maurice A. Moore, a nineteenth-century York County physician and local historian, "Col. W[m]. Hill was abt. 5 feet 9 in. in height, a thin spare made man [with] rather a round face, large nose and spoke slowly...Col. W[m]. Bratton was abt. 5 feet 8, short neck & high shoulders, a small spare made man [with a] sharp visage."[194]

Following the meeting at Bullock's Creek, it was clear that Colonels Watson and Bratton no longer wished to serve as commanders of the New Acquisition Regiment. If the men of the New Acquisition wished to continue to field a militia regiment, they would have to find new officers to lead them.

Wednesday, 7 June

In the middle section of the District between the Broad and Catawba Rivers, corresponding to the modern county of Fairfield, lived a prominent family of Whigs named Winn (or Wynn) that included two brothers, Richard and John. The Winns were of Welsh ancestry and had migrated from Fauquier County, Virginia, to South Carolina in the mid-1760s. They obtained thousands of acres in land grants on the east side of the Broad River and settled near the modern town of Winnsboro, which they founded. Before the war, Richard Winn established himself as a prominent planter, merchant, surveyor and land speculator in the Camden District. He enlisted in the Third South Carolina Regiment of Rangers in 1775 and served as a lieutenant and captain under Colonel William Thomson during the early period of the war. As one of Thomson's Rangers, Winn participated in the Snow Campaign of 1775 and the battles of Sullivan's Island in 1776 and Fort McIntosh in 1777. After his discharge from the Third Regiment, Captain Winn organized a militia company and fought at the Battle of Stono Ferry in 1779. He also represented the District between the Broad and Catawba Rivers in the General Assembly in 1779 and 1780.[195] By virtue of this service, Winn was well acquainted with the prominent Whigs from the New Acquisition and the upper portion of the District between the Broad and Catawba Rivers—including the Neals, Brattons, McClures and Laceys—and had fought alongside them during the first five years of the war.[196]

In early June, the British established a strong outpost at Shirer's (or Sherer's) Ferry on the east bank of the Broad River opposite the Dutch Fork, and summoned the inhabitants of the region to take the oath of allegiance to the king or be regarded as enemies.[197] Encouraged by the British presence, the Tories in the area began plundering Whig plantations, including the homes of Captains John and Henry Hampton, whom they arrested and sent to Camden under guard. In his memoirs of the Revolution written in 1812, Richard Winn stated that the Tories, under the command of Colonel Charles Coleman, set up camp at a meeting house near Little River. This site, known variously as Mobley's Meeting House or Gibson's Meeting House, was about twelve miles above the British post at Shirer's Ferry, which Winn referred to as "Shiroe's Ferry." When Winn learned of this Tory assembly, he set out to rally the Whigs in his neighborhood. Such was the fear of the British authority by this time that, as Winn later recalled in his memoirs, "he could not raise one single person to oppose them, [so he] set out himself for the New Acquisition to see if he could not raise men by the help of Cols. Lacey, Bratton and Nixson [John Nixon]." Winn arrived in the New Acquisition on 7 June and contacted the local militia commanders. Over the course of the day, the officers recruited a force of about one hundred volunteers, including John McClure and the thirty-two men who had attacked the Tories at Alexander's Old Field the day before. Colonel Bratton also raised a company of young volunteers from the Bethesda neighborhood, and his presence in the group, as testified by Winn and others, is proof that he had not simply retired from the field, as Hill implied in his reminiscences. With this strong force of militiamen, all well-mounted on good horses, Winn set out for Mobley's Meeting House.[198]

While these events were transpiring in South Carolina, another scenario was unfolding in North Carolina that was to have a profound influence on the war in the Backcountry. A Loyalist officer named John Moore, who lived about six miles from Ramsour's Mill on the South Fork of the Catawba River in Lincoln County, North Carolina, returned home after spending several months with the British Army. Moore had accompanied Lord Cornwallis's troops on their march up the country from Charleston and took his leave at Camden, arriving at his father's home on

7 June wearing an officer's sword and a well-worn British uniform. After assembling some of the loyal inhabitants in his neighborhood, Moore announced that he was now a lieutenant colonel in the Royal North Carolina Regiment, a Provincial regiment commanded by Lieutenant Colonel John Hamilton of Halifax County. He proceeded to describe the siege and capture of Charleston and the British occupation of Camden, and designated 10 June as the date for the Loyalists in the vicinity to assemble on Indian Creek, seven miles from Ramsour's Mill.[199]

Thursday, 8 June

The Whigs arrived in the vicinity of Mobley's Meeting House early that morning and scouted the area; there were already about two hundred people assembled there. Some were armed Loyalist militiamen commanded by Colonel Coleman, while others were local citizens complying with British proclamations to take protection and join the loyal militia. Coleman's men were posted both inside and outside the meeting house, a log structure with strong walls, but they were not really expecting any trouble. The Whigs, on the other hand, had come to fight. Their strategy was the same used at Alexander's Old Field: attack without warning and surprise the enemy. They fanned out through the woods and surrounded the meeting house on three sides. The fourth side faced a steep bluff, and the Whigs felt confident that none of the enemy would attempt to escape out that side of the building. In his reminiscences of the event, Winn stated that "as Capt. Winn was well acquainted with the strength and situation of the place it was left to him to bring on the attack." As the sun began to rise over the horizon, Winn and his party opened fire. The fight lasted for several minutes, and to the surprise of the Whigs, many of the Tories did in fact try to escape down the bluff on the back side of the building.[200] Maurice Moore later reported that "there was more of the British & Tories killed and wounded by their leep down this precipice than was by the American rifles."[201] Winn also remembered that "in a few minuits the body of Tories was drove from a strong House which answered for BlockHouse & totally defeated with a small loss of killed & wounded. The Wig party lost nothing."[202] Hugh Gaston of McClure's company, who was also present at the battle, recalled in his pension application that "[t]he battle was fought at break of day & lasted a short time—several negroes were killed & some tories were taken prisoners. After the battle the militia returned home."[203] Winn's party recovered a great deal of loot that the Tories had taken from Whig plantations, including some thirty slaves, several wagons and teams, thirty horses and a large quantity of household furniture plundered from John and Henry Hampton.[204] Following the battle, the Whig militia commanded by Bratton and McClure removed to the Upper Fishing Creek Presbyterian Meeting House and made camp there, while Winn, Lacey and Nixon returned to their own neighborhoods.[205]

Friday, 9 June

At Rocky Mount, the northernmost British outpost in South Carolina, Lieutenant Colonel George Turnbull was worried. The loyal subjects in the area kept him well informed of the rebel activities; they told him about the attacks at Alexander's and Mobley's almost as soon as they happened, although there is no mention of either incident in his letters to his superiors.[206] Turnbull realized that a show of force was going to be necessary to keep the rebels in check. The Whigs in the New Acquisition and the upper District between the Broad and Catawba Rivers still had not submitted to British authority, and their recent successes against the Tories made it obvious that they had no intentions of laying down their arms without a fight. Turnbull's spies had informed him that Bratton and McClure were camped at Reverend John Simpson's meeting house and were rallying men to their cause. Since taking post at Rocky Mount a few days earlier, Turnbull had been organizing a Loyalist militia regiment to reinforce his New York Volunteers and British Legion dragoons. The incidents at Alexander's and Mobley's had demonstrated the royal militia's lack of fortitude in the face of the more experienced Whigs, and Turnbull did not have a lot of confidence in their abilities.[207]

In addition to Henry Houseman, two men named James Ferguson and John Owens (or Owen) from the Fishing Creek and Rocky Creek settlements were also recruiting Loyalist militia in the Rocky Mount neighborhood. Ferguson, like Turnbull, was of Scottish ancestry, but unlike the Scotland-born Turnbull, Ferguson's family had been in the colonies since the early 1700s. Settling first in Essex County, Virginia, before 1717, the Fergusons obtained several land grants in what is now lower Chester County, South Carolina, during the 1760s. James Ferguson bore the same name as his father and grandfather, so he is sometimes referred to as "James Ferguson II" or "James Ferguson III."[208] The Fergusons were members of Simpson's Lower Fishing Creek congregation, but unlike most of Simpson's flock, the Fergusons stood firmly in the king's camp.[209] So did John Owens, a latecomer of Welsh ancestry who also moved down from Virginia and received several Craven County land grants on upper Fishing Creek in early 1773. Owens did not live far from Upper Fishing Creek Church, but whether he was a member of that congregation is uncertain.[210]

Following the fall of Charleston, Ferguson, Owens and Houseman raised several companies of Loyalist militia and reported to Turnbull at Rocky Mount. Turnbull was not overly impressed by these men, and his letters to Lord Cornwallis and Lord Rawdon during this period never mention any of them by name, although as noted earlier, he does refer to a captain from Cedar Creek who was probably Houseman.[211] Our knowledge of these Loyalists comes primarily from the accounts of Whig veterans and nineteenth-century local historians who listed them as commanders of Tory militia at Rocky Mount during the summer of 1780. John Craig of the New Acquisition Regiment referred to Ferguson as "Major Ferguson," but both Richard Winn and William Hill made it clear in their memoirs that by July 1780 Ferguson was a colonel in command of a regiment, and Winn further stated that Owens ranked as "major to Colonel Ferguson's Regiment of Tories."[212] As further confirmation of Owens's rank, "Major John Owens" also appeared as second-in-command on a payroll for the Rocky Mount Loyalist militia regiment commanded by Colonel William T. Turner in 1782.[213]

Although he was of Scottish parentage, Turnbull had little regard for the Scotch-Irish settlers who made up most of the inhabitants of the area. In his letters to Lord Cornwallis, Turnbull referred to them sarcastically as his "good friends the Bounty Irish," and described them as "the Greatest Skum of the Creation."[214] He was not particularly fond of South Carolina in general, especially the northern frontier, and bitterly resented being stationed at "the worst spot in it."[215]

The New Yorkers were unaccustomed to the heat, humidity and backwoods conditions of the Carolina frontier, and more than anything Turnbull wished to return to his wife and family in New York. But while he was stationed in the South, the colonel was resolved to do his duty as best he could, and that included attempting to train and discipline the Backcountry Loyalist militia. He resolved to send Captain Christian Huck and his dragoons, accompanied by the best equipped of the militia, to punish the rebels around Upper Fishing Creek Church, or "Simpson's Meeting House" as he referred to it.[216]

On the other hand, the Whigs in the area were greatly encouraged by their successes at Alexander's and Mobley's. In both cases they had been outnumbered and outgunned, but their years of experience in backwoods warfare, combined with the element of surprise, had given them two important victories. After the disastrous defeats at Charleston and the Waxhaws, these engagements provided a much needed morale boost for the residents of the Broad and Catawba Valleys and also reinforced the belief among the local Whigs that Providence was on their side. John Craig, who temporarily served in McClure's Rangers in early June, later recalled, "Our cause was a good one, and that nothing short of an Almighty Hand could have given us that which we were contending for, will appear to any reflecting mind. The race is not to the swift nor the battle to the strong; the Almighty was with us."[217] William Hill made a similar statement in his memoirs, "[T]here was a Providence that overruled the actions of men, who brought forth means to carry forth the great work."[218]

Saturday, 10 June

Lord Rawdon arrived in the Waxhaw settlement from Camden and made camp at the home of "Mr. Leslie," probably Samuel Leslie (or Lessley) who lived on the north side of Waxhaw Creek.[219] He was met by a delegation of local citizens who assured him of their "warmest desire to live under the British Government." Rawdon instructed the locals to appoint a committee of "principal inhabitants" with whom he could conduct all his business. He also recommended that the loyal subjects form a militia regiment for their own protection, but he was surprised to hear that the locals preferred to remain "on parole" and keep their arms in case they were attacked by rebel militia from nearby Mecklenburg County, which, like the New Acquisition, was settled chiefly by Presbyterians from the north of Ireland. Rawdon sensed that the Waxhaw inhabitants were reluctant to organize a Loyalist militia when the surrounding districts had not done so, fearing that if they did, they would almost certainly suffer the same fates as the Tory militia at Alexander's and Mobley's. The locals informed Rawdon that they feared not only the Whigs from the Charlotte, North Carolina, area but also the Catawba Indians, whose close attachment to the South Carolina government was well known. Rawdon decided to send an address to the citizens of Charlotte, warning them to keep the peace or risk British punishment. As for the Catawbas, who feared an attack by Cherokees and their British allies, Rawdon instructed the Waxhaw committee to inform the Indians "that if they return to their settlement & behave quietly, they shall receive protection; but that if they commit any act of hostility, their settlement shall be utterly destroyed." More than anything, Rawdon was eager for the Waxhaw settlers and the Indians to tend to their crops, as grain was rapidly becoming scarce in the region.[220]

The procurement of food from the surrounding countryside was extremely important to the British Army in the Carolinas, and the local Loyalist militia played an important role in requisitioning or confiscating such supplies from local planters. As Lord Cornwallis's commissary, Charles Stedman, noted in his history of the American Revolution: "From the time that the British army entered Camden...it was wholly supported by supplies from the neighbouring districts. The militia were employed in collecting Indian corn to be ground into meal, which, issued when new, made a good substitute for wheat. They were also employed in collecting cattle and sheep; they were allowed four shillings and eight-pence per head for cattle, and two shillings and eleven pence sterling per head for sheep (for driving only). The owners had either a receipt, or a certificate, given them (unless avowedly hostile)."[221]

The Loyalist militia in the Carolinas thus became "cowboys" and foragers for the British Army, which naturally did little to endear the militiamen to the local populace, especially their Whig neighbors. Commissary Stedman later praised their service in his memoirs and gave them no small credit for supporting the British Army during the Southern Campaign:

> *The militia, most of them being mounted on horseback...went in quest of provisions, which were collected daily from the country through which the army marched: Nor were their difficulties of this service trifling; they were obliged to ride through rivers, creeks, woods, and swamps, to hunt out the cattle. This service was their constant and daily duty; they were frequently opposed; sometimes worsted, and with no inconsiderable loss. In short, so essentially necessary was this unfortunate description of people, that it was impossible to have supported his majesty's army in the field without them. Cattle-driving was of itself a perfect business; it required great art and experience to get the cattle out of the woods. The commissary was under the greatest obligations to those people, without whose assistance he could not possibly have found provisions for the army.*[222]

The Whig militia, of course, was required to perform the same sort of duties in order to support its own operations in the field and to support the Continental Army when it arrived in the Carolinas.

Across the Catawba River at Rocky Mount, Turnbull dispatched Huck's dragoons and a detachment of mounted militia under James Ferguson with instructions to disperse the rebels at Fishing Creek. More than likely, Turnbull also gave Huck orders to establish a presence at Walker's Mill on upper Fishing Creek, where wheat and corn requisitioned from surrounding plantations could be ground for the garrison at Rocky Mount. Like Rawdon, Turnbull was also feeling the pinch for supplies, and with the hot weather just beginning, he was concerned about feeding his men and the large number of horses that the dragoons and militia brought.[223]

That same day, Rev. John Simpson—after once more encouraging his congregation to take up arms against the British—shouldered his rifle and joined the Fishing Creek militia. "There the pastor, taking his place in the ranks with the brave men of York and Chester, encouraged and stimulated them by his counsel no less than his services, performing the duties of a private soldier, and submitting to the rigorous discipline of the camp."[224] The South Carolina audited accounts for Revolutionary War service show that Simpson enlisted as a private in the mounted

South Carolina Audited Account of militia service for the Reverend John Simpson, documenting that he served as a private of mounted militia and a commissioner of public accounts from 10 June until 10 November 1780, and that he lost a gun and clothing at the Battle of Fishing Creek on 18 August 1780. *South Carolina Audited Account 7019. Courtesy of the South Carolina Department of Archives and History, Columbia, South Carolina.*

Deposition signed by Colonel Edward Lacey attesting to the militia service of the Reverend John Simpson. *South Carolina Audited Account 7019. Courtesy of the South Carolina Department of Archives and History, Columbia, South Carolina.*

militia under Captain Alexander Pagan and Lieutenant John Mills of Fishing Creek, in Colonel Edward Lacey's Regiment, on 10 June 1780.[225] Along with Simpson, about eighty men from the Fishing Creek and Bethesda congregations joined as well. Although their numbers were growing, they were still vulnerable to an attack from Rocky Mount if they remained at Fishing Creek Church. Having received word from their spies that Huck was advancing on their camp, Bratton and McClure decided to head for safer territory, specifically Hill's Ironworks in the northern section of the New Acquisition, which Turnbull referred to as "the mountains."[226] This area is in fact very hilly and includes several small mountains, among which are Nanny's Mountain, Henry's Knob and the Kings Mountain Range.

Hoping to capitalize on their success, a few of the Whigs from the New Acquisition went out into the district to recruit volunteers for the militia. One of these men, John Craig, was disappointed to learn that most of the men in the area were still afraid to take arms against the British. "The second defeat [at Mobley's Meeting House] had so exasperated the British and Tories that they turned into burning houses and plundering the Whigs," Craig later recalled, "so that at that moment times had but a gloomy appearance. Nothing but devastation and ruin appeared, and men were disheartened." Only seven men volunteered to join Craig.[227] However, word reached them that Colonel Francis Locke of the North Carolina Militia was raising volunteers at Salisbury to take the field against the enemy. A group of thirteen men from the New Acquisition—including Captain James Martin, Captain James Jamieson, Lieutenant William Robison, Private John Craig and Private Henry Rea—rode up to Salisbury to offer their services.[228]

One of the Whigs who immediately suffered the wrath of the Tories was Captain Richard Winn. Knowing that Winn had planned and led the raid on Mobley's, and that he was still in the field with the Whig militia, Loyalists from the Little River visited Winn's plantation, sacked it and put it to the torch. Describing the incident years later, Winn stated that "the British and Tories had all his houses Burnt to the ground & every negro plundered together with every other property he possessed in the world, his wife plundered of her clothes & she drove off with two Infant Children. When this was made known to me, my answer was it is no more than I expected."[229]

To the west of the Broad River, Colonel Thomas Brandon, commander of the Fair Forest Militia Regiment, was camped with seventy or eighty Whigs on Fair Forest Creek, about five miles below the present site of Union. While awaiting the arrival of the militia regiments commanded by Colonels John Thomas and James Lisle, Brandon's men had captured a Loyalist named Adam Steedham. One of Brandon's soldiers, Thomas Young, later noted that Steedham was "as vile a tory as ever lived." However, Steedham escaped on the night of 9 June and made his way to the camp of Captain William Cunningham, who commanded a force of Tories from the Saluda River. Before daybreak on the morning of 10 June, Cunningham's Loyalists attacked Brandon's camp and completely routed the Whigs.[230] Thomas Young, who was not in Brandon's camp that morning, recalled in his memoirs: "On that occasion, my brother, John Young, was murdered. I shall never forget my feelings when told of his death. I do not believe I had ever used an oath before that day, but then I tore open my bosom, and swore that I would never rest until I had avenged his death. Subsequently a hundred tories felt the weight of my arm for the deed, and around Steedham's neck I fastened the rope as a reward for his cruelties. On the next day I left home in my shirt sleeves, and joined Brandon's party."[231] Following Cunningham's attack,

Brandon's men retreated across the Broad River to the relative safety of the New Acquisition and took post at Bullock's Creek Meeting House.[232]

Further west in the Ninety Six District, General Andrew Williamson and other prominent Whigs officially surrendered to Captain Richard Pearis, the Loyalist officer acting on behalf of the British. In addition to the general, Colonel Andrew Pickens of the Long Cane Creek settlement and several other high-ranking officers also gave their paroles. These officers further agreed to give up the arms and ammunition stored in a fort at Whitehall, Williamson's plantation, as well as to disarm and discharge its garrison. The rebellion in the western part of the state seemed to many Whigs, including those in the New Acquisition, to be over.[233]

At Indian Creek near Ramsour's Mill in North Carolina, a group of Loyalists assembled on 10 June in response to the request from Lieutenant Colonel John Moore, issued three days earlier. The noted North Carolina partisan Joseph Graham, then a captain in the militia, recalled the incident in his memoirs:

> *Forty men assembled, and Moore told them it was not the wish of Lord Cornwallis that they should embody at that time, but that they and all other loyal subjects should hold themselves in readiness, and in the meantime get in their harvest; that before the getting in of the harvest it would be difficult to procure provisions for the British army; and that as soon as the country could furnish subsistence to the army, it would advance into North Carolina and support the royalists.*
>
> *Before this meeting broke up an express arrived to inform them that Major Joseph McDowell, of Burke County, with twenty men, was within eight miles of them, in search of some of the principal persons of their party. Confident of their strength, they resolved to attack McDowell, but some preparation being necessary, they could not march until next morning, when, finding he had retired, they pursued him to the ledge of the mountains which separate the counties of Lincoln and Burke, and not being able to overtake him, Moore directed them to return home and meet him on the 13th at Ramsour's Mill.[234]*

Events were rapidly moving toward a major clash between Whigs and Tories in the neighborhood of Ramsour's Mill, a clash that would undo much of Lord Cornwallis's careful planning for a campaign in North Carolina later that autumn.

Sunday, 11 June

Captain Huck arrived in the upper Fishing Creek settlement early Sunday morning with his dragoons and a detachment of Tory militia under James Ferguson. Turnbull's intelligence placed the rebel militia under Bratton and McClure in camp at the meeting house, and this included most of Simpson's congregation from Fishing Creek and Bethesda. Huck expected to find Simpson and his congregation attending worship service that morning and to catch them by surprise. As they approached the Fishing Creek Meeting House, Huck and Ferguson stopped at the neighboring home of Janet "Jenney" Strong. She was a widow and a sister of Justice John Gaston, and her family was well known to be staunch Whigs. Her oldest son, Christopher, was twenty and had served in the local militia for several years. Mrs. Strong's other son, William, was seventeen and had joined the militia company of Captain Jonathan Jones only nineteen days earlier.[235] There are two versions of what transpired next. Turnbull, in a letter to Lord Cornwallis, stated that Huck's men were reconnoitering the road leading to the meeting house when "two men with Rebell Uniforms were discovered running through a field of Wheat. The Militia fired upon them, killed one and wounded the other."[236]

Local traditions in the Fishing Creek community, recorded by Chester County magistrate and historian Daniel Green Stinson in the nineteenth century, told a much more gruesome (and probably exaggerated) story. The nineteenth-century writer Elizabeth Ellet incorporated Stinson's version into the third volume of her *Women of the American Revolution*:

> On Sunday morning, June 11th, the troops under Huck arrived at the house of Mr. Strong, near Fishing Creek Church. They immediately entered and plundered the house of everything, carrying away also the corn and wheat. Some of the grain being accidentally scattered in the yard, a tame pigeon flew down and picked it up. The brutal captain struck the bird, cutting off its head at a blow with his sword; then turning to Mrs. Strong, he said: "Madam, I have cut off the head of the Holy Ghost." She replied, with indignation: "You will never die in your bed, nor will your death be that of the righteous." The prediction thus uttered was in a month signally fulfilled. Mrs. Strong was a sister of old Justice Gaston.
>
> After this insult and blasphemy, some of Huck's men went to the barn, where her son, William Strong, had gone shortly before their arrival. He had taken his Bible with him, and was engaged in reading the sacred volume. They shot him dead upon the spot, and dragged him out of the barn. The officers then began to cut and hack the dead body with their broadswords, when Mrs. Strong rushed from the house, pleading with all a mother's anguish, to the officers, that they would spare the corpse of her son. They heeded not her agonized entreaties, till she threw herself upon the bleeding and mangled body, resolving to perish as he had done by the cruel hands of her enemies, rather than see her child cut to pieces before her eyes.[237]

A quarter of a mile away at the Simpson home, the reverend's wife, Mary Remer Simpson, was having breakfast with her children when she heard the sound of gunfire. As her husband and the rest of the local militia had departed the day before, she wondered what the noise was about.[238]

Following the incident at the Strong plantation, Huck's force proceeded the short distance up the road to Fishing Creek Meeting House. The Loyalists surrounded the building and went inside, but were disappointed to find it empty and no rebel militia in sight. Unknown to the British, the rebels had been tipped off that Huck was coming and had retreated north into the New Acquisition. Huck ordered his men to remount and proceed to the reverend's home, where they would "burn the rascal out." Several of Reverend Simpson's slaves were standing nearby and overheard Huck's comments; they hastened to the Simpson home and gave warning to Mrs. Simpson. Once again, Ellet's narrative tells the story, based on Stinson's research:

> Mrs. Simpson looked out, and saw a body of men coming down the lane. Stopping only to gather up a set of silver tea-spoons, most valued by her as a gift from her mother, she took her four

children and went out at the back door, concealing herself in the orchard in the rear. Here she was enabled to watch the movements of her enemies, without being herself discovered.

They rifled the house of everything valuable, took out four feather beds, and ripped them open in the yard; collected all the clothing, from which they selected such articles as they fancied for their own keeping, and having exhausted their invention in devising mischief, finally set fire to the house, which was soon burned to the ground. Just as they were going away, they noticed an outhouse, which contained a valuable library, and was usually occupied by Mr. Simpson as a study. This was soon also in flames. The men now left the premises, and as soon as they were out of sight, Mrs. Simpson hastened back to the house, rushed into the study and carried out two aprons' full of books. She could save no more, and in doing this, was much burned and had nearly lost her life. The feathers in the yard had taken fire, but she succeeded in saving enough for one bed. She then went to the house of one of her neighbors, where she remained till after her confinement, which took place in four weeks. As soon as she recovered, she returned to her own place, and took up her residence in a small outhouse which had escaped the enemy's vengeance.[239]

Confirmation for much of this account comes from the Camden District court records and also provides the names of two of the Loyalist militiamen who accompanied Huck and Ferguson on their trip to Fishing Creek. On 24 June 1785, Charles Lewis swore out the following deposition before Justice James Knox in Camden District Court:

Be it remembered that Charles Lewis appeared before me and being Sworn upon the Holy Evangelist of Almighty God, Saith upon his Oath that on or about the tenth Day of June in the year of our Lord one thousand Seven Hundred and Eighty this Deponent being put under Guard, by a Col. Turnbull, and a Capt. Hook and a party of Horse Compelled me to go on a Scout with s[d.] Hook, with a party of Tories from Rocky Mount up the Country, being Disarmed, Saith upon his Oath, that the Day After they Left Rocky Mount they Came to the House of the Rev. John Simpson, whose House was Burned, and Property Destroyed, and Carried off by the above mentioned Party. He further Saith upon his Oath that Burrel Burge and Jeremiah Burge were very Active, with the s[d.] Party, and at the House of the s[d.] Simpson, he Saw them take and Carry off Bed clothes and other articles out of s[d.] Simpson's House. Sworn and subscribed before me this 24 of June 1785. Ja[s.] Knox, J. P. /s/ Charles Lewis[240]

Several sources also indicate that Huck's men burned the meeting house itself that Sunday morning. The earliest statement to that effect comes from Winn, who had joined forces with Bratton and McClure a few days earlier. In his 1812 notes on the campaign of 1780, Winn stated that "Capt. Huck with his party...burnt the meeting house of the Rev[d.] M[r.] Simpson, who was at the head of a large Presbyterian congregation. The people in that Quarter [of] Fishing Creek immediately cried out they wanted no protection from such a set as burnt churches & the word of God."[241] Referring to the same congregation, William Dobein James stated in his 1821 biography of Francis Marion that Huck "burnt their church, their parsonage, and their bibles; and treated them with insult and cruelty."[242] Major Joseph McJunkin made a similar statement in his 1837 memoirs, asserting that Huck was sent by Turnbull "to punish the Presbyterian inhabitants of that place, which he did with a barbarous hand, by killing men, burning churches, & driving off the ministers of the gospel to seek shelter amongst strangers."[243]

Although Ellet made no mention of the meeting house being burned in her rendition of Stinson's research, Draper's notes include several quotes from his conversations with Stinson stating that "Fishing Creek Church [was] burned by Huck's party June 11th on his first trip up the country, & killed young Strong there."[244] Church history confirms that the original log church building was destroyed in 1780 and not rebuilt until 1785, and since the Fishing Creek Meeting House (like the Bullock's Creek Meeting House) was being used as a camp by local militia, it seems likely that Huck or some other Loyalists burned the building at the same time they destroyed Simpson's home and study.[245]

While Simpson and his congregation were not in church that Sunday morning, farther down on Rocky Creek, the Covenanters in Reverend William Martin's congregation turned out in large numbers. In fact, so many people showed up for church that morning that there was not room enough for them in the little log meeting house, so they moved Martin's pulpit out into the churchyard and assembled under the shade of the trees. Although the Covenanters were unaware of Huck's activities to the north, they were fully cognizant of Charleston's capitulation and, more importantly, the defeat at the Waxhaws on 29 May. That Sunday morning, Martin preached a sermon full of fire and anti-British sentiment that was long remembered in the Rocky Creek community. Daniel Stinson collected notes on the sermon from individuals who were there at the time; he in turn passed his notes on to Elizabeth Ellet, who put the story into her own colorful Victorian prose:

"My hearers," he said in his broad Scotch-Irish dialect—"talk and angry words will do no good. We must fight! As your pastor—in preparing a discourse suited to this time of trial—I have sought for all light, examined the Scriptures and other helps in ancient and modern history, and have considered especially the controversy between the United Colonies and the mother country. Sorely have our countrymen been dealt with, till forced to the declaration of their independence—and the pledge of their lives and sacred honor to support it. Our forefathers in Scotland made a similar one, and maintained that declaration with their lives; it is now our turn, brethren, to maintain this at all hazards." After the prayer and singing of the Psalms—he calmly opened his discourse. He cited many passages from Scripture to show that a people may lawfully resist wicked rulers; pointed to historical examples of princes trampling on the people's rights; painted in vivid colors the rise and progress of the reformation—the triumph of truth over the misrule and darkness of ages—and finally applied the subject by fairly stating the merits of the Revolutionary controversy. Giving a brief sketch of the events of the war from the first shedding of blood at Lexington, and warming with the subject as he went on, his address became eloquent with the fiery energy of a Demosthenes. In a voice like thunder, frequently striking with his clenched fist the clapboard pulpit, he appealed to the excited concourse, exhorting them to fight valiantly in defence of their liberties. As he dwelt on the recent horrid tragedy—the butchery of Buford's men, cut down by the British dragoons while crying for mercy—his indignation reached its height. Stretching out his hand

towards Waxhaw—"Go see," he cried, "the tender mercies of Great Britain! In that church you may find men, though still alive, hacked out of the very semblance of humanity: some deprived of their arms—mutilated trunks: some with one arm or leg, and some with both legs cut off. Is not this cruelty a parallel to the history of our Scottish fathers, driven from their conventicles, hunted like wild beasts? Behold the godly youth, James Nesbit—chased for days by the British for the crime of being seen on his knees upon the Sabbath morning!" etc. To this stirring sermon the whole assembly responded. Hands were clenched and teeth set in the intensity of feeling; every uplifted face expressed the same determination, and even the women were filled with the spirit that threatened vengeance on the invaders. During the interval of divine worship they went about professing their resolution to do their part in the approaching contest; to plough the fields and gather the crops in the absence of the men—aye, to fight themselves, rather than submit. In the afternoon the subject was resumed and discussed with renewed energy—while the appeals of the preacher were answered by even more energetic demonstrations of feeling. When the worship was concluded, and the congregation separating to return homeward, the manly form of Ben Land was seen walking among the people, shaking hands with every neighbor and whispering in his ear the summons to the next day's work.[246]

While these events were transpiring at Fishing Creek and Rocky Creek, Lord Rawdon was still camped in the Waxhaws. Unaware of the growing discontent across the Catawba, he was at the moment more concerned with the rebellious spirit of the Whigs in Charlotte and Mecklenburg County, many of whom were mustering in arms at Salisbury. As his first order of business, Rawdon composed a proclamation entitled "To the Inhabitants of Charlotteburg. N. Carolina," advising them to keep the peace and tend to their crops. Quoting the wishes of Earl Cornwallis, Rawdon advised the Charlotteans "to return immediately to their Farms; where they shall gather their Crops without Fear or Interruption: Provided always that they do demean themselves peacefully, & do not attempt to distress either in person or property any Friend to Government within their own or in the neighboring settlements." He ended the proclamation with a severe warning about the consequences of armed resistance to the crown.[247]

After dispatching the proclamation to Charlotte, Rawdon then wrote to Lord Cornwallis, who was still in Camden, giving him a detailed update of the events since his arrival in the Waxhaws on 10 June. Rawdon briefed Cornwallis on his meeting with the Waxhaw committee and their apprehensions about the Catawbas. Noting that the Indians had "good crops on the ground," he expressed his hope that they would soon return to their homes and bring in their harvest. There was little to gain by remaining in the Waxhaws, he observed, and no point in advancing any farther into the frontier. Promising to return to Camden in three or four days, Rawdon then gave a report on the status of the Waxhaws as to provisions. "The country tho' thickly settled is poor in itself and much drained," he reported. "I am regularly supplied with Cattle; tho' even in that article they plead poverty; but the neighborhood is totally destitute of grain or any kind of Dry Forage." Rawdon further informed Cornwallis that he would "send Five Waggons tomorrow for a reinforcement of Provisions" and noted that he had already written to Captain Alexander Ross, Cornwallis's aide-de-camp, informing him of the matter.[248]

Monday, 12 June

Early Monday morning, a group of Martin's Covenanters assembled at a muster ground seven miles from Rocky Mount and began drilling under the command of Captain Ben Land. Unknown to Land and his men, a local schoolmaster named Montgomery had tipped off the British at Rocky Mount regarding the muster. Montgomery was "a Scotchman" and a Loyalist, and had consistently refused to sign the state association or take any oaths of allegiance to the South Carolina government. Thanks to Montgomery's warning, a party of Huck's dragoons caught the Whigs by surprise, charged in upon them and put them to flight. Land was surrounded by the dragoons and attempted to defend himself with his sword. He wounded several of the cavalrymen but was soon cut down and killed.

About two miles above the muster ground, some half a dozen of the Covenanters assembled at the shop of a George Harris, "a Negro blacksmith," in order to get their horses shod. These men were also surprised by the dragoons, and James Boyd was killed in the shop. The dragoons then proceeded to the home of Martin, arrested him and took him back to Rocky Mount as a prisoner, from whence he was soon transported to the jail at Camden.[249]

In the New Acquisition, scattered Whigs from the west side of the Broad River began to collect at Bullock's Creek Meeting House. Reverend Alexander, the minister there, had left his home and sought refuge with his relatives in Mecklenburg County on account of his strong attachment to the Whig party. Thomas Brandon's men had gathered at Bullock's Creek after their defeat by William Cunningham two days earlier; they were joined there by Colonel John Thomas Jr., now leading the remnants of his father's Spartan Regiment; Colonel James Lisle, commanding the Whigs from the Dutch Fork District; and a handful of refugees from Georgia. Major Joseph McJunkin later recalled the meeting in his memoirs:

> Here after enumerating our dangers and trials past, & thinking of future dangers and hardships, with the offers of British protection before us—the question came up, what shall be done? Col. John Thomas Jr. (son of Col. John Thomas Sr.) addressed the meeting. He asked, shall we join the British, or strive like men to gain the noble end for which we have striven for years past? Shall we declare ourselves cowards and traitors, or shall we pursue the prize, Liberty, as long as life continues? He advised the latter course. After he had finished, I addressed the people to the same effect—shall we pursue Liberty, or give up? The question was put—all who were in favor of fighting the matter out, were to clap their hands & throw up their hats. The question came. The hats flew upwards, and the air resounded with the clapping of hands, & shouts of defiance to the armies of Britain and the foes of Liberty.
>
> We entered on this resolution—that he that through necessity of apparel, or a wish to see his family, desired to return home, was welcome to do so, if he would agree to meet us at Tuckasegee Ford, on the Catawba river, east side, whither myself and others immediately proceeded.[250]

Also on or about 12 June, another meeting took place in the New Acquisition at Hill's Ironworks. The residents of the New Acquisition anxiously assembled to learn the results of the envoy sent to Lord Rawdon the week before. Once again, our only detailed account of this meeting comes from William Hill's memoirs, although other sources like Samuel Gordon's deposition also refer to the incident. Hill tells us that a representative from Lord Rawdon's headquarters rode up to the ironworks to meet with the assembled Whigs of the New Acquisition. Exhibiting his commission "from under the great seal of Lord Rawdon," the officer informed the men that "he was empowered to take their submissions & give paroles & protections to all that choose to become British Subjects," the same offer already extended by Captain Richard Pearis in the Ninety Six District, Captain Henry Houseman at Alexander's Old Field, and by British representatives at Shirer's Ferry in the Dutch Fork District and Mobley's Meeting House on the Little River. According to Hill, the commissioner then proceeded to read a proclamation from Lord Rawdon stating that Congress had abandoned any hope of reclaiming "the two Southern states," Georgia and South Carolina. The proclamation also claimed that General George Washington's army was reduced to only a few men and that Washington had "fled to the mountains."

At this point, Hill interrupted the commissioner and addressed the citizens himself, disputing the claims made by the officer. Hill stated that Congress had not given up on any of the states, and that Washington "was in a more prosperous way than he had been in for some time." Furthermore, Hill told the assembly that Washington had in fact appointed one of his general officers to lead a Continental Army to relieve the Southern states and that this army was already on the move toward the Carolinas. Hill reminded the men that "we had all taken an oath to defend & maintain the Independence of the state to the utmost of our power and that if we could not raise a force to meet the foe, we had one open side, we c^d. keep in a body, go into No. Ca. meet our friends, & return with them to recover our State." After Hill finished his speech, the citizens of the New Acquisition were "visibly animated" and their spirits were considerably raised, so much so that Rawdon's commissioner was forced to depart in a hurry with his proclamation for fear of being accosted by the audience.[251]

As the operator of a large ironworks, Hill had extensive contacts with important officials and prominent citizens in Charlotte, Salisbury and throughout western North Carolina. These contacts undoubtedly kept him informed of developments further north, including Washington's plans for a new Southern army. As a result of these contacts, Hill's information about Washington's army was essentially correct, especially the part about a new Continental Army being sent to the aid of South Carolina. Before the fall of Charleston on 12 May, Washington ordered Major General Johann DeKalb, better known as Baron DeKalb, to march south with two brigades of Maryland and Delaware Continentals, some of the army's most experienced and disciplined soldiers. Along the way he was to pick up fresh drafts of Virginia and North Carolina militia. Meanwhile, Washington and Congress argued over who to appoint as commander in chief of the Southern Department. Congress wanted Major General Horatio Gates, the "Hero of Saratoga," but Washington preferred his more capable commissary officer, Major General Nathanael Greene. Congress would ultimately get its way, and Gates would be designated as commander in chief of the Southern army—an appointment that would be disastrous for the army.[252]

After Rawdon's commissioner left, the men of the New Acquisition expressed their desire to remain together as a regiment; however, since Watson and Bratton had resigned, they did not have any senior officers. Hill advised the men to ballot for a full colonel and a lieutenant colonel, as was the custom for militia regiments. Andrew Neal, one of the twin sons of the regiment's former commander, Colonel Thomas Neal Sr., was chosen as senior colonel, while Hill was chosen as lieutenant colonel.[253] Neal and Hill were members of the Bethel congregation, as were many of the men in the room, and both men were logical choices to lead the regiment. Andrew Neal had served under his father since the Snow Campaign and was undoubtedly the most experienced field officer in the room. In choosing Hill, the men were electing a well-known and influential citizen, but one without any significant experience as a field commander. However, because Hill owned and operated the ironworks, he was well respected, and Hill's Ironworks now became the headquarters for the reconstituted New Acquisition Regiment. The men proceeded to form companies and elect the necessary captains, lieutenants and sergeants. "We then formed a camp and erected the American Standard," Hill related. "And as soon as this was known there were men both of the states of Georgia and South Carolina adding daily to our numbers that we soon became a respectable body."[254]

While the New Acquisition Regiment was re-forming at Hill's Ironworks, down at Rocky Mount, Lieutenant Colonel Turnbull was composing a letter to Lord Cornwallis in Camden. His Lordship had suggested that Turnbull enroll three companies of independent South Carolina militia into his New York Volunteers. The companies Cornwallis referred to were almost certainly the Loyalist militia raised by Houseman, Ferguson and Owens in the vicinity of Rocky Mount, men with whom Turnbull was not especially enamored. The colonel was extremely reluctant to enlist such men in his elite Provincial regiment. As delicately as possible, Turnbull assured Cornwallis that his "zeal and attachment for His Majesty's Service [would] never be awanting" and that he would do his utmost to discipline and equip the Loyalist militia under his command in any way he could. "But I do imagine it would not answer to Enroll such People in a Corps with ours," he continued, "who are High Disciplined and not Indulged with the same Conditions." He went on to state that as soon as the province was "quieted," he would welcome the chance to return to New York with his regiment, where he felt he and his men could render much more useful service. Turnbull also missed his wife and family, so much so that he was considering leaving the army once peace was restored to South Carolina. "When I speak of that matter how it affects me Personally I Really have Scarce words to Express it," he wrote. "There is Surely a Duty which a man owes His Family and if I see no Relief after Settling the Peace and Quiet of this Province I shall be Drove to the Disagreeable Necessity to Quit the Service Intirely."[255]

Wednesday, 14 June

The New Acquisition Militia Regiment, now headquartered at Hill's Ironworks, received intelligence that a Tory named Matthew Floyd was raising men in the Broad River settlements to reinforce the British post at Rocky Mount. The report also stated that Floyd and his men were "distressing" the Whig inhabitants living along the east and west banks of the Broad River. Upon hearing this news, Colonel Neal collected as many men as he could and set off in pursuit of the Tories, leaving only a small garrison to guard the ironworks during his absence.[256]

Floyd was a prominent Backcountry Loyalist who migrated from Ireland to Pennsylvania around 1746, when he was seventeen years old, and moved to the Carolina Backcountry in 1754.[257] With his wife Sarah, he settled on 450 acres along Guyan Moore Creek in what is now York County, during the period when North Carolina claimed the region as part of Anson County. After the area was incorporated into Mecklenburg County, Floyd obtained several additional land grants on Turkey Creek and Bullock's Creek in present-day York County, as well as grants on the upper branches of the Broad River in territory that is still part of North Carolina.[258] During the Cherokee War of 1759–1760, Floyd served as a lieutenant in the North Carolina Militia, and in October 1759, he led a company of rangers on a campaign against the Cherokees in western North Carolina.[259] He was also active in the local county governments: Mecklenburg County appointed him justice of the peace in December 1762, and Tryon County appointed him tax collector in February 1770.[260] Throughout the 1760s and early 1770s, Floyd engaged in land speculation and made a considerable profit, not only selling some of his own grants but also buying and selling land along the Broad and Catawba Rivers in North and South Carolina.[261] Floyd eventually sold his property on the east side of the Broad River and moved across the river to what is now Union County, and when the Revolution broke out, he declared his allegiance firmly on the side of the king. As a result of his participation in the Loyalist revolt of November and December 1775, Floyd was arrested and imprisoned for three months in Charleston. In order to get out of jail, he took an oath not to take up arms against his countrymen. However, in the spring of 1779, he again angered the Backcountry Whigs by arresting some of the returning veterans of the Battle of Briar Creek. Following the surrender of Charleston, Floyd began actively recruiting Loyalist militia on the west side of the Broad River.[262] In early June, Floyd's militia began harassing the Whigs on the east side of the river, who immediately sent word of what was happening to the New Acquisition Regiment at Hill's Ironworks.[263] Meanwhile, Floyd collected about thirty of his most dedicated followers and set out for Rocky Mount to offer his services to Turnbull, not realizing that he was leaving his own neighborhood vulnerable to Whig vengeance.[264]

Huck returned to Rocky Mount that afternoon. After destroying Simpson's home (and probably the meeting house), Huck reconnoitered the area but was unable to find the Whig militia. Huck reported that the rebels had "fled to the mountains," a reference to the hilly area in the northern part of the New Acquisition where Hill's Ironworks was located. He also reported that his militia had killed one rebel and wounded another.[265]

In the Tory camp near Ramsour's Mill in North Carolina, some two hundred Loyalists had rendezvoused with Lieutenant Colonel John Moore the day before. On 14 June, reinforcements arrived under the command of Major Nicholas Welsh (also spelled Walsh or Welch), a native of the area who commanded a company in the Royal North Carolina Regiment under Lieutenant Colonel John Hamilton. Welsh had joined the British Army eighteen months before and had only recently left Lord Cornwallis's headquarters. Welsh brought news of Buford's defeat at the Waxhaws and the overall success of British operations in South Carolina:

> *He wore a rich suit of regimentals, and exhibited a considerable number of guineas, by which he sought to allure some, while he endeavored to intimidate others by an account of the*

success of the British Army in all operations of the South and the total inability of the Whigs to make further opposition. His conduct had the desired effect, and much more confidence was placed in him than in Colonel Moore. They remained in camp until the 20th, during which time a detachment, commanded by Colonel Moore, made an unsuccessful attempt to capture Colonel Hugh Brevard and Major Joseph McDowell, each of whom came into the neighborhood with a number of Whigs to harass the Tories, who were assembling.[266]

Thursday, 15 June

Early in the day, Turnbull composed another letter to Lord Cornwallis, giving an update on the situation in the area. He reported the results of Huck's excursion to Fishing Creek and informed the Earl that several of the "most violent" Whigs in the area—including Colonels Robert Patton, William Bratton and Richard Winn—had abandoned their plantations and "gone amongst the Catawba Indians." The rebels, he stated, were propagating a far-fetched story that the British seized all their young men and sent them to the "Prince of Hess," meaning the men were sent to join the Hessian army, which was causing great consternation in the Backcountry. Turnbull further informed Cornwallis that corn was becoming scarce, noting he only had about ten days worth of meal left. "It is difficult to support Dragoons without Corn," he complained. The colonel was aware of an "Irish settlement at Turkey Creek and Bullock Creek" about thirty miles to the west with abundant provisions; however, these people had become "very violent," and he proposed sending troops to settle them. Turnbull was eagerly awaiting the arrival of some of his New York Volunteers from Camden who were equipped with horses for mounted service, and if the militia continued to improve its performance, he suggested that he might be able to spare the Legion dragoons altogether if Lord Cornwallis had some other use for them. Clearly, Huck's troopers and their horses were becoming a burden to Turnbull, who also had to support his own soldiers and the Loyalist militia when they were in camp. Turnbull was expecting the local militia to show up on Saturday, 17 June, when he would continue his efforts to organize and train them, but he doubted whether he would find anyone fit to rank as a field officer.

Turnbull's briefing also addressed Hill's Ironworks, which was becoming a thorn in his side. "It has been a Refuge for Runnaways," he told the Earl, "a Forge for casting Ball and making Rifle Guns &c. I wou[l]d Propose with your Lordships permission to Destroy this Place. I think a small Party might be found against Saturday at the [militia] muster that wou[l]d Compleat this affair. Sending some of our own officers and men [New York Volunteers] with them." Lastly, Turnbull related that he had received a letter from Lord Rawdon, who was preparing to depart the Waxhaws. Rawdon was concerned about the "body of Rebell Militia still in arms between Charlotteburg and Salisbury, but as He [Rawdon] has no Dragoons or mounted men, He says He has no chance of giving them a blow. I Flatter myself your Lordship will see the Necessity of Dispersing those men for while such a Body of Rebells keep in arms so near us our Militia affairs will not go well."[267]

Later that day Turnbull received a pleasant surprise. Floyd and thirty of his Loyalist militiamen from the Broad, Tyger and Enoree Rivers arrived at Rocky Mount, "all Volunteers to serve the King." For once, Turnbull found a militia officer he could trust: Floyd seemed sensible and a staunch friend of the British government. After hearing of Floyd's persecution by the rebels and his time spent in the Charleston jail, Turnbull commissioned him a colonel and placed him in charge of the Upper or Spartan District Loyalist militia.[268] Floyd's son Abraham accepted a commission as a captain and company commander. Abraham Floyd had served under Colonel Thomas Neal Sr. in the New Acquisition Regiment prior to the fall of Charleston and was a veteran of the Cherokee Expedition of 1776. In February 1779, he went to Georgia with Major Frank Ross's battalion, was captured by the British at the Battle of Briar Creek, imprisoned at Savannah and escaped. After Charleston surrendered, he joined his father in the Loyalist militia.[269] Turnbull does not mention Floyd's second-in-command, but subsequent statements by Cornwallis and Lieutenant Colonel Banastre Tarleton make it clear that this position was held by Lieutenant Colonel John Lisle (or Lyle).[270] Lisle was a former Whig from the Dutch Fork District who had served as a lieutenant in the Third South Carolina Regiment from November 1775 until August 1779, and as an officer in the Dutch Fork Militia Regiment; he was a veteran of the Snow Campaign, the Cherokee Expedition and several other early battles of the war.[271] When General Benjamin Lincoln surrendered Charleston, Lisle and many other Whig officers were interned on the Sea Islands off the South Carolina coast, but Lisle gave his oath of loyalty and accepted parole in exchange for his freedom and service in the royal militia.[272]

While Turnbull was enjoying the company of Floyd and his officers, a couple of express riders came in bringing the news that Neal's regiment was wreaking havoc in the settlements where Floyd and his men lived. Writing to Lord Cornwallis the next day, Turnbull outlined this new intelligence to the Earl:

> *Our joy was very soon interrupted by a Couple of Expresses who assured us that a Party of Rebells had Sallyd forth from the Iron Works and had gone into the settlement of M^r. Floyd and His Company and were tearing everything to Pieces.*
>
> *I immediately Ordered Capt. Hook of the Legion to get Ready, that with Capt. Floyds Company and the other militia which we could assemble it was necessary to give these fellows a Check. The weather Prevented their Setting off last night. But they took the morning Early. I have taken the Liberty to give Capt. Hook Orders to Destroy the Iron Works they are the Property of a M^r. Hill a great Rebell. I hope the marching of this Party will do something towards Quieting our Frontier. Those Rebells Embodyd Between Charlotburg & Salisbury Over awes great part of the Country and Keeps the Candle of Rebellion still Burning. Lord Rawdens Retreat [from the Waxhaws] I dare Say Confirms them in the Belief that we are only here for a few days.[273]*
>
> *I Confess my Lord I have no Particular attachment to any Part in South Carolina but I wou[l]d not wish to Leave the worst Spot in it untill the Neck of Rebellion was broke.*
> *In my former Letter I mentioned to your Lordship that we had meal for about Ten or Twelve days, when that is done we shall be much at a Loss.*
> *The Inhabitants are Constantly turning [to] me for Proclamations. I wish your Lordship would Send me some.*

I meant tomorrow to have had a Gen.[l] muster of the Militia to arrange them in the best manner I could. This alarm will discompose it a good deal.[274]

Friday, 16 June

Captain Huck set out early in the morning from Rocky Mount with his Legion dragoons and about sixty militia under Captain Abraham Floyd, with the goals of destroying the ironworks and dispersing the rebels camped there. He did not proceed immediately to Hill's Ironworks, however. Because of the shortage of food and fodder at Rocky Mount, an equally important part of Huck's mission was foraging for supplies, and he established a forward camp at Major Brown's Crossroads.[275] This "Major Brown" was Joseph Brown, a veteran of the Cherokee Expedition and the Georgia Campaign. Before the fall of Charleston, Brown served as a major under Colonel John Winn and a lieutenant colonel under Colonel Edward Lacey Jr.[276] Brown's property adjoined the Nicholas Bishop plantation, where John McClure had organized his militia company earlier that spring, and was located near the intersection of Rocky Mount and Land's Ford Roads, about three miles southwest of Philip Walker's Mill (present-day Lando). This crossroads corresponds to the modern intersection of Highways 9 and 901, near the town of Richburg in Chester County.[277] From this location, Huck could requisition or confiscate corn and wheat from local plantations and quickly transport it to the mill to be ground into meal and flour. Turnbull, meanwhile, composed another letter to Lord Cornwallis, informing him of Huck's mission, reiterating his critical need for provisions and updating him on the status of the militia.[278]

From his headquarters in Camden, Lord Cornwallis wrote a letter to Turnbull, addressing the concerns Turnbull had expressed in his letter of 15 June. After promising to send salt, rum and the rest of the Legion cavalry and infantry from the New York Volunteers as soon as they arrived in Camden, Cornwallis added:

> *I should then advise you going to the Irish Settlement you mention, & staying there as long as you find it convenient & bringing back some Meal to your present Post. If the Horses of the Legion suffer for want of Corn, I wish you would send back immediately some of the best of them, & the remainder as soon as your people* [New York Volunteers] *join you. I likewise approve of your destroying the Iron work & beg you will take upon yourself to act in all those Matters as it shall appear to you to be best for the King's Service. You will give permission to the Militia to do what they please with the Plantations abandoned by the Rebels. If they can get in the Crops & turn them to their own use, it will be the best Plan, but if it is more convenient now & then to destroy one I have no objection, only I strictly forbid & will severely punish any act of cruelty to their wives & children.[279]*

At Hill's Ironworks in the New Acquisition, William Hill received word that Thomas Sumter was in Salisbury, recruiting men and "waiting for a reinforcement." After fleeing his plantation in the High Hills, Sumter had ridden up to Salisbury, which was the headquarters for the Salisbury District Militia Brigade. Picking up some of his veteran riflemen from the

Thomas Sumter (1734–1832) was lieutenant colonel commandant of the Sixth South Carolina Regiment (Riflemen) from 1775 to 1778 and brigadier general of Sumter's Brigade from 1780 to 1782. *Portrait by South Carolina artist Rembrandt Peale, 1796. Courtesy of the Collection of the Sumter County Museum, Sumter, South Carolina.*

old Sixth South Carolina Regiment as he rode through the Waxhaw settlement, Sumter arrived in Salisbury in early June and began to organize a command. The North Carolina civil and military authorities encouraged Sumter to rally the Backcountry South Carolina militia and issued him $19,000 in treasury certificates for procuring supplies and ammunition.[280] "I then wrote to him," Hill recalled in his memoirs, "informing him of our situation & that there was a probability of our making a handsome stand—and that we were about to form a junction with Gen[l]. [Griffith] Rutherf[d]. in N. Car[a]. [and] that we were going to attack a large body of Tories that had collected at a place called Ramsour's Mill." Hill made plans to rendezvous with Brigadier General Rutherford, commander of the Salisbury Militia Brigade, at Tuckasegee Ford on the Catawba River in North Carolina, not realizing that Sumter was already on his way there from Salisbury.[281]

Saturday, 17 June

After securing his camp at Brown's Crossroads, Captain Huck set out for Hill's Ironworks early Saturday morning. Employing a local Tory named John Dennis as their guide, Huck's men made their way into the New Acquisition.[282] The Loyalists stopped at the plantation of James Simril (or Simeral), whose property adjoined Colonel Samuel Watson on Rocky Allison Creek, a tributary that entered the much larger body of Allison Creek from the south. Simril was a Whig militiaman who had served as a lieutenant under Watson and Colonel Thomas Neal during the

Snow Campaign and the Cherokee Expedition. Huck's men confiscated what provisions they could find at Simril's plantation and set fire to his barn before they left.[283] The detachment then made its way to the home of Moses Ferguson, another Whig sympathizer who also resided on Rocky Allison Creek, about two miles south of the ironworks. Huck ordered Ferguson to show him the best route to take in order to outflank and surprise the rebels stationed at the ironworks. "If you refuse," Huck told Ferguson, "my men will make mince meat of you."[284]

As Colonel Neal and the New Acquisition Militia Regiment still had not returned from their foray into the Broad River settlements, Colonel Hill had only a small garrison on hand that day to defend the ironworks.[285] This left the camp in a very vulnerable situation. Having been apprised that Huck was moving up from Rocky Mount toward the New Acquisition, Hill dispatched Captain John Henderson to scout the area for signs of enemy movement. Henderson soon ran afoul of Huck's advance guard and was captured. Huck confiscated Henderson's horse ("a valuable five-year-old bay mare"), along with the bridle and saddle, and sent the prisoner under guard to Rocky Mount while he continued on to the ironworks.[286]

The ironworks proper, with its store, furnace and mills, was on the south side of Allison Creek, as was the Whig encampment. Since Huck was advancing up the road from the south, the Whigs accordingly prepared for an attack from that direction. Two of Colonel Hill's sons, Robert and William Jr., procured a one-pound swivel gun manufactured at the ironworks and

On 17 June 1780, the Loyalist forces under Captain Christian Huck destroyed Hill's Iron Works in the New Acquisition District. On 25 November 1785, Colonel William Hill signed this deposition attesting to the fact that Captain John Henderson was captured during the battle, and that his horse, bridle and saddle were confiscated by the British troops. *South Carolina Audited Account 3522. Courtesy of the South Carolina Department of Archives and History, Columbia, South Carolina.*

set it up on a hill overlooking the south road, where they could train it on the approaching Tories. Unknown to the Whigs, however, Huck had anticipated their defense and outflanked them. Rather than approach from the south, as the Whigs expected, Huck circled around the ironworks and attacked from the north, catching the defenders completely by surprise.[287]

As the Loyalists approached the ironworks, the Whigs saw that they were greatly outnumbered. Huck's detachment included his troop of dragoons and sixty Loyalist militia, while the defenders numbered only twelve to fifteen men. The Whigs hastily pulled down the bridge across the main branch of Allison Creek north of the ironworks, hoping to slow or stop the enemy horsemen. To their dismay, however, the Tory militia quickly repaired the wrecked bridge and Huck's men then charged in upon the rebels' position.[288] Daniel Stinton stated that the Whig garrison at the ironworks was commanded by Hill, Bratton and McClure, but Hill's memoirs are silent as to exactly who was present or in command of the garison. After trading several volleys with the Loyalists, the outnumbered Whigs mounted their horses and headed toward North Carolina. Huck overtook the rear of the Whig detachment and, according to his report, killed seven of the men and took four prisoners.[289] The Loyalists stripped the prisoners "of everything, even to the rings some of them wore on their fingers."[290] Sergeant Benjamin Rowan, a veteran of the Third and Sixth South Carolina Regiments, recalled in his state pension application that he "was at Col. Hills Iron Works, when they were burnt by the enemy; and narrowly made his escape when two other men were killed." Huck also captured Colonel Hill's two sons, although he eventually released them.[291]

One of the men taken prisoner by Huck was Hill's iron molder, an Irishman named Calhoun who was related to Patrick Calhoun, father of the famous South Carolina statesman John C. Calhoun. According to a nineteenth-century account, "[Calhoun] was caught by the British and hung to make him tell where Col. Hill was, but Calhoun was true to his employer and did not betray him. The British burned the building and left Calhoun hanging, who was cut down and restored to life by a very faithful negro of Hill's, who had witnessed the whole proceeding from his place of concealment."[292]

The Loyalists then proceeded to plunder the camp of everything they could carry away.[293] Once that task was completed, Huck ordered the ironworks and all of Hill's houses and outbuildings to be completely destroyed. Hill later recalled that the British "burned the forge, furnace, grist and saw mills together with all other buildings even to the negro huts, & bore away about 90 negroes all which was done before Col. Niel returned with the army to camp."[294] Some of these captured slaves became the personal servants of Turnbull's officers. Hill noted in his memoirs that two of his "very valuable young negroes" were taken by one of Huck's lieutenants "and were kept to wait on him."[295]

After demolishing the ironworks, Huck moved down to Fergus Crossroads, where the town of York is now located, and made camp for the night.[296] The destruction of Hill's Ironworks was another serious blow to the Whig cause in the Backcountry. The ironworks was a key producer of ammunition, guns and agricultural implements, and the people in the border area between the two Carolinas depended heavily on it. It was a "great calamity to the Whigs," wrote nineteenth-century historian Maurice Moore, "and a general misfortune to the farmers, for forty or fifty miles around; many of them expected that they would have to return to the wooden plough."[297]

Colonel Hill and the other Whig officers from the New Acquisition had already made plans to rendezvous with General Rutherford at Tuckasegee Ford on the Catawba River. Huck's attack on 17 June hastened their departure from the ironworks, and they arrived at the ford later that day. Here they found many of their comrades from the Spartan and Fair Forest Regiments, as well as some refugees from Georgia who had fled to North Carolina. Among the Backcountry militia commanders present at Tuckasegee Ford that day were John Thomas Jr., James Lisle, Thomas Brandon, Andrew Neal, William Hill, William Bratton, John McClure and Richard Winn. These men were surprised and heartened to find Colonel Thomas Sumter also camped at Tuckasegee. Some of the Whigs assembled there had served under Sumter in the Sixth South Carolina Regiment, while others had campaigned alongside him during the early campaigns of the war. To many of these men, Sumter seemed a natural choice to lead them in their efforts to drive the British from their homeland.[298]

Sunday, 18 June

Captain Huck and his task force moved back down Fishing Creek to Brown's Crossroads, where Huck sent an express to Lieutenant Colonel Turnbull informing him that he had defeated "150 rebels" and completely destroyed the ironworks.[299] Believing that he had dispersed the last body of armed troops in the district and that the region was now secure, Huck began sending his men throughout the area, posting notices and notifying the inhabitants of the region "that he desired to make terms with them, & that he would put them in the King's peace."[300] These notices informed the locals that Huck would be holding an assembly at the crossroads on the following Thursday, 22 June, where the citizens could sign the oath of allegiance and take British protection. Meanwhile, his men continued to forage the area for provisions.[301]

At Tuckasegee Ford, the Whig refugees from South Carolina began to discuss their future. Now that they were all assembled together, the various regiments from the Upcountry were eager to elect a suitable officer to command them, "being all on fire for the cause of our beloved country," as Joseph McJunkin put it. Captain Richard Winn asserted that he was chosen "without a dissenting voice," but that he suggested Colonel Sumter would be "the most proper person to take the command." Captain Winn and Colonel Robert Patton approached Sumter to see if he was willing to lead the men.[302] As McJunkin later recalled: "After an interchange of views, we said to Col. Sumter, 'if we choose you as our leader, will you direct our operations?' He replied, 'I am under the same promise with you; our interests are identical—with me, it is liberty or death.' An election was held, and he was chosen."[303]

The South Carolinians now had the nucleus of a viable militia brigade, with Sumter commanding them as acting general. This brigade included some of the most experienced officers and men in the Backcountry, the majority of whom were veterans of five years of warfare against Indians, Tories and British regulars. Some had served in the militia, some in the Continental regiments and some had served in both militia and Continental units. They were excellent horsemen, expert riflemen and used to the hardships of service in the Backcountry. John Adair, who was a twenty-three-year-old lieutenant in Lacey's Regiment at the time, later recalled the occasion in his Federal pension application, "[A]bout three hundred men who had fled from the Enemy, of which I was one, did assemble in North Carolina where the[y] had fled, and enter into a solemn obligation to place themselves under the command of Gen[l]. Thomas Sumpter and to continue in a body and serve under his command untill the war was at an end, or untill their services were no longer necessary, they were to find their own horses and arms, cloathing and all necessaries—it being absolutely necessary that they should act on horse back."[304]

As the afternoon wore on, General Rutherford arrived at Tuckasegee with the main body of his North Carolina militia, some five hundred men, bringing word that there were now more than one thousand Tories assembled at Ramsour's Mill.[305] McJunkin reported that when the South Carolina Whigs learned of the Loyalist force, they "could hardly be constrained from proceeding that evening to attack the above Tories; but Rutherford would not consent for [them] to start until next morning."[306] Rutherford composed a message ordering Colonel Francis Locke of Rowan County to meet him north of the ford on the evening of 19 June or the morning of 20 June. Rutherford planned to join forces with Locke and then attack the Loyalists assembled at Ramsour's Mill with the combined militia under his command. However, "the express was neglected," as Captain Joseph Graham put it, and Locke never received the message. Unaware of Rutherford's plans, Locke proceeded with his own endeavors to take on the Tories at Ramsour's with the men he had assembled.[307]

That evening, Graham and a party of Whig militia from the Steele Creek area of Mecklenburg County arrived at Bigger's Ferry on the east bank of the Catawba River. While attending worship services that morning at Steele Creek Presbyterian Church, Graham and his neighbors learned that "a party of British and tories were marching up the west side of the Catawba River" into the New Acquisition. Following the end of the church service, the men assembled their horses and weapons and headed down to Bigger's Ferry, where they expected to cross the river and reinforce the garrison at Hill's Ironworks. When they arrived at the hill overlooking the ferry, Graham and his men were greeted with a hellish sight: huge clouds of smoke ascending from the still smoldering ruins of the ironworks some four miles to the east. With grim determination, they turned their horses and galloped toward the rendezvous at Tuckasegee Ford.[308]

Monday, 19 June

The Whigs at Tuckasegee Ford awoke on the morning of 19 June to find that it was raining. General Rutherford decided it was too wet to proceed and ordered his men to wait for the weather to improve. At midday the weather cleared, and the men test-fired their guns. Many of the Whigs in the neighborhood, hearing the gunfire, assumed that the Tories were crossing the river and came to Rutherford's camp in arms. That evening, Rutherford's force crossed over to the west side of the Catawba River and marched to within about sixteen miles of Ramsour's Mill, where the general brought the column to a halt. The men hoped that they would march through the night and take up positions to attack the Tories at first light the next morning, but Rutherford had other ideas. Still believing that his express had reached Colonel Locke, he decided to wait for Locke to join him, in order to attack the next day with his entire force. At 10:00 p.m., Colonel James Johnston rode into Rutherford's camp. Locke had dispatched

Johnston to find Rutherford and notify him that Locke planned to attack the Tories at sunrise the next morning and to request Rutherford's cooperation. Rutherford, still confident that his express had reached Locke, sent Johnston on his way and continued to wait.[309]

At Rocky Mount, Lieutenant Colonel Turnbull sent a report to Lord Cornwallis detailing Huck's successful mission against the ironworks. After giving a few details of the battle from Huck's after-action report, Turnbull noted that the ironworks were "completely destroyed." Turnbull then continued with an update on the status of the loyal militia, a request for more provisions and the results of his interview with Captain John Henderson, the rebel scout whom Huck captured on the morning of 17 June:

> I am taking every step to arrange the militia although my Progress is but slow as most of their former officers are Run off. I can't get people to warn them and bring them together yet I Expect in the course of this week to do a good deal—
>
> I Beg Leave to put your Lordship in mind that when our Detachment passes We may not be forgot in the Articles of Rum and Salt.
>
> Some more Arms, Cartridges, Flint and a Barrel of Powder are Likewise wanted.
>
> A Capt. Henderson was taken some days ago. He was a great persecutor and Expected to be hanged. Some of his friends told him that He shou[l]d do something in favor of government to Intitle him to be Restored to favor. He proposed to Seize Govr. Rutledge and bring him a Prisoner. I told him if He Succeeded He shou[l]d Be Handsomely Rewarded and have sent him of[f] to try his luck. He assured me that Rutledge and [Colonel John] Twigg[s] from Georgia were at a Widdow womans house near Salisbury about ten days ago and that His guard had left him.
>
> Some times great Villains will do services at all Events. I thought it best to put it to the tryal.[310]

In spite of Turnbull's optimistic wishes, Henderson made no attempt to "seize Governor Rutledge and bring him in a prisoner." As soon as he was released from Rocky Mount, Henderson returned to the New Acquisition and within a few days was back in arms with his comrades in Sumter's newly formed partisan brigade.[311]

Tuesday, 20 June

As morning dawned, the Whigs under Rutherford and Sumter set out for Ramsour's Mill, located about sixteen miles up the South Fork of the Catawba River. As they neared the mill, they could hear the sounds of gunfire echoing down the valley; the battle had started without them. Having received no instructions from Rutherford and unwilling to risk waiting any longer, Locke launched a surprise attack on the Loyalists camped at the mill just as the sun started to rise. Although John Moore commanded about thirteen hundred Tories and occupied a very favorable position, the determined Whigs eventually prevailed after a protracted and bloody battle that involved a great deal of hand-to-hand combat. Both sides suffered considerable loss, but the Loyalists' resolve evaporated as the battle turned against them, and the majority of

Moore's force fled the field. By the time Rutherford and Sumter arrived on the scene, some two hours later, the battle was over.[312]

The disappointed Whigs from the New Acquisition found that a small group of their comrades had fought in the ranks with Locke's North Carolinians. These were the thirteen men under Captains James Martin and James Jamieson who left the New Acquisition on 10 June and went up to North Carolina looking for some action. They joined Colonel Locke's militia at Salisbury and went on an expedition against Tories in the forks of the Yadkin River. Following that excursion, they accompanied Locke to Ramsour's Mill, where they fought alongside the North Carolina militia. These men were the only South Carolinians who actually participated in the Battle of Ramsour's Mill. Following the conflict at Ramsour's, they rejoined the other Whigs from the New Acquisition and became a part of Sumter's command.[313]

Although Sumter arrived too late to participate in the fight, the battle provided an unexpected windfall for the impoverished South Carolinians. The Loyalists had stockpiled a huge quantity of supplies and material at Ramsour's Mill, which Rutherford's militia promptly seized after the battle. Sumter asked Rutherford if he could spare some of the goods for the South Carolina militia. The victorious North Carolinian graciously allowed Sumter to requisition whatever he needed, provided he issued receipts in the name of South Carolina for all the material he procured. Sumter quickly agreed, and his men obtained much-needed horses, wagons, and "provisions of all kinds."[314]

Sumter's men spent the night camped at Ramsour's Mill, celebrating the victory with the North Carolinians. The Battle of Ramsour's Mill was a more decisive engagement than the earlier skirmishes at Alexander's and Mobley's, and did much to raise the spirits of the Whigs. It also solidified Thomas Sumter's position as the overall leader of the resistance in the Upcountry of South Carolina.

As much as the Battle of Ramsour's Mill was a tremendous boost for the Whigs, it was a serious setback for the British. By assembling the Loyalists when he did, Moore disobeyed specific instructions from Lord Cornwallis to the contrary. After learning that North Carolina could not possibly support the British Army until after the wheat harvest, and taking notice of the heat of the season and the unsettled conditions in South Carolina, the Earl decided to postpone offensive operations in North Carolina until the end of August or the beginning of September. But Moore and his men were impatient and had no desire to wait two or three months for the British Army to show up. They had scores to settle, and the British occupation of South Carolina excited them to recklessness. When Cornwallis learned of the Ramsour's Mill debacle, he was furious with Moore for disregarding orders and seriously considered court-martialing him.[315]

On the same day that Moore was defeated by Locke at Ramsour's Mill, Major General Johann DeKalb arrived at Parson's Plantation, some thirty-five miles northeast of Hillsborough, North Carolina, with two brigades of Maryland and Delaware Continentals and a regiment of artillery.[316] The arrival of a new contingent of the Continental Army in North Carolina further strengthened the resolve of the Whigs in the region and added to the distress of the Loyalists. The Tories quickly informed the British commanders in South Carolina of DeKalb's presence, and also of the facts that Colonel Charles Porterfield was bringing state troops down from

Virginia, that Major General Richard Caswell was raising a large force of North Carolina militia and that Sumter was recruiting men on the Catawba. As Banastre Tarleton later recalled in his memoirs: "The news brought by these loyalists created some astonishment in the [British] military, and diffused universal consternation amongst the inhabitants of South Carolina.... These accounts being propagated, and artfully exaggerated, by the enemies within the province, caused a wonderful fermentation in the minds of the Americans, which neither the lenity of the British government, the solemnity of their paroles, by which their persons and properties enjoyed protection, nor the memory of the undeserved pardon so lately extended to many of them, had sufficient strength to retain in a state of submission or neutrality."[317]

As it turned out, the Battle of Ramsour's Mill was fought on the same day that Sir Henry Clinton's proclamation of 3 June officially released all of the Carolina militia from their former paroles. Clinton's instructions stated emphatically that after 20 June, all paroled militia must actively support the British crown or be considered "enemies and rebels to the same." The actions at Ramsour's Mill that day demonstrated in no uncertain terms the Backcountry Whig militia's response to Clinton's proclamation.[318]

Thursday, 22 June

After leaving Ramsour's Mill on 21 June, Sumter moved his men south of Charlotte and set up camp on Hagler's Branch, a tributary of Sugar Creek located in the northeast corner of the New Acquisition District, where his men were joined by additional South Carolina militia and another small party of refugees from Georgia.[319] Robert Wilson of the New Acquisition recalled that, after escaping from British captivity in Charleston, he made his way back home and joined Sumter's camp in June. "On reaching home I remained but a few days, & learning that Sumter, Hill & Bratton, three distinguished Whigs, were mustering a small force near the N°. Carolina line on a small stream called Hagler's Branch...I found with Sumter, Hill & Bratton one hundred & five Whigs."[320] Badly needed supplies also began to coming in. Sergeant Benjamin Rowan brought down a wagon loaded with 250 pounds of lead that Sumter had requisitioned from General Rutherford.[321] Local blacksmiths like Isaac Price of Steele Creek were enlisted to make swords and rifles.[322] Sumter and his men then began to discuss plans for their upcoming operations. As Joseph McJunkin remembered:

> Sumter summoned all of his commissioned [officers] to attend at his markee, which was composed of a wagon cloth & the broad canopy of heaven, under whose auspices we were certainly then, to hold a court-martial, the subject of which was to fall on a method of the then opening campaign, the general being president. One of the officers allowed that as soon as we got in proper order of defence, that the enemy would fly away; other officers held that as the British backed the Tories, that they would fight hard. Gen. Sumter said, "Gentlemen: You may depend upon it, that in order to regain our country, we must expect to fight hard, & that force must repel force, or otherwise we need not attempt to regain our beloved country." The conclusion was to gain our point, or die in the attempt.[323]

While Sumter's men were holding their court-martial near Charlotte, Captain Christian Huck was hosting a much different assembly on upper Fishing Creek. Since most of the younger men in the area were by that time in Sumter's camp, the citizens who attended Huck's assembly on 22 June were primarily the older men from the New Acquisition and the upper part of the District between the Broad and Catawba Rivers. William Hill later described the scene as it was reported to him:

> Accordingly they met him, he undertook to harrangue them, on the certainty of his majesty' reducing all the Colonies to obedience, and he far exceeded the Assyrian Gen[l] who we read of in ancient writ in blasphemy by saying that God almighty had become a Rebel, but if there were 20 Gods on that side, they would all be conquered, was his expression—Whilst he was employed in this impious blasphemy he had his officers & men taking all the horses fit for his purpose, so that many of the aged men had to walk many miles home afoot.[124]

One of the men whose property was seized by Huck's men was Daniel Williams of Turkey Creek, a nephew of Colonel James Williams, commander of the Little River Militia Regiment. Daniel Williams rode to Huck's meeting on a fine English stallion named Blanch, accompanied by his slave Weaver George. Much to Williams's dismay, Huck confiscated Blanch to serve as his personal mount and took Weaver George to serve as his body servant.[125] The dragoon captain's verbal assault on the old men and his seizure of their property produced the opposite effect from what he desired: very few of the men signed the oath of allegiance, and most of them left the meeting determined to resist the British with all their resources. One such individual was Daniel Collins of the New Acquisition, a native of Waterford, Ireland who had thus far remained neutral in the war. Collins came home from Huck's assembly resolved to join the Whig militia and take arms against the British, and he encouraged his sixteen-year-old son James to do the same.[126]

Hill's statement comparing Huck's blasphemy to that of the "Assyrian generals in ancient writ" is one of several Biblical references that crop up in the Whig accounts of the war in the Backcountry during this period, showing the unmistakable influence of Presbyterian ministers and elders who perceived the conflict as a "holy war." In fact, Hill may have been recalling an actual sermon preached by Reverend John Simpson in the New Acquisition that compared Huck and his officers to the Assyrian generals Tartan, Rabsarus and Rabshakeh in the Old Testament of the Bible. In Chapters 18 and 19 of the Second Book of Kings, the Assyrian King Sennacherib sends his army to surround Jerusalem, home of the Judean King Hezekiah. Standing outside the walls of the city, Rabshakeh taunts the people of Judah in their own language, telling them not to trust Hezekiah or their God to deliver them from the military might of the Assyrian army. Instead, he mocks the power of all foreign gods and orders the Judeans to surrender to the king of Assyria:

> Hath any of the gods of the nations delivered at all his land out of the hand of the king of Assyria?...Who are they among all the gods of the countries, that have delivered their country out of mine hand, that the Lord should deliver Jerusalem out of mine hand?...Thus

shall ye speak to Hezekiah king of Judah, saying, Let not thy God in whom thou trustest deceive thee, saying, Jerusalem shall not be delivered into the hand of the king of Assyria. Behold, thou hast heard what the kings of Assyria have done to all lands, by destroying them utterly: and shalt thou be delivered?[127]

The parallels between Huck's speech and that of Rabshakeh would have been obvious to anyone well versed in the Old Testament, and could easily have been used to portray Huck and other British officers in the Backcountry as blasphemous enemies of the devout God-fearing Christians of upper South Carolina.

Down at Camden, Lord Rawdon received a visitor, one of the Loyalist survivors of the Battle of Ramsour's Mill. This Tory first stopped at Rocky Mount and gave his report to Lieutenant Colonel Turnbull, who then sent him on to Rawdon. After interviewing the witness, Rawdon penned a letter to Lord Cornwallis, who by this time had returned to Charleston, informing him of the unfortunate setback at Ramsour's and blaming Colonel Moore entirely for the fiasco. "This man says the number of the Loyalists was about Eight Hundred; & that of the Rebels was estimated about Six Hundred," Rawdon informed the Earl. "He complains much of ill management on our side, & indeed, by his account, it seems to have been a sharpe business. He imagines the losses to have been exceedingly trifling on both sides; but says the Loyalists were completely scattered." Rawdon also noted that "in consequence of this disaster," Turnbull had left Rocky Mount earlier that day to join Huck at Brown's Crossroads and had requested a reinforcement of twenty British Legion dragoons from Camden. Turnbull hoped that the presence of a large force of British cavalry would impress the shaken Loyalist militia and give them renewed confidence in the aftermath of Moore's Defeat. Rawdon had his doubts about the necessity of such reinforcements, but nonetheless he dispatched sixty Legion dragoons under Captain David Kinlock to rendezvous with Turnbull at Brown's Crossroads. However, Rawdon made it clear to Kinlock that if his services were not needed, he was to return immediately to Camden, and if Turnbull's position seemed too dangerous, Kinlock was to prevail upon the colonel to fall back to Rocky Mount. Rawdon also sent several wagons of arms and ammunition to Rocky Mount, escorted by Major John Carden and one hundred men from the Prince of Wales Regiment, a northern Provincial corps stationed at Camden.[128]

Friday, 23 June

Moore's Defeat at Ramsour's Mill had prompted Turnbull to march north on 22 June in an effort to settle the "Bounty Irish" in the upper part of the district. Turnbull considered these Scotch-Irish settlers to be "the worst of the Creation," and he sincerely believed that "nothing [would] bring them to reason but Severity." Accompanied by a detachment of New York Volunteers and additional Tory militia under Colonel Matthew Floyd, Turnbull rendezvoused with Huck and Colonel James Ferguson at Brown's Crossroads on 23 June. Turnbull expected that a show of force, combined with the offer of paroles and protection, would bring the locals to heel. In this regard, he was disappointed. Captain Huck's previous exhibition had already alienated most of the locals, and those who did "submit and embody" soon abandoned their paroles and their plantations, and went over the river to Sumter's camp. While he was in the area, Turnbull decided to make good on his earlier threat to send some troops into the "Irish settlement at Turkey and Bullock Creek." As he noted earlier in a letter to Cornwallis, there was an abundance of provisions in the area but the people were "very violent," undoubtedly a reference to their recent attacks on the Broad River Tories. Turnbull dispatched Huck and Ferguson on an excursion to quiet the rebels on Bullock's Creek and Turkey Creek and to forage for corn and wheat.[129]

Saturday, 24 June

Lieutenant Colonel John Moore came into Camden and gave his version of the defeat at Ramsour's Mill to Lord Rawdon, who passed the details on to Cornwallis in Charleston. Moore tried to deflect as much of the blame as possible from himself and place it on others. He claimed that the Whigs had nearly one thousand men, two hundred of whom were Continentals, while the Loyalists numbered eight hundred men who were badly armed and severely lacking in ammunition. Only 20 or 30 Loyalists were killed or wounded, he claimed, and about 150 were taken prisoner; the rest fled the field, and Moore reported that he was sure they would soon join Turnbull. Moore had apparently stopped at Brown's Crossroads to see Turnbull before journeying on to Camden, where Colonel Floyd informed Moore that the Loyalist militiamen "were turning out in great spirit." Owing to the scarcity of food in the upper Catawba Valley, Rawdon did not think that either side could pursue the action any further, "for neither party could trust to the Country for provisions on a march." Finally, Moore stated that it was not really his idea for the Loyalists to embody at Ramsour's Mill; he did so only at the express urging of Major Nicholas Welsh, and "rather in contradiction to his own opinion." Rawdon noted in his letter that Welsh was expected to arrive in Camden at any time, when he could give his own account of the affair. In any case, Rawdon observed dryly, neither officer had waited on his Lordship's "final sentiments" concerning the plan.[130]

While Moore was giving his report to Rawdon, Captain Kinlock of the British Legion arrived at Brown's Crossroads with sixty dragoons to reinforce Turnbull. Turnbull ordered Kinlock to patrol along the west side of the Catawba while Huck swept through the settlements on Turkey Creek and Bullock's Creek. By this time, Turnbull was aware that the South Carolina militia was regrouping under Sumter in the New Acquisition. He was receiving exaggerated reports about the numbers of men coming in to Sumter's camp, and he was also aware that a large body of Mecklenburg and Rowan County militia was still in arms under Rutherford. In his forward position at Brown's Crossroads, Turnbull was vulnerable to a surprise attack, and he needed reliable intelligence on the movements of the rebels and the locations of their camps. He hoped Kinlock could provide this information.[131]

As Huck and Ferguson moved through the western part of the New Acquisition District, they ran into a small body of rebels at the ford where Quinn's Road crossed Bullock's Creek, on or about 24 June (the exact date is not given in sources). The resulting skirmish left several Whigs dead and several captured, and roused the ire of the local residents. J.M. Hope, the grandson of a local Whig soldier named James Hope, later described the incident in a letter to Revolutionary War historian Lyman Draper: "Robert Wilson, who was brother-in-law to

[Captain James] Jamison (having married his sister) came in from home (Southwestern York) and brought news that Furguson was sending squads all over the country between that and Broad River—Insulting, Robbing and murdering Whigs, male & female; that and Capt. Huck had killed a man at the ford on Bullocks Creek, and a mile above killed good old Mr. Fleming, a man of 70."[332]

The "Mr. Fleming" referred to was probably Robert Fleming of Bullock's Creek, who had four sons in the Whig militia: Alexander, Elijah, Robert Jr. and William.[333] A rare description of a skirmish between Ferguson's Tory militia and the Whig militia during this time comes from Charles McClure. McClure served under Captain John Steele from Fishing Creek, who by this time commanded a militia company of his own. Although McClure does not give a date for the incident, the skirmish fits well with J.M. Hope's description of Ferguson's activities during this period. In a deposition describing his Revolutionary War service, McClure stated that "during the Revolutionary War [he] volunteered and entered into the Militia Service under Capt. Steele, that shortly after he turned out aforesaid Steele & his company was attacked by Capt. Ferguson, Steele and most of his men retreated and escaped—two or three were killed, your petitioner and two others were taken prisoners, and conveyed to Camden Jail, and was there confined for Eight Months or near that time & suffered hunger, pain, cold and was during part of the time sick, treated with the utmost indignity and fed like a brute."[334]

Another one of the Whigs captured may have been Robert Fleming's son Alexander Fleming, who was taken prisoner by the British during this same period and imprisoned in the jail at Camden, where he eventually died.[335]

Thursday, 29 June

The Earl Cornwallis was none too pleased with the recent events at Ramsour's Mill. After receiving Lord Rawdon's reports on the affair, he wrote back to Rawdon on 29 June. "The affair of Tryon County has given me great concern," Cornwallis noted, "altho' I had my apprehensions that the Flame would break out somewhere, the Folly & Imprudence of our friends is unpardonable." Cornwallis ordered Rawdon to send instructions to Lieutenant Colonel John Hamilton, commander of the Royal North Carolina Regiment, to report to his headquarters in Charleston "immediately, & [I] would have him acquaint his Officers before he leaves the Regt. that if I hear of any more instances of Irregularity about recruiting or disobedience of Orders that I will put the Regt. into Garrison on Sullivan's Island. I likewise desire that you will examine Maj[r]. Walsh very strictly as to what passed between him & Col[l]. Moore."

After noting his approval of Turnbull's march up into the settlements of the "Bounty Irish," the Earl added some further orders to help motivate the Loyalist militia officers. "I think I mentioned to you that it will be proper to give higher rank to the Majors of Militia as soon as proper persons are found to succeed them as Majors, perhaps you need not wait even for that, as the being called Col. will help to give them Authority." Cornwallis concluded the missive with instructions to "continue to send on parole to the Islands all those [rebel prisoners] who come under the description of my Order."[336]

Friday, 30 June

From his headquarters in Charleston, Lord Cornwallis sent a letter to Sir Henry Clinton in New York describing the events of the past month in South Carolina, in which he confidently stated that the entire state had been brought under British control. He admitted, however, that his affairs in North Carolina had not gone so smoothly. The Earl emphasized his need to wait for the harvest to be completed before moving north, and put the blame for Ramsour's Mill squarely on the shoulders of Colonel Moore:

> The submission of General Williamson at Ninety Six, whose capitulation I enclose with Captain Paris's letter, and the dispersion of a party of rebels, who had assembled at an iron work on the north-west border of the province, by a detachment of dragoons and militia from Lieutenant-colonel Turnbull, put an end to all resistance in South Carolina....
>
> I have established the most satisfactory correspondence, and have seen several people of credit and undoubted fidelity from North Carolina. They all agree in the assurances of the good disposition of a considerable body of the inhabitants, and of the impossibility of subsisting a body of troops in that country till the harvest is over. This reason, the heat of the summer, and the unsettled state of South Carolina, all concurred to convince me of the necessity of postponing offensive operations on that side until the latter end of August, or beginning of September; and, in consequence, I sent emissaries to the leading persons amongst our friends, recommending, in the strongest terms, that they should attend to their harvest, prepare provisions, and remain quiet till the King's troops were ready to enter the province.
>
> Notwithstanding these precautions, I am sorry to say, that a considerable number of loyal inhabitants of Tryon county, encouraged and headed by a Colonel Moore, rose on the 18th instant, without order or caution, and were in a few days defeated by General Rutherford with some loss.[337]

Cornwallis's letter demonstrates once again the British Army's critical need for supplies during this period and its keen interest in the success of the harvest in the Backcountry. Cornwallis simply could not bring in enough supplies through Charleston to feed his soldiers. If large numbers of men were absent from their plantations, regardless of whose camp they were in, there would be no one to harvest the corn and wheat, and the British soldiers would starve along with the rest of the country.

Chapter IV

"English Sanity is thrown away"

Saturday, 1 July 1780

The first day of July brought another depressing development for the Whig cause in South Carolina: the city of Georgetown surrendered to Captain John Plumer Ardesoif of the Royal Navy.[338] Located at the head of Winyah Bay, Georgetown was the second largest city in South Carolina during the eighteenth century and was the state's major shipping port for rice and indigo.[339] Although the surrender of Georgetown did not carry the same emotional shock value as the fall of Charleston, it was another important victory for the British and seemed to confirm Lord Cornwallis's boast that South Carolina was a conquered province.

On the same day that Georgetown surrendered, General Thomas Sumter moved down from Hagler's Branch and established a new base in one of the Catawba Indians' old fields at Catawba Old Town, situated fourteen miles south of Charlotte on Clem's Branch of Sugar Creek. The large numbers of men coming into Sumter's camp meant that he had to move periodically in order to procure food for the troops and pasturage for their horses. Joseph McJunkin recalled that the men referred to the camp at Clem's Branch as "Poor Hill" or "Starved Valley" because of the great difficulty they had in obtaining provisions and "money that would do us any good."[340] According to McJunkin, Sumter's men depended greatly on the generosity of the North Carolinians during these lean times: "When we went over into North Carolina to half buy & half beg provisions, the inhabitants asked us, why we didn't stay at home, & defend ourselves there? We got some barley meal, & made batter—we put it into a kind of crock—dug a hole in the ground, set the crock in it, and covered it over with hot ashes and embers—cooked it without salt, beef or bacon, and it tasted mighty sweet."[341]

In spite of the poor accommodations, Whigs from North and South Carolina continued to filter into Sumter's camp, steadily increasing the number of soldiers under his command. Many of the new volunteers were officers and enlisted men whom the general had known during the Snow Campaign and the Cherokee Expedition, including about eighty veterans of the old Sixth South Carolina Regiment. The men organized themselves into companies and regiments, elected their officers and did what they could to prepare for the coming campaign.[342]

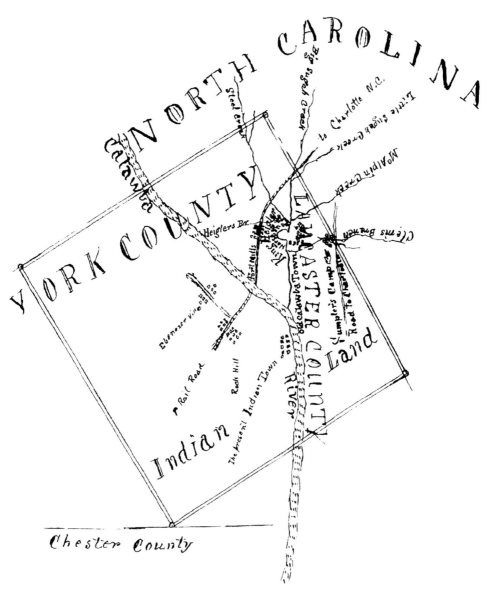

Map of the Catawba Indian Land showing Hagler's (Heigler's) Branch and Clem's Branch of Sugar Creek, sites of Thomas Sumter's camps in June and July 1780. Drawn by Daniel G. Stinson for Lyman C. Draper, 21 March 1872. *Thomas Sumter Papers, 5VV46, Draper Manuscript Collection. Image 27320. Courtesy of the Wisconsin Historical Society, Madison, Wisconsin.*

Sunday, 2 July

After riding some twelve miles along the Catawba on reconnaissance patrol, Captain David Kinlock and his dragoons returned to Lieutenant Colonel Turnbull's camp at Brown's Crossroads with news of Sumter's militia. Kinlock's sources had deliberately misled him as to Sumter's strength and location, and his intelligence report, according to Turnbull, "was none of the Best." Kinlock reported "that the Rebells Were Thirteen Hundred strong and that they were at a Great Distance." In reality, Sumter's strength was fewer than half that number and he was certainly not "at a great distance," but it was in the local Whigs' best interests to keep Turnbull misinformed, and Kinlock, being new to the area, was easily deceived. Kinlock was a veteran cavalry officer who had served as a commander of Provincial light dragoons since 1778.[343] At the Battle of the Waxhaws on 29 May, Kinlock carried Lieutenant Colonel Banastre Tarleton's offer of surrender to Colonel Abraham Buford, and during that battle he charged the center of the American line at the head of troopers from the British Legion and Seventeenth Light Dragoons.[344] Although born in Scotland, Kinlock lived in the town of Jamaica on Long Island before the war and, like most of his fellow soldiers from New York, he was not used to dealing with the Backcountry Carolinians or their hot, oppressive summers.[345] "He Returned and Complained so much of the heat of the weather and the Tiredness of their Horses," reported Turnbull, "that I let him go down [to Rocky Mount] and sent home the militia to Reap their Crops, which [they] was losing for want of Reapers."[346]

At about this same time, Lord Rawdon, working in conjunction with Lord Cornwallis's aide-de-camp Captain Alexander Ross, began sending emissaries into the Backcountry settlements, making "liberal offers of Secret Service Money" in exchange for pledges of loyalty and information on rebel movements. One of the men whom these emissaries contacted was Edward Lacey Sr., the Loyalist father of the prominent Whig militia commander Colonel Edward Lacey Jr. Rawdon hoped that the elder Lacey could persuade or bribe his son to support the British cause.[347]

Tuesday, 4 July

By the Fourth of July, Sumter's Brigade had established a new camp on the east side of the Catawba River about four miles from the Old Nation Ford.[348] Sumter dubbed it "Camp Catawba," and Joseph Graham of Mecklenburg County later described the layout of the camp as follows:

> *The position being favored for collecting supplies of provisions* [Sumter] *determined to occupy it for a few days; but doubtful of being visited by the Enemy's cavalry, the ground being hilly and covered with oak timber, the General ordered the timber to be felled in different directions round the Camp some what in the form of an Abatis and the body of the trees split and leaned over a strong pole supported by forks or some high stump, the other end on the ground at an angle of 30 degrees elevation and facing the avenues left through the brush or abatis for passage, so that they would answer the double purpose for the men to lay*

under and for defence. If the enemy's cavalry had come, unless they were supported by a large
body of Infantry or artillery, they could not have forced the Camp.[549]

Among the officers in Sumter's camp that day was Colonel James Williams, commander of the Little River Militia Regiment, who showed up a few days earlier with a small party of men from his regiment. In a letter to his wife dated "Camp Catawba, Old Nation, July 4, 1780," Williams was optimistic about the state of affairs for the South Carolinians. He gave highly exaggerated reports about the numbers of reinforcements coming from Maryland, Pennsylvania and Virginia to join Major General Richard Caswell and Brigadier General Griffith Rutherford, and mentioned that there were "some South Carolina militia commanded by Col. Sumter, to the amount of 500, now in camp at this place, and are expected to cross the river to-day, with about 500 of the Mecklenburg militia." He went on to give his wife the following encouragements:

> *From this you may see, under the blessing of God that we will soon relieve our distressed*
> *families and friends; so bear up with fortitude till that happy day comes. I hope in God*
> *this will find you, my dear wife, and my children all well. My compliments to you and my*
> *children and friends that inquire about me. Myself and Capt. Hays, Daniel and the boys are*
> *all hearty; God be blest for His mercy to us.*
>
> *The uncertainty of your situation is my great mortification; but let our joint prayers meet*
> *in Heaven for each other and our bleeding country. The Rev. Mr. Simson has had his house*
> *and every thing he had but the clothing the family had on destroyed, and he is in camp with*
> *me and Mr. Croghead, and is part of my family in camp. Mr. Simson, Mr. Croghead, and*
> *Capt. Hays, join me in our compliments to you, my love and friends.*[550]

"Capt. Hays" was Captain Joseph Hayes, from Williams's Little River Regiment. "Daniel" was Daniel Williams, Colonel James Williams's son (not to be confused with his nephew of the same name mentioned earlier), who also served in the Little River Militia.[551] "The Rev. Mr. Simson" was, of course, Reverend John Simpson of Fishing Creek, who had officially joined the militia company commanded by Captain Alexander Pagan and Lieutenant John Mills on 10 June.[552] "Mr. Croghead" was probably Reverend Thomas B. Craighead, one of the two sons of Reverend Alexander Craighead (or Cragehead) of Mecklenburg County. Until his death in 1766, Alexander Craighead was the only full-time Presbyterian minister in Mecklenburg and Rowan Counties, and throughout his ministry, he was an outspoken critic of the British church and state. Thomas Craighead had been preaching at the Waxhaw Meeting House since 1778 and was ordained its pastor in 1779. Following Buford's Defeat and the British movement into the Waxhaw community, Craighead abandoned his church, fearing that he would be arrested by the British; he eventually made his way to the comparative safety of Virginia, but he never returned to Waxhaw. Thomas's younger brother, Captain Robert Craighead, commanded a company of militia from Sugar Creek; he joined Sumter's partisans about this same time.[553]

Meanwhile, Turnbull, still camped at Brown's Crossroads, received word that Sumter had taken post at the Old Nation Ford with six hundred men, threatening "Death and Destruction to us all." It was clear to Turnbull that the rebels wanted him to retreat back to Rocky Mount, and because he was in an exposed position and was substantially outnumbered, he realized that he had little choice but to comply.[354]

Wednesday, 5 July

In order to force Turnbull to withdraw from his post at Brown's Crossroads, Sumter sent a detachment of men down the east side of the Catawba River toward Rocky Mount. Sumter's men advanced as far as George Wade's Mill in what is now Lancaster County, about ten miles northeast of Rocky Mount, and set up camp. Word reached Turnbull that Sumter's entire force of five hundred men was at Wade's Mill, so Turnbull hastily left Brown's Crossroads and retreated back to his fortified position at Rocky Mount. Upon returning to Rocky Mount, Turnbull received a second report that Sumter only had about forty men at Wade's Mill. Nonetheless Sumter's feint had achieved its desired goal: it had forced Turnbull to withdraw his men from Brown's Crossroads and return to Rocky Mount. Turnbull also received an express from Lord Rawdon stating that he had dispatched Major Thomas Mecan and the Twenty-third Regiment of Foot from Camden to the Waxhaws with orders "to disarm such of the Inhabitants as did not enroll in the Militia; [and] to collect grain which I proposed to store at Rugeley's Mills [near Camden]."[355]

Thursday, 6 July

In a letter to Lord Cornwallis, Turnbull gave the Earl an update on the events of the last two weeks. A lot had happened since his last communiqué of 19 June, including Moore's Defeat at Ramsour's Mill and his own march up to Brown's Crossroads. The defeat of the Loyalists at Ramsour's was particularly unsettling, he noted to the Earl:

> *The last time I had the Honor of writing your Lordship our affairs in this Quarter were in a very Prosperous way and had it not been for that Weak Silly man Moore who led a Parcell of those poor Innocent Devils of North Carolina into a Scrape, we shou[l]d have been now in Perfect Peace and Quietness on this Frontier.*
> *Moores Defeat made me march some days sooner than I intended up amongst my good Friends the Bounty Irish. I wish I cou[l]d say something in their favor. I Believe them to be the worst of the Creation – and Nothing will Bring them to Reason but Severity. Numbers had left their Plantations and severall have Run of[f] since I was amongst them after Submitting and Embodying.*[356]

After passing on the results of Kinlock's excursion and what he had learned of Sumter's movements, Turnbull summed up his disgust with the unruly Scotch-Irish settlers in Mecklenburg, Rowan and the New Acquisition. He also expressed his sincere desire to return to the more civilized environs in Charleston and to either visit his wife in New York or leave the army altogether:

I now find Major Mecan has marched against them and if He will only Remain as long at the Waxhaws as I have done here, I Really Believe we shou[l]d feel the good Effects of it thou[gh] Mecklenburgh, Ro[w]an, and my Friends the Irish above are perhaps the Greatest Skum of the Creation. English Sanity is thrown away when there is not Virtue to meet it half way. If some of them Could be Catched who have submitted and Run off and join[e]d the Rebells an Example on the Spot of immediate Death and Confiscation of Property might perhaps make them submit.

I am now to thank your Lordship for the attention you have had for this Little Corps, in about a Couple of months they will be so Ragged that I shou[l]d be very happy that the service might Permitt our being moved to [Charles]Town. – I should then Embrace your Lordships Generous offer to make a short visit to M^r. Turnbull and Either Bring her or Quit the Army.[357]

Friday, 7 July

Having received intelligence that the British were once again moving toward the Waxhaw settlement, Sumter broke camp and marched down to intercept them with his entire force. Once he reached the Waxhaws, however, Sumter found no trace of the reported British troops, so he returned to the Old Nation Ford. After consulting with his officers, the general decided to allow his troops to go home for a few days to obtain provisions, recruit more volunteers and, above all else, secure the wheat crop, which was ready for harvest. Most of them did so, although a few men remained in camp to guard the supplies and ordinance.[358] Sumter took advantage of the opportunity to ride into North Carolina, where he hoped to procure rifles from the Gillespie brothers, a family of famous gunsmiths who lived at the foot of the Blue Ridge Mountains. According to tradition, it was the Gillespie brothers who gave Sumter the nickname "Gamecock."[359]

At his headquarters in Camden, Lord Rawdon wrote a long, detailed letter to Lord Cornwallis, complaining bitterly about the bad effects of Sir Henry Clinton's final proclamation. "The majority of the Inhabitants in the Frontier Districts, tho' ill Disposed to us, from circumstances were not actually in arms against us," he reported. "They were therefore freed from the Paroles imposed by Lt. Colonel Turnbull & myself; & nine out of ten of them are now embodied on the part of the Rebels." The rebel force included "the greater part of the Waxhaw people," he stated, as well as "the Irish Settlement on the West of the Catawba River." Rawdon went on to give a detailed report on Sumter's encampment at Old Nation Ford, Turnbull's return to Rocky Mount and DeKalb's movements in North Carolina, speculating on what direction the rebel army might take and what, if anything, he could do to stop them.

Rawdon also informed the Earl of his progress in trying to buy off some of the local rebels. "Lacey is the only one of Capt. Ross's emissaries who has returned to me and given me any information," he reported, referring to his ally Edward Lacey Sr. "I fear the rest have been taken up. I have been making liberal offers of the Secret Service Money; but should your Lordship have to pay any of my Drafts in that line, I hope you will find that the object has been adequate to the expense." He also noted that he had transferred Major Mecan and the Twenty-third Regiment to Hanging Rock instead of the Waxhaws, but had left Captain Kinlock and his dragoons in the Waxhaw area to try to "purchase a Detachment of the Enemy from the Waxhaw people. Gold will, I think, outweigh the spirit of rebellion; tho' it is very strong in my old friends," a reference to his countrymen from the north of Ireland. After noting that Colonel Henry Rugeley's Loyalist militia regiment from Camden was embodied and had joined Kinlock's command, he remarked that "Turner's militia were mostly with the rebels," probably a reference to Colonel William T. Turner's Loyalist militia regiment from the Rocky Mount area.[300]

The British commander was especially eager to capture or kill General Sumter, and in a letter written the same day to Colonel Rugeley, Rawdon gave Rugeley the names of several prominent Whig officers and authorized him to offer five hundred gold guineas to anyone who would lead Sumter into an ambush. Knowing that Lacey Sr. was a dedicated Loyalist, Rawdon suggested that Rugeley use the elder Lacey to try to win over his son, the Whig militia commander Colonel Edward Lacey Jr.[301] In his nineteenth-century biography *The Life of Gen. Edward Lacey*, Maurice Moore confirmed that "a British officer," using the elder Lacey as an agent, offered Colonel Lacey "a large amount of gold, to abandon the Rebels and join the Loyalists. Although poor, Lacey indignantly spurned the offer."[302] One of Colonel Lacey's brothers, Reuben, was apparently not so resilient. Although Reuben had served as a Whig soldier under his brother during the early years of the Revolution, he evidently gave in to pressure from his father and bribes from Lord Rawdon and joined ranks with the Loyalists at Rocky Mount.[303] Colonel Lacey never accepted any such bribes and remained a staunch Whig throughout the war; nevertheless, the activities of his father and brother cast a cloud of doubt over him during this period and caused many of his comrades to regard him with suspicion.[304] As Joseph McJunkin stated in one of his narratives, "About this period there were some doubts respecting the soundness of the principles of Col. Edward Lacey's, fearing he would join the Enemy; but Sumter sent an armed party & brought him into camp—he was detained some time a prisoner in camp, & there declared himself on the American cause, & he was set at liberty & joined Sumter, & proved ever after a good soldier & a good officer, & was reinstated in his command."[305] Also adding to Colonel Lacey's troubles was the large number of Loyalists in the upper Sandy River neighborhood where he lived. The Chester historian Daniel Stinson noted that "after the fall of Charleston, Lacy did not join [Sumter's Brigade] immediately. The reason assigned is that most of his neighbors on Sandy River were Tories, and that being the case, he knew that if he left home it would be unsafe for him to return again."[306]

Saturday, 8 July

The Whig soldiers returning to their homes from Sumter's camp soon learned of Captain Christian Huck's activities in the area, especially the meeting at the crossroads where he harangued the men and confiscated their horses. As William Hill recalled in his memoirs, "This ill behaviour of the enemy made an impression on the minds of the most serious men in this little band and raised their courage under the belief that they would be made instruments in the hand of Heaven to punish this enemy for his wickedness and blasphemy—and no doubt the recent injuries that many of their families received from the said Hook and his party had an effect to stimulate this little band to a proper courage."[307]

While these events were transpiring on the west side of the Catawba, Major William Richardson Davie was establishing a Whig outpost on the north side of Waxhaw Creek, in what is now Lancaster County, South Carolina. Davie arrived with his own troop of mounted militia from Mecklenburg and Rowan Counties, and was soon joined by Major Robert Crawford with a company of militia from the Waxhaw settlement and some North Carolina militia under Lieutenant Colonel William Haggins. Another group of unexpected recruits also came in to Davie's camp in the Waxhaws: a company of Catawba Indian warriors under their chief, General Newriver, newly returned to their homes after removing their families to Virginia early in June.[308]

At age twenty-four, Davie was already one of the best cavalry commanders in the Carolinas. He was the nephew and adopted son of Reverend William Richardson, an influential Presbyterian minister from England who was the pastor at the Waxhaw Meeting House until his death in 1771. After being wounded at the Battle of Stono Ferry in June 1779, Davie retired to Salisbury to study law under Judge Spruce Macay. When the British Army moved into the South Carolina Backcountry in June 1780, Davie abandoned his studies and joined the Rowan County Militia, rapidly becoming one of the Whigs' most capable field officers.[309] While stationed in the Waxhaw settlement, Davie employed the services of two young brothers named Robert and Andrew Jackson, aged sixteen and thirteen. Davie did not use the Jacksons as front-line troops but rather as mounted orderlies and scouts, delivering messages and gathering intelligence on enemy movements. Andrew Jackson would later become the seventh president of the United States, and he always mentioned Davie as one of the men he held in greatest esteem. Jackson's traumatic experiences in the Backcountry during the summer of 1780 were to greatly influence his personality and actions during the War of 1812 and his later years as president.[310]

While Davie was busy setting up a Whig militia camp in the Waxhaws, Lieutenant John Adamson was joining the Loyalist militia at Rocky Mount. Adamson, from Colonel Henry Rugeley's Camden Militia Regiment, probably arrived at Rocky Mount around 8 July. He was born in County Antrim, Ireland, in 1744 and, sometime between 1765 and 1770, settled in Camden, where he became a prominent merchant in the years before the Revolution.[311] In early June 1780, Adamson assisted Rugeley in raising a regiment of Loyalist militia and accepted a lieutenant's commission in that regiment.[312] Although he had remained loyal to the British government since the beginning of the war, Adamson had strong ties to the Whig community in the Camden District, and after the British occupied the Upcountry, he used his influence to protect his friends in the Whig party. A petition presented to the South Carolina House of Representatives in 1784 on his behalf stated that Adamson accepted the lieutenant's commission in Rugeley's regiment "at the Earnest request of his Neighbours (now Subjects of this State) to prevent its falling into the hands of a person whose intentions was well known was to oppress them." The petition further stated that "he used all the Influence he had with the British in favour of Such persons as avowed their attachment to the American Cause."[313] Similarly, Adamson's great-grandson, Dr. Edward M. Boykin, maintained that Adamson assisted distressed Whigs by "protecting them from the oppression and pillaging of the 'Black riders' and 'Cowboys' who under the sanction of the British Flag were common thieves."[314]

Sunday, 9 July

Captain Kinlock, patrolling up the east side of the Catawba, belatedly received word that a large body of Sumter's rebels were camped somewhere in the Waxhaws. He set out with his troop of dragoons in an attempt to find them, but was unsuccessful; the rebels, who had returned to their homes on the west side of the river, were busy harvesting wheat and rounding up volunteers for Sumter's Brigade.[375]

Monday, 10 July

For once, Turnbull's spies brought him intelligence that was accurate and timely. They informed the British colonel that many of Sumter's men—including Captain John McClure and Colonel William Bratton—had returned to their neighborhoods for a few days. Turnbull was pleased to learn that the "noted Partisan McClure was come home and Reaping his grain" and that Colonel Bratton "was publishing Proclamations and Pardons to who should return to their duty." This is, incidentally, another confirmation that Bratton did not simply resign his commission and retire from active service, as William Hill implied in his account. Rather, Turnbull's statement makes it clear that Bratton was actively recruiting volunteers for Sumter's Brigade by posting recruitment notices and offering pardons to men who would desert the royal militia and rejoin the Whigs.[376]

Turnbull ordered Captain Huck to ride up to the South Fork of Fishing Creek to see if he could apprehend the two rebel leaders while they were still nearby. Knowing that the rebel militia had grown considerably since Huck burned Hill's Ironworks, and that McClure and Bratton were probably traveling with a sizeable force, Turnbull ordered twenty mounted New York Volunteers and some fifty mounted militia to accompany Huck's troop of thirty-five dragoons. Huck willingly accepted the mission and began preparing his men to move out. Along with the additional troops, Turnbull also gave Huck the following written orders:

> You are hereby ordered with the Cavalry under your command, to proceed to the frontier of the province, collecting all the royal militia with you in your march, and with said force to push the rebels as far as you may deem convenient.
>
> To Capt. Christian Huyck.[377]

After getting the various contingents ready for a march of several days' duration, Huck set out that evening with about 110 men under his command, with the anticipation of collecting further Loyalist militia along the way. Huck, as senior commissioned officer in the Provincial troops, was in overall command. Riding with Huck as second-in-command of the British Legion dragoons was Lieutenant Benjamin Hunt, a seasoned officer from Westchester County, New York. Hunt had served as a lieutenant in Captain John Althause's rifle company of Emmerick's Chasseurs during 1778 and 1779, and was reassigned to Huck's troop of dragoons in the summer of 1779.[178] Commanding the mounted infantrymen of the New York Volunteers were Lieutenant John McGregor and Ensign Allan Cameron.[179] McGregor was a native of Scotland who settled in Tryon County, New York before the war; he joined the Volunteers as an ensign in 1777 and participated in the British capture of Savannah in 1779.[180] Like McGregor, Cameron was also of Scottish ancestry; he joined the Volunteers in 1779 and participated in the capture of Savannah.[181] Colonel Matthew Floyd commanded the Loyalist militia from the Upper (Spartan) District, probably accompanied by his son Captain Abraham Floyd and Lieutenant Colonel John Lisle.[182] John Craig remembered another Loyalist officer whom he referred to as "Major Robison" or "Major Robertson" (he used both spellings). This officer is otherwise undocumented; assuming that Craig was not mistaken in his reminiscences, Major Robison may have been part of Floyd's regiment.[183]

Commanding the Rocky Mount Militia were Colonel James Ferguson and Major John Owens of the Fishing Creek and Rocky Creek communities.[184] Captain Henry Houseman may have accompanied the expedition, although no source confirms this. Lieutenant John Adamson of the Camden Militia Regiment also went along, attached to one of the militia commands.[185] Although Adamson held a lieutenant's commission at the time, the Whig accounts universally referred to him as "Captain Adamson" and erroneously stated that he was Huck's second-in-command. Turnbull's letters also mentioned a "Lt. Lewis of the militia" who accompanied the mission; this may be a reference to Charles Lewis, who was involved in the incident at Fishing Creek Church on 11 June.[186]

After leaving Rocky Mount, Huck's detachment proceeded up the Rocky Mount Road toward Walker's Mill. The men stopped for the night at the plantation of Nicholas Bishop, located about four miles southwest of Walker's Mill near Brown's Crossroads.[187] The Bishops were a Whig family and the four oldest sons—Henry, James, William and Nicholas Jr.—were all veterans of the early campaigns of the war. Henry Bishop, the eldest son, had departed Sumter's camp a few days earlier and returned to his home on Fishing Creek to visit his wife, who had just given birth to their first child. The rest of the Bishops, who still lived at home with their father, received word that Huck was approaching their plantation on the afternoon of 10 July. They hurriedly evacuated their home and went to Henry's plantation, loaded his wife and newborn infant into a wagon and made haste for Sumter's camp, where sixteen-year-old John Bishop, the youngest son, promptly joined the militia. The Bishops quickly gave the men in the camp the news that Huck was in the area.[188]

When Huck arrived at the Bishop plantation, he and his officers discussed the feasibility of pursuing the Bishops, who were certain to raise the alarm. Colonel Ferguson, who probably knew the family, opposed the idea. "Let them be killed in battle," he told Huck and the other officers. Huck took Ferguson's advice, and the British made camp for the night at the Bishop plantation.[189]

Tuesday, 11 July

Captain Huck broke camp on the morning of 11 July and proceeded toward upper Fishing Creek, fully expecting to catch McClure and Bratton at their plantations. He was also on the lookout for wheat and corn that he could take back to Walker's Mill. His first stop was at McClure's home, located in what is now the Rodman community of northeastern Chester County. Unaware of Huck's pursuit, John and Hugh McClure had already left and were headed toward Sumter's camp with their men, but their mother—Mary Gaston McClure, one of the sisters of Justice John Gaston and a widow for many years—was at home, along with her youngest daughter Mary, her son James, and Edward "Ned" Martin, the husband of her daughter Olive. The family was in the process of building a new room onto the house, and much of the room was still under construction.[390]

James McClure and Ned Martin were busily employed melting Mrs. McClure's pewter dishes and casting them into bullets for the militia; they probably planned to catch up with the rest of the militia once they were finished. When they observed the approaching soldiers, James's first impulse was to open fire on them, but Ned protested that they were hopelessly outnumbered, and that their resistance would only result in their defeat and the destruction of the family home. Reluctantly, James agreed. Huck's soldiers entered the house, apprehended both men, took them outside and searched them. Their pockets were full of pewter bullets, proof enough that they were members of the rebel militia. Huck ordered them to be bound with ropes and then sentenced both men to be hung at sunrise the next morning.[391]

Captain Huck then entered the house and demanded to know the whereabouts of Mrs. McClure's other two sons. Once again, Elizabeth Ellet gives us a colorful, romanticized account of the incident, based on the traditions of the McClure and Gaston families collected by Daniel Stinson:

> When they [McClure and Martin] were secured, Huck stepped up to her and said, rudely, "You see now, Madam, what it is to oppose the King! Where are your other sons—John and Hugh? I should like to have them in company with this Jemmy of yours, who impudently says if it had not been for Ned Martin, he would never have been bound as he now is. We'll hang your son, Madam; that is his doom! Where are John and Hugh? Come, out with it! Search, men; they are hid some where—grand cowards!"
>
> "That is a lie!" exclaimed the indignant mother, casting upon the brutal captain a look of intense scorn. "You, sir, know better! You have never yet stood to meet them; and if John were here now, you would be afraid to face him!"
>
> "D—n him!" cried Huck, "tell me where I may meet him!"
>
> "Go to Gen. Sumter's camp," was the reply; "there you may possibly meet with him."
>
> In scrutinizing the different objects around the room, Huck laid his hands upon two books on the table. Taking them up, he asked, "What book is this?"
>
> "That, sir, is the 'Afflicted Man's Companion.'"
>
> "A good title—one which the d—d rebels will soon have need of."
>
> "It is a good book, sir," replied Mrs. McClure.
>
> "And what book is this?"
>
> "It is the Family Bible."
>
> "Do you read them?"
>
> "Yes, sir."

"It is these books," said Huck, furiously, "that make you such d—d rebels!" and he threw them both into the fire. The matron sprang forward to recover them, and though he would have prevented her, succeeded in dragging them from the flames. One corner of the Bible was badly burned. It was long kept in the family as a relic.

Enraged at her saving the books, Huck struck Mrs. McClure with the flat of his sword. She said to him, nothing daunted by his brutality, "Sir, that will be a dear blow to you!"

The soldiers set fire to the new house, but Mrs. McClure succeeded in extinguishing the flames. It was but little, however, that her unassisted strength could avail, and they soon entered and began pulling down the plank partition. It happened that she had wrapped a few gold guineas in a cloth, and hid them in a crevice. Knowing where they were concealed, she rushed in through the soldiery amidst the falling plank, and when the cloth fell, placed her foot upon it, stooped down as if hurt, and saved the money. The others, meanwhile, were busily engaged in destroying her property, carrying off whatever articles it suited their inclination to take. A quantity of nails had been purchased for the new building; these they took and scattered them broadcast over the field as they departed from the premises, driving James and Ned before them.

No sooner were the intruders gone, than Mrs. McClure despatched her daughter Mary in all haste to Sumter's camp, to carry the news of the outrage she had suffered and the captivity of the young men. The young woman made her way to the camp, arriving late in the evening. The Americans had heard from different persons for several days past, of the march of Huck's party through the country, their progress being marked by cruelty and spoliation, and some from the vicinity of Mrs. McClure's had fled to the camp for safety. The news of the capture hastened their preparations for the expedition against him, and just after sunset the companies of John McClure and [William] Bratton—the York and Chester men—headed by their captains and under the command of Col. Neil, left Sumter's camp.[392]

The Loyalists proceeded from the McClure home to Walker's Crossroads, near the present site of Lewis Turnout in Chester County. At the crossroads, they turned north back onto the Rocky Mount Road, which would take them to the Bratton plantation in the New Acquisition.[393] Still foraging for food and supplies, they made several stops along the way. One of these stops was the home of John Price, a prominent Whig landowner and "respectable man" who lived just south of the modern border between York and Chester Counties.[394] They also visited William and Mary Adair, whose property adjoined Price to the north and west.[395] The Adairs were a Scotch-Irish family who moved down from Pennsylvania about 1758. William Adair Sr. was a bricklayer, and his apprentice in the years before the Revolution was the young Edward Lacey Jr.[396] Lacey's father lived about a mile north of the Adairs, but unlike the elder Lacey, the Adairs were Whigs. Two of their sons, John and James, served in Colonel Lacey's Militia Regiment—John was a lieutenant at the time—while another son, William, was in the Continental service. The couple's daughter, Mary, was the wife of Captain John Nixon, who commanded the militia from Rocky Creek.[397]

Huck's men confiscated all of the Adairs' cornmeal and flour as well as any other food and valuables they could find.[398] "After having taken the silver buckles from Mrs. Adair's shoes, the rings from her fingers, and the handkerchief from her neck," Ellet states, "they took her husband out, put a rope about his neck and were about to hang him up because his sons were out with the rebels, when some of the tories pleaded in his behalf that the old man was not so much to blame; it was the mother who had encouraged her sons, and urged them to their rebellious course." Adamson then pulled Mrs. Adair aside to have a private talk with her. He told her that he understood her sons were all "fine young men" and that she exerted a great deal of influence over them. If she could persuade them to join the royal militia, he promised to obtain officers' commissions for all of them. "The matron replied that her sons had a mind of their own, and thought and acted for themselves." The British force then moved on, although, according to one source, two of the Loyalist militia officers elected to spend the night at the Adairs' house.[399]

After leaving the Adairs, Huck stopped at the home of Edward Lacey Sr., knowing that the old man would be only too glad to assist him on his mission. While Lacey didn't have any direct information on the whereabouts of his Whig son, he welcomed Huck warmly and provided him with enough food to give the captain and his officers "a fine breakfast."[400]

The next stop for the Loyalists was the plantation of John Moore Sr. Known locally as "Gum Log" Moore, he resided on a branch of the South Fork of Fishing Creek called Gum Log's Branch.[401] Moore was busy processing his freshly harvested wheat crop and had set up a threshing floor to separate the wheat from the chaff. Assisting Moore were William Moore, one of his younger sons, and Isaac Ball, a nephew of Moore's neighbor Samuel Rainey. (Rainey was one of the men serving in Colonel Bratton's militia command, and his daughter Harriet would later marry Bratton's son John Simpson Bratton.) Old "Gum Log" was a staunch Whig himself, and three of his older sons—John Jr., Samuel and Nathan—were also serving with Bratton. Huck arrested the old man and placed him with the other prisoners, James McClure and Ned Martin; he then confiscated the horses belonging to the two young men, William Moore and Isaac Ball.[402] More than likely, Huck also seized the threshed wheat stacked on the threshing floor.

By this time it was late in the afternoon, and Huck proceeded on to the Bratton plantation, hoping to catch Colonel Bratton at home. Bratton's wife, Martha, had been in the field reaping wheat that day, with the assistance of several of the older men from the neighborhood, including Thomas Clendennon, Charles Curry, Robert McRandall and Colonel Bratton's older brother Robert.[403] During June and July 1780, when most of the young men were in arms with the militia, the women and older men assumed the responsibility of gathering the wheat harvest so essential to their survival. Daniel Stinson, who knew most of the folks in the area, recalled that the "young women went day after day from one farm to another, and reaped the crop with the assistance of the matrons and a few old men."[404]

The most detailed account of Huck's visit to the Brattons was recorded by Colonel Bratton's oldest son, Dr. William Bratton Jr., who was not quite seven years old at the time. According to Dr. Bratton, the family had already been warned that the "Red Coats" were on their way "and were on the lookout for them."[405] Family tradition states that Martha instructed Watt, the family's African-American slave, to ride to Sumter's camp and warn her husband of Huck's presence in the area.[406] Since Martha was advised of Huck's approach earlier in the day, she most likely dispatched Watt on his mission before Huck's men arrived.

A British dragoon threatens Martha Bratton with a reaping hook on the front porch of her home as Lieutenant John Adamson comes to her rescue, from a nineteenth-century lithograph. *Courtesy of the Culture & Heritage Museums, York County, South Carolina.*

"At last they were seen coming up the road, a long line of 'Red Coats' followed by a great multitude of 'Tories,'" Dr. Bratton recalled. Huck and the dragoons apparently brought up the rear of the column. A small squad of soldiers under Lieutenant Adamson was the first to arrive at the Bratton home. Martha met them on her porch, or "piazza" as Dr. Bratton referred to it, and asked what they wanted. Adamson stated that they were looking for her husband, Colonel Bratton, and asked where he was.[107] When Martha informed him that she did not know her husband's whereabouts, a "red-headed Irishman" named Henry "swore that he would make her know, seizing a sickle that was hanging on a peg in the Piazza, he placed it in a position around her neck and drawing his sword swore that, 'if she did not immediately tell where her Husband was that he would cut her head off and split it.'" Young William, clinging to his mother's dress, was "transfixed with horror and fright" as his mother calmly replied, "I told the simple truth and could not tell if I would, but I now add that I would not if I could." However, before Henry could carry out his threat, Adamson struck him hard with the side of his sword. Henry immediately released Martha and begged for his own life as Adamson "beat him with the flat of his sword and kicked him headlong down the steps." Adamson then turned to Martha, apologized for Henry's behavior and assured her of his protection. Martha turned without a word and went into her house with young William still clinging to her dress.[108]

Following Adamson's intervention, the Loyalist soldiers waited on Huck's arrival, which according to Dr. Bratton "was not long after." Huck stepped up to the door and asked for an interview with Mrs. Bratton, which she granted. At first, Huck was "very courteous and polite," and when William approached him Huck sat the boy on his knee and treated him kindly, even allowing him to play with his watch and seals. Huck told Martha that he was authorized to offer her husband a commission in the royal militia commensurate with his current rank in the rebel forces, and urged her to use her influence to persuade Bratton to accept the offer. Martha replied that "she had no influence with her Husband in such matters," but Huck continued to press her, extolling the advantages that a British commission would bring to Bratton and his family. At this point, Martha told Huck, "It is useless to prolong the interview if that is its purpose. My husband is in Sumter's Army and I would rather see him die there, true to his Country and cause, than have him live a traitor in yours."[409]

"Huck then behaved very badly," Dr. Bratton recalled. "[He] sprang up from his chair and stamped about the room swearing fearful oaths of vengeance against the Rebels, and my Father particularly. The suddeness of his movement threw me from his knee on my face on the hearth, and the result of my misplaced confidence will attend me to my grave in the shape of a broken nose." Captain Huck then ordered Martha to prepare supper for him and his officers, which she did.[410] Martha briefly entertained the idea of poisoning the food, but thought better of the idea and abandoned it.[411] Huck also stated his intention to burn the Brattons' house just as he had the Simpson and McClure homes, but decided to let that task wait until the next day.[412]

Following supper, Huck made sure "all the women and children in the house were confined in the garret and held prisoners."[413] In addition to Mrs. Bratton and young William, the family at that time included Elisa or "Elsie," age thirteen; Jane, age twelve; Martha, age nine; and Elizabeth, age one.[414] Bratton family records do not state definitely whether the family had any female slaves or indentured servants during the Revolution, but it is possible. Huck also arrested the "old men" who were assisting with the wheat harvest, probably fearing that they might try to warn the Whig militia of his presence.[415] But instead of camping for the night at the Bratton plantation, Huck made a fateful decision: he moved his force to the plantation of James Williamson, a neighbor of the Brattons who lived about one-quarter of a mile to the southeast. Lieutenant Colonel Turnbull later stated that the reason Huck camped at that particular spot was because of "an Oat Field that was near."[416] Evidently Huck had learned about this oat field during one of his earlier stops that day or from one of his scouts. As a cavalry officer in charge of a large detachment of mounted men, Huck undoubtedly jumped at the opportunity to graze his horses on something besides grass, and Williamson's oat field provided that opportunity.

It is possible to reconstruct Williamson's plantation as it existed in July 1780 based on later descriptions. The Williamson family lived in a "strong log House two stories high," as Richard Winn described it.[417] The house was situated on the south side of a small creek branch that flowed into the South Fork of Fishing Creek, close to a spring where the family could draw water. A short road known as Williamson's Lane ran from the Armstrong Ford Road past Bratton's house down to Williamson's, stopping just short of the South Fork. Situated along the north side of the lane were Williamson's house and outbuildings, which included a corncrib and a stable or barn.[418] A wooden fence surrounded the house and also lined both sides of the lane.[419] This fence served to keep cattle, which were allowed to roam free in those days, from approaching too close to the house. Directly in front (to the south) of the Williamson house was a large field, at least a portion of which was planted in oats, and to the south of the field was woodland. The New York Volunteers apparently set up camp in the lane, and the Tory militia was posted along the edge of the field, about three hundred yards from the house, with their horses turned out to graze.[420] To the rear (north) of the house was a "clear open old field," where the Legion dragoons were posted with their horses close at hand, "prepared to mount in a moment if required."[121] A peach orchard bordered the western side of the old field.[122] In front of the house, adjacent to the field where the Tories were camped, were some apple trees, and there was also reportedly a "clump of plum trees" nearby.[123]

Williamson's corncrib became a makeshift jail for the prisoners taken during the day. These prisoners now included Robert Bratton, Thomas Clendennon, Charles Curry, Robert McRandall and John "Gum Log" Moore from the Bethesda congregation, as well as James McClure and Ned Martin from the Upper Fishing Creek congregation. The Loyalists locked the men inside the corncrib and posted a guard to make sure they did not escape.[124] Huck also posted four sentinels: one up the Armstrong Ford Road to the north near the creek branch; one down the road about one hundred yards south of the Williamsons; one guarding the east end of the lane, near the South Fork; and one watching the west end of the lane, halfway between the Williamsons and Brattons. Having thus secured his men and prisoners, Huck informed the Williamsons that he was spending the night in their house. Playing unwilling hosts to Huck that night were James Williamson, the sixty-seven-year-old head of the family; his wife; several daughters (and perhaps daughters-in-law) whose names are presently unknown; and four-year-old James Williamson Jr. Williamson's other sons—Adam, George, John and Samuel—were old enough to serve in the militia and were in fact with Colonel Bratton's unit at the time.[125]

Chapter V

"A good dressing before day light"

Tuesday, 11 July 1780

The news that Captain Christian Huck was once again out in force reached General Thomas Sumter's camp on the east side of the Old Nation Ford during the night of 10 July or early morning hours of 11 July by way of the Bishop family and perhaps other informants.[426] Later that morning, the militia companies commanded by John McClure, William Bratton, William Hill and Andrew Neal arrived at the ford. John Craig, who by this time had returned to Colonel Neal's regiment, later recalled:

> We started early and in high spirits to go over from Chester into York District. We numbered one hundred and thirty-three, when we arrived at Catawba river, the far [east] bank was lined with women and children, who had been ordered from their homes by the British and Tories on account of their relations generally having joined themselves to the Whig party.
>
> These women who had been forced to leave their homes informed us that Col. Floyd, Capt. Hook, and Capt. Adams[on], with other officers, commanding about four hundred British and Tories, were lying at White's [Walker's] mill in Chester county. The situation of these women and children driven from their firesides, excited in every bosom a sympathy for the distressed, and an indignation against the hard-hearted foe who could perpetrate such an inhuman deed. We received our orders to set these distressed people over the river which we did. Then we received orders to turn out our horses to graze, and meanwhile the officers called a council and soon determined to risk all consequences and attack the inhuman ruffians.[427]

The refugees lining the east bank of the Catawba were primarily from the Waxhaw settlement and the upper districts between the Broad and Catawba Rivers, including "some from the vicinity of Mrs. McClure's [who] had fled to the camp for safety." Many families had abandoned their plantations when the British advanced into their neighborhoods, and some had seen their homes burned by Loyalist raiders.[428]

Since not all of Sumter's men had yet returned to camp, Richard Winn—recently promoted to colonel and now acting as Sumter's adjutant—dispatched Lieutenant Charles Miles to locate those militia officers who were still absent. Winn's message instructed the officers to round up as many men as they could and to return to camp as quickly as possible. Not everyone was eager to go after the British Legion; as Winn recalled, "both officers & men seemed loth to engage the Horse, as they had cut Buford's men to pieces so shortly before but about 130 agreed to follow & try the business." In addition to the men commanded by Bratton, McClure, Neal and Edward Lacey, the ad hoc task force included militia companies commanded by Captain John Moffett (or Moffitt) of the Beersheba congregation; Captain John Nixon and Captain John Steele from Catholic Presbyterian; Major Michael Dickson and Captain Alexander Pagan from upper Fishing Creek; and Captain Jacob "Jack" Barnett from the Bethel congregation. The officers decided to wait until sunset and then march to Walker's Mill, where they expected to take Huck's force by surprise.[429] Late in the afternoon, John McClure's sister Mary rode into camp, bringing word that Huck had stopped at their home. As evening approached, the companies commanded by McClure, Bratton, Neal, Lacey and the other officers left Sumter's camp and headed toward Walker's Mill.[430]

Sunset of 11 July 1780 was at 7:40 p.m., with twilight ending at 8:09 p.m. In spite of the darkness, visibility was good that night. The moon was waxing gibbous, between half moon and full moon, with about three-fourths of its visible disk illuminated.[431] In addition, there was another source of illumination that night. According to William Bratton Jr., a brilliant aurora borealis made the night of 11 July "about as light as day."[432] The aurora borealis was (and still is) rare this far south, and it must have lent an eerie, supernatural aura to the night sky.

The Whigs arrived in the vicinity of Walker's Mill around sunset. The men halted about a quarter of a mile from the mill, and the officers held a short consultation. They decided to send a small mounted group under Captain McClure ahead to scout the mill site, while the rest of the men dismounted and marched to the mill on foot, ready for battle. John Craig later recalled that "every man received the countersign and watchword, which were—*Washington: Good luck.* Capt. Hugh Bratton was Captain of the guard." The dismounted troops tied their horses in some woods and proceeded on foot in a column six abreast, while McClure's men rode on ahead. Lieutenant John Adair of Lacey's Regiment later stated that he could not remember whose plan it was to organize the troops so. "The men seemed to act more by instinct than by order or command," he recalled.[433] According to Ellet's account:

> *McClure took twenty mounted men, and went up the* [mill] *pond, intending to go round its head about half a mile; but found a ford where they could pass through the pond. McClure, putting himself at the head of his men, gave command to swim their horses, and having reached the other side, issued his orders in a loud voice, and the party, spurring their horses, dashed up the hill. The tramp of their feet on the rocky ground, broke the dead silence of night. No British were found on the hill....*[434]

As McClure's men came back down the hill they met a "mill boy," a young African-American slave who worked at Walker's Mill. John Moore Jr., who was riding in front, asked the boy where the British had gone. "Up to Colonel Bratton's" was the reply.[435]

As the dismounted Whigs under Colonels Neal, Bratton and Lacey neared the mill, they saw a body of mounted men approaching. Not expecting McClure's men to be returning so soon, they at first mistook these troops for the enemy.[436] Colonel Lacey was one of the six men in the front of the column, and as the riders approached, he called out in a low voice, "Is that you, McClure?" Reining in his horse, McClure replied, "It is," and then added, "The British have gone to Bratton's." Lieutenant Adair, who was directly behind Lacey in the second row, heard the exchange between McClure and Lacey, and was a witness to what happened next: "When McClure said the Brittish are going to Brattons, the word was passed back, 'March to your horses' and before it passed far, it was changed to 'run to your horses' and in great confusion they ran and...between one and two hundred never joined them any more. Those that were willing to pursue the Brittish mounted their horses and took their trail."[437]

Apparently the men at the back of the column misunderstood the reason for the order to mount up and thought the British cavalry was attacking. In "great confusion and excitement," these men raced to their horses, mounted them and rode pell-mell back to the camp at Old Nation Ford or on to Charlotte. The exact number of men who departed is not known; John Craig thought it was twenty-three, while John Starr Moore put the figure at fifty. Adair's statement put the number even higher, at about 150, although some of these men may have dropped out later during the march from Walker's to Bratton's. The officers held another consultation; in spite of their loss, they unanimously decided to continue their pursuit of Huck into the New Acquisition.[438]

Wednesday, 12 July

Midnight found the Whig column winding its way up the Rocky Mount Road toward the Bratton plantation. At about 2:00 a.m., they stopped at the home of John Price and inquired if he had seen Huck and his party. Price informed the men that Huck had stopped there "a little before night but had gone on to Colᵒ. Brattons on the main road." Winn later asserted that at this point Colonels Lacey, Hill and Bratton placed him in overall command of the detachment by virtue of his prior experience in the Continental service.[439] None of the other accounts mentions this detail, and in the years following the battle, the honor of "overall command" of the Whigs at Huck's Defeat was assigned by various sources to other officers, including Bratton, Lacey and Neal. More likely, the officers continued to make their decisions by joint consultation, which was standard militia protocol in situations where so many different officers and militia commands came together for one purpose.

After leaving Price's, the Whigs proceeded to the plantation of William Adair Sr., about three miles south of Bratton's, where they found the old man still awake and wandering in the yard. Lacey asked if they could get some refreshment. Adair informed him that Huck had passed by earlier that evening and had taken everything that he and his wife had to eat, not even leaving them enough cornmeal to make a hoecake. When Lacey informed Adair that they planned to attack Huck at Bratton's house, the old man warned him "that the Brittish would cut them all to pieces if they pursued and attacked them." Lacey's reply to the old man was, "We will give them a good dressing before day light."[440]

Local historian Daniel Stinson later maintained that two of Huck's officers spent the night at the Adair home and were asleep in the family's bed when the Whigs arrived.[441] John Adair did not mention any British officers billeted at his parents' home in his account of the battle;

however, Richard Winn confirmed that the night before the battle, the Whigs captured Major John Owens of Colonel James Ferguson's Tory militia regiment and took him along with them as a prisoner.[442] Owens actually lived on the Rocky Mount Road not far below John Price, so it is possible that the Whigs captured him at his own home instead of at the Adairs'.[443] None of the other sources mentions where Owens was captured.

As the Whigs were leaving, John Adair's parents took hold of him and attempted to detain him by force. The Adairs were convinced that Huck's force was superior and that the Whigs had no chance of defeating them. The parents pleaded with their son not to go, but he broke free from them, jumped on his horse and took off after the rest of the men, leaving his mother screaming and crying behind him.[444]

Edward Lacey Sr. lived about a mile up the road from the Adairs. Maurice Moore recounted what happened when the Whigs passed by the elder Lacey's residence: "Col. Edward Lacey detailed four men to guard [his father] all night, and tie him, if necessary, so as to prevent him from going to the enemy and giving them notice of the intended surprise. Old Lacey, by some artifice, eluded the guard, and started for Huck's camp, only two miles from his residence; fortunately, before he had gone two hundred yards, he was overtaken, brought back, and absolutely tied in his bed till morning."[445]

The Whigs approached to within about a mile and a half of Colonel Bratton's, dismounted and tied their horses in the woods. From here, they proceeded on foot.[446] At this time, Bratton began to have second thoughts about attacking the British so near his home. Unaware that Huck was actually at Williamson's, Bratton feared his family might get caught in the crossfire. He called a council with McClure, Neal, Hill, Lacey and the other officers, and proposed that the Whigs parley with the British in an effort to avoid a fight; the council rejected this idea immediately. Bratton then proposed that the Whigs fire some warning shots into the air to draw the British out from around his home; the enemy could then be engaged without jeopardizing the lives of his family. Several of the other officers present, most notably Lacey and McClure, expressed vehement objection to this plan as well. The Whigs' original plan was to surround the enemy and attack without warning at daybreak, just as they had done at Alexander's Old Field and Mobley's Meeting House. McClure argued that sounding an alarm would allow Huck to form his troops and prepare them for battle, "the very thing that they should endeavor to prevent." Still Bratton insisted that they fire some shots. At this point, Lacey stated sharply, "Bratton, if you fire a warning shot, I'll blow your brains out." Bratton backed down, and the Whigs proceeded toward the Bratton plantation with their original plan intact.[447]

Colonel Lacey's brother Reuben, like his father, was a Tory, although he had been a Whig earlier in the war and would change sides again before the war was over.[448] Lacey knew that his brother was with Huck's militia that night and would probably be returning to his nearby home before daylight. He also knew that Reuben was blind in one eye and would have difficulty seeing clearly in the dark. Lacey therefore conceived a plan to discover the layout and disposition of Huck's force with the unwitting cooperation of his disadvantaged sibling. Accompanied by Lieutenant John Mills, Lacey moved in advance of the main force and laid in wait for his brother about twenty paces off the road. Sure enough, before long Reuben came riding along on his horse, accompanied by his dog; both horse and dog were, according to tradition, blind in one eye as well. Disguising his voice, Lacey called out to his brother and pretended to be a "friend of the King" who had fallen behind the main force and wished to enter Huck's camp before reveille. Employing this ruse, Lacey and Mills ascertained that Huck was actually camped at Williamson's plantation and that there were only four sentinels guarding the camp. After obtaining details of the sentinels' disposition, the two men allowed Reuben to pass on, and then returned to the main body of troops.[449]

It was now about 3:00 a.m. The new intelligence that Huck was at Williamson's undoubtedly came as a relief to Colonel Bratton and called for a change in plans. According to Winn's account, "Capt. Read, a bold daring officer, was ordered to pick out twenty five men & file of[f] to the left of Colonel Brattons plantation & as soon as the action began in front he was to attack the rear of the Enemy & take all strag[g]ling parties. At the same time Capt Read received his orders the remaining part of the men commenced their march to bring on the action." This "Captain Read" was undoubtedly James Read (also spelled Reed or Reid) of the New Acquisition Militia Regiment, an experienced officer who was wounded twice on the Cherokee Expedition under Colonel Thomas Neal Sr. and who served as a captain under Bratton and Sumter in the summer of 1780.[450]

As the Whigs approached the Bratton plantation, they met two young men coming toward them. Colonel Winn later remembered them as "two tories in search of their Horses," but in that detail he was mistaken.[451] They were, in fact, William Moore and Isaac Ball, whose horses were confiscated the day before by Captain Huck at Gum Log Moore's threshing floor. Determined to get their horses back, the young men waited until the British were asleep, sneaked into their camp, retrieved their horses and then slipped away without being detected.[452] The boys informed the Whig officers "that Col. Furguson with his party lay in the Edge of a field which was in advance of the British Horse about three hundred yards," and that Huck and his dragoons were posted in and around the Williamson house.[453]

The officers held another consultation and took a head count; out of the original detachment, there were now only 133 left to take on the British. They decided to split their remaining force into two groups and attack the enemy from both ends of Williamson's Lane, thus cutting off any chance for the British to escape once the attack was launched. One group—comprised primarily of men from present-day York County under Colonels Bratton, Neal, Hill and Winn, and Captain Moffett—would attack from the west end of the lane. The other group—chiefly men from what is now Chester County under Colonel Lacey and Captain McClure—would attack from the east end of the lane. The two groups then separated, with Bratton's group continuing northward and McClure's group leaving the main road to cut across through the woods to the east end of the lane. The men agreed that, as soon as either group fired the first shot, they would all "raise the war-whoop" and rush simultaneously to the attack.[454]

The group led by Bratton and Neal had little difficulty getting into position for the attack. As the men proceeded on toward the lane, they passed one of the sentinels sound asleep at his post. Samuel Williamson was detached to guard the sentinel, with orders "to shoot him if he should stir."[455] The rest of the men took cover behind the fence along the lane and the field, preparing for the battle to come.[456]

Unfortunately, the going was not so easy for the second group led by McClure and Lacey. Having left the road, the men soon found their progress impeded by trees, bushes, briars and the small, swampy branches of the South Fork of Fishing Creek. Captain James Moore and seventeen-year-old David Sadler, both of who lived in the immediate vicinity, volunteered to guide Lacey and McClure through the difficult terrain, but in spite of their assistance, the group was delayed getting into position for the attack.[457]

Daybreak on the morning of 12 July 1780 was at 4:52 a.m. By this time, Huck's men were awake, preparing breakfast and getting their horses ready for the day's ride. There was not enough light for them to notice the Whigs creeping through the trees and taking up positions behind the fences around the Loyalist encampment. However, the sounds and smells of the morning activities did cause the sleeping Tory sentinels to begin waking up. Samuel Williamson, standing guard over the sentinel on the main road, noticed that the man was beginning to stir. As soon as the guard woke up, Williamson shot him dead, as per his orders. At almost the same instant, Colonel Neal took aim at the sentinel on the west end of the lane and shot him down. Lacey's men were within twenty-five paces of the sentinel on the east end of the lane when he began to wake up. They dropped him as well. On the far side of the Williamson house, closest to the dragoons, the Whigs under Captain Read were moving through Williamson's peach orchard when they were spotted by the fourth sentinel. The Tory fired at them and fled back toward the house.[458] The Battle of Williamson's Plantation had begun.

Captain Huck spent the night with the Williamson family, whose house had an upper floor like the Brattons'. Huck probably locked the family upstairs and posted a guard, while he and some of his officers slept downstairs in relative security. After awakening that morning, Huck ordered the family to come down and prepare him some breakfast. As old James Williamson led his wife, children and daughters-in-law in a morning devotional, Huck seized the opportunity to harangue the family.[459] He flourished his sword over the heads of the frightened country folk and threatened them all with destruction unless they convinced their husbands and sons to quit the rebel militia and take British protection.[460] As he was about to walk out the door of the house, Huck stopped and turned to the family. "We have driven the Regulars out of the country," he boasted, "and I swear that if it rained militia from the Heavens, I would not value them." No sooner did these words leave his mouth than the first shots of the battle echoed up and down the lane. When Huck dashed outside to see what was happening, the Williamsons barricaded the two doors, thus preventing him from retrieving his dragoon jacket and any other personal gear still in the house.[461]

Just as the sun was about to rise over the eastern horizon, the Whigs under Bratton and Neal raised the "war-whoop" and commenced their attack, "every man his own commander." Using the fence line as cover, the Whigs directed their fire at the Tory militia in the field and the New York Volunteers camped in the lane. The fence "formed a kind of breast-work," Maurice Moore noted, "and gave the Whigs some little protection against the enemy's musketry, and afforded them a good rest for their rifles, with which they took unerring aim." Moore also stated that Colonel Ferguson led the Tory militia in three ineffective bayonet charges against the Whigs. A bayonet charge by untrained Loyalist militia is extremely unlikely, but it is precisely the type of tactic that the New York Volunteers were trained to use. However, no other source mentions such a charge.

In his *Autobiography of a Revolutionary Soldier*, James Collins of upper Bullock's Creek, who was a sixteen-year-old recruit fighting in his very first battle, alluded to several charges by the mounted dragoons, and it may be that later writers confused the two detachments.

Instead of mounting bayonet charges, the Tory militia for the most part abandoned their horses and weapons and fled the battlefield. Winn recalled that "Colo. Ferguson and some of his men were killed in the first onset, the rest run & chiefly left their horses tho sad[d]led and ready to mount." Ferguson was marked by the Whigs for particular vengeance because he commanded the squad that killed young William Strong at Fishing Creek Church. John Craig remembered that Ferguson "stood at the end of the lane and was shot down, and his clothing was blackened with the gun powder," indicating that he was killed at very close range. "We heard the words, 'boys take over the fence,'" Craig continued, "and our men rushed after the Tories and British as they fled before us."[402]

One of the Tories who quickly departed the battle was Colonel Matthew Floyd. When Floyd saw the Whigs approaching and his men taking to the woods, he and his young African-American slave, Sam (later known as Miller Sam), mounted their horses and took off at a gallop. As they escaped the field, Floyd dropped his valise or saddlebag, and ordered Sam to stop and get it. Sam doubled back to pick up the bag and was spotted by the Whigs, several of whom took aim at him, mistaking him for a Tory. Thinking fast, Sam pulled off his slouched hat so that the Whigs could see his face, and one of the soldiers shouted, "Don't shoot him, it's only a Negro!" Sam was thus spared and was taken prisoner along with the other slaves accompanying the Loyalist soldiers.[403]

The remaining Loyalist militia and New York Volunteers quickly surrendered, and the Whigs then turned their attention to the Legion dragoons positioned around Williamson's house. The officers detached some men to guard the prisoners and secure their arms, while the rest proceeded to attack the dragoons. "Here we did not stop one minuit," Winn stated, "but went on to commence an attack on the British horse in a clear open old field. We was paraded in about one hundred yards from them." Another detachment of men, probably Captain Read's group, advanced through the orchard behind the house, "thinking the peach trees would be a good safeguard, against the charge of the horsemen," as James Collins later remembered. Young Collins was one of the soldiers chosen to attack the dragoons through the peach orchard. Armed with a "blue barrel shot gun," he was about to get his first taste of battle. By this time, the dragoons had mounted their horses and paraded, which Collins recalled "was a very imposing sight, at least for me, for I had never seen a troop of British horse before, and thought they differed vastly in appearance from us—poor hunting-shirt fellows." After a short delay, Captain Huck arrived, but he had been unable to retrieve his dragoon jacket from inside the Williamson house and his white shirt made him stand out among the rest of his men. As Collins watched from behind the trees, Huck "drew his sword, mounted his horse, and began to storm and rave, and advanced on us; but we kept close to the peach orchard. When they had got pretty near the peach trees, their leader called out, 'disperse you d—d rebels, or I will put every man of you to the sword.'" The Whigs, however, had not come this far in order to disperse, and instead opened fire on the dragoons. Urged on by Huck, the dragoons made several ineffective charges against the Whigs but could not penetrate the trees where the rebels were hiding.[404]

More Whigs from the main group arrived and also opened fire on the dragoons. At this point, Huck and four other dragoons tried to break out of the trap and escape to the main road near Bratton's house. John Craig, John Carroll and Lieutenant Charles Miles took off after them. "John Carroll led the way, I was next to him, and Charles Miles next," Craig noted in his memoirs. "We halted to fire and both Miles and Carroll fired at the same time, and brought down the Captain of the British Dragoons." As Huck fell from his horse, he clung to his saddle horn so tightly that he pulled off the saddle and his still-holstered dragoon pistols along with it.[405] James Collins, who witnessed the scene, recalled that:

> *Hook was shot off his horse and fell at full length; his sword flew out of his hand as he fell and lay at some distance, and both lay till some of his men gathered about him and around him two or three times. At length one halted and pointed his sword downward, seemed to pause a moment, then raising his sword, wheeled off and started at full gallop. We then moved on to the house without opposition, but all had disappeared. In the yard sat two good looking fellows bleeding pretty freely, their horses standing at no great distance: one of them was shot through the thigh.[466]*

Lieutenant Benjamin Hunt, Huck's subaltern, was one of the dragoons who tried to break out with his captain; he was wounded by Whig gunfire and surrendered to Winn. Lieutenant John Adamson, who may have been with Huck at the Williamson house, tried to rally the men and lead another charge after Huck fell. Spurring his horse, Adamson attempted to jump a ditch in the old field and was thrown from his mount. As he fell to the ground face first, he landed on the broken stump of a pine sapling and was impaled through the chest. Seriously wounded, he lay bleeding on the ground as the rebels rushed forward.[407]

The triumphant Whigs gathered around Huck's body, which lay not far from Williamson's barn, and Carroll and Miles immediately began to argue over which of them fired the fatal shot. Both men presented their rifles, described the part of Huck's body that they had aimed at and claimed Huck's sword as a trophy. Miles had a large-bore rifle, while Carroll's rifle was of a smaller caliber. Collins, standing nearby, heard Carroll proclaim, "I shot him! I shot him! I shot two balls which entered close under the ear!" Huck's body was then examined, and two bullet holes were found in the back of his head above his neck, one about half an inch above the other, just as Carroll described. Another militiaman, Sergeant James Stephenson of Bullock's Creek, came running up and also claimed to have fired the killing shot, but the evidence of Huck's wounds was conclusive and the group conceded that Carroll had fired the shot that brought Huck down.[408] Carroll lived on upper Fishing Creek in the New Acquisition, and the tradition that he killed Huck remained strong in that neighborhood for many years. In an interview with historian Dr. John H. Logan in the late 1850s, local resident John Starr Moore recalled that "John Carroll killed Hauk from a clump of plum trees," and in 1871, Colonel Bratton's grandson Dr. James Rufus Bratton told historian Lyman C. Draper that "John Carroll was the one who killed Capt. Hook."[409]

Meanwhile, the second group of Whigs under McClure and Lacey, slowed by the difficult terrain they were forced to cross, finally broke out of the woods and joined the battle. They arrived in time to fire a couple of volleys at the retreating Loyalists and dragoons, and were able to capture some of the men who tried to escape down the east end of the lane. Advancing up the lane toward Williamson's with seventeen-year-old David Sadler in the lead, they approached the corncrib where Huck's prisoners spent the night. McClure was especially anxious to learn the fate of his brother James and brother-in-law Ned Martin, whom Huck had planned to hang. The men were joined on the way by John Moore Jr., who was looking for his father, "Gum Log" Moore. As they reached the corncrib, they were astonished to find that the prisoners had turned the tables on their captors. As John Starr Moore later recalled, during the battle the elder Moore "had pushed off the top of the crib, & gave a hurra[h] for the Whigs, when one of the guard raised his gun to shoot him, & was prevented by the Captain of the Guard." As the guard became distracted by the battle, the inspired prisoners grabbed his musket from him and took the Tory prisoner.[470]

McClure's unavoidable delay in reaching his position did allow some of the Loyalists to get away. Colonel Hill maintained in his memoirs that if McClure's party "had made good their march in time very few of them w^d. have escaped."[471] However, McClure was determined to pursue the fleeing Tories as far as possible. He and some of his men rushed to the spot where they had left their horses, mounted up and took off after the retreating Tories. Although the Loyalists had a head start, McClure's men pursued them at full speed for some thirteen or fourteen miles back toward Rocky Mount before finally giving up and returning to the battlefield.[472]

The engagement at Williamson's plantation did not last very long; in fact, Winn remembered that "we was in full possession of the field in five minuits without the loss of a single man either killed or wounded, as I am well convinced the enemy during the action never fired a single gun."[473] This five minutes of work left the battlefield covered with dead, wounded and captured Tories, but the rebels had emerged nearly unscathed. Most of the surviving accounts of the battle indicate that the Whigs suffered only one casualty, although the accounts differ in some of the details.[474] According to John Starr Moore, a Whig soldier from Chester District named Campbell had escorted a Tory prisoner up to the Bratton house; as Campbell turned away, the prisoner "drew a pistol from his cloak, shot Campbell dead, and made his escape."[475] On the other hand, Daniel Stinson thought that the lone Whig casualty was a man from Chester District named Cameron, and Winn remembered that he was one of McClure's men who, "being a little advanced before the rest was, I was informed, killed by one of his own party."[476] There is evidence supporting another Whig casualty as well. John Forbes Jr. stated in a Federal pension application that his father, John Forbes of York District, "was wounded while in an Engagement with the Enemy at Williamson Plantation" and received an invalid pension from the state of South Carolina for his disability.[477] The military historian Francis Heitman stated that Colonel Bratton was "severely wounded" in the action at Williamson's Plantation, but there is no evidence whatsoever to verify that Bratton was wounded in this or any other battle, and the source of Heitman's statement is unknown.[478]

The Whig soldiers were surprised by the number of familiar faces they spotted among the Tories. George Neely, one of McClure's men, recognized many of the Loyalists, "some of whom were my acquaintances and men I had never suspected of toryism."[479] Someone—perhaps one of the prisoners in the corncrib—told Colonel Bratton about the reaping hook incident the day before and incorrectly informed him that it was Lieutenant Adamson who threatened Martha Bratton with the hook. Enraged, Bratton and Captain John Chambers searched the battlefield and found Adamson, still lying on the ground where he fell; he was bleeding profusely and the wound appeared mortal. Bratton confronted Adamson with the accusation against him, and Adamson informed the colonel that he was innocent of the charge. The Whig officers thought he was lying and told him so; they pulled their swords and were about to finish him off, when the wounded Tory addressed them. "My life is of little consequence to me, Sir," Adamson told Bratton, "for you can only hasten the end which I feel is fast approaching, but I beg of you to consult Mrs. Bratton before you perpetrate so great a wrong." At this point Bratton realized that he had forgotten all about his family. They were not with the Williamsons, so Bratton dispatched Lieutenant John Adair to locate his wife and children.[180]

Unknown to Colonel Bratton, Martha and the children had passed the night in the darkness of their upstairs prison. Martha had little reason to be hopeful that Huck would show them any kindness the next day; at the very least, he would certainly make good on his threat to burn their house as he had done the Simpson and McClure homes. The family had no inkling of what was transpiring so near to their home until just before daylight, when the sounds of gunfire signaled that a battle was close at hand. Some of the bullets began hitting the side of the Bratton house, so Martha took the smallest children and placed them inside the upstairs fireplace for protection. At one point during the battle, a bullet passed through one of the walls of the upper story, struck the side of the chimney and fell to the floor. Seven-year-old William darted out and grabbed the bullet, after which his mother seized him and thrust him back into the fireplace. William kept the ball and treasured it for many years.[181]

As daylight approached, Martha and the children peered through the cracks of the house and tried to see what was happening outside. Martha felt certain that it was her husband attacking the British, but her limited view afforded her no way of seeing what was transpiring. As dawn broke, the aurora borealis faded away, the gunfire ceased and the family waited anxiously for someone to release them from their captivity. Presently they heard the clatter of horses coming up the lane, and shortly afterward, someone entered the house and called out for Mrs. Bratton. Martha answered and heard the stairway door open. John Adair ran up the steps and said tersely, "Your husband has sent for you." He turned and headed back down the steps, leaving Martha wondering if Colonel Bratton was wounded or even dying at that very moment. She moved quickly down the steps, leaving young William upstairs crying to go with her. Martha paused and held out her hands to him, but Adair told her to go on, ran back up the stairs, took the boy under one arm and started after her. According to Dr. William Bratton Jr.'s account, the floor of their home was covered in dead and dying Tories, placed so close together that there was no way to get to the door without stepping on them. Dr. Bratton does not explain how all these men were placed in the house without the family hearing the noise; other evidence suggests that the Tories were actually placed in the house later that morning, after the Brattons were released from captivity, and that Dr. Bratton remembered the scene out of sequence.[182]

Adair escorted Martha and young William to where Colonel Bratton and Captain Chambers stood over the wounded Adamson. Bratton asked his wife if she recognized the man on the ground. Martha was at once overcome with relief at seeing her husband alive and at the same time shocked by the battlefield scene in front of her. Adamson was so pale and blood-soaked that she did not recognize him from the day before. "Madam, you were sent for at my request," he said with great difficulty, "more to save your husband from a cruel injustice to himself than for any service you may be able to render me. He has heard that it was I who threatened your life." At that moment, Martha realized who he was and comprehended why her husband and Captain Chambers were standing over him with drawn swords. Hastily, she confirmed his story to Colonel Bratton and, as William Bratton Jr. later recounted, "all of their savage fierceness changed into tender care." Bratton and Chambers then knelt down beside Adamson and gave him some rum, "the panacea of our Revolutionary Fathers."[483]

By the time the sun rose above the eastern horizon at 5:21 a.m. on 12 July 1780, the Battle of Williamson's Plantation was over.[484] The engagement soon became known as Huck's Defeat, an epithet that spread rapidly throughout the Backcountry. The victors now proceeded to the important tasks remaining at hand: the proper disposition of the Loyalist prisoners, and the division of the spoils. The men first took an inventory of the prisoners, horses and captured gear. To protect the wounded from the heat of the rising July sun, the Whigs carried them to the Bratton home and laid them on the downstairs floor.[485] After Bratton and Chambers had fortified Adamson with several shots of rum, Martha recruited Adair and some other men to transport the wounded lieutenant to the house. By this time the floor was covered with other battlefield casualties, some of whom had already died. Adair then cleared out a place for Adamson, as William Bratton Jr. recalled: "I remember well how Adair and another man took up Redcoats, one by the head and the other by the heels, and threw them out of the house like dead hogs, and laughed at my Mother when she remonstrated with them. A room was cleared of dead and wounded (of whom the house was full) and a bed was prepared, and [Adamson] was brought in. My Mother, who was skilled in concocting healing salves and poultices, dressed his wound and he was made as comfortable as circumstances would permit."[486]

Lieutenant Hunt, as Huck's second-in-command, gave parole for himself and the rest of the Loyalist prisoners, promising that they would not take up arms for the duration of the war or until exchanged. Hunt then applied to the Whig officers for three wagons to transport him and the rest of the wounded back to Rocky Mount. The Whigs rounded up the necessary wagons and made plans to send the wounded down the next day.[487] Colonel Hill's memoirs describe in some detail a conversation he had with "Hook's lieutenant," who, according to Hill, was "wounded & died afterwards." This is apparently a reference to Lieutenant Hunt, although Hunt did not die of his wounds after the battle. According to Hill, "two very valuable young negroes belonging to yr. author were taken by the wounded Leut. already mentioned, and were kept to wait upon him." While Hill was busy rounding up wagons and guards to take the wounded back to Rocky Mount, the slaves disappeared. Hill informed the lieutenant that he knew the slaves had "gone to Rocky Mount" and insisted that the officer send them back with the Whig escort after he returned to the British encampment. "He appeared to be very warm that I should have any doubt of his doing so," Hill recounted, "and said, that he would be a D—n scoundrel to keep my property, after receiving such human treatment from me."[488]

Another officer who also gave his parole was Major John Owens. After witnessing Huck's Defeat firsthand, Owens appeared eager to cooperate with the Whigs. He informed Winn that he had been at Rocky Mount the day before the battle; Winn asked him if he would be willing to gather intelligence for the Whigs, and Owens readily agreed to serve "as a spy without fee or reward." Winn then instructed Owens to return to Rocky Mount, "count the number of men, & report the state & strength of the place." He also made arrangements to meet Owens on 20 July at a specified location, where Owens was to give him a full report on the status of the British fort.[489]

The Whigs were left with a large quantity of spoils from the battle. According to Winn, "about one hundred horses, saddles, bridles, pistols, swords, and many other things...[were] divided among the officers and men, much to their satisfaction; but Winn did not take to himself a copper's worth of the spoil."[490] John Craig stated that the men held an auction for the most valuable items. "We gathered up all the British and Tory spoils, and sold them," he recalled.[491] At the auction, John Nixon purchased Sam, Matthew Floyd's African slave.[492] Adair received "a fine silver-mounted gun, and a roan horse," while his cousin Alexander Moore obtained "a fine English grey mare."[493] James Collins remembered that the men in Captain Moffett's company "took three swords, three brace of pistols, some powder and lead, perhaps my Lord Hook's watch, and but little else."[494]

There are several references in the battle accounts to the division of Huck's "armor." Craig noted that Carroll "claimed [Huck's] armour and David like, took it and wore it."[495] Adair also mentioned "Huck's armor," but could not recall who received it.[496] The "David" metaphor crops up in other accounts as well; Joseph McJunkin compared Carroll to "a little David" when he slew Captain Huck.[497] The references to Huck's armor should not be taken literally; as the David metaphor demonstrates, they are almost certainly poetic allusions derived from the Biblical account of the battle between David and Goliath. The First Book of Samuel states that, after killing Goliath with his sling, young David claimed the Philistine giant's armor and put it in his tent, and it is obvious that all these patriotic references were intended to cast John Carroll in the same heroic light as David.[498]

Most of the accounts indicate that Carroll claimed Huck's sword and some of his other personal effects. Carroll's grandnephew, Lemuel Carroll, told Revolutionary War historian Lyman Draper that "John Carroll got [Huck's] horse and accoutrements as trophies."[499] However, Colonel Bratton's grandson, Dr. James Rufus Bratton, asserted that "Hook's cap & sword & holsters were long owned by Col. Bratton."[500] It was probably also Bratton who found Lieutenant Colonel Turnbull's written orders to Huck, and it appears that the document remained in the Bratton family for many years.[501] Captain John Steele bought Huck's razor at the auction, and that instrument later passed into the possession of the Gaston family.[502] The Whigs also captured many horses and slaves that had been confiscated by the British and restored them to their previous owners. Daniel Williams eventually recovered his English stallion Blanch and his "negro man" Weaver George, both of whom Huck had taken earlier in the month.[503] The McClure brothers reclaimed three or four of their horses, which Huck's men had carried off from the McClure plantation the day before.[504]

About two hours after sunrise, a group of Bratton's neighbors came up to see what all the noise was about. Samuel Killough and a party of reapers had gone out at daybreak to harvest wheat and heard the gunfire of the battle as they headed into their field. But finishing the harvest was more important than investigating the shots, and it was several hours before the reapers could leave their work. Arriving after the battle was over, Killough saw the "troops and prisoners there" and was briefed on the engagement by his friend, Major John Wallace of Bratton's battalion, with whom he had served in some of the earlier campaigns. Killough was one of many men from the area who joined Sumter's Brigade immediately after Huck's Defeat.[505]

A number of local women also came to the Bratton plantation that afternoon and, along with Martha Bratton, administered aid to the wounded prisoners. The Whig officers made arrangements to billet some of the most seriously wounded Tories in the homes of neighbors who were sympathetic to the British cause.[506] Colonel Lacey dispatched Lieutenant Adair to retrieve a local doctor named Turner, who lived about a mile away. Adair could not find Turner and returned to the battlefield; Lacey then sent him and his brother James to bring their parents, William and Mary Adair, up to the Bratton home. Lacey made plans to take the Adairs to North Carolina, where they would be safe from Loyalist retribution. When the Adairs arrived at the battlefield, Mrs. Adair alighted from her horse and went to see "Captain" John Adamson inside the Bratton's house. As John Adair Jr. later related to Maurice Moore: "When the old lady saw him, she remarked, 'well Cap'. you ordered me last night, to bring in my rebel sons, here sir, are two of them, and if the third had been within a days ride he would have been here also.' (Uncle William was not at Hooks defeat, he belonged to the regular service and was not in that part of the country.) The Cap'., a good deal chagrined, replied 'yes madam, I have seen them.'"[507]

Most of the Whig soldiers were dismissed and allowed to return to their homes for a few days to visit their families, obtain supplies and secure their harvests.[508] The one-sided victory over Captain Huck energized the Whigs and raised their spirits tremendously. Whereas before Huck's Defeat many of the militia were "loathe to engage the Horse," they now realized that the British Legion dragoons could be beaten. "Thus ended a glorious day for So. Carolina," Colonel Winn summed up, "as it put what few men we had in high spirits as many often told us they had rather fight the Horse than the foot, I can say on this day both officers & privates behaved brave in the defence of their country."[509] Colonel Hill stated in his memoirs that Huck's Defeat "was of greater consequence to the American cause than can be well supposed from an affair of [so] small a magnitude – as it had the tendency to inspire the Americans with courage & fortitude & to teach them that the enemy was not invincible."[510]

Later that morning, a young Whig soldier named William Wylie was walking up the Rocky Mount Road toward his home in the upper Fishing Creek community. Wylie had entered the military service early in the war, at the age of sixteen, and served under General Andrew Williamson in the Cherokee Expedition. He was with General William Moultrie during the retreat from Black Swamp in 1779 and with Captain John McClure and Lieutenant Colonel William Washington at Monck's Corner in April 1780. Wylie joined Sumter's Brigade at Clem's Branch in late June 1780, and when Sumter dismissed the men for a few days in early July, he and a comrade set out for home to visit their family and friends. As he neared his home, Wylie lay down to take a nap and was awakened "by a British soldier standing over him with a bayonet presented to his bosom." The soldier took Wylie to Rocky Mount as a prisoner, but after being held there for several days, he made his escape and once more set out for home. As he walked up the Rocky Mount Road, Wylie heard the sound of horses approaching at high speed and was startled to see about a dozen British Legion dragoons, and as many Tory militiamen, gallop by him as if they were being pursued by the devil himself. After they passed, Wylie continued on his journey, but a little farther up the road, he was even more surprised to see a squadron of mounted Whig militia in hot pursuit of the Tories. The young man recognized Captain McClure and some of his rangers, and he hailed them as they approached. Recognizing him, McClure reigned in his horse and asked Wylie if he had seen the fleeing Tories. Wylie answered in the affirmative, and McClure realized that the Loyalists would reach Rocky Mount before he could catch them. The Whig patrol included a few Loyalist prisoners, men whom McClure had overtaken and captured during the pursuit from Bratton's. He sent the prisoners on to Rocky Mount, stating that he considered them a fair exchange for Wylie, and with Wylie now mounted, McClure and his men headed back to the battlefield.[511]

The first Loyalist survivors of Huck's Defeat—those troops who had escaped the ambush on horseback—arrived back at Rocky Mount several hours after daybreak, commanded by Ensign Allan Cameron of the New York Volunteers and "Lieutenant Lewis of the militia," possibly a reference to Charles Lewis of the Camden District. Lieutenant Colonel Turnbull was shocked when he heard the details of the battle and saw how few of his men had returned. He was especially dismayed by the fact that none of his New York Volunteers had made it back to Rocky Mount. At 1:00 p.m., he sat down and composed a short letter to Lord Rawdon in Camden. He started off by outlining the intelligence that had prompted him to send Huck up into the New Acquisition and then continued with a brief report of the battle and his losses:

> *By Intelligence from the other side* [of the Catawba River] *that Kinlock had pursued the Rebells partly up the Waxhaws on Sunday last and hearing that a Noted Partisan M*^c*Clure was come home and Reaping his Grain about Twenty Two miles above and that Col. Bratton who Lived about Twelve miles farther was publishing Proclamations and Pardons to who should return to their duty, I proposed to Capt. Huck that I wou*[l]*d mount twenty of our men* [New York Volunteers] *and give him some militia to the amount of fifty to Beat up those two Quarters.*
>
> *The party marched from this* [post] *Monday Evening and found only one of the M*^c*Clures and no person at Brattons. My orders to him was not to go farther than Prudence should Direct him. He very unfortunately Encamped about a Quarter of a mile Beyond this and was attackd this morning about Sunrise By a Large Body of Rebells and has been Totally Defeated. Capt. Huck they Inform me is killed. Cornet Hunt is wounded and supposed to be prisoner. Lt. Adamson and Lt. McGrigor of the New York Volunteers, and all our Twenty* [NY Volunteers] *are Missing. Ens. Cameron of the New York Volunteers, Lt. Lewis of the Militia and Twelve Dragoons and Twelve Militia are Returned.*

Knowing that Major Patrick Ferguson was camped near Fair Forest Creek in the lower Spartan District, Turnbull recommended that Rawdon send Ferguson against the rebels before they could move against Rocky Mount or Ferguson's force. Since the fall of Charleston, Ferguson had been slowly making his way up the western part of the state, recruiting and training a large body of Loyalist militia as he went. Turnbull felt certain that the rebels' success at Williamson's

Left: First page of Lieutenant Colonel George Turnbull's initial letter to Lord Rawdon, dated 1:00 p.m., 12 July 1780, giving preliminary details of Huck's Defeat. See appendix B for a complete transcription of this letter. *Cornwallis Papers, PRO 30/11/2/285. Courtesy of the National Archives of Great Britain (Public Record Office).*

Center: Second page of Turnbull's initial letter to Rawdon on 12 July. *Cornwallis Papers, PRO 30/11/2/285. Courtesy of the National Archives of Great Britain (Public Record Office).*

Right: Third page of Turnbull's initial letter to Rawdon on 12 July. *Cornwallis Papers, PRO 30/11/2/286. Courtesy of the National Archives of Great Britain (Public Record Office).*

plantation would encourage them to make further attacks against the isolated crown forces in the Backcountry. He concluded the letter by stating that neither Lieutenant Colonel John Moore nor Major Nicholas Welsh had been to Rocky Mount since the debacle at Ramsour's Mill:

> *This is a very Unfortunate affair, my Lord. If Major Ferguson does not advance from Fair Forest, or some Larger Body of Troops makes head against them I am afraid they will give us Trouble. Their success will no doubt Encourage them to pay us a Visit, and they may Distress us in Provisions.*
>
> *I hope your Lordship will be assured that whatever I Plann[e]d I thought could have been Executed without much Danger. Mr. Cameron Says the Ground they were on was not very favourable and* [the rebels] *advanced so Rapidly that the Dragoons had not time to mount.*
>
> *Lt. Col. Moore nor Major Walsh is neither of them here nor do I know where they are.*[512]

Note that in Cameron's account, as quoted by Turnbull, the dragoons did not have time to mount before they were overwhelmed, while in the Whig accounts the dragoons were mounted and made several courageous but ineffective charges.

Turnbull also dispatched an express to carry the "disagreeable news" of Huck's Defeat to Major Ferguson and warn Ferguson that he might be attacked next. The rider arrived in Ferguson's camp on Padget's Creek, a branch of the Tyger River in what is now southern Union County, on the evening of 12 July and brought the news that Huck's party had been defeated "at Col^l. Brat[t]on's [on] Fishing Creek."[513] Unknown to Turnbull and Ferguson, another group of rebels had also engaged in a battle with Loyalist militia that same morning, about thirty miles from where Ferguson and his men were resting on Padget's Creek. This battle took place at Cedar Springs in the Spartan District, at the same time as the Battle of Williamson's Plantation occurred in the New Acquisition; like Huck's Defeat, it was a success for the Backcountry Whigs.

Jane Black Thomas, the wife of Colonel John Thomas Sr. of the Spartan District, had ridden to Fort Ninety Six on 11 July to visit her ailing husband, who was imprisoned in the Ninety Six jail for refusing to take the oath of allegiance. While there, Jane overheard some Tory women describing a planned ambush on the camp of her son, Colonel John Thomas Jr., at Cedar Springs near present-day Spartanburg. Jane slipped away, mounted her horse and rode the sixty miles from Fort Ninety Six to her son's camp in order to warn him of the imminent attack. This warning allowed Colonel Thomas to prepare an ambush for the Tories, who attacked before daylight on the morning of 12 July. The Loyalist detachment, consisting of about one hundred and fifty militiamen, outnumbered Thomas's force of sixty men by better than two-to-one, but the Whigs had prepared their position well. After a brief battle, the Tories were driven off with several casualties and the Whigs had another victory.[514]

As the day wore on, more survivors of Huck's Defeat came into the British camp at Rocky Mount and brought further intelligence concerning the battle. At 9:00 p.m., Turnbull wrote another letter to Lord Rawdon, updating him on the news from Williamson's plantation. "I was Unfortunate enough to be obliged to tell you a very Disagreeable story some hours ago," he began regretfully. He then proceeded to the details. Nine of his New York Volunteers and one dragoon had returned since the arrival of the initial survivors; these were probably the prisoners brought down by McClure. A young slave who was captured by the Whigs and then escaped also made his way back to Rocky Mount; this "very intelligent Negro boy" may in fact have been one of the "two very valuable young Negroes" mentioned by William Hill in his memoirs. The slave told Turnbull that Lieutenant Adamson fell off his horse and "being much bruised [was] taken prisoner." He also informed the colonel that seven New York Volunteers, as well as a sergeant and two privates of the Legion, were wounded and still in the hands of the rebels, who would send them down with Adamson the next day. "Lt. McGregor and Cornet Hunt we suppose have made their escape but have not yet arrived," he continued. "Capt. Huik is the only person who was killed dead on the spot. My Militia are so allarmed it will be some days before they recover their spirits." By questioning Ensign Cameron and the other survivors, Turnbull tried to ascertain the reason that Huck had decided to camp at Williamson's. "By what I can learn the only bait which led Huik to encamp at this cursed unlucky spot was an Oat Field that was near," he told Rawdon. "But by every account the position was very unfavourbl."[515]

Turnbull then informed Rawdon that he was sending the wounded militia to Camden by wagon to be treated by Dr. Hugh Hill, the senior medical officer of the Volunteers of Ireland. Turnbull's doctor, James Murdoch, had resigned the previous week, and he had no medical staff at Rocky Mount except Surgeon's Mate Nicholas Humphreys, who was "not very Regularly Bred" and in whom Turnbull had no confidence. He noted that he had written to Dr. Wynne Stapleton, chief surgeon of the British Legion, and Dr. Thomas Gibbs, chief surgeon of the

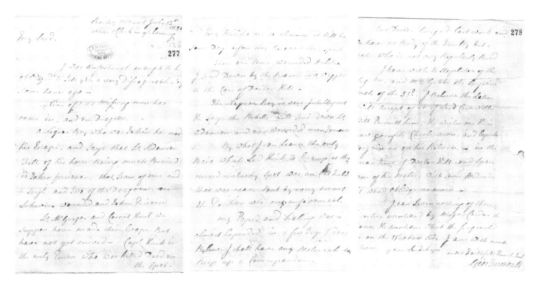

Left: First page of Lieutenant Colonel George Turnbull's follow-up letter to Lord Rawdon, dated 9:00 p.m., 12 July 1780, giving further details of Huck's Defeat. See appendix B for a complete transcription of this letter. *Cornwallis Papers, PRO 30/11/2/277. Courtesy of the National Archives of Great Britain (Public Record Office).*

Center: Second page of Turnbull's follow-up letter to Lord Rawdon on 12 July. *Cornwallis Papers, PRO 30/11/2/277. Courtesy of the National Archives of Great Britain (Public Record Office).*

Right: Third page of Turnbull's follow-up letter to Lord Rawdon on 12 July. *Cornwallis Papers, PRO 30/11/2/278. Courtesy of the National Archives of Great Britain (Public Record Office).*

Thirty-third Regiment of Foot, for assistance at Rocky Mount. "I believe the latter will accept of it if Lord Cornwallis will permitt him," Turnbull stated. "He writes me he is now going to Charlestown and expects to join us on his return. In the mean time if Doctor Hill cou[l]d spare one of his mates with some Medicine it wou[l]d oblige us much."[516]

While Turnbull's letters of 12 July provide some important details about the losses among Huck's men, they leave many questions unanswered. Turnbull's accounting of the dragoons and militia is especially incomplete, and gives little indication of the actual casualties. Captain Huck was certainly not the only man "killed dead on the spot," nor was he the only fatality among the dragoons. While Turnbull's concern for his own New York Volunteers is obvious, his disdain for the Tory militia is also evident: he says nothing about the status of Colonel Matthew Floyd, Colonel James Ferguson, Lieutenant Colonel James Lisle, Major John Owens, Captain Abraham Floyd or any other militia officer except Lieutenant Lewis, and he gives no information about what happened to most of the privates. His figures for the number of men who returned to Rocky Mount on 12 July and the number of wounded who were to return the next day still leave many men unaccounted for.

Over the course of the next week, the Whigs found a significant number of dragoons and militia who were wounded during the firefight and died of their wounds in the woods surrounding the Bratton and Williamson plantations. In a subsequent letter to General Johann DeKalb, General Sumter stated that the British losses were one colonel, one captain and twelve privates found dead on the battlefield, along with one major, one lieutenant and twenty-seven privates captured. He did not say how many of the Loyalists were wounded and subsequently perished, but noted that since the battle, the number of dead amounted to twenty-one, "the loss considerable amongst the dragoons."[517] William Hill mentioned in his memoirs that the enemy's losses included a "considerable number of privates the number not known, as there were many of their carcasses found in the woods some days after."[518] Dr. Maurice Moore recorded his family tradition that the British losses numbered "between thirty and forty killed, and about fifty wounded."[519]

Thursday, 13 July

True to their word, the day after Huck's Defeat, the Whigs sent the wounded men down to Rocky Mount along with an armed escort. However, Lieutenant Adamson was still in no condition to be moved, and he remained a prisoner of the Whigs. After arriving at the British fort, the captain of the Whig guard unsuccessfully attempted to recover Colonel Hill's two slaves from Lieutenant Hunt. Hill recalled the incident unhappily in his memoirs: "The Cap.* of the guard, knew the negroes, & found that he the said Liu.* had them again in his service, and when he was ready to leave the place applied to him for the negroes; but he threatened him and the rest of the guard with confinement, if he would say any thing about them, & it was with a great difficulty he obtained a pass to return back to me—These two negroes have never been recovered by me [or] by any other for me.[520]

Later that same day, Lieutenant Hunt of the British Legion rode into Major Patrick Ferguson's camp, located at the plantation of Captain Jonathan Frost on Padget's Creek in the lower Spartan District. Two of Ferguson's officers, Dr. Uzal Johnson and Lieutenant Anthony Allaire, recorded the incident in their diaries.[521] The entries in both diaries are almost identical, and since the two men were good friends, it seems likely that Allaire copied Johnson's entries at the time.[522] These journal entries give some interesting details concerning Huck's Defeat, including the numbers of men under Huck's command. However, the figures given by Johnson and Allaire differ significantly from the figures given by Turnbull, Lieutenant Colonel Banastre Tarleton and Lord Cornwallis for the same battle.

The first news of Huck's Defeat had actually come to Patrick Ferguson on the evening of 12 July, when an express rider brought word from Rocky Mount. Johnson's entry for that day refers to "seventeen of the British Legion, eighteen New York Volunteers and twenty Militiamen being defeated at Col.* Brat[t]on's [on] Fishing Creek."[523] Allaire's entry for the same incident refers to "seventeen of the Legion, eighteen York Volunteers, and twenty-five militia being defeated at Col. Bratton's, at Fishing Creek."[524] The discrepancy between the numbers given in the two otherwise identical accounts is echoed in the entries for 13 July. Johnson's diary, as transcribed by Dr. Bobby Moss, states:

> *Lieu.* Hunt of the British Calvary came to our Quarters at Cap.* Frost's. He was one of the party defeated the 12.*th Instance. He gave us but an imperfect account of the affair. Cap.* Huck commanded the party, consisting of one Subaltern and seventeen Privates of the British*

Legion, two Subalterns and eighteen New York Volunteers and twenty-five Militiamen. They were sent in pursuit of a Rebel party and arrived at twelve o'Clock Tuesday night the 11th Instance. Very much fatuged, they thought to rest themselves. Unfortunately, a Rebel party commanded by Col' Lacey came upon them at four in the Morning of the 12th, were in amongst them, and had possession of every pass before they were apprized of it, except a Road leading to North Carolina where Cap' Huck with four Dragoons endeavored to make off. Cap' Huck was shot through the neck, of which he died. M' Hunt with one Dragoon took a foot path leading to a Swamp. The Militia, he could give no account of.[525]

Allaire's entry, as transcribed and edited by Dr. Lyman Draper, reads as follows:

Lieut. Hunt of the Legion Cavalry came to our quarters at Capt. Frost's. He was one of the party defeated the twelfth inst. He gave an imperfect account of the affair. Capt. Huck commanded a party consisting of one subaltern and seventeen dragoons of the Legion, three subalterns and eighteen New York Volunteers, twenty-five militia men. They were sent in pursuit of a Rebel party, and arrived a twelve o'clock, Tuesday night, the 11th instant, at Col. Bratton's, at Fishing Creek, and were very much fatigued. They thought to rest themselves. Unfortunately a Rebel party commanded by a Col. Lacey came upon them at four o'clock in the morning of the 12th, who were in amongst them, and had possession of every pass before they were apprised of it—except a road leading towards North Carolina, where Captain Huck, with four dragoons, attempted to make off. Huck got shot through the neck, of which he died. Mr. Hunt, with one dragoon, took a foot path leading to a swamp. The militia he could give no account of.[526]

As noted earlier, Lieutenant Colonel Turnbull stated in his first letter of 12 July to Lord Rawdon that he sent twenty New York Volunteers and fifty militiamen to accompany Huck. He did not specify how many dragoons of the British Legion were under Huck's command. However, Lord Cornwallis, in a subsequent letter to Sir Henry Clinton, stated that Turnbull "sent Captain Huck of the legion, with a detachment of about thirty or forty of that corps, twenty mounted men of the New-York Volunteers, and sixty militia" to disperse the rebels at Fishing Creek.[527] Tarleton noted in his memoirs that Huck's detachment "consisted of thirty-five dragoons of the legion, twenty mounted infantry of the New-York volunteers, and about sixty militia."[528] The statements made by Cornwallis and Tarleton, based as they were on the after-battle reports from Turnbull or Rawdon, should be more accurate than the "very imperfect account" that Hunt gave to Patrick Ferguson and his officers. While Hunt might not be expected to know the exact number of militia on the expedition, it seems odd that he apparently did not know how many dragoons there were. Furthermore, the numbers of dragoons and militia reported to Ferguson by the express rider and Lieutenant Hunt were precisely one-half of the number reported by Turnbull, Tarleton and Cornwallis, while the number of New York Volunteers was the same. But strangely, Johnson and Allaire disagreed on the number of subalterns (lieutenants and ensigns) commanding the New York Volunteers: Johnson reported two, which along with eighteen privates made a total of twenty; Allaire said three, which would bring the total of

New York Volunteers to twenty-one. This difference is difficult to explain considering that Allaire's account seems to have been copied almost verbatim from Johnson's. Lacking further information, it is impossible to account for the discrepancy between the accounts of British and Loyalist officers whose information was ultimately derived from the same source, Lieutenant Colonel Turnbull and Lieutenant Hunt.

Another discrepancy exists between Hunt's statements as recorded by Johnson and Allaire, and those made by Turnbull, Winn and Hill. Turnbull reported in his first letter of 12 July that "Cornet Hunt" was wounded and supposed to be a prisoner. In his second letter, he referred to a sergeant and two privates of the dragoons who were wounded and taken prisoner, and added that "Cornet Hunt" and Lieutenant McGregor were supposed to have escaped but had not yet returned to Rocky Mount. (Although Turnbull referred to him as a cornet, Hunt was in fact a full lieutenant.) Colonels Winn and Hill seemed to verify that Hunt was wounded and captured, but said nothing about his escape. Winn indicated that Hunt was wounded in battle, gave his parole and agreed to accompany the rest of the wounded prisoners back to Rocky Mount on 13 July. This concurs with Turnbull's statement that the rebels planned to send the wounded prisoners down the next day. Hill's account, while not mentioning the wounded officer's name, stated that "Hook's lieutenant" returned to Rocky Mount the day after the battle along with the wounded and then reneged on his promise to restore Hill's slaves. On the other hand, Johnson and Allaire recorded that Hunt claimed to have escaped the battle on a footpath leading to a swamp, along with another dragoon. Furthermore, neither Johnson nor Allaire said anything about Hunt being wounded, and because Johnson was a surgeon, this is just the sort of detail he would typically have noted in his diary. In spite of Hunt's claim that he escaped the battle on horseback, the weight of the evidence suggests that he was wounded (although not seriously), gave his parole and accompanied the other wounded soldiers back to Rocky Mount the day after the battle. After reporting to Turnbull, Hunt then rode over to Ferguson's camp on Padget's Creek and informed him of the affair.

From his headquarters in Charleston, Cornwallis penned a note to Rawdon regarding the increasingly unsettled nature of the Backcountry. Not yet aware of Huck's Defeat, the Earl expressed his regret that Rawdon's post at Camden was turning out "more troublesome that we apprehended when I left you." He emphasized that Rawdon should take the "greatest Care" of his detachments operating on the frontier and "keep everything as compact as possible." Clearly, Cornwallis knew the danger of sending small groups of British soldiers into the hostile settlements of the upper districts. He promised to march north with his army as soon as possible and, in the meantime, to do "everything in my power to hasten the Stores to Camden, and to procure Waggons." Finally, in response to Rawdon's requests to pay drafts for "secret service," the Earl noted, "Any Demands you may have on me for Secret Service shall be duly answered. That is not in my opinion a proper article for economy."[529]

Two other events happened on 13 July that were significant for the burgeoning conflict in the Backcountry. In the Spartan District, Colonel John Thomas Jr. led his men north and linked up with Colonel Charles McDowell of Burke County, North Carolina. Fearing an invasion of western North Carolina by Ferguson and his Loyalist corps, McDowell brought some three hundred to four hundred North Carolina militiamen to Earle's Ford on the North Pacolet River in the Spartan District, just south of the border between North and South Carolina. Although he did not realize it at the time, Thomas was followed from Cedar Springs by a band of about forty Tories, who halted at Gowen's Old Fort on the South Pacolet River, just west of the old Cherokee Line (now the border between Greenville and Spartanburg Counties). Unknown to the Tories, one of McDowell's officers, Colonel John Jones of Burke County, was in the vicinity escorting about thirty-five Georgia militiamen to McDowell's camp. Disguising themselves as Loyalists, Jones and his men discovered the location of the Tory encampment, surrounded the fort and attacked the Loyalists at about 11:00 p.m. After a brief engagement, the Tories surrendered and were paroled. Jones and his men confiscated their weapons, destroyed what they could not carry and made off with the best of the Tories' horses.[530]

Meanwhile, in Philadelphia, the Continental Congress commissioned Major General Horatio Gates to command the Southern Department. Members of Congress believed that the "Hero of Saratoga" would be able to rally the Southern militia to support the Continental Army, a task that they mistakenly believed he accomplished before the Battle of Saratoga in New York. George Washington opposed giving Gates the command of the Southern Department and greatly desired to see that command go to his very able commissary, Major General Nathanael Greene. But the Continental Congress did not consult Washington in the decision, and its choice of Gates over Greene was to have disastrous consequences later that summer.[531]

Friday, 14 July

The news of Huck's Defeat spread quickly through the Backcountry, and large numbers of fresh recruits began coming in to Sumter's camp at the Old Nation Ford. Within a few days of the battle, there were more than four hundred men at Camp Catawba. The Whigs found it necessary to move their camp once again, and relocated a few miles to the north on Steele Creek near the Knox plantation.[532] On or about this date, an incident occurred that typified the unsettled nature of warfare in the Backcountry in late 1780. Shortly after the battle at Williamson's plantation, Lieutenant Colonel John Lisle, second-in-command of Colonel Matthew Floyd's Upper District Loyalist Militia Regiment, seized the opportunity to return to his former allegiance and defected to Sumter's Brigade, taking with him most of Floyd's regiment as well as its newly issued arms and ammunition. Cornwallis mentioned the incident in a subsequent letter to Clinton.[533] Tarleton later complained that the affair destroyed the British Army's confidence in the Loyalist militia:

> *An instance of treachery which took place about this time, ruined all confidence between the regulars and the militia: The inhabitants in the districts of the rivers Ennoree and Tyger had been enrolled since the siege of Charles town, under the orders of Colonel Floyd; Colonel Neale, the former commanding officer, having fled out of the province for his violent persecution of the loyalists. One Lisle, who had belonged to the same corps, and who had been banished to the islands, availing himself of the proclamation to exchange his parole for a certificate of his being a good citizen, was made second in command: And as soon as the battalion was completed with arms and*

ammunition, he carried it off to Colonel Neale, who had joined Colonel Sumpter's command in the Catawba.[534]

Tarleton was mistaken in one detail of his report: Colonel Andrew Neal did not command the Whig militia in the Tyger and Enoree River region in 1780. That area fell within the confines of the Spartan and Dutch Fork Districts and was under Colonels John Thomas, Thomas Brandon and James Lisle. Tarleton's information may have been derived from knowledge that Neal's father, Thomas Neal Sr., commanded militia from the Tyger and Enoree area when he was colonel of the Tryon County Militia Regiment and the New District Regiment before 1775.[535]

On the west side of the Broad River, the conflict continued to escalate. Lieutenant Colonel Alexander Innes, commanding a Loyalist garrison at Fort Prince on the North Fork of the Tyger River (now in Spartanburg County), decided to send a Loyalist force against Colonel John Jones and the Georgia militia camped at Earle's Ford, some twenty miles away. Unaware that Colonel Charles McDowell was also camped at the ford with more than three hundred men, Innes dispatched Major James Dunlap, with fourteen mounted infantry of the American Volunteers, and Colonel Ambrose Mills, commanding sixty Loyalist militia, to attack the rebel camp. Dunlap crossed Earle's Ford during the night of 14 July and attacked Jones's militia, which was camped just across the river on the east side of the ford. The Whigs quickly rallied and counterattacked Dunlap, who then found himself badly outnumbered. Dunlap beat a hasty retreat, but his men succeeded in killing eight rebels and wounding thirty. Colonel Andrew Hampton of the Whig militia, who lost a son in the battle, blamed McDowell for the Whig losses. Hampton had urged McDowell to place videttes on the west side of the ford to guard against just such an occurrence. McDowell, however, had sent his brother, Major Joseph McDowell, on a scouting expedition earlier that day, and as the major had not reported back with news of any Tory activity, the colonel believed it safe to retire his men without posting guards.[536] As Captain Huck had discovered two days earlier, and as General Sumter would subsequently learn at Fishing Creek and Fishdam Ford, it was foolhardy and dangerous to encamp large bodies of men in the Backcountry without posting adequate guards against surprise attacks. It was a mistake that both sides would continue to make during the war.

Later that day in Camden, Lord Rawdon penned a letter to Lord Cornwallis in Charleston stating that "nothing particular" had occurred since his last letter, "excepting that I have had notice of the junction being formed between De Kalb & Caswell at Coxe's Settlement." This was a reference to a link up between DeKalb's Continentals and Major General Richard Caswell, senior commandant of the North Carolina Whig militia. Rawdon added that Dr. Hill had cured him of "a little fever which had attacked me." Having enclosed Turnbull's second letter on Huck's Defeat, he added that "the misfortune of Huck's Party has not been so bad as it first appeared. In the course of this day, I hope to learn with certainty something respecting the Enemy Movements; an account of which I should immediately dispatch."[537]

That same day, Lord Cornwallis sent a letter to Sir Henry Clinton in New York, assuring Clinton that he was busily employed "in the internal regulations of the province, and settling the militia of the lower districts, both of which are in great forwardness; and I have kept up a continual correspondence with the frontiers, and the internal parts of North Carolina, where the aspect of affairs is not so peaceable as when I wrote last." The Earl then proceeded with a detailed summary of the rebel troop movements: DeKalb was in Hillsborough with two thousand Continentals, moving toward Salisbury; Colonel Charles Porterfield was near Salisbury with three hundred Virginians, along with General Rutherford and some North Carolina militia; and General Caswell was on Deep River between Hillsborough and Salisbury with another fifteen hundred North Carolina militiamen. He added that "Sumpter, with about the same number of militia, is advanced as far as the Catawba settlement. Lord Rawdon reports to me, that many of the disaffected South Carolinians, from the Waxhaw, and other settlements on the frontier, whom he has put on parole, have availed themselves of the general release of the 20th of June, and have joined General Sumpter."[538]

Cornwallis added that twenty-five hundred Virginia militiamen were supposedly following DeKalb, and that members of the Virginia Assembly had voted to draft another five thousand men and had given Governor Thomas Jefferson "absolute power during their recess." The North Carolina government, Cornwallis added, was "likewise making great exertions to raise troops, and persecuting our friends in the most cruel manner." In spite of the Earl's orders to the contrary, Loyalist Colonel Samuel Bryan had "lost all patience" and had ridden down from the Yadkin River to the Cheraw District with eight hundred Loyalists to join Major Archibald McArthur and the Seventy-first Regiment there; only about two-thirds of his men were armed, and those "but indifferently." Cornwallis concluded his letter by noting that the reports of enemy activity in Virginia and North Carolina were undoubtedly exaggerated. "I am using every possible dispatch in transporting to Camden rum, salt, regimental stores, arms, and ammunition," he added, "which, on account of the distance and excessive heat of the season, is a work of infinite labor, and requires considerable time."

But Cornwallis was confident in the ultimate success of his plans: "[T]he measures I have directed Lord Rawdon to take will, I trust, put it out of the power of the enemy to strike a blow at any of our detachments, or to make any considerable inroads into this province. I have the satisfaction to assure your excellency, that the numbers and dispositions of our militia equal my most sanguine expectations." Events in the Backcountry would soon prove his lordship's confidence in the safety of his detachments and the effectiveness of his militia to be overly optimistic.[539]

Saturday, 15 July

Not long after sending his confident letter to Clinton on 14 July, Cornwallis received the first reports from Rawdon and Turnbull on Huck's Defeat. The Earl was none too pleased with the way things were going in the Backcountry, first with Ramsour's Mill and now with Huck's debacle. Writing to Rawdon on 15 July, Cornwallis reemphasized the danger of sending small detachments into the frontier settlements, noting that "if the enemy come within any possibility of reaching you, be compact, & prefer that to any other considerations." He then addressed his plans to move into North Carolina and the destruction of Huck's expedition, with some rather cutting comments about Huck's abilities as an officer:

I forsee that it will be absolutely necessary to act aggressively very soon, to save our friends in N. Carolina, & to preserve the Confidence, in which is included the friendship of the South Carolinians. I am hastening our preparations but we must do it ready or not ready rather than submit to any serious insult. I will come to you as soon as possible, and I think it will be very soon....

Lt. Col. Turnbull's Letter gave me very serious concern, & it is indeed a very serious misfortune. Cavalry acts chiefly upon the Nerves, & if ever it loses its terror it loses its greatest force. Tarleton will join us in a few days, in the mean time let me conjure you to take care of the Cavalry & to give the most positive orders against small Detachments; they are always dangerous, especially under ignorant & careless officers....

If in consequence of that unlucky officer of the Legion, the Rebels should be troublesome between the Wateree & Broad River, Your Lordship will please to send to [Lt. Col. Nisbet] Balfour [at Fort Ninety Six] for every Militia assistance he can give you.[540]

Later on the afternoon of 15 July, some Whig soldiers from the Spartan District under Major Joseph McJunkin transported a supply of gunpowder into Sumter's camp. They also brought intelligence that Captain William Cunningham, the Tory officer who defeated Colonel Brandon in early June, was once again causing trouble on the west side of the Broad River. A young Whig named James Knox, who moved to the Spartan District from Captain John McClure's neighborhood the year before, was captured and executed by Cunningham, and it was reported that the Tories were planning to cross the river and raid the New Acquisition. General Sumter had just returned to camp from North Carolina with his newly acquired rifles, and he promptly dispatched McClure and some of his rangers to intercept Cunningham. McClure picked up Cunningham's trail and attacked his camp, but most of the Tories escaped. McClure took four prisoners and pursued Cunningham some thirty miles toward Ninety Six, but he eluded capture.[541] Sumter mentioned the incident in a letter to Baron DeKalb two days later.[542]

Following Major Dunlap's attack on the troops at Earle's Ford, Colonel McDowell sent fifty-two mounted militiamen under Captain Edward Hampton after the Tory party. Not expecting any pursuit, Dunlap was in no hurry to return to Fort Prince and stopped to rest along the way. Hampton set out before daylight and, after two hours of hard riding, overtook Dunlap on the Blackstock Road near the present site of Shiloh Methodist Church, not far from the modern town of Inman in Spartanburg County. Eager to avenge the death of his nephew, Hampton attacked without warning and killed eight of Dunlap's men with his first volley. The Loyalists were taken by surprise and thoroughly routed; Dunlap and the rest of his men fled in great haste back to Fort Prince. Hampton advanced to within three hundred yards of the fort but, realizing he was significantly outnumbered by the Loyalist garrison there, broke off his attack. "At two o'clock in the afternoon, Hampton and his men returned to McDowell's camp," Lyman Draper wrote, "with thirty-five good horses, dragoon equipage, and a considerable portion of the enemy's baggage, as the trophies of victory, and without the loss of single man." Fearing an all-out attack by McDowell, Colonel Innes abandoned Fort Prince.[543]

After receiving Lord Rawdon's letter of 14 July, Cornwallis dashed off another letter to Clinton. "De Kalbe has certainly joined Caswell at Coxes' plantation on Deep river," he wrote;

"his lordship in consequence has withdrawn Major McArthur's detachment over the Black creek, when he means to join him with two battalions, and post Lieutenant-colonel [James] Webster on Hanging-rock creek." He also gave Clinton the news about Huck's Defeat and did not hesitate to place the blame on Captain Huck:

> Lord Rawdon likewise inclosed to me a letter from Lieutenant-colonel Turnbull, at Rocky mount, on the west bank of the Wateree, thirty miles from Camden, who reports, that having heard that some of the violent rebels, about thirty miles in his front, had returned to their plantations, and were encouraging the people to join them, he sent Captain Huck of the legion, with a detachment of about thirty or forty of that corps, twenty mounted men of the New-York volunteers, and sixty militia, to seize or drive them away. Captain Huck, encouraged by meeting with no opposition, encamped in an unguarded manner, was totally surprised and routed. The captain was killed, and only twelve of the legion, and as many of the militia, escaped.[544]

Lieutenant Colonel Tarleton was also in Charleston with Cornwallis when he learned of Huck's Defeat. Tarleton disliked having his dragoons split off into small detachments and sent into the Backcountry where they could be easily ambushed and "cut to pieces," and he was furious at Rawdon for what he perceived to be a careless misuse of this valuable military resource.[545] However, like Turnbull and Cornwallis, Tarleton did not hesitate in assigning the blame to Captain Huck. Writing about the incident years later in his memoirs, he reflected on the battle:

> The state of the country, and the exaggerated reports of the Americans, occasioned frequent patroles of cavalry and mounted infantry from the advanced British posts; one of which experienced both disgrace and defeat. Lieutenant-colonel Turnbull, on some intelligence from Fishing creek, sent Captain Huck of the legion to investigate the truth : The detachment committed to his care consisted of thirty-five dragoons of the legion, twenty mounted infantry of the New-York volunteers, and about sixty militia. On his arrival at the cross roads, near the source of Fishing creek, Captain Huck neglected his duty, in placing his party carelessly at a plantation, without advancing any pickets, or sending out patroles : Some Americans who were assembled in the neighbourhood heard of his negligent situation, and with an inferior force surprised and destroyed him, and a great part of his command.[546]

Tarleton was clearly drawing on the same report as Cornwallis, and it is interesting to note that even at this late date, he still maintained that "a great part" of Huck's command was destroyed, in obvious contradiction to Turnbull's follow-up letter downplaying the defeat.

Monday, 17 July

In his camp on the Catawba River, General Sumter composed a long letter to General DeKalb that brought him up to date on the events in the Backcountry. In his letter, Sumter included a breakdown of the numbers of British troops in the state that almost certainly came from some of the prisoners taken at Huck's Defeat. He also provided a detailed account of the British losses at the battle, and a strategy that he believed would prevent the scattered British forces from combining and overwhelming the Whigs. This was the first and only letter that DeKalb received from any of the South Carolina officers still in the field. Datelined "State So. Carolina, Camp Catawba River, 17th July, 1780," it read as follows [all spelling is verbatim]:

Having been well informed that you are Marching to the Reliefe of this Country, I think it my Duty to give you the Earliest Intelligence of the situation and force of the Enemy, together with such other things as appear the Most Interesting. From the best accounts the Number of the British Are as follows, vize.: at George Town, 250; C. Town, 800; Beauford, 12; Savanah, in georgia, 300; Agusta, 500; Sennica Fort, 70; Ninety-Six, 250; fair forest, 30; Rockey Mount, 200; Hanging Rock, 280 foot, 70 Dragoons; Camden & its Vicinity, 700; Cheraw's said to be 600; Total, 3,482. This Number I Conceive to be equal to the whole of the Brettish force, Provided every man fit for Duty was brought together from the Defrent posts, Which, if attempted, Coud not Posably be effected en less than twelve or fifteen days' time, as to their Tory or Militia Force, Nothing Certain Can be Said, that Depending Solely upon Circumstances, and is a Matter of Very Serious nature to this Country and Indeed to the Continent, for if they are permitted to Retreat slowly to Charles Town, or have an opportunity of Collecting the Tories and imbodying the militia, who they Compell to do Duty, I say if they are suffered to do this they will by that means add above ten thousand men to their army—and thereby become so strong as Not only to Keep possession of Charles Town, but also a Great part of the State besides, and to Obviate this evil your Excellency will, I hope, pardon me for the freedom I take in giving my opinion, the Method I Shoud purpose to Prevent this Junction & accumilation of force, Woud be to Detach a Body of Light Troops to take post upon the South Side of Santee River, at Neilson's [Nelson's] and Manigalute's [Manigault's] Ferries, this woud effectually Cut of[f] their Retreat to Towns and thereby prevent them from forcing the Militia to retreat with them, or from their Gathering together the Forces, and also from Striping the Country of all its Resources, Which they are with the Greatest Diligence Doing; and if Not Shortly Pervented Will Leave it in a Situation Not Acceptable for Giving Scarce any Support to an army.

When it is Considered how Vastly Weak the enemy is by being so Detached in Small parties, and the Impossibility of their being collected in a Short Time, and the certainty of their being anoyed if that Shoud be attempted, Leaves No Room to Doubt but that one thousand or fifteen hundred Troops Might, With the Greatest propriety, Take Post at the place before mentioned, and woud unfailable answer the end Designed, Not only by perventing them from forcing the Militia into their Service and Carring off all the Horses, stock and other provisions that the country offers, But woud Render their own Retreat exceeding Difficult, if not impossible, as it Coud be effected only by the way of Georgia, the Distresses of the people of this country have been for Some Time past almost beyond Conception, in the Northerein part of the State they have Now Some Respite, I having Collected a party of men, attacked and Dispersed the enemy, So As to Cleare two Regiments of them, the Most Considerable Scirmish Happened on Wednesday Morning. The enemy's loss, Kild upon the Spot, was one Col., one Capt. and Twelve others; one Majr., one Lt. &

Left: First page of General Thomas Sumter's letter to General Johann DeKalb dated 17 July 1780, giving details of British troop strength in South Carolina. DeKalb's answer is noted at the top of the page. *Horatio Gates Papers. Courtesy of the Collection of The New-York Historical Society.*

Center: Second page of Sumter's letter to DeKalb on 17 July, giving details of Huck's Defeat and engagement with Tories on Broad River. *Horatio Gates Papers. Courtesy of the Collection of The New-York Historical Society.*

Right: Third page of Sumter's letter to DeKalb on 17 July. This is the only known letter from a South Carolina field officer written to DeKalb before his death at the Battle of Camden on 16 August 1780. *Horatio Gates Papers. Courtesy of the Collection of The New-York Historical Society.*

Twenty-Seven others taken prisoners, Since Which the Number found Dead aMounts to Twenty-one; the Loss very considerable among the Dragoons. I had about one hundred and thirty men in the action, the enemy twice that Number, Seventy of which were Brittesh. We Released a Number of our friends, who were fast bound with Cords and otherways Treated with Great Severity. On Saturday last I sent a party over Broad River, who Broke up an encampment of Tories that were forming there, to Secoure a passway over the River. They did them but Little Damage, except that of Taking their post, which was of Consequence to them, and not easy to be maintained by me, as the Tories are Very numerous in that quarter and are Supported by Brittish. I am destitute of almost every Requisite for war; but, notwithstanding, Can Counteract some of their Designs untill your army arives, which I have the Greatest hopes will be soon, if Not Disagreeable, [I] shoud be exceedingly obliged by having the Route of your army for this few days to Come, as I might thereby be the better inabled to act aGainst the enemy With a probability of success.[54]

Thursday, 20 July

True to his word, Major John Owens kept the appointment he made with Colonel Richard Winn after Huck's Defeat. After acting as a spy and collecting information on the British fort at

Rocky Mount, Owens—who still considered himself to be on parole after Huck's Defeat—met Winn at a secret location and gave him a detailed report on the number and disposition of the British forces stationed there. According to Winn, Owens "reported that Colo. Turnbull commanded—had about 300 men & was posted in a Strong Block house two stories high, properly prepared for defence & sufficient Abbatis." Winn then passed the information on to Sumter, and Sumter began planning an attack on the British fort.[548]

Owens accurately reported that Turnbull's headquarters at Rocky Mount was in a large framed house with thin clapboard walls, and the Whigs assumed their musket and rifle balls would pass through the walls without difficulty. Since Sumter did not have any artillery, the Whigs hoped that their small arms would be sufficient to reduce the British to submission. However, Turnbull must have suspected that Owens was acting as a spy for the Whigs, because after Owens left Rocky Mount, Turnbull immediately began strengthening his fortifications there. As Colonel Hill later reported, "From the time we rec'd. this information until the time the attack was made the Enemy had wrought day & night and had placed small logs about a foot from the inside of the wall and rammed the cavity with clay." This reinforcement rendered the walls of the main building impervious to small arms fire, as the Whigs would soon discover to their dismay.[549]

Friday, 21 July

At his post on the north side of Waxhaw Creek, Major William Davie received intelligence that a British supply convoy carrying "provisions, spirits and clothing" was heading from Camden to Hanging Rock in order to resupply that post. As Davie related in his memoirs, the British had "improvidently consumed all the grain between that post and Camden and were now obliged to draw their supplies from that place; to cut off these became an object of importance." Davie and his dragoons left their camp on the evening of 20 July and, by riding all night, reached the main road to Camden on the morning of the next day. The Whigs took up a position about five miles south of Hanging Rock at a place called Flat Rock, in modern Kershaw County, and waited on the convoy. The convoy "appeared in the afternoon & were captured with little trouble, the spirits, provisions and waggons being destroyed, the escorts and waggoners were mounted on the captured horses, and about dark the party commenced its retreat." Fearing that he might fall prey to an ambush if he returned to his camp by the same route he had taken earlier, Davie instructed his guides "to take the most unfrequented route to prevent the detachment from being attacked in the night, the whole country being covered with thick woods and dangerous defiles."[550]

Later that day, General DeKalb received Sumter's letter of 17 July at his camp in North Carolina and read it immediately. However, knowing that Major General Horatio Gates was on his way south to take command of the army, DeKalb decided to take no action. He sent a message back to Sumter stating simply, "I will lay the letter before General Gates at his arrival."[551]

Saturday, 22 July

At about 2:00 a.m., Davie's detachment, with the prisoners and captured supplies, approached a plantation on the principal branch of Beaver Creek in what is now Lancaster County.

Anticipating an ambush, Davie sent an advance guard forward under one of his officers, a Captain Petit, "to examine the Houses and a narrow lane through which the road led, and also the ford of the Creek and with express directions to secure the family." The scouts reported the way clear, and the detachment entered the lane. About the time that the rear of the column came into the lane, Captain Petit spotted some enemy soldiers "concealed under the fence and some standing corn; on challenging a second time he was answered by a discharge of Musquetry, which commenced on their right and passed like a run[n]ing fire towards the rear of the Detachment." Major Davie tried to rally his men, but they fell back and retreated down the lane and into the woods. In spite of the fact that the Tories possessed the element of surprise, most of Davie's men escaped the ambush unharmed and made their way back to camp later that morning.[552] Davie concluded his narration by emphasizing the lessons he had learned regarding carelessness in partisan warfare—costly lessons that would have served Captain Huck equally well ten days earlier:

> The loss was slight considering the advantage of the British, Cap.[t] Petit and two men wounded and Lie.[t] [Elliot] killed; the fire fell principally among the prisoners, who were confined two upon a horse and mixed with the guard presented a larger object than a single dragoon; the advance guard with the prisoners nearly filled the lane, it was owin to these circumstances that the prisoners were all killed or wounded except three or four. The object of surprising the convoy was effected the slaughter of the prisoners could not be considered a loss; but the ambuscade might have been fatal to the whole Detachment; a misfortune solely occasioned by the officer of the advance guard not having executed his orders; this may furnish a useful lesson to the officers of partizan corps who should never forget that every officer of a detachment on command may at some moment have its safety and reputation committed to him, and that the slightest neglect of duty is generally severely punished by an enemy.[553]

Sunday, 23 July

Major Thomas Blount, a North Carolina Continental officer in Hillsborough, sent a letter to North Carolina Governor Abner Nash apprising him of the recent Whig victories in the Backcountry. Blount had already reported on the Loyalist defeat at Ramsour's Mill in an earlier letter the same day; his second letter went into detail about two subsequent actions. The first was Huck's Defeat, while the second was an engagement at Colson's Mill on the Peedee River between North Carolina Whigs and Tory militia on 21 July:

> Three successful attacks have been made on the Enemy. The particulars of the first [Ramsour's Mill] I gave you in a former letter. The second was on a Party of about one hundred and thirty tories, Commanded by Colo. Ferguson, a noted tory from the Northward, and seventy Light Horse of Cathcart's Legion, Commanded by a Capt. Hook on the 12th Inst. by a party of 80 or 90 Militia, under the command of Colo. Neale. The surprise was compleat. Ferguson, Hook, a Lieut. and 11 others were killed on the ground, and a major, 2 Lieuts. & 27 taken, many of whom are since dead of their wounds; the remainder are dispersed. Some accoutrements for

Light Horse & a number of Horses were also taken; of the exact number we have not yet a certain account, but it is supposed the whole. Our loss was only one man wounded.

Lieut. Col. Williams, Lieut. [Colonel William Lee] Davidson, of the Continental Line, with a Detachment of One Hundred & sixty Light Horse from Brig. Genl. Rutherford's Brigade, on the 21ˢᵗ Inst. made the third attack on about 500 or 600 tories, Commanded by the infamous Sam Bryan, near Colson on P. D., killed three or four, took Forty, & put the remainder to flight with more precipitation than we fled from Bryar Creek; none halted until they reached the Enemy's next Post at the Waxhaws, where they threw the whole into the utmost confusion and Consternation. Their whole time since has been employed in constructing Fortifications for their safety. Colo. Davidson was wounded in the Body, 'tis feared mortally; two Privates were also slightly wounded, but not a man killed. To Davidson's misfortune may probably be attributed their escape.[554]

Blount's letter contained several mistakes in the details, although the information was for the most part correct. He incorrectly assumed that Colonel James Ferguson was in overall command of the detachment at Huck's Defeat, and mistakenly referred to Ferguson as a Northern Tory; it was of course Captain Huck who was the "noted tory from the Northward." "Cathcart's Legion" was the original name of the British Legion, which was organized by Sir William Cathcart of the British Army prior to its deployment in the Southern Department. And although William Lee Davidson, who was actually a brigadier general by this time, was badly wounded in the action at Colson's Mill, the wound was not mortal. Davidson would continue to serve North Carolina with distinction until he was killed in battle on 1 February 1781, fighting against Lord Cornwallis's troops at Cowan's Ford on the Catawba River.

Monday, 24 July

The Whigs in Sumter's camp decided that the time had come to make Sumter's leadership official, and to establish the "rules of war" that they were to operate under. As the South Carolina government had been replaced by British military rule and the governor was in exile in North Carolina, the Whigs decided to convene a convention, legalize their status as state militia and officially confirm their earlier election of Colonel Sumter as brigadier general. They also established commissioners to oversee the disposition of requisitioned and confiscated supplies, weapons, ammunition and other stores. Richard Winn described the convention in his memoirs:

As the laws of the state had subsided about this time it was thought necessary to call a convention of the people which met in or near the Catawba Indian land, when the business of the meeting was opened, it was thought necessary to chose a President when Colo Richard Winn was called to the chair....

The first thing that was taken under consideration was the critical situation of the State, & here it was solemnly agreed on by the Convention what they would support the laws both civil & military by every means in their power & called on the good people to aid them in this undertaking.

Secondly, that they would oppose the British & Tories by force of arms, which arms was never to be laid down untill the British Troop was drove from the St of So Carolina & the Independence of the United States acknowledged. It was then moved & seconded, that Colo Thomas Sumter should be appointed a Brigadier General, & that the President be directed to make out a Commission to that effect, & to sign the same in due form which was accordingly so done....Several other officers being promoted mov.d Secon.d & agreed to.

That all such persons that would oppose the Common Enemy under the Command of Gen.l Sumter should inlist for six weeks under proper officers sign an attestation & take the oath for their faithful perform[ance] with the Execution of the officers, in a day or two Gen.l Sumter found himself at the head of four or five hundred men.

That all property of the Enemy taken in the field of Battle or else where, shall be divided among the officers & men who shall serve as above, but it shall be clearly understood that no such property shall be divided until first condemned by three Commissioners which is hereby appointed for that purpose, which said Commissioners shall keep Books, & make regular Entries of the property as aforesaid.

The people then directed the Pres.t to adjourn their convention (to meet again).[555]

The appointment of commissioners to record and condemn confiscated property was an effort to deter looting by the militia. One of the commissioners appointed to this task was Reverend John Simpson. His South Carolina audited account, certified by Colonel Edward Lacey, shows that he served from 24 July until 10 November 1780 as a "Commissionar to Settle Publick matters in Camp @ ³⁄₁₀ p.r Day," the same pay rate as a captain of rangers or mounted militia.[556]

Tuesday, 25 July

Major General Horatio Gates arrived at Coxe's Mill, North Carolina, and assumed command of the Southern Department from Major General DeKalb. Gates's Southern army at this time consisted of 1,200 Maryland and Delaware Continentals, 120 dragoons of Armand's (formerly Pulaski's) Legion, and three artillery companies. Armed with Sumter's estimate of only seven hundred British soldiers at Camden, Gates decided to march into South Carolina and retake Camden from the British.[557]

Wednesday, 26 July

Earl Cornwallis in Charleston wrote to Lord Rawdon in Camden, complementing him on the way he was handling events in the Backcountry. "The preserving of so extensive a frontier, & surmounting so many difficulties both in & out of the Province, can only be attributed to the Prudence and Firmness of your Conduct," he noted. Cornwallis then addressed the problem of prisoner exchanges with the rebels, in particular officers of the British Legion, and expressed concern about Lieutenant John Adamson, who was still being held by the rebels. The Earl had met Adamson during his stay in Camden, and was evidently impressed enough with him to take special interest in his release:

I do not care to propose to the Enemy an Exchange of any of the Prisoners here, as the General [Clinton] in his Instructions to me seems very averse to it; but Tarleton by my Consent, before I had received those Instructions wrote to the Command. *Officer in North Carolina to propose an Exchange of some of the officers taken at Waxhaw, for some of the Legion taken at Sea; he received no answer, De Kalbe was not then come into N. Carolina & I doubt whether any Continental officer was there. Tarleton will by with you in a few days, & will give you further account of this business; when I can see no impropriety in your writing to de Kalbe to renew the Proposition & to add L*. *Adamson; if he should be this means get released before I come down, I beg your Lordship will give what orders you think proper about his Company. If however any Lieut. of the Rebels should be actually or should hereafter fall into your hands (those taken by the Legion excepted, who certainly should not be exchanged without the release of the Officers of the Legion, who by all accounts have been most cruelly treated) you have my leave to negotiate L*. *Adamson's immediate exchange.*[558]

Friday, 28 July

By 28 July, General Sumter had some six hundred men under his command and was eager to launch his own campaign to drive the British from Rocky Mount and Hanging Rock. On Friday morning, he broke camp at Old Nation Ford and moved his brigade down to Land's Ford, an important crossing on the Catawba River between modern Chester and Lancaster Counties. He was joined at Land's Ford by Major Davie and his dragoons as well as by additional troops from Mecklenburg, Rowan and the Waxhaws. McClure was elected colonel and John Nixon was elected lieutenant colonel of the regiment from the upper portion of the District between the Broad and Catawba Rivers. Colonels Neal and Hill commanded the reconstituted New Acquisition Militia Regiment, while Colonel Bratton commanded a smaller battalion of volunteers from Bethesda, Beersheba and Bullock's Creek congregations.[559]

Sunday, 30 July

In his first letter to Lord Rawdon on 12 July, Lieutenant Colonel Turnbull had predicted that Huck's Defeat would encourage the rebels to "pay us a visit." Eighteen days later, Turnbull's prediction came true. Early on the morning of 30 July, General Sumter commenced operations against Rocky Mount. He dispatched Major Davie's troop to make a diversionary attack on Hanging Rock while he attacked Rocky Mount with most of his brigade. Davie and his dragoons struck the camp of Colonel Samuel Bryan's North Carolina Royalists at Hanging Rock and inflicted heavy casualties, capturing Bryan's supplies and sixty horses in the process. Meanwhile, Sumter's Brigade attacked Rocky Mount. During the initial attack, a brazen frontal assault on the fort, Colonel Andrew Neal and seven privates were killed. Sumter realized to his regret that the fort was more heavily fortified than he was originally led to believe. The Whigs tried unsuccessfully for several hours to take Rocky Mount, and even succeeded in setting the main building on fire, but were forced to break off operations when torrential rain began to fall.[560]

In the Spartan District, Colonel McDowell had moved his camp to Cherokee Ford on the Broad River. Among the Whig militia officers in his camp were Colonel Isaac Shelby from North Carolina's "overmountain" settlements (now eastern Tennessee) and Lieutenant Colonel Elijah Clarke, an excellent field commander who led the Whig refugees from Georgia. On the same day that Sumter attacked Rocky Mount, McDowell detached a party of militia under Shelby, Clarke, Colonel Andrew Hampton, and Major Charles Robertson to attack a Loyalist outpost called Thicketty Fort (or Fort Anderson) on Thicketty Creek, a branch of the Pacolet River in modern Cherokee County. Captain Patrick Moore, a Loyalist officer, commanded the fort and its garrison of ninety-three Tory militiamen. On the morning of 30 July, the Whig militia appeared at Thicketty Fort without warning, surrounded the fort and demanded Moore's surrender. Moore, believing he had no other choice, surrendered the entire garrison and a large supply of arms without firing a shot.[501]

The end of July saw the rebels taking the offensive on both sides of the Broad and Catawba Rivers. Against all odds, the Whig militia in the Backcountry had transformed itself from a few scattered groups of refugees driven from their settlements into several brigades of well-equipped troops capable of taking the fight to the enemy—and winning. And the British, who two months earlier had boasted that South Carolina was a conquered province without any rebel troops in the field, now found their detachments being ambushed, their outposts under attack and their base at Camden threatened by a new Continental Army being assembled in North Carolina.

Chapter VI

"Their success will no doubt Encourage them"

The Whig attacks of June and July marked the beginning of a counteroffensive that continued to ramp up during the month of August. On 6 August, exactly one week after his repulse at Rocky Mount, General Thomas Sumter attacked Hanging Rock, inflicting serious casualties on the Loyalist forces there and taking a great deal of supplies and ordinance.[502] That same day, Lord Cornwallis sent a letter to Sir Henry Clinton in New York providing further details on Huck's Defeat and the other rebel activities in the Carolinas. "The affair of Captain Huck turned out to be of less consequence than it appeared at first," Cornwallis assured Clinton. "The captain and three men of the legion were killed, and seven men of the New-York volunteers taken."[503] Although the Earl downplayed the seriousness of Huck's Defeat and completely ignored the Tory militia casualties, he provided an important detail lacking in Lieutenant Colonel Turnbull's earlier letters to Lord Rawdon: in addition to Captain Huck, three other dragoons of the British Legion were killed in the battle.

Throughout the month of August, the Whig attacks in South Carolina continued. On 8 August, militia from the Carolinas and Georgia under Colonel Isaac Shelby, Lieutenant Colonel Elijah Clarke and Captain Joseph Graham defeated a large force of Loyalists under Major James Dunlap and Major Patrick Ferguson near Wofford's Iron Works in the Spartan District. The battle lasted most of the day and was spread out over several miles.[504] A week later at Wateree Ferry in what is now Kershaw County, Sumter captured a British supply convoy headed from Ninety Six to Camden.[505] The following day, 16 August, Major General Horatio Gates finally met Lord Cornwallis in a pitched battle near Camden and suffered a disastrous rout at the hands of the British Army. The Battle of Camden proved to be the worst defeat the American Army would suffer until World War II.[506] Two days later, Lieutenant Colonel Banastre Tarleton attacked Sumter's camp on lower Fishing Creek and dispersed his command in a battle that became known throughout the Backcountry as "Sumter's Surprise." Once again, a large body of troops—this time, Sumter's Brigade—had camped in the open without posting adequate guards and paid a heavy price for their commander's negligence.[507] But in spite of these back-to-back defeats, the rebels refused to lay down their arms and surrender. In fact, the defeats at Camden and Fishing Creek seemed to spur the Whigs on to further retaliation.

On 18 August, the same day that Sumter was attacked by Tarleton at Fishing Creek, the Whig militia won an important victory over a portion of Ferguson's command at Musgrove's

Mill on the border between the Little River and Spartan Districts. The Loyalist force included detachments of two Provincial corps from the North, the First Battalion of DeLancey's Brigade and the Third Battalion of the New Jersey Volunteers, both under the command of Lieutenant Colonel Alexander Innes, as well as a detachment of the South Carolina Royalists militia regiment under Major James Fraser. At Musgrove's Mill on the Enoree River, Innes and Fraser attacked the Whig militia under Colonels James Williams, Thomas Brandon and Isaac Shelby, Lieutenant Colonels Elijah Clarke and William Farr, and Major Joseph McDowell. The Whigs repulsed Innes's attack and routed the Loyalists, whose casualties included sixty-three killed in action, ninety wounded and seventy taken prisoner. The Whigs suffered four men killed and eight wounded.[508]

The news of Huck's Defeat and the other victories in the South slowly spread north during August and September, and notices about the battles appeared in Whig newspapers in Virginia, Maryland, Pennsylvania and New Jersey. The earliest printed report on the Battle of Huck's Defeat appeared on Wednesday, 23 August 1780, in the *Virginia Gazette*, based on information received from Major General Richard Caswell's headquarters at Cross Creek (now Fayetteville), North Carolina, that incorrectly placed the battle in Mecklenburg County:

> *Richmond, August 23...Extract of a letter from Cross Creek, August 3...*
>
> *With pleasure I congratulate you on our success to the southward, the particulars as has been received at this place by express, are as follows; that on Wednesday week, Col. Sumpter with a party of the South Carolina militia surprised a post of the enemy, composed of British and tories, commanded by Ferguson, in which Ferguson was killed, together with a Capt. Hook, and 12 privates. Taken 1 Major, 2 Captains, 2 Lieutenants and 27 privates, with a number of horses and all the baggage. This party consisted of 180 under Ferguson, and posted at Twelve Mile Creek in Mecklenburg county in this state, at about 16 miles above where Col. Buford was defeated. The party under Sumpter consisted of 130, all militia, which has since been reinforced from that state to 1000, and lie near the enemy's post at Hanging Rock.[509]*

On Wednesday, 30 August 1780, a report on Huck's Defeat appeared in the *Pennsylvania Gazette and Weekly Advertiser* under the headline "Extract of a letter dated at Hillsborough, North-Carolina, July 23, 1780." The information in this article was taken almost verbatim from Major Thomas Blount's 23 July letter to North Carolina Governor Abner Nash, and described the patriot victories at Ramsour's Mill, Williamson's Plantation and Colson's Mill:

> *A second attack was made on a party of about 130 Tories, commanded by col. Ferguson, a noted Tory from the northward, and 70 Light horse of Cathcart's legion, commanded by a Captain Hook, on the 12 instant, by a party of 80 or 90 militia, under the command of Col. Neale, the surprize was compleat, Ferguson, Hook, a Lieutenant and seven others were killed on the ground, and a Major, two Lieutenants, and 27 taken, many of whom are since dead of their wounds, the remainder were dispersed, some accoutrements for Light horse, and a number of horses were also taken—of the exact number we have not certain accounts—our loss was only one man wounded.[510]*

waggons, &c. are all loft "

BALTIMORE, September 5.

Early in July laft, Col. Fergufon, with 200 Men, in the Britifh Service, were met with, and defeated, near the Catawba-River, in South-Carolina, by a Party of American Militia, under the Command of Col. Sumpter. Col. Fergufon, Capt. Hook, and 11 others, were killed on the Spot. One Major, one Lieutenant, and 27 Privates, were made Prifoners.

On the 20th of July Ult. about 500 Tories, collected from the Brufhy Mountains (South-Carolina) headed by a Mr. Bryan, were defeated by 160 American Cavalry, commanded by the Continental Col. Davidfon, who, it is faid, was mortally wounded in the Action.

About the laft of July, a Body of 102 Britifh Invalids, with a Lieutenant, Enfign, and Surgeon's-Mate, being on their Way down Pedee River, to George Town, South-Carolina, were made Prifoners by a Captain and 25 Militia, of that State, who had taken the Oath to the Britifh Government.

Extract of a Letter from St Euftatius, dated Auguft 10, 1780.

" We have to acquaint you with the Information.

Period newspaper account of Huck's Defeat, from the *Maryland Journal and Baltimore Advertiser* (Baltimore, Maryland), 5 September 1780. *Courtesy of the Culture & Heritage Museums.*

Extract of a letter dated at Hillfborough North Carolina, July 23, 1780.

A party of our militia, commanded by feven Captains of Light horfe, made an attack on a body of Tories under the command of one Col. Moore: the eldeft of our Captains, Gilbrett Hall, together with five others, fell in the engagement; the other Captain and one Lieutenant were wounded ; 70 of the enemy were killed, 100 taken prifoners, with 300 horfes, and a confiderable quantity of baggage.

" A fecond attack was made on a party of 130 Tories, commanded by col. Fergufon, a noted Tory from the northward, and 70 Light horfe of Cathcart's legion, commanded by a Captain Hook, on the 12 inftant, by a party of 80 or 90 militia, under the command of Col. Neale, the furprize was compleat, Fergufon, Hook, a Lieutenant and feven others were killed on the ground, and a Major, two

First column of another period newspaper account of Huck's Defeat, from the *New-Jersey Journal* (Newark, New Jersey), 6 September 1780. *Courtesy of the Culture & Heritage Museums.*

Lieutenants, and 27 taken, many of whom are fince dead of their wounds, the remainder were difperfed, fome accoutrements for Light horfe, and a number of horfes were alfo taken—of the exact number we have not certain accounts—our lofs was only one man wounded. Lieutenant Colonel William Lee Davidfon of the Continental line, with a detachment of 100 Light horfe, from B. Gen. Rutherford's brigade on the 21ft inft. made the third attack on about 5 or 600 Tories commanded by the infamous Samuel Bryan, near Collier's on Pee Dee, killed 3 or 4, took 40, and put the remainder to flight with more precipitation than we fled from Bryan Creek, none halted till they had reached the enemy's poft at the Waxaws, where they threw the whole into the utmoft confufion and-confternation. Their whole time fince, has been employed in conftructing fortifications for their fafety Col. Davidfon was wounded in the body, is feared mortally, 2 privates wounded flightly, but not a man killed—to Davidfon's misfortune may probably be attributed their efcape.

Second column of the *New-Jersey Journal* newspaper account of Huck's Defeat, 6 September 1780. *Courtesy of the Culture & Heritage Museums.*

On Tuesday, 5 September 1780, a brief dispatch appeared in the *Maryland Journal and Baltimore Advertiser*, which read as follows:

> *Early in July last, Col. Ferguson, with 200 Men, in the British Service, were met with, and defeated, near the Catawba River, in South Carolina, by a Party of American Militia, under the Command of Col. Sumpter. Col. Ferguson, Capt. Hook, and 11 others, were killed on the spot. One Major, one Lieutenant, and 27 Privates, were made Prisoners.*[571]

The following day, the *New-Jersey Journal* reprinted the earlier *Pennsylvania Gazette* report verbatim.[572] It is interesting to note that all of these accounts incorrectly assumed that because James Ferguson was a colonel, he was in overall command of Huck's detachment. As noted earlier, "Cathcart's Legion" was the original name for the British Legion, which was organized by Sir William Cathcart in the North before its deployment in the South.[573]

Following their respective defeats at Camden and Fishing Creek in August, Gates and Sumter slowly rebuilt their commands in preparation for renewed offensives in the fall. Although Gates was eventually replaced as its commander, the Continental Army in the South was far from finished. Under the command of Major General Nathanael Greene, the Continental Army reorganized and once again took the field against Cornwallis. And after a short period of regrouping and recruiting, Sumter's Brigade also returned to the field, continuing Sumter's plan of harassing the enemy's forts and outposts, and attacking its supply trains.

Captain Huck's defeat at Williamson's plantation had a major effect on the war in the Backcountry. The victory boosted the morale of the dispirited Whigs and demonstrated that the British troops were not invincible; furthermore, it brought hundreds of men into the camps of Sumter and other Backcountry militia commanders. Recruitment became easier, and many lukewarm Loyalists renounced their allegiance to the king and came over to the Whigs. Early historians of the American Revolution in the South were almost unanimous in their assessment of the importance of Huck's Defeat. As Benson J. Lossing stated in 1852, "The defeat of Huck had an important bearing upon the future condition of the state. It encouraged the Whigs, and many joined the standard of Sumter; while the Tories, abashed, were fearful and silent."[574] In 1901 Edward McCrady, a former Confederate general, went even further, calling the battle "one of the turning-points in the Revolution."[575]

In spite of its importance, Huck's Defeat was not, as some of these historians once claimed, the first victory over British forces in South Carolina after the fall of Charleston.[576] That credit rightly goes to the skirmish at Alexander's Old Field, followed closely by the engagement at Mobley's Meeting House. The significance of Huck's Defeat lies in the fact that it was the first victory over British Provincial troops after the surrender of Charleston and Buford's Defeat. While Alexander's Old Field and Mobley's Meeting House pitted Whig militia against Tory militia, Huck's Defeat put Whig militia up against some of the Provincial Corps' finest troops. The New York Volunteers and the British Legion had been instrumental in the British victories at Savannah, Charleston, Monck's Corner, Lenud's Ferry and the Waxhaws, and seemed invincible to many residents of the Carolinas. Huck's Defeat proved that they were not invincible, and demonstrated once and for all that the rebel militia could defeat the Provincial regiments in battle.

As a rallying point and a morale booster for South Carolina Whigs, the influence of Huck's Defeat was unmistakable. There can be little doubt that it directly contributed to the even greater defeats of crown forces at Kings Mountain on 7 October 1780 and Cowpens on 17 January 1781. At Kings Mountain, the victors of Ramsour's Mill, Huck's Defeat and Musgrove's Mill came together in what has been called the Southern militia's finest hour. In fact, the Battle of Kings Mountain was, both tactically and strategically, a virtual replay of Huck's Defeat, only with larger numbers of men. In both cases, an arrogant and overconfident commander of Provincial troops pitched his camp in a vulnerable location in the Backcountry, and in both cases, he was surrounded by an ad hoc coalition of Whig militia and overwhelmed in a surprise attack that left the commander dead and large numbers of his men killed, wounded or captured.[577]

The Whig soldiers who fought in Huck's Defeat continued to serve in the militia and state troops throughout the war, and many distinguished themselves during the hard-fought battles of 1780, 1781 and 1782. A considerable number of these soldiers made the ultimate sacrifice for their country's freedom. Colonel Andrew Neal was killed leading the frontal assault at the Battle of Rocky Mount on 30 June; his twin brother Thomas Neal Jr. died in an engagement with Tory militia on 6 March 1781. Colonel John McClure was badly wounded during the Battle of Hanging Rock on 6 August and died of his wounds in Charlotte twelve days later. Two of his cousins from the Gaston family, David and Ebenezer, along with their comrades Lieutenant Henry Bishop and John Millar were killed in the same battle. Lieutenant Colonel John Nixon was killed in a skirmish with Tories in the Dutch Fork District (now Newberry County) in late November 1780, shortly after the Battle of Blackstock's Plantation.[578]

John Carroll, the man who killed Huck, was another soldier who did not survive the conflict. While scouting for Tories near the end of the war, Carroll ducked into a seemingly abandoned cabin to light his pipe and was shot dead by a Tory hiding inside. In his later years, Carroll's brother Thomas claimed that he was the man who killed Huck and even carried a sword that he alleged to be Huck's sword. Thomas apparently managed to convince at least a few people, including his sons and Dr. Maurice Moore, that it was he and not his brother who killed Huck. However, as Dr. Moore pointed out, Thomas Carroll was an old man by then "and entirely in his second childhood," which certainly made his claims suspect. Moore also noted that most of the people in the area still gave John Carroll the credit for shooting Huck. Thomas's grandson Lemuel Carroll told Lyman Draper in no uncertain terms that it was John, not Thomas, who killed Huck. "John Carroll got [Huck's] horse and accoutrements as trophies," he told Draper, "and not Thomas Carroll, as Dr. Moore mistakenly states."[579]

However, most of the Huck's Defeat veterans survived the war and resumed their lives as respected citizens and community leaders once hostilities were over. Many of them became local church and community leaders, state legislators, and even governors and U.S. Congressmen. All of the patriots who fought in Huck's Defeat remembered the battle proudly for the rest of their lives, and as the years passed, their exploits took on almost legendary status, as the many surviving accounts testify.

Samuel Williamson, who fired the first shot of the battle, became an elder at Bethesda Presbyterian Church, raised a large family and owned a plantation on the South Fork of Fishing Creek, where he passed the rest of his days as a planter. He lived to see two of his sons, John and Samuel Jr., become Presbyterian ministers. His other children included two elders, a deacon "and five daughters who were exemplary members of the Presbyterian church." Samuel Jr. studied at the University of South Carolina and South Carolina College, obtained a doctor of divinity degree, taught mathematics and natural philosophy at Davidson College in North Carolina and served as Davidson's president from 1841 to 1854.[580]

Most of the Presbyterian congregations whose members fought at Huck's Defeat and the other Backcountry skirmishes recovered and thrived after the war. In the modern counties of York and Chester, Bethesda, Bethel, Beersheba, Bullock's Creek and Catholic Presbyterian Churches are all still in existence and still active in the Christian ministry. On the other hand, William Martin's church at Rocky Creek was never rebuilt after it was destroyed by the Loyalists, and of the two Fishing Creek churches, only the upper church remains. The Lower Fishing Creek congregation was irreparably divided by the war and never recovered; it finally disbanded in the early nineteenth century. Area families who supported the crown—such as the Fergusons and Featherstones—were severely ostracized by their Whig neighbors and eventually joined the Baptist and Methodist churches that sprang up in the area during the 1790s and 1800s.[581]

It took five years for the Upper Fishing Creek Church to rebuild after the 1780 destruction of the original meeting house, and the church continued to experience financial and organizational hardships for years to come. In September 1790, Reverend John Simpson accepted a call from Roberts Presbyterian Church in the Pendleton District, a new district formed from the old Cherokee Territory in western South Carolina. Simpson and his family, along with other local families, moved to the Pendleton District and settled in what is now Anderson County. Simpson died 15 February 1808 and is buried in the Roberts Presbyterian Church cemetery.[582] On 3 October 2004, the Lewisville Preservation Society and the congregation of the present-day Fishing Creek Presbyterian Church, along with local historians and members of Roberts Presbyterian Church, unveiled a new monument at Fishing Creek Church dedicated to the memory of Simpson and his service during the Revolutionary War.

Many of the other Revolutionary War veterans and their families moved west in the years following the war. Some relocated to the former Cherokee Indian territory of western South Carolina and northern Georgia, while others pushed farther west in Alabama, Mississippi and Louisiana, or to the northwest into Tennessee, Kentucky, Ohio, Illinois and Indiana. John Craig served under General Sumter and Sumter's successor, Brigadier General William Henderson, until the end of the war and then moved to the newly created Pendleton District, where he settled in what is now Pickens County. His reminiscences of Huck's Defeat were published in the *Pendleton Messenger* in November 1839 and were republished by several other newspapers in the Upcountry in later years, generating a great deal of interest whenever they appeared in print. Craig died in Pickens District on 11 February 1842, at the age of 81.[583]

David Sadler also served until the end of the Revolution, and after returning home, he courted Colonel William Bratton's oldest daughter, Elisa "Elsie" Bratton. Colonel Bratton opposed the union, so the couple eloped; according to family tradition, they were aided in their rendezvous by the Brattons' slave, Watt. The Sadlers moved west with the Simpsons, Craigs and other area residents, and settled in the part of Pendleton District that later became Anderson County, where they lived the rest of their lives in the community around Roberts Presbyterian Church. Elsie died on 22 November 1825 at the age of 59, while David lived to the age of 86 and passed away on 18 February 1848.[584]

The Bratton slave, Watt, outlived his master Colonel Bratton by twenty-two years. Local tradition states that, as a reward for his faithful service to the Bratton family during and after the American Revolution, "Watt never had to work another day for the rest of his life. He merely rode his horse around the plantation." Bratton family history also states that Watt "served the Bratton family as long as he lived. He was tenderly cared for by them in his old age and when death came to him was buried not far distant from the Bratton home." Watt's grave is marked with a fine marble tombstone that bears the following inscription: "Sacred to the Memory of Watt, Who Died December, 1837. During the Revolutionary War He Served His Master, Col. William Bratton, Faithfully, and His Children With the Same Fidelity Until His Death. Also Polly his wife who died July 1838 Who served the same family With equal faithfulness."[585]

Colonel Matthew Floyd's slave, Sam, became the slave of Captain (later Lieutenant Colonel) John Nixon after Huck's Defeat. Following the end of the war, Sam remained in the possession of the Nixon family, became a miller and "made a good living." He was well known throughout Chester District as "Miller Sam" and "took great pleasure all his life in the bravery of his Master," Colonel Nixon. Even in his old age, Sam loved to tell the story of Huck's Defeat to Nixon's daughters and right up until his death he would visit the Nixon home "to carry his 'young mistresses' through the war." As Elizabeth Ellet stated, "That battle field of July 12th, 1780, made Sam decidedly a whig, and he gives it as his opinion that 'the whigs can whip the whole world chock full of redcoats and tories too.'"[586]

James Collins had many adventures after the Battle of Huck's Defeat. He continued to serve under Captain (later Colonel) John Moffett and fought in some of the most famous battles of the South Carolina upcountry, including Fishing Creek, Kings Mountain and Cowpens, as well as numerous skirmishes with Tory militia. He also typified the restless spirit of many Revolutionary War veterans, moving not once but several times after the war, always pushing farther west. Collins relocated first to Georgia in 1785, where he lived in Franklin and Jackson Counties, and served in several campaigns against the Cherokee and Creek Indians during 1790 and 1791. In 1810, he migrated to the Tennessee River Valley and made a reputation for himself as a deer hunter. He moved to Louisiana in 1820, settling first in St. Helena Parish; two years later, he moved for the last time, to East Feliciana Parish, where he finished his memoirs in 1836 and died on 14 April 1840. His memoirs were published in 1859 by the Feliciana *Democrat*.[587]

Following the death of John McClure, Edward Lacey Jr. once again took over command of the regiment from the upper District between the Broad and Catawba Rivers. He remained in the field with Sumter's Brigade until the British withdrew from Charleston in December 1782. Lacey led his troops in the battles of Kings Mountain, Cowpens and Eutaw Springs, and in numerous other hard-fought engagements of the Southern Campaign. In April 1785, he received a commission to serve as one of the original justices of the peace for the newly created Chester County, and in July 1785, he was elected the first sheriff of that county. He also represented his district in the state legislature and was a brigadier general of South Carolina militia. In 1797, he moved to Montgomery County, Tennessee, and then to Livingston County, Kentucky, in 1799. In his later years, he suffered cataleptic fits, and on 20 March 1813, while suffering from such a seizure, he fell off his horse and drowned in Deer Creek, a tributary of the Ohio River.[588]

John Adair continued to serve under his friend Edward Lacey throughout the Revolution and was a major in Lacey's Regiment when the war ended. After Lacey was elected sheriff of Chester County, Adair took Lacey's position as a justice of the peace. A few years later, Adair moved to Mercer County, Kentucky and commanded a company of Kentucky riflemen during the Indian Wars of 1791 and 1792. He also served in the Kentucky state legislature and one term in the U.S. Senate, and while in the Senate he unwittingly supported Aaron Burr's attempt to overthrow the U.S. government. Adair was subsequently cleared of any wrongdoing, and during the War of 1812, he served as an aide to Kentucky Governor Isaac Shelby (of Musgrove's Mill and Kings Mountain fame), before being promoted to brigadier general of state militia. As commander of the Kentucky Rifle Brigade, Adair fought the British once again along with his old comrade General Andrew Jackson at the Battle of New Orleans in 1814. His final political service was as governor of Kentucky (1820–1824) and as a U.S. congressman in the early 1830s. On 12 July 1832 (the fifty-second anniversary of Huck's Defeat), Adair filed for a Federal pension at Harrodsburg, Kentucky. President Andrew Jackson signed a deposition supporting Adair's claim and noted that he and Adair were "schoolfellows at Waxhaws Academy." John Adair died at his home on 19 May 1840.[589]

William Bratton, William Hill and Richard Winn all commanded regiments in Sumter's Brigade until the end of the Revolution. Bratton led his troops in many of Sumter's famous attacks on the British forts and outposts along the Congaree and Santee Rivers during 1781, and continued to serve under General William Henderson when Sumter resigned his command in early 1782. Following the end of the war, Bratton was one of the original justices of the peace for York County, along with Hill and John Moffett. Bratton also served as a state legislator until 1795, when he was elected sheriff of the newly created Pinckney District. Bratton was a successful planter and operated a tavern, store and stagecoach station at his home, which eventually became the nucleus of a nineteenth century community called Brattonsville. He died at his home on 9 February 1815 and is buried at Bethesda Church. His wife Martha died a year later and is buried beside him. One of his grandsons—Brigadier General John S. Bratton, the son of William Bratton Jr.—commanded a brigade in the Confederate Army during the War Between the States.[590]

William Hill was wounded at Hanging Rock but nonetheless took part in the battles of Kings Mountain and Cowpens. In 1781, he formed a mounted regiment of state troops and commanded them in the field until the end of 1782. He then rebuilt his ironworks and once again became a prosperous industrialist, in addition to serving York County as a justice of the peace and a state legislator. Along with Thomas Sumter, Hill worked as a commissioner to open the Broad and Catawba Rivers for navigation and trade. Hill experienced financial difficulties in his later years and was forced to sell his ironworks, which finally closed in the early 1800s. He finished his memoirs of the Revolution in 1815 and died on 1 December 1816, less than two years after the death of his old rival William Bratton. Hill and his wife Nanny are both buried at Bethel Church, along with other Revolutionary veterans, including Samuel Watson and Thomas Neal Sr. Like Bratton, Hill also had a grandson who became a famous general in the Confederate Army, Lieutenant General Daniel Harvey (D.H.) Hill.[591]

Richard Winn became commander of his own regiment in Sumter's Brigade in late 1780 and remained in the field with his troops until the end of the war. After the Revolution, he continued to serve his district and state as a justice of the peace, brigadier general and major general of militia, lieutenant governor, state legislator and U.S. congressman until leaving South Carolina. He also served the Federal government as the U.S. superintendent of Indian affairs in the Southern Department and donated one hundred acres of land for the establishment of a school near Winnsboro, which still exists today as the Richard Winn Academy. In 1813, he moved to Maury County, Tennessee, where he died on 19 December 1818. His daughter Christina married Dr. William Bratton Jr.[592]

Thomas Sumter retired from active military service in February 1782. Following the war, he had a long and distinguished career as a planter, businessman and politician. He served in the South Carolina House of Representatives, the U.S. House of Representatives (until defeated by his old comrade Richard Winn) and finally the U.S. Senate. When Sumter died at the age of ninety-eight on 1 June 1832, he was the last surviving American general of the Revolutionary War, and in his memory, the state of South Carolina erected a fort at Charleston that still bears his name. The city and county of Sumter were named in honor of him, and the University of South Carolina "Gamecocks" still bear his epithet.[593]

During and after the Revolution, the governments of the thirteen United States confiscated the property of thousands of Loyalists and banished many of them from the country. In 1778, Christian Huck was "attainted of treason and [his] property confiscated" by the State of Pennsylvania (see appendix E for a biography of Huck).[594] In South Carolina, similar punishment was suffered by several of the Loyalist officers who were at Huck's Defeat, including Colonel Matthew Floyd, Major John Owens and Lieutenant John Adamson. After the South Carolina General Assembly reconvened at Jacksonboro in January 1782, one of its first acts was to draw up lists of Loyalists who were then sentenced to banishment and confiscation of property. Other Loyalists were sentenced to amercements, or fines based on the value of their property.[595] Floyd, Owens and Adamson all found their names on one of these lists.

After the British evacuated Charleston in December 1782, Matthew Floyd fled to St. Augustine in the British colony of East Florida. The Assembly at Jacksonboro banished him from South Carolina and ordered his property to be confiscated. In August 1783, Floyd filed a memorial with the British government seeking compensation for the loss of twenty-three hundred acres in the Camden District and nine "Negro slaves," at an estimated value of £3,078. His claim made no mention of his property west of the Broad River. After the British ceded East Florida back to the Spanish in 1783, Floyd left St. Augustine and set sail for England. Arriving in London in October 1784, he found that the Commissioners of American Claims had no record of his original memorial, and he was forced to resubmit his claim. Lord Cornwallis and other prominent British officers vouched for his loyalty. The Public Claims Court awarded Floyd an annuity of £25 commencing on 10 October 1784. In June 1787, he sent a letter to the commission stating his intention to relocate to Nova Scotia, Canada, and requested that his annual subsistence be paid to his attorney in London. However, there is no evidence that Floyd ever went to Canada, and in fact it appears very likely that he actually returned to the United States and lived with his son William in Lincoln County, Kentucky, where his Loyalist activities were unknown. There are no records of Floyd's activities after 1796, and he may have died soon afterward.[590]

Matthew Floyd's son Abraham, who served as a captain in his father's royal militia regiment, moved from South Carolina to Burke County, North Carolina in 1784. In April 1786, Colonel William Hill successfully sued Floyd and several other Loyalists in York County court, apparently in an effort to recover compensation for the destruction of his ironworks and personal property. Abraham Floyd moved to Madison County, Kentucky in 1796, and then to Indiana in 1828. On 9 May 1834, while living in Decatur County, he applied for a Revolutionary War pension from the U.S. government, based on his service in Colonel Thomas Neal's New Acquisition Militia Regiment from March 1776 until July 1779. He did not mention his service in the royal militia after the fall of Charleston or his captain's commission from Lieutenant Colonel George Turnbull, and although he referred to his parents in his pension application, he did not mention either of their names. The Federal government granted him a pension of $35.55 per month which he drew until 1844, at which time it appears that he died in Floyd County, Indiana.[597]

Following the British evacuation of Charleston, John Adamson went to Jamaica, where he attempted to reestablish himself in the good graces of the South Carolina government. During the British occupation of the state, a Loyalist officer named Colonel James Cary confiscated a large number of slaves belonging to the Camden merchant Joseph Kershaw and other prominent Whigs in the area. When the British evacuated Charleston, Cary fled to Jamaica with the confiscated slaves. Adamson used his influence to recover some of these slaves and return them to their former masters.[598] Because of these and other efforts, some influential Whigs such as Colonel Thomas Taylor and Colonel William Bratton petitioned the legislature on Adamson's behalf. On 28 January 1783, the Journal of the South Carolina House of Representatives noted the following:

> Col. Taylor presented to the House two Petitions in behalf of John Adamson
>
> [Viz. Setting forth That from the Commencement of the War to the reduction of Charles Town, he always did his duty as a good Citizen. After that time he took a Lieutenants Commission under the British, that he accepted of it at the Earnest request of his Neighbours (now Subjects of this State) to prevent its falling into the hands of a person whose intentions was well known was to oppress them.
>
> A petition, Signed by a Number of Inhabitants of the district in favour of Said John Adamson Setting forth That from principles of humanity and gratitude, they are led to declare that they verily believe the petitioner was not an Enemy to the freedom of america. That he used all the Influence he had with the British in favour of Such persons as avowed their attachment to the American Cause, that to the utmost of his power he protected the distressed families of Such Americans as were banished this State by the British.][599]

On 14 March 1784, thanks to the petitions of his neighbors and friends, the state removed Adamson's name from the banishment and confiscation list, and absolved him from all fines and other punishments.[600] Adamson eventually returned to Camden, but he was barred from holding public office in South Carolina for a period of seven years.[601] In gratitude to William and Martha Bratton for their efforts on his behalf, Adamson sent the family a pair of expensive crystal bowls, which have remained in the possession of Bratton descendants since that time. Adamson lived in Camden until his death on 25 May 1816 and is buried in the Quaker cemetery there.[602]

John Owens continued to oscillate back and forth in his loyalties for the duration of the war. After assisting Sumter's troops during the Rocky Mount campaign, Owens seems to have retired from active service for a while, but in June 1782 he once again entered the Loyalist militia and served as a major in Colonel W. T. Turner's regiment of Rocky Mount Militia until December 1782. Ironically, the only surviving payroll for that regiment includes a note that "Major Owens deserted to the rebels on 19 Sept. 1782."[603] In consequence of his Loyalist activities, the General Assembly placed Owens' name on the confiscation list in late 1782. A year later, a special committee of the South Carolina House of Representatives reduced the confiscation to a 12-percent amercement of the total value of Owens's estate. On 4 March 1785, the House committee considered a number of petitions from "Sundry persons" requesting that Owens and the other ex-Tories be released from the amercement.[604] After further inquiry into the conduct of these individuals, the committee reported on 14 March that "[i]t appears that they accepted Governor [John] Matthew's proposals set forth in his invitation and Complied with all his demands and having rendered essential Services to the distressed Americans who were Prisoners in their Vicinity, Your Committee recommend that their Names be taken off from the Amerced List, and that they be restored to every Priviledge of a Citizen of this State."[605] In 1785, Owens purchased 350 acres on the headwaters of Sandy River, and in 1790, he received a state grant of 530 acres in the same location, near the present town of Lowrys. He lived there for the rest of his life and died in 1819. Interestingly, Owens' daughter Priscilla married Dempsey Winborne Jr., the grandson of a well-known New Acquisition Loyalist named John Stallions (or Stallings). Owens had two sons who were well educated and studied law, but because of their "tory descent," they were not very popular among the people of Chester County. They eventually moved to Charleston in order to escape the stigma of their father's loyalism.[606]

Following the death of Captain Huck, Lieutenant Benjamin Hunt transferred to Captain David Ogilvy's company of British Legion cavalry and appeared on the muster roll for that company from 25 October 1780 until 24 December 1780. He then transferred to Captain Thomas Sandford's troop of British Legion light dragoons and served in that unit during 1781 and 1782. At the end of the war, Hunt returned to his native New York, where he died on Long Island in 1834.[607]

Lieutenant Colonel George Turnbull remained in command of the New York Volunteers until the end of the war, serving a total of seven years in the Provincial Corps. He and his regiment helped Lord Cornwallis defeat General Horatio Gates at Camden on 16 August 1780 and served with Lord Rawdon against Continental General Nathanael Greene at the Battle of Hobkirk's Hill on 25 April 1781. After the British evacuated Charleston, Turnbull and his regiment returned to New York and were stationed at Foster's Meadows on Long Island until the peace treaty was signed in 1783. Turnbull continued his career as an officer in the British Army after the Revolution ended and also kept his home in New York, where he was still living as late as 1798. He died in New Jersey in October 1810, and the *Boston Centinel* noted his passing on 17 October 1810: "Died in Bloomingdale, N.J., Lieut. Col. George Turnbull; he had served in the British army over sixty years—highly respected."[608]

Lieutenant John McGregor also remained with the New York Volunteers for the duration of the war and served a total of five years in the Provincial Corps. From September 1780 until June 1781, he served in Major John Coffin's troop of mounted infantry "in the country" of South Carolina. (This same troop burned the Waxhaw Meeting House and Academy on 10 April 1781.) McGregor's name also appeared on the muster rolls of Captain Bernard Kane's light infantry company at Camden and Johns Island in South Carolina between February and December 1781. He was captured by General Greene's troops at the Battle of Hobkirk's Hill but was quickly exchanged for American prisoners held by Lord Rawdon. By January 1783, he was back in New York, serving with Captain Archibald McLean's company of the New York Volunteers at Foster's Meadows on half-pay. When the British troops left New York, McGregor and his family of four moved to Canada, where the crown granted him a town lot in Port Shelburne, Nova Scotia.[609]

Ensign Allan Cameron of the New York Volunteers transferred to the British Legion and was promoted to lieutenant sometime before December 1781, when his name appeared on a muster roll of Captain Nathaniel Vernon's troop of British Legion dragoons. He continued to serve in the British Legion until at least December 1782. At the end of the war, he also moved to Canada, and in 1785 he received a grant of one hundred acres at Port Hebert, in the East District of Queen's County, Nova Scotia.[610]

The Loyalists who remained in the United States after the end of the Revolution had less reason to extol their services during that war than did their Whig counterparts, and consequently their fidelity to the crown generally went unheralded. Those who returned to the British Isles or immigrated to Canada apparently preferred to put the war behind them, and they also left little record of their activities. The consequent lack of documentation from the Loyalist camp has created a very one-sided historical record of battles like Huck's Defeat and the Southern Campaign in general. It is my fervent hope that this book has in some small way corrected that unbalanced record, and that it will be followed by many more detailed and objective studies of the important battles in the South.

Epilogue

Some observations on the South Carolina Backcountry militia

When I began this book, I originally envisioned it as a comprehensive historical account of Huck's Defeat and the galvanizing effect that the battle had as a "morale booster" in the South Carolina Backcountry in 1780. As the project evolved, it became clear that there was a need for a more comprehensive history of the events leading up to the battle, many of which had not been treated in great detail before now. As the work continued, I also saw a need to refute the claims made by some historians that the residents of the Backcountry did not take an interest in the Revolution until after the fall of Charleston. The first chapter of this book is my effort to sum up the events in the Backcountry before May 1780 and to demonstrate that the people in the upper districts of South Carolina did not remain on the sidelines during the first five years of the war.

As the book neared completion, another aspect of the war in the Backcountry seemed to demand some attention, preferably in the form of a conclusion to the main body of the book. Most of the battles that took place in the Backcountry during the final three years of the Revolution involved the militia. Some engagements—such as those at Alexander's, Mobley's, Ramsour's and Cedar Springs—were fought entirely between Whig and Tory militia. But an even larger number of battles—including Huck's Defeat, Rocky Mount, Hanging Rock, Fishing Creek, Musgrove's Mill, Kings Mountain, Fishdam Ford and Blackstock's Plantation—involved Whig militia attacking, or being attacked by, some combination of British regulars, Provincials and Loyalist militia. That so many of these battles in the Carolina Backcountry were won by the Whig militia is extraordinary, and allows us to make some general statements about the effectiveness of the militia in the South.

Historians have often downplayed and even maligned the performance and usefulness of the militia during the American Revolution. In an article about the Revolutionary War militia, military historian Mark M. Boatner III sums up the conventional wisdom when he states, "Being part-time soldiers, subject only to state authority, militia troops generally were unreliable." He goes on to provide several examples of occasions where the militia in the Northern campaigns proved to be both undependable and ineffective.[011] But he then goes on to state, "Southern militia probably did as much to defeat the British as did the American regulars, once the latter had to be ordered into the theater. At Bunker Hill, Cowpens, and Guilford the militia showed that *if commanded by experienced officers who understood their inherent weakness* they could fight like regular soldiers [italics are those of Mr. Boatner]."[012]

The poor performance of the militia in George Washington's army, and in the Northern campaigns in general, has led many historians to label all militia, including the Carolina Backcountry militia, as worthless. It is true that during several of the large land battles in the South, especially at Camden in August 1780 and Guilford Courthouse in March 1781, large numbers of North Carolina and Virginia militiamen dropped their weapons and fled the battlefield without firing a shot. In both of those cases, the men who ran were for the most part inexperienced and untrained, and their commanders did not use these soldiers effectively as Daniel Morgan did at the Battle of Cowpens in January 1781. And in spite of the Carolina militia's contribution to Morgan's victory over Banastre Tarleton at Cowpens, Morgan's view of the militia in general was not very complementary. Speaking about his choice of terrain at Cowpens, Morgan stated, "I would not have had a swamp in the view of my militia on any consideration; they would have made for it, and nothing could have detained them from it."[013]

Morgan's comments were based on his difficulties with the militia in the Northern campaigns. However, in spite of his military experience with Washington's army, Morgan was not a veteran of the war in the Carolinas and had never worked with the Backcountry militia prior to his arrival in the New Acquisition in December 1780. More traditionally trained Continental officers—particularly those from the North such as Nathanael Greene—were frequently exasperated by the Southern militiamen, who were understandably reluctant to give up their horses and serve as foot soldiers in the regiments of the Continental Army. As historian John Buchanan noted in his classic history of the Southern Campaign, *The Road to Guilford Courthouse*, this was not how the men of the Backcountry wanted to fight a war. "The key to their effectiveness as guerilla warriors was their mobility, but now they were engaged in joint operations with regulars, and when dismounted for action and required to move to another position their first thought was to retrieve their horses and vanish."[014] It was precisely the inflexibility and rigidity of Continental service that most mounted militiamen disdained and that contributed to their poor reputation among Continental commanders. The Continental generals were interested in fighting the British Army using classical European battle tactics, which militia troops regarded as a recipe for disaster.

In a widely publicized study that almost completely ignored the entire Southern Campaign of the Revolution, historian Michael Bellesiles of Emory University maintained that all of the Revolutionary War militia were totally worthless:

> *Even when the nation's very security was at stake, the militia just did not turn out when ordered...Even late in the war, after long experience with many humiliations, the militia remained largely an abstraction....And if the militia did turn up, they were, in the opinion of the best-informed sources, largely useless....It was no wonder that Greene, one of the most insightful military commanders of the war, thought the militia completely inappropriate for warfare...The Battle of Camden brought home the danger of placing any reliance on the militia...Even [at Cowpens], Morgan repeatedly had to cajole and even beg the militia to keep their part of the bargain in the face of Banastre "Butcher" Tarleton's English forces.[015]*

Camden and Cowpens are the only two examples from the Southern Campaign that Bellesiles can give to support his claims about the uselessness of the Southern militia, and he gives them only cursory notice. He ignores the fact that at Camden all of the militia did not instantly drop their weapons and flee the battlefield; in fact, some of the North Carolina militia under Brigadier General Isaac Gregory stood their ground and fired several volleys before being overwhelmed by the British regulars; General Gregory was in fact wounded himself during the battle.[616] And Bellesiles dismisses the stellar performance of the militia at Cowpens with a perfunctory statement that they only fired one volley and then ran from the field, when other authors state that they fired two or even three volleys and then withdrew in accordance with General Morgan's orders.[617] Bellesiles apparently made no attempt to study the pension applications and memoirs of the soldiers who actually fought at these and other battles in the Carolinas, and instead bases his assumptions on the statements of men far removed from the action and on the opinions of like-minded historians.

Using this type of reasoning, many modern historians have concluded that the American militiamen were not "true soldiers" and that Revolutionary War militia service should not be construed as actual military service. To cite another example, a recent television documentary on the Battle of Cowpens repeatedly referred to the Backcountry Carolina militia as "simple farmers and hunters" who had "no military experience."[618] But it was not "simple farmers and hunters" who defeated Loyalist militia, Provincial soldiers and British regulars at Ramsour's Mill, Williamson's, Hanging Rock, Musgrove's Mill, Kings Mountain, Fishdam Ford and Blackstock's, and the Backcountry riflemen who formed Morgan's skirmish lines at Cowpens were not "an abstraction." My own research on the soldiers who fought at the Battle of Huck's Defeat has led me to depart from the generally accepted beliefs about the lack of experience and overall worthlessness of the Revolutionary War militia, especially the Whig militia in the Carolina Backcountry. During the course of this project, I examined the military service records of every soldier known or thought to have been at Huck's Defeat. This was much easier for the Whigs than it was for the Loyalists, since virtually all of the Whigs left some kind of documentation that can be studied. These records range from brief claims against the South Carolina government for back pay and reimbursement of losses, to detailed pension applications and personal memoirs. This research is summarized in appendix F, "Roster of soldiers at the Battle of Huck's Defeat."

What I found during my research was that by July 1780 all of the Whigs, with only a few exceptions, were veterans of five bloody years of conflict in the Backcountry. In spite of Dr. Maurice Moore's assertion that the Whigs at Huck's Defeat were "raw militia,"[619] the record shows that many of them served anywhere from one to three years in the Third or Sixth South Carolina Continental Regiments and then joined the militia once their enlistments had expired, often becoming militia officers. Of the 142 Whig soldiers listed in appendix F, all of whom were placed in the Battle of Huck's Defeat by at least one reliable source, 25 were veterans of the Third South Carolina Regiment, 10 had served in the Sixth South Carolina Regiment and two men (John Mills and James Mitchell) were veterans of both regiments. Another soldier, Edward Doyle, had seen service with the Continental dragoons at Stono Ferry in June 1779. However, the majority of these soldiers were pure militiamen who had been fighting against British regulars, Provincials, Tory militiamen and Cherokee Indians since the fall of 1775.

Following the fall of Charleston in May 1780, these men quickly went on the offensive against the British and Loyalist forces in the Backcountry, and the majority of them were veterans of the siege of Charleston and the battles at Alexander's Old Field (Beckhamville), Mobley's Meeting House, Hill's Ironworks and Ramsour's Mill before they showed up at James Williamson's plantation in the early morning hours of 12 July 1780. Only four Whigs on this list do not appear to have had any prior military experience: William Hill, the proprietor of Hill's Ironworks; Reverend John Simpson, the Presbyterian minister; and sixteen-year-old James P. Collins and his father Daniel, who were fighting in their very first battle that day. On the other hand, seventeen-year-old David Sadler, who later married Colonel Bratton's daughter Elisa Bratton, had served in the Florida Expedition, the skirmish at Bacon's Bridge, the Battle of Stono Ferry—where his commander, Colonel Neal, was killed—and the attack on the Tories at Mobley's Meeting House. Unlike young Collins, Sadler was one of several teenaged soldiers at Huck's Defeat who was already a seasoned veteran by July 1780.[020]

Conventional wisdom also states that the militiamen came and went at will; that they only fought when they felt like it and went home whenever it suited them; and that the "regular officers" could never depend on them when they were needed. But when one reads the actual records of their service—the South Carolina audited accounts, Federal pension applications and firsthand accounts of the war—a much different picture emerges. One finds that the militia soldiers who officially enlisted or were drafted by the officers of their districts almost always served out the terms of their enlistments or drafts, and that they remained in service until discharged by their commanding officers, most of whom vouched for the men's service in the official records. Anyone who thinks that the Carolina militiamen were useless vagabonds who rarely fired a shot in battle would do well to spend some time reading the actual records of their service.

It is beyond the scope of this book to go into detail about all of the military service of the Whig militia at Huck's Defeat. Appendix F provides a brief overview of some of that service, but those wishing to learn more should consult the state and Federal records referenced in the bibliography, or the condensed abstracts of those records published in Dr. Bobby Gilmer Moss's books, including his *Roster of South Carolina Patriots in the American Revolution*, *The Patriots at the Cowpens* and *The Patriots at King's Mountain*. As these titles suggest, many of these soldiers went on to distinguish themselves in the later battles of the Revolution and served bravely until the last British troops left Charleston in December 1782. To state that these men were "simple farmers and hunters with no military experience" is to do them a terrible disservice.

The Loyalist militia at Huck's Defeat presents a more difficult problem, since most of their names are still unknown and their service records are poorly documented. In general, most of the Loyalist militiamen at Huck's Defeat do not appear to have had a great deal of military experience before June of 1780, unlike their Whig counterparts. Many of them had probably tried to stay out of the fight until after Charleston fell, when, encouraged by the British successes, they joined the crown forces. Of the known Loyalist militia officers at Huck's Defeat, only Matthew Floyd, Abraham Floyd and John Lisle appear to have had prior military service. Matthew Floyd served in the colonial militia and the Loyalist militia before 1780, but there is no indication that he had much actual battle experience. Abraham Floyd and John Lisle were Whig veterans who accepted British protection and joined the Loyalists after the fall of Charleston, although Lisle rejoined the Whigs immediately after Huck's Defeat. I have found nothing to indicate that James Ferguson, John Owens or John Adamson had any military experience before June 1780.

The record of the Whig militiamen in the Carolina Backcountry is a record of success, not failure—especially when they served under their own officers and were free to fight the enemy on their own terms. The battles and campaigns where they suffered the greatest setbacks—the Florida Campaign, Briar Creek, Stono Ferry, Camden and Guilford Courthouse—were all battles where they were placed under the command of Continental generals. Even at Fishing Creek, one of their worst defeats, the militia under Edward Lacey and John Moffett stood their ground and gave a good accounting of themselves before withdrawing from the battlefield. Most of Tarleton's casualties in this battle were inflicted by the militia serving under Lacey and Moffett.[621]

Lastly, and perhaps most importantly, the Backcountry militia in the Southern Campaign of the Revolution created a new type of warfare that owed little to the formalized eighteenth-century battle tactics of the European armies. Utilizing the lessons learned during the French and Indian War, the Cherokee War and the Regulator Wars, the militia perfected new and unconventional tactics of their own in order to defeat the British Army. Speed and mobility, surprise attacks, ambushes and hit-and-run tactics, combined with the judicious use of cover and accurate rifle fire, were all techniques adopted from the Indians, perfected during the Revolution and then all but forgotten by the regular American and European armies until World War II brought them to the forefront once again. Historian Russell F. Weigley has compared the partisan war in South Carolina during the Revolution to the irregular or guerilla wars fought in Nazi-occupied Europe during World War II and in Southeast Asia during the Vietnam War.[622] Most of the unconventional tactics so successfully employed by the militia in the Carolina Backcountry during the Revolution are now standard military tactics used by professional armies all over the world.

In conclusion, the evidence of Huck's Defeat and dozens of other battles and skirmishes in the Backcountry clearly demonstrates the effectiveness of the Whig militia in the Carolinas. Operating on their own with little support from the Continental Congress or state governments, forced to provide their own weapons, food and clothing, the militiamen kept up the fight and refused to surrender until the final battle was won. In spite of what many modern historians have claimed, the Backcountry Whig militiamen of the Carolinas and Georgia were a courageous, highly effective, highly motivated military force, and when led by their own officers and allowed to fight on their own terms, they were capable of meeting and defeating larger, better-equipped forces of the British Army on almost every occasion. They successfully waged a partisan war against the most powerful army on earth, and in the process, they not only helped win their country's independence, but they also helped push warfare out of the eighteenth century and into the modern age.

1. The Third South Carolina Regiment, or Thomson's Rangers, was a regiment of mounted troops that patrolled the South Carolina Backcountry during the Revolution. Hundreds of men from the upstate served in this regiment between 1775 and 1780. *Drawing by South Carolina artist Darby Erd from research by Fitzhugh McMaster. Plate 494, Military Uniforms of America, Company of Military Historians. Reproduced by permission of the artist.*

2. By the summer of 1780, the Whig militia in the South Carolina Backcountry comprised experienced veterans of Continental and militia service. The militia depended on horses for mobility but fought primarily as foot soldiers. *Photograph by the author, from a reenactment at Historic Brattonsville, McConnells, South Carolina.*

3. Lieutenant Colonel Banastre Tarleton (1754–1833) commanded the British Legion, a mix of Provincial corps of cavalry and infantry, during the Southern Campaign of 1780–1781. *Portrait by South Carolina artist Robert Windsor Wilson, 1976. Courtesy of the Culture & Heritage Museums, York County, South Carolina.*

4. Captain Christian Huck (1748–1780) commanded a troop of dragoons in the British Legion from August 1779 to July 1780. In this photograph, Huck is portrayed by historical reenactor Joe Hinson. *Photograph by the author, from a reenactment at Historic Brattonsville, McConnels, South Carolina.*

5. John Adair (1757–1840) was a lieutenant in Colonel Edward Lacey's regiment in the early summer of 1780. Adair moved to Kentucky following the end of the Revolution, commanded a rifle brigade in the War of 1812 and served as Kentucky's governor from 1820 to 1824. *Governor's portrait of John Adair, oil on canvas, by Nichola Marshall. Courtesy of the Kentucky Historical Society.*

6. The Reverend John Simpson (1740–1808) was the pastor at Upper and Lower Fishing Creek Presbyterian Churches and Bethesda Presbyterian Church during the Revolution. An ardent Whig, he encouraged his congregation to resist the British occupation after the fall of Charleston, South Carolina. In this photograph, Simpson is portrayed by the Reverend Donald Lowery, a historical reenactor and Episcopalian minister. *Photograph by the author, from a reenactment at Historic Brattonsville, McConnels, South Carolina.*

7. On Sunday morning, 11 June 1780, Captain Christian Huck arrived at Upper Fishing Creek Presbyterian Church looking for the Whig militia. Huck's British Legion dragoons and Colonel James Ferguson's Loyalist militia burned the home and library of the Reverend Simpson and probably burned the church as well. *Photograph by the author, from a reenactment at Historic Brattonsville, McConnels, South Carolina.*

8. After destroying Hill's Iron Works on 17 June 1780, Captain Huck held an assembly on Upper Fishing Creek where he harangued the local citizens and demanded they take British protection. In this photograph, Huck (portrayed by reenactor Mark Schneider) reads Sir Henry Clinton's proclamation while flanked by his British Legion dragoons. *Photograph courtesy of Nancy Sambets, from a reenactment at Historic Brattonsville, McConnels, South Carolina.*

9. While Captain Huck addressed the locals at Fishing Creek, his men confiscated all horses deemed fit for military service. Deprived of their horses, those men who did not join the king's troops were forced to walk many miles back to their homes. In this photograph, British Legion soldiers disperse the recalcitrant rebels at bayonet point. *Photograph by the author, from a reenactment at Historic Brattonsville, McConnels, South Carolina.*

10. Whig militia officers at the Battle of Huck's Defeat, portrayed by members of the New Acquisition Militia reenactor group: Colonel Edward Lacey (John Misskelley), Captain John McClure (Ed Darby), Colonel Andrew Neal (Joe Hinson), Colonel William Bratton (Bob McCann) and Colonel William Hill (Kip Carter). *Photograph by the author, from a reenactment at Historic Brattonsville, McConnels, South Carolina.*

11. The Colonel William Bratton House at Historic Brattonsville, McConnells, South Carolina. This house was inhabited by the family of William and Martha Bratton during the Revolution and was the scene of Captain Huck's visit on the evening of 11 July 1780. *Courtesy of the Culture & Heritage Museums, York County, South Carolina.*

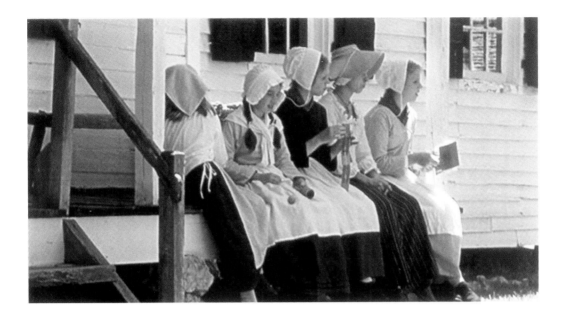

12. Reenactors (left to right) Dory Faris, Ellen Dewey, Amelia Thompson, Laura Melton and Alyson Thompson portray the Bratton children at Historic Brattonsville. *Photograph courtesy of Nancy Sambets, from a reenactment at Historic Brattonsville, McConnels, South Carolina.*

13. During the summer of 1780, groups of young women went from plantation to plantation in the Backcountry, assisting the shorthanded families in performing essential chores while the men were serving in the militia. In this photo, reenactors (left to right) Alyson Thompson, Anna Bortner, Amelia Thompson, Erin Allison, Jean Bessey, Ronda Robinson and Jaymie Benton are shown "walking the wool." *Photograph by the author, from a reenactment at Historic Brattonsville, McConnels, South Carolina.*

14. Martha Bratton, Robert Bratton and several older men from the neighborhood had just finished a long day of harvesting wheat when they received word that Captain Huck's detachment of Loyalist troops was approaching the Bratton plantation. Left to right, Cheryl Miller, Jim Jentz, Fred Moss, Sam Faris, Walter Thompson and Elizabeth Funderburk portray the Bratton reapers. *Photograph courtesy of Nancy Sambets, from a reenactment at Historic Brattonsville, McConnels, South Carolina.*

15. A small squad of Loyalist militiamen, commanded by Lieutenant John Adamson (Donald Lowery), arrives at the Bratton plantation, looking for Colonel William Bratton. Martha Bratton (Ronda Robinson) meets them in front of her house. *Photograph by the author, from a reenactment at Historic Brattonsville, McConnels, South Carolina.*

16. As seven-year-old William Bratton Jr. (Sam Faris) looks on in horror, a Loyalist militiaman (Kevin Lynch) places a reaping hook around the neck of Martha Bratton (Elizabeth Funderburk) and threatens to cut off her head if she does not reveal her husband's whereabouts. Lieutenant John Adamson (Watson Gunderson), the "honorable Tory," moves to intercept him. *Photograph courtesy of Nancy Sambets, from a reenactment at Historic Brattonsville, McConnels, South Carolina.*

17. Angered at the stubborn resistance of Martha Bratton (Elizabeth Funderburk), Captain Huck (Joe Hinson) storms out of the Bratton house as young William (Sam Faris) clings to his mother's side. *Photograph courtesy of Nancy Sambets, from a reenactment at Historic Brattonsville, McConnels, South Carolina.*

18. After leaving the Bratton plantation, Captain Huck's detachment camped at the nearby plantation of James Williamson. In this photo, Loyalist militiamen muster before the Battle of Huck's Defeat. *Photograph by the author, from a reenactment at Historic Brattonsville, McConnels, South Carolina.*

19. Provincial soldiers of the New York Volunteers assemble at the Williamson plantation early on the morning of 12 July 1780. *Photograph by the author, from a reenactment at Historic Brattonsville, McConnels, South Carolina.*

20. British Legion dragoons, camped around the Williamson plantation, prepare to move out on the morning of the battle. *Photograph by the author, from a reenactment at Historic Brattonsville, McConnels, South Carolina.*

21. Colonel Bratton (Bob McCann) assembles his men as they emerge from the woods around the Williamson plantation on the morning of 12 July. *Photograph by the author, from a reenactment at Historic Brattonsville, McConnels, South Carolina.*

22. New York Volunteers mount a bayonet charge against the rebel lines as smoke fills the air from the Whig volleys. *Photograph by the author, from a reenactment at Historic Brattonsville, McConnels, South Carolina.*

23. Whig militiamen form a line along the edge of Williamson's field and lay down heavy fire on the Loyalist militia camped there. *Photograph by the author, from a reenactment at Historic Brattonsville, McConnels, South Carolina.*

24. Loyalist militiamen flee the battlefield or ground their arms in surrender as the Whigs overrun Loyalist positions. *Photograph by the author, from a reenactment at Historic Brattonsville, McConnels, South Carolina.*

25. The second detachment of Whig soldiers under Captain John McClure (Chuck LeCount, far right) and Lieutenant Hugh McClure (Dale Loberger, second from right) enters the battle after a difficult trek through woods and creek swamps. *Photograph by the author, from a reenactment at Historic Brattonsville, McConnels, South Carolina.*

26. As the Whigs close in, several dragoons spur their horses and try to escape the battlefield. *Photograph by the author, from a reenactment at Historic Brattonsville, McConnels, South Carolina.*

27. Captain Huck (Joe Hinson) goes down as Whig rifle bullets find their mark. *Photograph by the author, from a reenactment at Historic Brattonsville, McConnels, South Carolina.*

28. The man who shot Captain Huck, John Carroll (Ken Ketchem), claims the captain's hat and sword as battlefield trophies. *Photograph by the author, from a reenactment at Historic Brattonsville, McConnels, South Carolina.*

29. Seriously wounded, Lieutenant John Adamson (Don Lowery) is dragged toward the Williamson home by (right to left) Colonel Edward Lacey (John Misskelley), Colonel William Bratton (Bob McCann), Captain John Chambers (David Chambers) and other Whig soldiers. *Photograph by the author, from a reenactment at Historic Brattonsville, McConnels, South Carolina.*

30. Martha Bratton (Ronda Robinson) joins her husband in order to save John Adamson from the vengeance of the Whig soldiers, who are convinced that he is the man who threatened her life the day before. *Photograph by the author, from a reenactment at Historic Brattonsville, McConnels, South Carolina.*

31. The victorious Whigs take stock of the battlefield, now littered with dead and dying Tories. The Battle of Huck's Defeat is over. *Photograph by the author, from a reenactment at Historic Brattonsville, McConnels, South Carolina.*

Appendix A

Accounts of Huck's Defeat in pension applications

The Federal and state Revolutionary War pension applications of the men who served in Sumter's Brigade contain numerous references to the Battle of Huck's Defeat. These accounts range from brief to highly detailed, and are a tremendous resource of information regarding the battle itself, the events leading up to it and the aftermath. Most of the pension applications include statements by the veteran himself and fellow soldiers who served with him. A few applications were filed after the death of the soldier by his widow and/or children in an effort to draw the pension due the deceased veteran, and included statements about the soldier's service by his heirs and others who knew him. These brief quotations do not represent the totality of service for most of these veterans; for the majority, military service began long before the fall of Charleston in May 1780 and covered the entirety of the war. Only those comments related to the battles and skirmishes in the spring and summer of 1780 are transcribed here. All comments in brackets those of the author.

1. John Adair, Federal pension application W2895.

Statement by John Adair dated 12 July 1832:

> I hereby certify that in the month of April or May 1780, Charles town having been surrendered to the Enemy, with all the regular Troops under the command of General Lincoln, and the gov'. of the State having fled from the States—there being then no legal authority in the State—and the British Troops under the command of Tarleton, Rawdon and other officers, were marching through and taking possession of all parts of the State about three hundred men who had fled from the Enemy, of which I was one, did assemble in North Carolina where the[y] had fled, and enter into a solemn obligation to place themselves under the command of Gen'. Thomas Sumpter and to continue in a body and serve under his command untill the war was at an end, or untill their services were no longer necessary, they were to find their own horses and arms, cloathing and all necessaries—it being absolutely necessary that they should act on horse back—they immediately returned into South Carolina and made their first attack on a party of British and Torys amounting to between five and six hundred men commanded by Cap'. Hoock or Huck of the Horse & a Col'. Ferguson who commanded the Torys at Williamson's

Plantation—the Enemy were defeated—Hoock & Ferguson both killed and a Cap[t]. Adamson who commanded the British Infantry wounded and taken with between thirty and forty men—Our numbers increased daily after this action and two or three weeks after we were led to an attack on a British garrison at Rocky Mount. And the Gen[l]. finding the works too strong to be taken without cannon (of which he had none) he abandoned the enterprise—and eight days after (having a reinforcement of 30 men from North Carolina under a Cap[t]. Ervin) we attacked a strong British force at the Hanging Rock. This I believe was the hardest fought Battle, during the war in the South. I continued in service untill the end of the war and fought many Battles which it is not necessary to name.

2. John Bishop, Federal pension application S9279.

Statement by John Bishop dated 24 November 1832:

When the British troops overrun the country after the fall of Charleston in May 1780, he was then he thinks about 15 or 16 years of age, but was grown. That himself and 4 other brothers (2 of them having families) retreated from home towards North Carolina. It was on the morning he thinks afore Hook's defeat, as they met the troops near Old-Nations fourd on the Cataweba River, going on the pursuit of the Enemy. That his older Brother Henry Bishop (who was a captin) returned with the troops to the attack. That he with the others went on with the women and children, and left them with some friends near Charlotte, North Carolina; and then returned and joined General Sumter in the Indian Land, Col. Lacey's Regiment. That he continued in the service until after the Battle of the Hanging Rock. At which Brother s[d]. Henry Bishop was wounded. That he then went with the wounded to Charlotte, where his Brother died of his wound. That when the troops collected again after Gates' and Sumter's defeats, he joined he thinks in Capt. Miller's Company.

3. Archibald Brown, Federal pension application S39249.

Statement by Archibald Brown dated 28 March 1822:

Immediately after the fall of Charleston when the enemy came into the back country he joined Gen[l]. Sumter at Clems Branch in the Indian Land, Capt. Nixons company, was at Hooks defeat near Colonel Brattons, was at the battle of the Hanging Rock, was with Gen[l]. Sumter when attacked by the British at Fishing Creek, was at the Battle of Blackstocks.

4. Walter Carson, Federal pension application S32165.

Statement by Walter Carson dated 13 May 1833:

In the year 1780 he again entered the service of the United States, at Ramsaur's Mills in the State of N. Carolina under the command of General Sumpter—that he marched thence back to Camden District S. C. where he was appointed by his company with the approbation of Colonel Andrew Neel who commanded the Regiment, a Captain, and that he served as Captain of his company during the whole remainder of his present tour of duty—that he continued in said Camden District during marching and countermarching in pursuit of Tories until his discharge—that during which time he was in many battles and skirmishes with British and Tories, some of which were as follows, to wit, a Battle with Captain Hook of the British and Col. Floyd of the Tories at a place near Col. Bratton's—another at Rocky Mount, another at Hanging Rock, another at Camden ferry on the Wateree river, another at Sumpter's defeat.

5. William Carson, Federal pension application S9305.

Statement by William Carson dated 22 May 1821:

He entered the Militia in the service of this state at the commencement of the Revolutionary War and served during the whole of the war under General Sumter, Coln. Neal, and Coln. Graham [probably Bratton]. That he was in the battles at the Congaree, at Hook's defeat, and the battle of King's Mountain and a number of skirmishes. That at the battle of Friday's Fort on the Congaree he was severely wounded being shot through the wrist of the right arm, and much disabled.

Statement by B.S. Carson, son of William Carson deceased, dated 12 April 1850:

Said William Carson entered the service shortly after the fall of Charleston South Carolina in the militia as a volunteer under Capt. Walter Carson, Col. Bratton's Regiment, Gen. Sumpters Brigade (Militia) and served in said company for some weeks as a fifer after which he was discharged and returned home and in a few days he again volunteered under Capt. John Hood and remained under him for a short time and was again discharged and that soon after said discharge he joined Capt. Cunningham's company who with others were in pursuit of Col. Furguson whom they overtook and defeated at Kings Mountain in the month of October 1780. That from the time he first volunteered in the month of June until the battle of Kings Mountain in October he was but a very few days out of the army and that during the above service he was in the following engagements viz, 1st a skirmish at a place called the Big Glades in the low country where they captured fourteen wagons laden with military stores—Huck's defeat—the taking of Fridays fort on the Congaree and the battle of Kings Mountain and that his next tour of service was in the fall of the year 1781. He volunteered for three months under Capt. John Hood, Col. Bratton.

6. James Clinton, Federal pension application S2437.

Statement by James Clinton dated 20 May 1833:

Just about the time of the fall of Charleston, the British and Tories became very bold, and had established forts throughout the country. Under this aspect of things the Whigs began to think of organizing themselves into volunteer companies, and entering the field against these invaders of the country. In the month of June, as my memory now serves me—it might have been earlier of that year (1780)—I again entered the service of the militia of the state as a volunteer private, and from the same district under Lt. [William] Davis, Captain Joseph Howe and Colonel Andrew Neal (son of my first Colonel [Thomas Neal] mentioned above). As soon as our troops assembled, we went first in search of one Captain Hook a British officer, whom we found at the plantation of Colonel Bratton, and instantly commenced the attack, in which Hook was killed with others and his party dispersed.

Supporting statement by Samuel Gordon dated 6 July 1833:

In the month of March 1780 the said [James] Clinton & [Samuel] Gordon again entered the service together as volunteers—the said Clinton as a private, and the said Gordon as sergeant aforesaid from the same county, under Captain Joseph Howe and Colonel Watson in a Regiment of horse, all volunteers. That during this service we defeated a party of Tories at Mobley's meeting house near Winnsboro, and a party at one Stallion's on fishing creek—that after the fall of Charleston in May 1780, Colonel Hook of the Brittish army came up into the interior, and defeated us at Hill's Iron works. After this defeat Col. Watson despaired and told his men to seek better service, & attach themselves to the American army—that upon this, the said Clinton, the said Gordon, and 25 others made Andrew Neal (son of said [Col.] Tho'. [Neal]) their colonel, and said Howe captain, and proceeded to join themselves to some other troops. On their way, they met Col. Sumpter & Winn, and put themselves under the command of Sumpter, who was proceeding on the same march. Sumpter stationed himself first [at] Ramsour's where he greatly [increased] his force, and then moved to the old Nation ford, where he recruited his force to 450, including 75 Catawba Indians. In a short time afterwards Sumpter attacked the Brittish post at Rocky Mount, and was repulsed. That in this attack Col. Neal was killed—that it was fought about the last of June 1780 as well as he remembers;—that in a few days we fought the Brittish and Tories at Hanging rock.

7. James P. Collins, Federal pension application R2173.

Statement by James Collins dated 8 April 1834:

I joined the service of my country in the year 1780, not long after the fall of Charleston, South Carolina, and in what is now called York District under the command of Col. John Moffet, a militia colonel, [and] was always under his command, while in service. We were nothing more than Militia Volunteers—and a scouting party that scoured the Districts of York and Chester, sometimes crossing Broad River to the west, in Union, and the Districts above [Spartanburg], and sometimes passing into Rutherford, Lincoln, and Mecklenburg in North Carolina. The first action I was witnessed was with Lord Hook, as he was called, near Fishing Creek, after he had burnt Hill's Iron Works, where his party was defeated and himself killed. My Captain was John Henderson.

Additional statement by James Collins:

> On having the declaration which I made in this court on the 8th day of April last, read to me to-day, I find it might be understood that I intended to say Col. Moffet commanded in chief when we defeated Lord Hook. Col Moffet was in the action; it was fought in a peach orchard near Col. Bratton's, who was the oldest Colonel, and commanded. Col. Bratton's Christian name was William. Col. Thomas Neal [Jr.] of [South] Carolina, was also in the action.

8. John Craig, Federal pension application W22864.

Statement by John Craig dated 3 October 1832:

> I entered the service under Col. Thomas Neile at fifteen years of age, in York Dist. S[l]. Carolina. I joined Gen[l]. Williamson's Army at the Seneca Fort (now of Pickens Dist.), went on under Williamson and assisted in defeating the Cherokee Indians on the waters of Highwasse. My next tour was under the same Col. Neale on Savanna River, Capt. [Richard] Sadler [was company commander], still against the Cherokees. My next tour [was] under the same Col. and rendavoused at Orangeburg S[l]. Carolina, was ordered to join Gen[l]. Moultrie at Black Swamp, retreated to Coosahatchee [Coosawhatchie] where there was a call for 130 men to burn down Tulifinny Bridge under Col. John Laurence [Laurens] who was wounded in the engagement. Retreated to the Main Army, marched to Charleston, from Charleston marched to Stono to join Gen[l]. Linkhorn [Lincoln], then followed the Battle of Stono near Charleston. My next service was at Rocky Mount [Alexander's Old Field] after the Fall of Charleston, commanded by Capt. J. McClure, Lieut[s]. Hugh McClure and John Steele. Succeeded in defeating the Tories, marched to Mobley Meeting House, defeated the Tories again. By permit I went to York County in order to get recruits to join us but was disappointed. Only finding seven men willing to join me we went to N[o]. Carolina near Salisbury, joined Col. Lock, pursued on after Col. Bryan to S[o]. Carolina, was not able to overhall him. Marched to Ramsours Mills, there defeated the Tories, then marched to Charlotte N[o]. Carolina, joined Gen[l]. Sumter & returned to S[o]. Carolina then went on a scout after the Tories under Col[s]. A. Neile, Lacy, Bratton & Maj. Dickson. Defeated the Tories and British at Williamsons Lane, killed Maj. Robison [and] Capt. Hook. Then returned to main army, then marched to Rocky Mount, attacked the fort but was driven back, lost Col. Andrew Neile killed. Marched from thence to Hanging Rock, stormed the encampment, drove the British and Tories, lost Capt. McClure killed.

Additional statements by John Craig:

> Commanded by Colonels Andrew Neal, Lacy, Bratton and Major Dickson our first engagement was with a set of Tories and British at Williamsons Lane. Our number was something to the sum of one hundred and thirty five men. There were of the Tories about three hundred men commanded by Col. Floyd. Capt. Hook commanded fifty dragoons, Capt. Adams[on] fifty Light Infantry which made one hundred British in addition to the three hundred Toreys. Among the slain on the part of the Tories were

Major Robertson and Capt. Hook, we took Capt. Adams[on] prisoner. Several were killed and taken prisoner besides, we lost but one man in the engagement. We went back and joined camp again with General Sumpter, we then marched to Rocky Mount where the British and Tories were Forted....

[After his early tours] this applicant was in no service until after the Fall of Charleston when in the last of May 1780 he turned out with Capt. McClure and was with him in the two engagements set forth, though he did not continue with him longer than one week when he went off in quest of recruits. Being disappointed in raising a sufficient number of recruits, in company with a few others he retired to North Carolina where in June 1780 he joined Col. Lock with whom he continued in active service two weeks and until this applicant heard that Sumter was at Charlotte embodying his forces. Very early in July (1780) he joined Gen'. Sumter and under him returned into South Carolina.

This applicant is informed that the War Department requires him to set forth more 'specifically' his service from the year 1780 to 1782—as it regards this service he declares most unequivocally from the time he first joined Sumter in Charlotte in July 1780 until the evacuation of Charleston in December 1782 he was in service and under arms during the whole time attached to the command of Sumter when he was able to be in the field or those who acted by his command or under the command of Gen'. Henderson during the time Sumter was confined on account of his wound. In his original declaration he has detailed the battles in which he was during this service. He was with Sumter immediately (sometimes sent off by him on some short scout as soon as performed always returning again to Sumter) from the first of July 1780 until he [Sumter] was wounded at Blackstocks in November 1780, the 20th day of that month. During this time he was commanded by Capt. James Jameison [Jamieson] until the battle of the Hanging Rock in which he [Jamieson] was wounded, when Lieutenant William Hilhouse succeeded to the command of the company. He belonged to Col. Neil's Reg'. who was killed at Rocky Mount & was afterward commanded by Col. Lacy.

9. Edward Doyle, Federal pension application S32216.

Statement by Edward Doyle dated 18 September 1832:

He was in the Battle at Col. Brattons House against a party of British and Torries and defeated them and killed a British officer called Capt. Hook of the Light Horse—at this battle Col. [Andrew] Neal was our commanding officer—he is the same officer that was killed afterward at Rocky Mount in South Carolina—which by mistake in this narrative said he was killed at the Hanging Rock. In this action at Brattons we took several horses, guns, swords and pistols, and took thirty or forty prisoners. He was with Gen'. Sumter.

10. John Forbes, Federal pension application R3645.

Statement by John Forbes Jr., son of John Forbes deceased, dated 16 June 1846:

This declarant the aforesaid John Forbes in the behalf of himself & the other heirs of John Forbes late Revolutionary Soldier dec'. States, that the said John Forbes was a private and Lieutenant in the Army of the Revolution the heirs understand and as such he served the United States against the Common Enemy—That he the said John Forbes Entered the Army of the Revolution in 1779 or 1780, as Lieut. under Capt. Moffit & Col. Watson of the Militia, after which he joined Col. Hills Company of the Cavalry where he served as a Lieut. for sometime and General Sumpter, after the above service he served some time in the Militia during which time he was wounded while in an Engagement with the Enemy at Williamson Plantation and that for many years before the death of the said John Forbes he received an Invalid Pension which was paid him by the State of South Carolina, the State in which he resided when he rendered the above service.

11. Hugh Gaston, Federal pension application S10729.

Statement by Hugh Gaston dated 25 April 1834:

While under the command of Capt. McClure he was at an engagement with the Tories at Mobley's Meeting House, where the Tories were defeated. Afterwards at Monk's Corner they were surprised by the enemy and compelled to retreat.[623] They retreated up the Santee River where they were reinforced by a party of men from North Carolina. He was at the battle at James Williamson's plantation near the south fork of fishing creek where the Tories and British were defeated. Col. Lacy was commander at this place. He was also at a battle at Rocky Mount where General Sumpter was highest in command.

Additional statement by Hugh Gaston dated 13 November 1834:

[After the fall of Charleston] he was called out in the militia under the command of Capt. McClure when he was at the battle at Mobley's meeting house where the tories were defeated. The battle was fought at break of day & lasted a short time several negroes were killed & some tories were taken prisoners. After the battle the militia returned home.

He was afterwards called out to defend & guard provisions stored at Monks Corner where Capt. McClure with the militia were surprised by the enemy's horsemen & compelled to retreat up the Santee river where they were reinforced by a party of men from North Carolina. Afterwards hearing of the fall of Charleston they returned home. He was afterwards at the battle at James Williamson's plantation. The night previous to the battle they encamped at Clems Branch when they crossed the Catawba river and attacked the united forces of the British & Tories about day break. The action continued but a few minutes. Capt. Hook a British officer was killed. Several of the enemy were killed & some taken prisoners.

12. William Gaston, Federal pension application S32265.

Statement by William Gaston dated 24 September 1832:

After Charlestown fell into the hands of the British in 1780, he entered the service as a mounted volunteer, under Capt. John McClure, Col. Lacy, & Gen. Sumpter, field officers. After several skirmishes he fought at the Battles of Rocky Mount, Hanging Rock, Hook's Defeat, and King's Mountain. (When Gen. Sumpter was surprised at McDonald's ford on Cataba river, this applicant's horse fell into the hands of the Enemy for which he never was compensated.)

13. James Hemphill, Federal pension application S21277.

Statement by James Hemphill dated 16 October 1832:

Some time in the summer of 1780 having moved to Mecklenburg County in North Carolina after the taking of Charleston by the British, our regiment then under the command of Lt. Col. Watson and Major Bratton (Col. [Thomas] Neel having died) joined the forces commanded by Col. Sumpter and a few days afterward moved down to Hagler's Branch in S.C. and after staying there between one and two weeks went about eighteen or twenty miles to the mountains having understood that there were several British Dragoons and Tories in that neighborhood and when we had a battle with about four hundred British and tories commanded by a Capt. Huck of whom we defeated very badly.

14. John Henderson, South Carolina audited account AA3522.

Statement by Colonel William Hill dated 25 November 1785:

This is to Certify that on 17th June 1780 when a Great part of the State of South Carolina was overrun by the British, that there was a party of Our friends made a Stand at the Iron works in York County in Said State, & that I Sent Capt. John Henderson to endeavor to make discovery of the Enemies movements, who in the execution of that endeavor, was Taken prisoner by the british, by which means he lost a large bay horse about five feet high, five years old which mare together with a Saddle & Bridle lost at the Same time was appraised to three hundred pounds old Currency, as will appear by an appraisement signed by Tho. & Joseph Henderson.

15. William Hillhouse, Federal pension application S7008.

Statement by William Hillhouse dated 3 February 1832:

In May 1780 I again went into actual service, and continued till October 1781. I entered as orderly sergeant, in which capacity I served a short time, when I was elected lieutenant of the company in which I had hither done duty. Brigadier General Thomas Sumpter now commanded the Brigade, and Col. Andrew Neil the Regiment to which I belonged, and Capt. J. Jamison the company. During this campaign I marched through the greater part of the middle and lower sections of S. Carolina, and through a considerable part of North Carolina. As well as I can now recollect, I was, during this term of duty in the following battles, viz, at Williamson's Plantation in the district of York S. Carolina, I was in a Battle in which the British and Tories were commanded by the British officers, Captains Hook and Adams [on], and most gloriously defeated, by a few militia Boys, my companions in arms, commanded by Col. Neil.

16. Samuel Houston, Federal pension application W7810.

Statement by Samuel Houston dated 6 May 1834:

In the year 1780 and in the latter part of the month of April or the first of the month of May, he again entered the service of the United States as a private, and believes as a volunteer, in Chester district South Carolina, under the command of Lieutenant Col. Joseph Brown, who then had the Command of Colonel Lacey's Regiment of the So. Carolina militia, in Captain Frost's Company of which Michael Gore was a Lieutenant, that he was marched to Camden and thence toward Charleston, but before we reached that place, we were met by Governor Rutledge with the information that Charleston had fallen into the hands of the British and Lt. Colonel Brown at the suggestion of Govr. Rutledge returned with us to Camden, where he was discharged by Col. Brown having been in the service not less than two weeks.

Immediately after he returned to his Father's in Chester district So. Carolina, in the month of May 1780 he volunteered and joined the Company of South Carolina militia Commanded by Capt. John McLure of which Hugh McLure was first Lieutenant, John Steele second Lieutenant, and James Johnston third Lieutenant, of Colonel Lacey's Regiment, as a private, and was marched to Mobley's Meeting House where we had a skirmish with some Tories. Thence he was marched into North Carolina near Charlotte in Mecklenburg County, at which place General Sumpter joined us and was appointed to the Command in Chief, thence we marched to Phifer's where Genl. Davidson of the North Carolina militia joined us. Capt. McLure's Company, in which he was, at Phifer's were detached by Genl. Sumpter to cross the Catawba River into Lincoln County against some Tories embodying in that County, at Ramsour's Mills, where we had a Battle with and defeated the Tories, in this Battle Captain Falls who Commanded a Company of Cavalry was killed. From the Battle ground at Ramsour's Mills he was again marched across the Catawba River into the Catawba Indian's Land and encamped for some time at a place called Clem's branch in Lancaster district South Carolina. From thence in Captain McLure's Company under the Command of Col. Lacey he was detached to cross the Catawba River into York district to meet some British & Tories, whom we met and defeated at Col. William Bratton's. Capt. Hook, a British officer, and Col. Ferguson a Tory, was killed & a Capt. Edmonson [Adamson] of the British Infantry was taken prisoner. From Col. Bratton's we were again marched across the Catawba & joined Genl. Sumpter at Clem's Branch. Thence he was marched with Genl. Sumpter to Rocky Mount where we had a battle with some British & Tories under the Command of Col. Turnbull of the British army.

17. William Jenkins, Federal pension application S31774.

Statement by William Jenkins dated 3 August 1832:

> He entered the service of the United States under the following named officers: Colonel William Bratton and Captain Thomas Jenkins,—thinks it was in the opening of 1780 that he volunteered; he then resided in York County South Carolina; the army embodied on the east side of the Cottawba river, from where he lived—and on the first evening after he arrived at the camp he was appointed a sergeant.
>
> In a short time they were informed that about one hundred and fifty tories and about thirty Dragoons of the British army had assembled near the residence of Colonel William Bratton, that Col. Bratton and Capt. Jenkins with about one hundred men, him being one of that number, started and traveled all night and about day discovered the main guard and fired upon them. When they retreated they advanced to the mouth of a lane, where an engagement took place with the dragoons in which one them, to wit Capt. Hook was killed, the balance then fled. He sometime after that engagement joined the army under the Command of General Sumpter, was not engaged in any other battles during that campaign.

18. Jonathan Jones Jr., South Carolina audited account AA 4109.

Supporting statement by William Knox dated 15 August 1826:

> I have been well acquainted with Jonathan Jones the applicant in the Revolutionary War and knew him to be a firm friend to (and grate sufferer for his Country) and was with him at the Battle of the Congaree fort, Black Stocks and Hookes Defeat and I realize him to be at a number more actions that I was not along.

19. James Kincaid, Federal pension application R5929.

Statement by James Kincaid dated 1 July 1833:

> He entered the service as a volunteer under General Sumpter and Colonel Bratton and was attached to Captain Moffet's company sometime about the month of May A.D. 1780 for thirty days and that he served under said officers during his term of thirty days and at the expiration of that time he immediately enrolled himself again for forty days which term he served under the above named officers (having volunteered first in York District South Carolina). That he was first marched into Lancaster District South Carolina in the indian Land at Clem's branch. That he was shortly after his first enrolment marched to Fishing Creek in York District South Carolina and was there in the engagement under Capt. Moffet and Col. Bratton, at Hooks defeat, and that shortly thereafter he was then marched to Rocky mountain and was there in that engagement under the command of Genl. Sumpter, Col. Moffet [actually Bratton] and Capt. Moffet where Genl. Sumpter's army was repulsed.

20. Thomas Lofton, Federal pension application S17114.

Statement from Thomas Lofton dated 10 December 1822:

> *After Charleston was taken by the British, they embodied under Col. John Moore and encamped at Ramsour's Mill—Col. Sumpter had left his home and come into the back part of S.C. where numbers joined him and amongst the number my brother and myself and marched for the tories at the above named Mill. I was at this time 1st Lieut. in Captⁿ. Joseph Howe's Company commanded by Col. Andrew Neel; we joined General Rutherford of the N.C. Militia, and about two hours before we got to Ramsour's the tories were completely defeated by Col. Francis Locke who commanded the militia of Rowan County. Col. Neel then marched from thence with 110 men and defeated Captⁿ. Huck of Tarleton's Dragoons. Huck was killed, Captⁿ. Adamson of the infantry wounded and taken prisoner, and the whole party were either killed wounded or dispersed. Our next affair was at Rocky Mount.*

21. James McCaw, Federal pension application S18117.

Statement from James McCaw dated 21 September 1833:

> *After the fall of Charleston in the year 1780 volunteered in Captain Pagan's Company Col. Lacy's Regiment under Genl. Sumpter, was at the Skirmish at Williamson's Plantation when Capt. Huck was killed, was at the battle of Rocky Mount, Battle of Hanging Rock and at the skirmish at Fishdam Ford on Broad River, Served Six months when dismissed.*

22. James McElwee, Federal pension application W9553.

Statement from James McElwee dated 26 September 1832:

> *In the year 1780 the state of South Carolina was infested with the British army and the Torys. Sumpter was alicted* [elected] *general of the South Carolina militia immediately after the Battle at Ramsour. He then in the month of July in said year enrolled himself in a company commanded by Capt. John Moffitt whose company was attached to the command of Col. W^m. Bratton. The troops were immediately marched down to Catawba river and was engaged in the battle fought with Capt. Hook and defeated them. This engagement took place in the month of August 1780 where a number of prisoners were taken by the Whig party. A few days afterwards he was again engaged against the Torys and every man of the company was taken but himself* [probably a reference to the Battle of Fishing Creek]. *In making his escape at that time he crippled one of his feet and returned home. He did not recover from his injury until after Ferguson's defeat* [the battle of Kings Mountain].

23. James Martin, Federal pension application S9391.

Statement from James Martin dated 16 October 1832:

> *In June 1780 he left the state for N°. Carolina with thirteen men where he joined Col. Lock of N°. Carolina, and then proceeded with him to attack the Tories at Ramsour's Mills in the said State, where they defeated them, this engagement was about the 20th of June 1780. After this battle he returned to S°. Carolina and joined Gen¹. Sumpter at Hagler's Branch, crossed the Catawba and defeated the British under Captain Hook at Williamson's this was in the month of July [then] marched to Rocky Mount and attacked the British under Col. Turnbull and drove them into their garrison. He then crossed the Catawba River, and one week after the battle of Rocky Mount defeated the Tories and British at the Battle of Hanging Rock.*

Additional statement by James Martin:

> *On the tenth of June 1780 he left this state for North Carolina (with thirteen men) where he found Co¹. Lock of the North Carolina Militia, and then proceeded with him to attack the Tories at Ramsour's Mills in the said state, when they defeated them, this engagement was fought the 20th of June 1780. After this battle he returned to So. Ca. and joined Gen¹. Sumter of the So. Ca. Militia at Hagler's Branch, Crossed the Catawba and defeated the British under Captain Hook at Williamson's, this was in the month of July. He then marched to Rocky Mount So. Ca. and attacked the British under Co¹. Turnbull.*

24. John Mills, Federal pension application W9194.

Statement by Mary Mills Pagan, daughter of John Mills deceased and Mary Mills deceased, dated 30 June 1846:

> *Captain John Mills was a Lieutenant and Captain of horse, South Carolina Militia, Sumter's Brigade and a Captain of Cavalry, State Troop under an enlistment for 10 months which expired the spring of 1782 and afterwards Captain of a company of rangers which he continued to command until the end of the war...and as such he served the United States against the common enemy from the time he entered the service in June or July 1780 until the close of the war as above stated, and received two negroes Prince and Bella for his service as Captain in the State Troop (10 months).*

Supporting statement by Robert Wilson dated 11 November 1847:

> *He was in the days of the Revolution well and intimately acquainted with John Mills an officer and soldier in the Army of the Revolution that resided in Camden [District] but now Chester District South Carolina. That the deponent was in the service during the*

172

Revolution on different occasions with the said John Mills that their first service together was in the Early Part of the war at Seneca Fort. Their next service that deponent now recollects was in the summer of 1780 after the fall of Charleston they were together some two or three months under General Sumter who had the command of the Militia Forces, which had congregated together after the fall of Charleston to oppose the Enemy. That during this service under Sumter in 1780, the said John Mills belonged to and served as a Commissioned Officer, Either as Lieutenant or Capt. in Col. Edward Lacy's Regiment of Mounted Militia or horse, for the whole force was mounted, that said Lacy was Col., Patrick McGriff [was] Lieut. Col. and Charles Miles [was] Major which constituted said Regiment, and was under the command of General Sumter. That deponent was with the said Army from the middle of July till December at which time he left Sumpters Army and went on an expedition to Newbern N. C. for military stores, and did not return till March following, about the time of the raising of Sumter's State Troops, and that deponent does not now recollect of being in service after 1781....This deponent also states on his oath, that the sd. Col. Edward Lacy's Rgt. was not a Regiment of State Troops, but belonged to the Militia, nor did said Col. Lacy ever command a Regiment of State Troops to deponent's knowledge.

Supporting statement by D.W. Wallace dated 1 December 1847:

Capt. John Mills enlisted in the service in July 1780 as a Lieutenant in which capacity he served about three months and was then promoted to the Rank of Captain in the Militia & served three or four months in Sumpter's Brigade. He [Mills] was then Comᵈ. Captain in the State Troops which was raised the spring of 1781 for ten months enlistment which expired in the month of April 1782. For his services in the state troops he got two negroes, Prince and Bella, Confiscated Property. He then commanded the company of Rangers as before stated until the close of the war making in all 340 days service as Captain in the militia and ten months Captain in the State Troops of Cavalry.

Supporting statement by John Bishop dated 1 December 1847:

John Bishop also verifies...that Capt. John Mills Commanded a Company in Col. Laceys Regiment of Militia and was generally in the Service from the fall of Charleston till the end of the war.

Supporting statement by David Morrow dated 8 January 1851:

David Morrow aged 75 years sworn saith that Captain John Mills husband of Mary Mills late of Chester District deceased commanded a company called rangers in the war of the revolution after the command of the state troops under the command of General Sumter, in which he continued until the close of the war. Deponents father was in Mills company of State Troops and was killed in that service...Deponent distinctly recollects seeing Captain Mills on patrol service at the house of his mother Mary Morrow after his (Mills') marriage and that he carried a rifle called a Yager which name he distinctly recollects. Deponents mother and Captain John Mills were full cousins and very intimate.

25. David Morrow, Federal pension application S7253.

Statement by David Morrow dated 22 September 1833:

He volunteered the 1ˢᵗ of June 1780, as well as he now recollects, under Capt. John McClure—had a skirmish at a place called the old fields, another at Mobley's meeting house—Sumpter then formed a flying camp—we fled to N. Carolina returned and defeated Hook at Williamson's or Bratton's and fought the British and toreys at Rocky Mount then to a place called hanging rock—had a hard fight & Capt. McClure was killed—then was attached to Capt. Hugh Knox, Lacy our Colonel.

26. Joseph Morrow, Federal pension application S21892.

Statement by Joseph Morrow dated 19 December 1832:

[He was] drafted again for three months under Wᵐ. Jones Capt., Hugh McClure Liut. marched to go to Charleston met the army on its retreat from Charleston after it was captured by the British Served this time three or four weeks. The country became so overrun with the British and Tories so that all the Whigs were obliged to be in the army for their own Safety and the Safety of their country he then volunteered in Capt. John McClure's company John Steel Liut. Joined Sumter's Army under Col. Lacy & Col. Winn continued with Sumter's army in this State and North Carolina was at the defeat and utter Rout of Capt. Huck at Williamson's where Huck was killed and many others. Continued with Sumter till the Battle of Hanging rock where he had his arm shattered by a Ball by reason of which he had near lost his arm and still remains a cripple. This wound put an end to his Services being peace made by the time his arm healed which was about two years, this last tour lasted or he continued in the army from May till August three or four months. He further saith that he was at the Skirmish at Mobley's Meeting house & the Battle at Rocky Mount these last places he says he forgot to put them in their places.

27. George Neely, Federal pension application S4613.

Statement by George Neely dated 30 September 1832:

He entered as a volunteer while living in Camden district S. Carolina in the year 1780 and in his 19ᵗʰ year of age. He thinks it was about the 20ᵗʰ of May, soon after Charleston was taken by the Brittish. After that event the tories began to hold Musters and do great damage in Camden district, and the adjoining counties. There being a call for men to put them down he entered as a volunteer in Capt. John McClure's Company and marched with this company up to fishing crek 10 or 12 miles to a Mr. Bishop's near the Cross Roads where the company was properly organized. He marched about for some time, preventing the tories from committing depredations. Then on hearing a body of tories and Brittish had collected at Bratton's or William's farm, under Col. Furguson a tory and Capt. Hook a Brittish officer, a detachment including Capt. McClure's Company under Major John Adair marched to rout them. We came upon them after marching the whole night, about day break and took them by surprise, killing Capt. Hook and Col. Furguson with several others, some of whom were my acquaintances and men I had never suspected of toryism. After we had routed them we then disbanded and joined in companies of 7 or 8 men each (the country being somewhat relieved of these tories) and went about in the neighborhood still retaining our arms and guarding the property and lives [of] our countrymen. Soon after the company collected under Capt. McClure and joined Col. Lacey's regiment & marched about from place to place until he was marched with this regiment up to Mecklenburg County N. Carolina and encamped on Steel Creek near one Knox's. In this month the regiment suffered greatly for provisions. After laying here some time he was marched towards the upper end of S. Carolina still continuing on the west side of the Catawba river. There he was marched about against small bodies of tories, until Col. Lacey's hearing that the Brittish and tories had collected at the Rocky Mount down in South Carolina under a Col. called Turnbull, he was marched there and the regiment joined Gen. Sumpter who took the command of the men in the besieging of that place, a very strong position. We were repulsed with considerable loss including Col. Andrew Neal.

28. Robert Pattison, Federal pension application S3654.

Statement by Robert Pattison dated 27 August 1832:

At the age of 18 years and some months, he volunteered and entered the service under the command of Capt. McMullin & he thinks in the Regiment of Col. Wᵐ. Hill [actually Col. Thomas Neal Sr.] as a militia man & marched from York County in South Carolina where he volunteered to Reedy River in said state of South Carolina—they had a skirmish with the Tories on said River and took one hundred and three prisoners, & dispersed the rest of them. He was then marched back to said York County & discharged after a six week term of service. He next volunteered in North Carolina, and went on an expedition against the Tories in Ramsours settlement, he does not remember under the command of what officers, they scouted the country themselves for sometime without meeting the enemy & returned back into South Carolina and was discharged. The term of this service he does not recollect. He remained inactive until the spring of 1780. He then joined Capt. Moffit's company in the Militia service in South Carolina York County in which company he continued in service as minute man during the remainder of the Revolutionary War. They made a strong stand at Hills Iron works in said county of York, but were in a short time driven from there by the enemy. Then they fled to North Carolina and joined the command of General Sumpter. He continued a soldier in said command till the end of the war, which was 18 months. While he was under the command of General

Sumpter he marched to Ramsours settlement the second time, & reached there on the same morning immediately after the battle fought there between the American troops and the enemy thence he was marched to Lancaster County South Carolina below the Waxsaw settlement & were forced to retreat back into North Carolina & thence back into South Carolina & fought a battle in Williams Lane defeated Capt. Hooks party of the enemy & some of the said Hooks troops was killed in that action.

Then they marched to Rocky Mount where they had a severe engagement with the British & Torys.

29. John Patton, Federal pension application W162.

Statement by John Patton dated 10 August 1832:

After returning home & being discharged from the Campaign against the Indians, he with fifteen or twenty others from the said District of York South Carolina determined to enter the service again, and traveled up to the State of North Carolina and on the battle ground at Ramsour's Mills which was in Lincoln County joined Genl. Sumpter's brigade as a volunteer under the command of Capt. [Robert] Thompson and remained a volunteer in Sumpter's brigade so long as the british and Tory hostilities existed in that section of the Country, with the exception of a tour of duty he performed in what was called the Siege of ninetysix in which expedition he was under the command of Col. [Robert] Anderson, at this place Genl. Greene commanded in person.

After joining Sumpter's brigade at Ramsour's Mills he went with said brigade into South Carolina and at a place called Bratton's farm attacked & defeated a detachment of British and Tories under the command of Col. Turnbull. In this engagement they killed & wounded a considerable number of Turnbull's men & took near thirty prisoners. After disposing of the dead wounded & prisoners, they continued their march after Turnbull, who had fortified his regiment at Rocky Mount on the Catawba river, at this place we again attacked Turnbull but were unable to dislodge him he being advantageously posted.

30. Henry Rea, Federal pension application W9246.

Statement by Henry Rea dated 16 October 1832:

In 1780 [he] volunteered in scouting parties to suppress the tories, sometimes under Capt. [James] Jamieson, and sometimes under Capt. [Jacob] Barnet, and sometimes unofficered and continued in this Service about Eleven Months. During this Eleven months tour we went to North Carolina and while there served under Coln. Lock against the tories in the forks of the Yadkin, and from thence to Ramsour's under Capt. Jamieson of South Carolina.

Then volunteered and joined General Sumpter at Hagler's Branch. Thence sent in a detachment under Coln. Bratton against Capt. Hook on Fishing Creek. The next Battle was under General Sumpter at the Hanging Rock.

31. Joseph Robinson, Federal pension application W10246.

Statement by James G. Robinson, son of Joseph Robinson deceased, dated 24 December 1846:

> *His next tour of service was in 1780, after the Fall of Charleston as a private & Lieutenant in Capt. John McCools company Genl. Sumpters Brigade, as a volunteer & served until the end of the war; but the particulars of his service he is unable to give. He was in the following Battles viz. at the Battle of Briar Creek in the state of Georgia where he was slightly wounded & our forces were defeated—Also at the Battles of Hanging Rock, Fish Dam Ford, Blackstock & Hooks defeat, in the state of South Carolina—and in 1781 he was at the battle of Eutaw Springs.*

32. William Robison, Federal pension application S21452.

Statement by William Robison dated 25 March 1833:

> *In June 1780 he volunteered and served as a Lieutenant under Capt. [James] Jamieson & Col. [Francis] Lock and went on an expedition against the Tories in North Carolina in the forks of the Yadkin river and at Ramsours. He joined General Sumpter at Hagglars Branch N. C. crossed the Catawba river and defeated the British under Capt. Hook at Williamsons. Went to Rocky Mount and attacked the British under Col. Turnbull without success— recrossed the Catawba and defeated the British and Tories at the Battle of Hanging Rock.*

33. George Ross, Federal pension application S1717.

Statement by George Ross dated 14 November 1832:

> *He was first drafted in the militia of the State of South Carolina in the District now called York District under the command of Col. Andrew Neel first Colonel & William Bratton Lieut. Colonel, John Moffet Maj. & in Captain John Millar's Company and that he went into Service under the above named officers sometime in the Summer of the year 1780 and continued in service until Colonel Andrew Neel was killed at Rocky mount battle and after that he served under Col. Wm. Bratton first Colonel and John Moffet Lieut. Col. & Major Hawthorn & in Capt. John Millar's Company & continued until Cap. John Millar was killed at the Battle of Hanging Rock then continued untill the End of the war under the Command of the last mentioned field officers & Captain John Peters Company untill the End of the revolution...that during his Service he was in the following Engagements (to wit) first at the Battle at Col. Bratton's when Cap. Hook was defeated Second at the Battle of Rocky Mount when Col. Andrew Neel was killed Third at the Battle of Hanging Rock where Cap. John Millar was killed.*

34. David Sadler, Federal pension application S9471.

Statement by David Sadler dated 6 March 1833:

> When he was sixteen years and four months old [he] was drafted to serve his country in support of American Independence and under Lieutenant Hemphill marched to the neighborhood of Bacon's Bridge, forces commanded by Gen[l]. Williamson.[024] Recollects that the Picket was attacked the night after he got into camp and that they were out for some time but cannot recollect how long, thinks three months. Second tour went off in quest of British in the direction of Stono—was sick at the battle though in the immediate neighborhood. He was again in a battle at Mobley's Meeting House commanded probably by Col. Neil, and near Col. Bratton fought the Tories who were commanded by Hook and who was killed, the American forces commanded by Bratton & Neil as Colonels. Having served these two tours which he thinks consisted of three months each he joined as a volunteer one Capt. [Hugh] McClure with whom he served two tours of two months and three months but does not recollect very distinctly what they done nor where they went to being but a boy & going where he was ordered.

35. James Stephenson, Federal pension application W596.

Statement by Rosanna Stephenson, wife of James Stephenson deceased, dated 26 August 1839:

> James Stephenson, her husband, enlisted in the Army of the United States as a Sargeant in the Company commanded by Captain Lacey, in the year and month not recollected, in York County [South] Carolina and served under the following named officers General Sumpter, General Washington, Col. Bratton & Lacy, said James Stephenson was in the battles at Brandywine, Cow Pens, Eutaw Springs, Hanging Rock & perhaps others. Said James Stephenson was in the army a sargeant at the close of the war and rendered many meritorious services during the war, he always thought he was the man who killed a celebrated Tory by the name of Hook, the number of the Regiment & the line affiant cannot now recollect, that he was more than two years as a Continental soldier, where he enlisted for & during the war, besides was a considerable time with the volunteers & militia of South Carolina before he enlisted a Continental soldier. That affiant and the said James Stephenson were married in the County of York and the state of South Carolina shortly after the close of the war, she thinks as well as she can now recollect they were married in the month of June 1784.

Supporting statement by William A. Stephenson, son of James Stephenson deceased, dated 26 August 1839:

> He is the son of the said James Stephenson dec[d]. & the foregoing applicant Rosanna Stephenson, that he has often in the life time of the said James Stephenson heard him recount & state to various persons his services in the war of the Revolution, that he was a Sargeant in Capt.

Lacy's Company & enlisted in York County South Carolina, for & during the war and was more than two whole years in actual service and was a sargeant & in service at the close of the war. Affiant has often heard his Father speak of being in the battles of Brandywine, Euta Springs, Cow Pens, hanging rock, & other battles & skirmishes with the Tories and Brittish, and repeatedly heard him say that he believed that his shot killed a celebrated Tory by the name of Hook. Affiant has often seen the discharge that the said James Stephenson received after the close of the war, he remembers it was a discharge to his said Father as a Sargeant in the Continental Army after the close of the war and was assigned by Genl. Sumpter as well as he can now recollect.

36. John Wallace, Federal pension application W 955.

Statement by Sarah Wallace Locke, wife of John Wallace deceased, dated 24 November 1838:

She is a widow of John Wallace deceased, who was a Major in the Revolutionary War...He was in the battle at the Cowpens, at Briar Creek in Georgia, at Ramsours, at Gates defeat near Camden, at the Skirmish with Captain Hook in York County, at one time while Major Wallace was in the service and making a forced march with his troops, he met in the night a tory & not knowing who he was asked "who was there?", the tory replied "friend." "Friend to whom?" asked Major Wallace, "Friend to King George", said the tory with an oath, upon which Maj. Wallace shot him down. Declarant remembers that he was at the Battle of the Eutaw Springs and a skirmish at Fishing Creek in York County [probably Stallions' or Stallings' Plantation]. This last was with the Tories. He served as Major in all these engagements, as declarant has been often informed by her husband. She has often seen his commission as Major & she thinks, as adjutant.

Supporting statement by Samuel Killough dated 20 November 1838:

At harvest time 1777, or 1778 [1780] Captain Hook a British officer, having under his command a number of British troops, came into York County South Carolina & made proclamation that all who would come to him to take protection should have Leave to remain at home. By this means he had gathered around him some two or three hundred Tories. The Whigs of York being somewhat terrified at this force retired to North Carolina in Mecklenburg county. They got a reinforcement, and under the command of Maj. John Wallace marched to the number of some four hundred men against Captain Hook. Between day light and sun rise, this deponent & some others, who were going out to reap, heard the guns firing, and shortly after heard that Maj. Wallace and command, had come suddenly upon Capt. Hook, when not expected, and after killing & wounding some (Captain Hook being one of the killed) took the whole group of British & Tories prisoners. Deponent arrived on the ground in two hours after the battle, and saw the troops & prisoners there. Maj. Wallace was a faithful soldier, & served from the breaking out of the war in South Carolina till it ended. He was constantly in service being seldom at home for more than a day or two at a time. The war was always hot in York County, so that a Whig was safer in camp than at home.

37. Samuel Wallace, Federal pension application W6408.

Statement by Samuel Wallace dated 13 February 1834:

> *He enlisted in the army of the United States in the year 1778 about the middle of June say 15th of that month with Capt. Thomas Brown & in the 40th Regiment of the ___ line under the following named officers—*
>
> *Applicant enlisted as a regular soldier a common private for five years at the time above stated under Capt. Thomas Brown in Col. or Genl. Sumpters army or Regiment. He enlisted in York County South Carolina, was in a battle called Hooks defeat on the waters of Fishing creek a water of Kattawba river in South Carolina he is not entirely certain but thinks this engagement was with a part of Cornwallaces army, date of the battle not recollected. From Fishing creek he was marched on to the state of Georgia to a place called Mt. Pelier where we built a station on the Ocona [Oconee] river.*
>
> *Applicant remembers that their muskets were branded with the No. 40 which he was informed was for the No. of the Regiment to which he belonged if his memory is correct as to that point.[625]*

Supporting statement by Clairborne Gentry dated 4 November 1833:

> *In the year 1780 then a citizen of Stokes County N. Carolina[626] he volunteered in the service of the United States under Col. Martin Armstrong & was marched from N. Carolina to South Carolina & joined Genl. Sumpter's army in York County in said State. Affiant was at the battle of Hooks defeat and about five months before that battle he became acquainted with Samuel Wallace the present applicant for a pension...he formed his acquaintance with him in the army when they were soldiers together & were together in the battle of Hooks defeat...Witness volunteered for nine months & after the battle of Hooks defeat his time was out & he was discharged & went home.*

Supporting statement by William Maxwell dated 11 February 1834:

> *In the latter part of the year 1779 or fore part of the year 1780 affiant was a citizen of Mecklingburg County North Carolina...and under Captain William Alexander called Black Bill Alexander marched from York County South Carolina the adjoining county to Mecklingburg in North Carolina...General Rutherford of Ro[w]an County N. C. was our general and General Lincoln had the full command at Charles Town during the time I was stationed in and about that place during the time I was their I was frequently sent out in scouting parties while a soldier at that time in Charles Town I formed an acquaintance with the said Samuel Wallis who was from York County South Carolina then at Charles*

Town a private soldier in the Regular Army of the United States...after my term of service was out I was discharged and left said Wallis then at Charles Town with the army. After this their was another call for me to go to South Carolina I again inlisted rather as it was called volunteered for another tour and marched under my olde Captain Alexander. He was sick part of the first tour and did not command me the whole time we marched from North Carolina joined the Regular Army as well as I can now recollect near Whites Mill on Fishing Creek South Carolina where I again saw my friend and acquaintance Samuel Wallis still a Brave soldier in the Regular Army not long after we joined the Regular Army we was both in the Battle called Hooks Defeat in South Carolina from Hooks Defeat we marched to a place called the Poor Hill.

38. Samuel Watson Jr., Federal pension application S17187.

Statement by Samuel Watson Jr. dated 27 September 1832:

In the year 1777 he entered the service of his country as a volunteer in Col. Brattan's regiment of militia under Genl. Sumter for the term of one year or upwards and from the end of that period he served different officers in Genl. Green's army sometimes as an officer but principally as an private still as a volunteer under the command of militia officers and found his own horse and accoutrements untill the end of the war....[I]n the month of March as he now thinks in the year 1777 [1780] in said district of York in South Carolina he again enrolled himself as a private in a company of volunteers commanded by Capt. John Moffitt the company was attached to the regiment commanded by Col. Brattan those troops were horsemen or mounted troops and were marched from York District to a place called Rocky mount with a view to rout a part of British and Tories assembled at that place. At that place he was engaged in a battle at which time the troops under command of Col. Brattan was defeated by the British and Tories. During the engagement Lieutenant Colonel Neall was killed and another officer belonging to Brattan's regiment by the name of [Captain Robert] Leaper was mortally wounded with several privates. As soon after the engagement as the troops collected together Col. Brattan directed Capt. Moffitt to raise as many volunteers as he could with a view specially to rout a gang of tories assembled in the neighborhood of Kings Mountain. He went with Capt. Moffitt in that forlorn hope. When they had reached the neighborhood of the tories not being on their guard were surprised by them and a considerable engagement ensued in which he had his horse shot down from under him they succeeded however in putting the Tories to flight and pursued them to an almost impenetrable cane brake and left them and immediately returned to the balance of the troops with Col. Brattan who were then encamped on a creek he thinks called Clams Creek [Clem's Branch]. At this place there had assembled a good many volunteers some from Georgia who were commonly called refugees. This place was selected as a place of greater safety from the Tories than any other known at the time and the place from which several important sorties were made during those times. In a short time he does not remember how long, the troops under command of Col. Brattan the company of Capt. Moffitt among them crossed over the Catawba River leaving a number of troops at Clam's Creek and marched a distance of twenty *eight or thirty miles in the dead of night and early next morning had an engagement with a party of British and Tories under command of a British officer whose name was Hook, and defeated them. This engagement was called Hook's defeat and he thinks Hook was killed and several others also among them a Tory Col. whose name was Cunningham* [actually James Ferguson]. *He further says that not long after this period the precise time he cannot recollect, Capt. Moffitt's company he among them joined Gen. Sumpter and remained with Sumpter a long time doing and performing many services for his country against the British and Tories.*

Supporting statement by James McElwee dated 27 September 1832:

I the said James McElwee do hereby further certify that the said Samuel Watson was a soldier in the same company in the year 1776 to which I was attached the company commanded by Capt. W[m]. *Byers when company belonged to Col. Neel's regiment....That he the said Watson belonged to the same company towit Capt. Moffet's company of militia and were engaged together in a battle fought with a Capt. Hook where Hook was defeated, and I further certify from my own personal knowledge of services rendered by said Watson that in the days of the revolutionary struggle the times when all men were required to take part the said Sam*[l]. *Watson was ever ready to serve his country and do his duty.*

39. Thomas Woods, Federal pension application S32614.

Statement by Thomas Woods dated 22 October 1832:

Again after the capture of Charleston in South Carolina, in 1780, under the command of Cap[t]. *Andrew Neil and Col*[l]. *Thomas Sumpter, as a volunteer horseman, for a term of between four & five months, in which time I was at the defeat of Cap*[t]. *Huck of Tarleton's dragoons at Williamson's Lane, in York District, S.C. & again at the battle of Rocky Mount, & again at the battle of Hanging Rock.*

Additional statement by Thomas Woods dated 9 December 1833:

In 1780 Charleston fell, I fell in as a volunteer under Andrew Neile, as a horseman for four months, who acted as a Colonel under Sumpter and was present when we defeated and killed Cap[n]. *Hook of the British Dragoons in Williamson's lane. I was at the battle of Rocky Mount and Hanging Rock and many skirmishes with the Tories.*

40. Francis Wylie, Federal pension application S21592.

Statement by Francis Wylie dated 8 October 1834:

In the year 1780 [he] *marched under Capt. McClure* [and] *Col. Lacey to a place called Mobleys Meeting House where they routed a party of Torys, then under same Capt.*

McClure, Col. Lacey, Col. Bratton & Col. Hawthorne surprised a party of British & torys at Williamson's plantation when Capt. Hook was killed; then under said Capt. McClure, Col. Lacey, Col. Neal [and] Gen'. Sumpter marched to & was at the Battle of Rocky Mount & when Col. Neal was killed then under same officers marched & was at the Battle of Hanging Rock when his Capt. McClure was killed.

Supporting statement by Joseph Gaston dated 25 October 1834:

When the last visage of armed force in SC were destroyed by Tarleton's massacre of Col. Buford's men in Lancaster District in this state about May 1ˢᵗ [29ᵗʰ] 1780, this applicant [Francis Wylie] was one of the veteran band of thirty two volunteers who joined Captain John McClure a few days afterward, and routed the Tories at Beckhamville and Mobley's meetinghouse and never grounded their arms until their state was recovered from the Enemy.

Appendix B

British Army correspondence June–July 1780

The collected correspondence of Lieutenant General Charles, Earl Cornwallis is an important primary source for information on the Revolutionary War in South Carolina. Much of this correspondence deals directly with events in the South Carolina Backcountry. Of particular interest to the history of the Revolution in the upper districts of South Carolina are letters written by two of Cornwallis's field officers, Lieutenant Colonel Francis, Lord Rawdon and Lieutenant Colonel George Turnbull. Lord Rawdon was in charge of the British garrison at Camden, South Carolina, and was overall commander of British forces in the Camden and Cheraw Districts, while Lieutenant Colonel Turnbull commanded the important British outpost at Rocky Mount, located at the confluence of Rocky Creek and the Catawba River in present-day Fairfield County, South Carolina. These letters give a detailed picture of the events in the South Carolina Backcountry during this crucial period in the summer of 1780 and include firsthand descriptions of the British attempts to pacify the "bounty Irish" in the Broad and Catawba River basins. They also reveal the British perspective on such local actions as the raid on Fishing Creek Church in what is now Chester County (11 June 1780) and the Battle of Williamson's Plantation, or Huck's Defeat, in what is now York County (12 July 1780). Equally interesting are the personal opinions and viewpoints expressed by two British officers who found the South Carolina Backcountry to be "the worst spot in the country" and to whom the local inhabitants seemed to be "the Skum of the Creation, without sense or reason." The verbatim transcriptions published here are all taken from a microfilm copy of the Cornwallis Papers located in the South Carolina Department of Archives and History in Columbia, South Carolina. The originals are in The National Archives of Great Britain, Public Record Office, Kew, Surrey, England, and are transcribed here with the permission of that agency.

1. Lieutenant Colonel Francis Lord Rawdon to Lieutenant General Charles Earl Cornwallis, 11 June 1780 (PRO 30/11/2/123–125):

> *Leslie's House, Waxhaw*[627]
> *June 11ᵗʰ 1780*

My Lord

I have the honor to report to your Lordship that I arrived at this Settlement yesterday; & have fixed my Camp in a spot the most centreal within the District. Being met by a number of the people, I required that they should appoint among themselves a certain number of the principal Inhabitants with whom I might transact all business. This Committee has been with me today & they professed the warmest desire to live under the British Government, I strongly recommended them to take up arms for their own defence. But this they declined, wishing rather to be considered as Prisoners. I believe in this instance, the sound of the word Parole, decided their judgement; for with a very curious & nice distinction they impressed their desire that their arms might be left with them, & that they might be empowered to use them against the Rebel Militia of Mecklenburg County, in case the latter should make inroads into the district. To this request they did not find me inflexible. I am very sure that if they were convinced any other district in the Province had arranged a Militia, they would immediately follow the example; but they fear to take a step which they imagine others have refused. I think it would be very expedient that M^r. Rugeley[628] (if he can be spared) should come hither before I quit the place. The idea of an administration of Justice by a Conservator of the Peace is very pleasing to them; & I think M^r. Rugeley may induce them to stand forth in support of that regularity.

They are apprehensive here, that they shall be troubled by the North Carolina Militia & by the Catawba Indians. Many people have quitted Charlotteburg, & retired in arms to the pass in the Mountains near Salisbury. To induce them to behave peaceably, I have sent them an address, a copy of which is enclosed. I have taken the liberty of mentioning your Lordships name in it, but it was on a point which I knew to be accordant with your sentiments. I took this step principally on account of a number of People who came in to me from N. Carolina, & who on account of their families, cannot well remain with the army till it should penetrate thither. I have recommended to them to remain quietly at home for the present; & they think my Paper may secure them from molestation. The Catawba Indians have retired into North Carolina with their families, & every thing which they could carry away. Lest they should be troublesome by coming down to Camden for support, I have empowered the Committee here to assure them that if they return to their settlement & behave quietly, they shall receive protection; but that if they commit any act of hostility, their settlement shall be utterly destroyed. As they have good crops on the ground, & fled from an apprehension that a body of Cherokees were advancing with some detachment of our troops, I dare say they will return. I do not see that by prolonging my stay here any advantage can accrue; nor do I at present observe any point to be gained by advancing further.

Therefore if anything particular happens, or if I do not receive your Lordships orders to the contrary, I shall in three or four days set out for Camden. The country tho' thickly settled is poor in itself, & much drained. I am regularly supplied with Cattle; tho' even in that article they plead poverty; but the neighborhood is totally destitute of grain or any kind of Dry Forage. I send Five Waggons tomorrow for a reinforcement of Provisions; upon which head I have written to Capt. Ross.[629] I have this day written to L^t. Colonel Turnbull. The Inhabitants here insist that the Party which attacked Leonard & his Companions[630] were not disaffected to the king; & only *defended their property against the unwarranted depredations of a set of those who have long lived in a loose manner. They wish much that Evidence should be heard upon it.*

I have the Honor to be My Lord
With sincere respect & affection
Your very faithful Serv
Rawdon
Colonel Vol. of Ireland

Earl Cornwallis
&c &c &c

2. Lord Rawdon's enclosure to Lord Cornwallis—a copy of his proclamation to the people of Charlotte dated 11 June 1780 (PRO 30/11/2/127–128):

To the Inhabitants of Charlotteburg. N. Carolina

Being informed that many of the Inhabitants of Charlotteburg & its neighborhood have deserted their Plantations thro' apprehension of suffering for their late association; I think it necessary to give them the following instruction.

It is the generous wish of Lieut. General Earl Cornwallis to reclaim rather than to subdue the Country; to incline the Inhabitants to Peace by giving them time & encouragement to consider their own interest, rather than to make them sigh for it from suffering the Scourges of War.

In obedience to the Instructions which I have received from his Lordship, I do earnestly recommend to the Inhabitants of the District above mentioned, to return immediately to their Farms; where they shall gather their Crops without Fear or Interruption: Provided always that they do demean themselves peacefully, & do not attempt to distress either in person or property any Friend to Government within their own or in the neighboring settlements.

After this warning, should any Person be unadvised enough to foment further disturbance in the Country, or to instigate his neighbors to a ruinous & unavailing show of opposition, to him alone must be charged the Severities which such misconduct may draw upon the District.

Given at Waxhaw, this Eleventh of June 1780
Rawdon

3. Lieutenant Colonel George Turnbull to Lord Charles Cornwallis, 12 June 1780 (PRO 30/11/2/147–148):

My Lord

In Answer to your Lordships Proposal of joining Three Carolina Independent Companies to the New York Volunteers—

I hope you will be well assured that my zeal and attachment for His Majestys Service will never be awanting to forward His Interest.

If your Lordship will do me the Honor to put any number of Companies under my Command I will do my Utmost to Discipline them and give them every assistance in my Power. But I do imagine it wou[l]d not answer to Enroll such People in a Corps with ours who are High Disciplined and not Indulged with the same Conditions.

I do Flatter myself when this Province is Quieted that your Lordship will Espouse our cause by Taking our case into consideration and if the Service Permitts to send us to our own Province, where we not only wou[l]d have an Opportunity of Compleating the Corps But our Services in a Place where we are known must Exceed that of Strangers.

When I speak of that matter how it affects me Personally I Really have Scarce words to Express it. There is Surely a Duty which a man owes His Family and if I see no Relief after Settling the Peace and Quiet of this Province I shall be Drove to the Disagreable Necessity to Quit the Service Intirely.

Forgive me the Expression it may be Improper Language for an Officer on Duty—But I have already Declared that I will see this Service out, and the Peace of the Province Established. I Do Venture to say your Lordship will have Compassion for one in my Situation. I am with the Greatest Respect

Your Lordships
most obedient and
most humble Servant
Geo: Turnbull
Rocky Mount June 12ᵗʰ 1780

The Right Honbl Lord Cornwallis

4. Lieutenant Colonel Turnbull to Lord Cornwallis, 15 June 1780 (PRO 30/11/2/158–159):

My Lord.

Captain Hook and His Party Returned yesterday having made a circular Tour of about Forty miles to the Westward. The Rebells who were Embodyed Fled so fast to the Mountains that He could not come up with them. From information that some of them had Taken Post at Simson's meeting, He surrounded the house and finding them gone, But in Recoinoitring the Road which Led to it, Two men with Rebell Uniforms were Discovered running through a field of Wheat. The Militia fired upon them, Killed one and Wounded the other.

Cols. Patten, Bratten, Wynn[631] and Number of Violent People have abandoned their Habitations it is believed they are gone amongst the Cataba Indians and some say that the Indians Likewise have Retired further Back.

The Rebells have Propagated a story that we Seize all their young men and send them to the Prince of Hesse, it is inconceivable the Damage such Reports has done.

Corn Begins to be Scarce. I have now about ten Days meal But when that is out I Don't know which Rout to take.

There is an Irish settlement at Turkey and Bullock Creek which abounds with Provision but it is Thirty miles westward. I do believe those fellows wou[l]d be much the Better for some Troops to keep them in order for a Little, they have become very Violent.

It is Difficult to Support Dragoons without Corn. I am in hopes if our own mounted men arrive and the Militia continue their good Countenance when they meet here against Saturday, that in such case we might spare the Legion altogether if your Lordship has any Service for them.

I forgot to mention an Iron works about Fifty miles to the westward, it has been a Refuge for Runnaways, a Forge for casting Ball and making Rifle Guns &c. I wou[l]d Propose with your Lordships permission to Destroy this Place. I think a small Party might be found against Saturday at the muster that wou[l]d Compleat this affair. Sending some of our own officers and men with them.

I have given no Receipts for any Provisions as yet. But I fancy it will be necessary on some Occasion to give Receipts.

While I am waiting I have Received a Letter from Lord Rawden Dated yesterday. He mentions that He is about Returning to Camden and that there is a Body of Rebell Militia still in arms Between Charlottburg and Salisbury but as He has no Dragoons or mounted men, He says He has no chance of giving them a blow. I Flatter myself your Lordship will see the Necessity of Dispersing those men for while such a Body of Rebells keep in arms so near us our Militia affairs will not go well.

I have appointed one Capt. of Militia at Cedar Creek until your Lordships Pleasure is further known. Indeed He was the Choice of the People and I thought him Deserving.

I shall Endeavor to make some arrangement on Saturday forenoon when I Expect them all at Rocky mount. But am much afraid I will not be able to get any body fit to make a Field officer. I have the Honor to be with the Greatest Esteem and Respect

> *Your Lordships*
> *most obedient and*
> *most Humble Servant*
> *Geo: Turnbull*
> *Rocky mount Jun. 15th 1780*

The Right Honb^l. Lord Cornwallis

5. Lord Cornwallis to Lieutenant Colonel Turnbull, 16 June 1780 (PRO 30/11/77/11–12):

> *Camden 16 June 1780*

Sir

I have just received your Letter and am sorry to find that Meal grows scarce already, I shall send you some Salt & Rum, & your Cavalry & Infantry as soon as they arrive. I should then advise your going to the Irish Settlement you mention, & staying there as long as you find it convenient & bringing back some Meal to your present Post. If the Horses of the Legion suffer for want of Corn, I wish you would send back immediately some of the best of them, & the remainder as soon as your people join you. I likewise approve of your destroying the Iron work & beg you will take upon yourself to act in all those Matters as it shall appear to you to be best for the King's Service. You will give permission to the Militia to do what they please with the Plantations abandoned by the Rebels. If they can get in the Crops & turn them to their own use, it will be the best Plan, but if it is more convenient now & then to destroy one I have no objection, only I strictly forbid & will severely punish any act of cruelty to their wives & children. You are to give receipts for provisions to all Friends, & I would have you take the utmost pains to settle a Militia & if possible to appoint a Major Commandant to each District where the Enemy had a Field Officer, a very plain Man with a good Character & tolerable Understanding will do, He is to act more in a civil than a Military Character, & as we are not at present troubled with Law, all that is required of him is to have sense enough to know right from wrong, & honesty enough to prefer the former to the latter. I send you a form of a Commission which you may sign & deliver to the Field Officer till I can have an opportunity of sending one. I do not apprehend any great danger from the Enemy's Militia which you mention said to be posted between Charlotte & Salisbury; they are above an hundred miles from us & would certainly retire on our approach & the Country between us & them is a perfect desart. I think whilst we keep, which I promise to do, a strong Post at this Place with a large Body of Cavalry, the Militia on this Frontier of S. Carolina need not fear being properly supported. I wish you would endeavour to explain this to them, & to instill as much confidence as possible into them.

I am Sir,
Your most obedient
& most humble Serv.
[Cornwallis]

I inclose you two late Proclamations, they do not materially affect my Plan, only those who have not served in the Army or Militia or acted as Magistrates, will be released form their Paroles on the 20th of this Month accord. To S. Henry's Proclamation of the 3rd of June.

6. Lieutenant Colonel Turnbull to Lord Cornwallis, 16 June 1780 (PRO 30/11/2/162–163):

My Lord.

Yesterday Afternoon I was favoured with a Visit from a M. [Matthew] Floyd who Lives about Sixty miles to the Westward. He appears to be a Sensible man and a Staunch Friend to Gov. Has been Persecuted and lain some time in Charlestown jail. He Brought about Thirty men with him all Volunteers to Serve the King.

I appointed His Son Cap[t]. of the Company as He was their choice and I thought I could not get so good a man to Command that upper District as Mr. Floyd so that I appointed him Col.

Our joy was very soon interrupted by a Couple of Expresses who assured us that a Party of Rebells had Sallyd forth from the Iron Works and had gone into the settlement of M[r]. Floyd and His Company and were tearing everything to Pieces.

I immediately Ordered Cap[t]. Hook of the Legion to get Ready, that with Cap[t]. Floyds Company and the other militia which we could assemble it was necessary to give these fellows a Check. The weather Prevented their Setting off last night. But they took the morning Early. I have taken the Liberty to give Cap[t]. Hook Orders to Destroy the Iron Works they are the Property of a M[r]. Hill a great Rebell. I hope the marching of this Party will do something towards Quieting our Frontier. Those Rebells Embodyd Between Charlotburg & Salisbury Over awes great part of the Country and Keeps the Candle of Rebellion still Burning. Lord Rawdens Retreat I dare Say Confirms them in the Belief that we are only here for a few days.[632]

I Confess my Lord I have no Particular attachment to any Part in South Carolina but I wou[l]d not wish to Leave the worst Spot in it untill the Neck of Rebellion was broke.

In my former Letter I mentioned to your Lordship that we had meal for about Ten or Twelve days, when that is done we shall be much at a Loss.

The Inhabitants are Constantly turning [to] me for Proclamations. I wish your Lordship would Send me some.

I meant tomorrow to have had a Gen[l]. muster of the Militia to arrange them in the best manner I could. This alarm will discompose it a good deal. I am with great Esteem

> *your Lordships*
> *most obedient and most*
> *Humble Servant*
> *Geo: Turnbull*
> *Rocky mount June 16th 1780*

> *The Right Honb[l]. Earl of Cornwallis*

7. Lieutenant Colonel Turnbull to Lord Cornwallis, 19 June 1780 (PRO 30/11/2/171–172):

My Lord

I have the Pleasure to Acquaint your Lordship that by a Letter from Capt. Huck of the British Legion Dated yesterday some miles this side of the Iron Works. That the Rebells were assembled at that Place about one hundred and fifty strong that He with his Detachment of the Legion and about Sixty militia attacked them. The Rebells had time to pull down a Bridge very near the Iron Works which Impeded them for some time. That Repairing the Bridge they were Lucky enough to overtake their Rear Killed seven and took four Prisoners the Rest Fled to the mountains.

I am Likewise to Inform your Lordship that Cap.[ ] Huck has Completely Destroyd the Iron works which has been the Head Quarters of the Rebells in arms for some time past.

I am taking every step to arrange the militia although my Progress is but slow as most of their former officers are Run off. I can't get people to warn them and bring them together yet I Expect in the course of this week to do a good deal—

I Beg Leave to put your Lordship in mind that when our Detachment passes We may not be forgot in the Articles of Rum and Salt.

Some more Arms, Cartridges, Flint and a Barrel of Powder are Likewise wanted.

A Cap.[ ] Henderson[633] was taken some days ago. He was a great persecutor and Expected to be hanged. Some of his friends told him that He shoud do something in favor of government to Intitle him to be Restored to favor. He proposed to Seize Gov.[ ] Rutledge and bring him a Prisoner. I told him if He Succeeded He shoud Be Handsomely Rewarded and have sent him of to try his luck. He assured me that Rutledge and Twigg from Georgia[634] were at a Widdow womans house near Salisbury about ten days ago and that His guard had left him.

Some times great Villains will do services at all Events. I thought it best to put it to the tryal. I have the

Honor to be with the greatest Respect and Esteem
your Lordships
most obedient and most
Humble Servant
Geo: Turnbull
Rocky mount June 19th 1780

The Right Honb.[ ] the Earl of Cornwallis

8. Lord Rawdon to Lord Cornwallis, 22 June 1780 (PRO 30/11/2/179–182):

Camden June 22.[d] 1780

My Lord

It grieves me that the first intelligence which I have reason to transmit to you should be of unpleasing tenor. M.[ ] Moore, in spite of your Lordships earnest advice & in contradiction to your express direction, has called forth the Loyalists in Tryon County.[635] The consequence was that early on the 20th Ins.[ ], the second day after their assembling, they were attacked near the South Fork of the Catawba River by General Rutherford, & entirely dispersed.[636] I received the intelligence this morning thro' L.[ ] Colonel Turnbull, who forwarded to me a person that had been in the engagement. This man says the number of the Loyalists was about Eight Hundred; & that of the Rebels was estimated about Six Hundred. He complains much of ill management on our side, & indeed, by his account, it seems to have been a sharpe business. He imagines the losses to have been exceedingly trifling on both sides; but says the Loyalists were completely scattered. L.[ ] Colonel Turnbull informs me that in consequence of this disaster, he was just going to march for Major Brown's,[637] where Cap[t]. Huck with the Dragoons lay; & he requests a reinforcement of Cavalry. The reason given for this step (which, as far as I can judge, I do not think adviseable) is, that the advantage on the part of the Rebels may shake the fidelity of our new-found Militia on the Borders, unless the troops are present to awe them to their duty. Brown's is five & thirty miles advanced from Rocky Mount. I should conceive L[t]. Colonel Turnbull would not have made the movement had he not been thoroughly convinced there was no risk in it, &, as I am unacquainted with the circumstances of that district, I repose myself on his prudence. I have, however, very fully signified my doubts to him: and, lest this accident should encourage any turbulence, instead of sending twenty Dragoons as L[t]. Colonel Turnbull requested, I have detached Cap[t]. Kinlock with Sixty of the Cavalry[638] to visit that District, & to return immediately if he sees no cause of apprehension. If he thinks the Post stranded, he is to prevail upon Turnbull to fall back. As I had some Arms & Ammunition to send to Rocky Mount, I have detached an escort of one hundred Men under Major Carden,[639] with it. They are to meet L[t]. Colonel Turnbull's directions at that place; &, according to them, are either to join him should he find it necessary, or to return immediately. I thought that if no more actual purpose was to be effected by this movement, a report of the March of troops might probably fix any wavering spirits. The Proclamation strikes hard at us now, for these frontier districts who were before secured under the bond of Paroles, are now at liberty to take any steps which a turn of fortune might advise. However, from the present disaster I foresee no consequences; unless that it may possibly tempt some of the Rebel Militia within Kinlock's reach. The Detachment of the 71st Regt. which was at Rocky Mount, arrived here this day; the party belonging to the New York Volunteers having rejoined their Corps. The 2[d]. Battalion of the 71st marches in the course of this night to reinforce Major McArthur.[640] As the Inhabitants of Waxhaw still endeavor to temporize, I have bidden Major Rugeley to instruct them to take up arms immediately, under his Majesty's Standard. If they hesitate, he is directed to require that they shall surrender all their Arms & Ammunition; demanding military execution against any person who shall presume to secrete either.

I have just received a quantity of Bacon & Flour with some Rum, belonging to Colonel Kershaw,[641] at a House about ten miles off. We narrowly missed a box containing a very large quantity of Gold. Kershaw unfortunately saw the Man who gave me the intelligence; & suspecting the matter, sent for his Box; which was brought hither safely to him, before the Commissary of Captures arrived at the hoard. I shall not fail to give your Lordship the earliest information respecting the event of that affair in Tryon County. In the mean time I have the Honor to profess myself, My Lord,

Your most obed[t].
& affect[t]. Humble Serv[t].
Rawdon

Earl Cornwallis
&c &c &c

9. Lord Rawdon to Lord Cornwallis, 24 June 1780 (PRO 30/11/2/189–190):

Camden, June 24th 1780

My Lord

I have just received the fullest account of the misfortune in Tryon County, concerning which I had the Honor of writing to you yesterday. For Colonel Moore, who commanded the party, has arrived here. He says that he had collected about Eight Hundred Men. The Rebels had nearly a thousand; two hundred of which were Continentals. The Loyalists were badly armed; & had little ammunition so that they retired after a very slight action. Colonel Moore thinks that between twenty & thirty were killed or wounded; & he believes that an hundred & fifty may have been made Prisoners. The rest separated & fled; they were not pursued, so that Moore thinks most of them will join L. *Colonel Turnbull. Colonel [Matthew] Floyd was at Brown's; & told Moore that our Militia were turning out with great spirit. The affair, I fancy, must necessarily stop here, for neither party could trust to the Country for provisions on a march. Colonel Moore says that he embodied those unfortunate people at the express instance of Major Walsh,*[642] *& rather in contradiction to his own opinion. By this account, Major Walsh appears to have acted diametrically opposite to his instructions. He has escaped, & is hourly expected here. It should be observed, that they assembled on the 18*th*; altho' their plan, had your Lordship approved it, was not to have risen till the 24*th*. So that they did not wait to have your final sentiments.*

I have the Honor to be
My Lord, with great respect
& affection
Your very faithful serv.
Rawdon

Earl Cornwallis
&c &c &c &c

10. Lord Cornwallis to Lord Rawdon, 29 June 1780 (PRO 30/11/77/18–19):

Charlestown 29 June 1780

My dear Lord

The affair of Tryon County has given me great concern, altho' I had my apprehensions that the Flame would break out somewhere, the Folly & Imprudence of our friends is unpardonable.

I desire you will inform L[t]. Col[l]. Hamilton[643] that I wish him to come to town immediately, & would have him acquaint his Officers before he leaves the Reg[t]. that if I hear of any more instances of Irregularity about recruiting or disobedience of Orders that I will put the Reg[t]. into Garrison on Sullivan's Island. I likewise desire that you will examine Maj[r]. Walsh very strictly as to what passed between him & Col[l]. Moore, you will likewise please to inform yourself whether Cap[t]. M[c]Neal[644] of that Corps went without leave into North Carolina & if he did, you will send him up to me to answer for his conduct. You will please to order Maj[r]. Doyle[645] to examine all recruits, that are brought to any of the provincial Corps, & if it appears that any of them are Rebel Prisoners, they must be sent to [Charles]town escorted by an Officer & Party of the Corps which has inlisted them, & you will report to me the name of the Officer by whom they were inlisted.

I approve perfectly of everything you have done relative to L[t]. Col[l]. Turnbull's March & the Detachment you have made. I think I mentioned to you that it will be proper to give higher rank to the Majors of Militia as soon as proper persons are found to succeed them as Majors, perhaps you need not wait even for that, as the being Col. will help to give them Authority.

You will please to give orders to all the Districts with which you have any communication to continue to send on parole to the Islands all those who come under the description of my Order.

There is nothing new, they talk of several Actions in the West Indies, but none decisive. I have received from my Brother a very pleasing & satisfactory account of his Engagement with La Motte Piequet.

I am My dear Lord
Most sincerely Your's
[Cornwallis]

R[t]. Honble Lord Rawdon.

11. Lieutenant Colonel Turnbull to Lord Cornwallis, 6 July 1780 (PRO 30/11/2/250–251):

My Lord

The last time I had the Honor of writing your Lordship our affairs in this Quarter were in a very Prosperous way and had it not been for that Weak Silly man Moore who led a Parcell of those poor Innocent Devils of North Carolina into a Scrape, we shoud have been now in Perfect Peace and Quietness on this Frontier.

Moores Defeat made me march some days sooner than I intended up amongst my good Friends the Bounty Irish. I wish I coud say something in their favor. I Believe them to be the worst of the Creation – and Nothing will Bring them to Reason but Severity. Numbers had left their Plantations and severall have Run of[f] since I was amongst them after Submitting and Embodying.

Cap[t]. Kinlock Brought a Reinforcement of the Legion to Major Browns Cross Roads where I was Encamped. I added a Pretty Large Body of Militia and mounted men of our

Reg^t. which made a Respectable Detachment.^{646} – and in order that Kinlock should have a full Scope I Did not Tye him Down by Written Orders. He marched about Twelve miles and Received Some intelligence which I found afterwards was none of the Best. Viz. that the Rebells Were Thirteen Hundred strong and that they were at a Great Distance. He Returned and Complaind so much of the heat of the weather and the Tiredness of their Horses that I let him go down and sent home the militia to Reap their Crops which was losing for want of Reapers. – They were not Two days gone when the Rebells Begun to be Saucey and Encamped on the East Side the Cataba River about four miles from the old Nation Ford to the amount of about six Hundred Commd^d. by Col. Sumpter – and threatened Death and Destruction to us all. I conceived they wanted that I shoud move Back to Rocky mount and Indeed they Effected it by Sending a party of Forty men down as low as George Wades Mill on the East Side the River Within ten miles of Rocky mount which number was given me to the Amount of Five Hundred.

I now find Major Mecan^{647} has marched against them and if He will only Remain as long at the Waxhaws as I have done here, I Really Believe we shoud feel the good Effects of it thou[gh] Mecklenburgh, Ro[w]an, and my Friends the Irish above are perhaps the Greatest Skum of the Creation.^{648} English Sanity is thrown away when there is not Virtue to meet it half way. If some of them Could be Catched who have submitted and Run off and joind the Rebells an Example on the Spot of immediate Death and Confiscation of Property might perhaps make them submit.

I am now to thank your Lordship for the attention you have had for this Little Corps in about a Couple of months they will be so Ragged that I shou[l]d be very happy that the service might Permitt our being moved to [Charles]Town. – I should then Embrace your Lordships Generous offer to make a short visit to M^{rs}. Turnbull and Either Bring her or Quit the Army. – The Bearer of this L^t. Peterson was appointed to Major Sheridans Company which is to be Raised.^{649} I now send him to his assistance. I am with much Esteem

your Lordships
most Faithfull Humbl Servt.
Geo: Turnbull
Rocky mount July 6th 1780

The Earl of Cornwallis

12. Lord Rawdon to Lord Cornwallis, 7 July 1780 (PRO 30/11/2/252–255):

Camden July 7th 1780

My Lord.

That unfortunate Proclamation of the 3rd of June has had very unfavourable consequences. The majority of the Inhabitants in the Frontier Districts, tho' ill Disposed to us, from circumstances were not actually in arms against us. They were therefore freed from the

Paroles imposed by Lt. Colonel Turnbull & myself; & nine out of ten of them are now embodied on the part of the Rebels. I must own that several likewise who were excepted from the indulgence have, not withstanding their Paroles, taken the same native part against us. Yet here again the Proclamation wounds us; for should any person in this predicament fall into our hands, his guilt, which before could not have been controversed, becomes matter of nice disquisition; & the punishment due to his crime, may by this representation furnish a pretext to the Rebels for exercising inhumanity upon some friend of ours in their hands. Perhaps, I ought not to question the expediency of that Proclamation; but I so immediately feel the effects of it that I may fairly be excused. The greater part of the Waxhaw people have joined the Rebels; the rest live under the Enemy's protection. The Irish Settlement on the West of the Catawba River has taken the same part. General Sumpter is encamped near the old Ford, in the Catawba Lands with from a thousand to fifteen hundred militia. Upon his assembling that force, & upon general symptoms of disaffection among the people around him Turnbull fell back to Rocky Mount, much to my satisfaction. By advancing in force, I could remove Sumpter immediately; but that alone is not a real object and the bare credit of making him retire cannot be put in competition with what I think I might argue by the move. He is sixty miles from us; so that I could not hope to make the march undiscovered. He would retire to Salisbury; & when I fell back to Camden as I should be obliged to do, he would retire to his post. The reason for my not being able to leave any considerable force in that Country is that I have not lately had any exact account of De Kalb.[650] My last intelligence was that stores were preparing for him in Salisbury. If he comes thither whilst a principal part of my Force is at Waxhaw, he has good [advantage to assemble?]. He may advance to Charlotteburg, as if intending to oppose my Detachment; which would not be equal to seek him there. Then he might strike suddenly into a cross road which leads by the heads of Brown's Creek into the Cheraw road, aiming at McArthur. Having thus two days march of me, he might rout that Corps before they could be sustained. This struck me some time ago, & in consequence I sent directions to McArthur, that as soon as he should hear of the arrival of De Kalb's Army at Salisbury, he should immediately fall back with his Infantry behind Black Creek, leaving only Light troops in the Pedee. Exclusive of the cross road from Charlotteburg, there is only one cut from the Waxhaw road; which makes a small slough to Linches Creek. But it is a rough and difficult track. Should the Enemy think of taking an offensive part, I imagine they would advance to Camden by two routes; the Waxhaw & the Brown's Creek roads, but there is an intermediate position by which you can cover both. The letters, which I have the honor to transmit, make De Kalb's force, when his parties are united, near Six Thousand Men; without including the Mecklenburgh & Rowan Militia. I should not think his numbers so great at present; but they will probably be completed to that amount when the Virginians are delivered from their fear of invasion. I am tampering with his Commissaries; & think I shall succeed. Lacey[651] is the only one of Capt. Ross's emissaries who has returned to me and given me any information. I fear the rest have been taken up. I have been making liberal offers of the Secret Service Money; but should your Lordship have to pay any of my Drafts in that line, I hope you will find that the object has been adequate to the expense. Mecan is stationed at Hanging Rock; & Kinlock with the Cavalry is to try if any thing can be done. I have bidden him try to purchase a Detachment of the Enemy from the Waxhaw people. Gold will, I think, outweigh the spirit of rebellion; tho' it is very strong in my old friends.[652] As I claim a particular interest in those Gentlemen, I wish your Lordship would let me forward as many of them as I can pick up, to the Commanding Officer of the Navy in Charleston. I think two hundred of my Countrymen would be admirably placed aboard your Brother's Squadron; & it would be the only chance that any one of them would ever have of doing a meritorious action. I am not without hope of drawing Sumpter forward a Day's march; in which case, I shall try to get at him. Upon that scale I should be confident enough; but I should be very much concerned were the parrying of more decisive covenants & rest upon my little experience. The post with which your Lordship has honored me is not an idle one at present, but the advance of an Enemy in force would make this a critical Command: For there is no position to maintain; & the station, tho' a most useful one, is awkwardly circumstanced. The want of communication between the roads leading from the town is a real difficulty. The Militia in a line with us, & those in our rear, seem not only well disposed, but very zealous: Many of them, however, want arms. Rugeley's Militia are embodied; & advanced with Kinlock; but Turner's have for the most part joined the Rebels.[653] I am apprehensive that your Lordship will find it necessary to move earlier than you professed. To advance upon the Enemy would be the surest stile of defense for this territory, if you did us the honor to observe it here, but it will be attended with more difficulty should the Enemy make a similar move first. I know your Lordship will excuse my stating my sentiments with such freedom; & I think it right to mention which opinion I favor from the course which I see affairs take in this quarter. I have sent Balfour[654] notice, that some Rebels in Georgia, are pressing Sumpter to advance to Ninety-Six; promising to join him with a number of men. There is one Levi Allen gone to Charlestown, upon a Parole & Pass from me. Since his departing I have learned that he is brother to Ethan Allen:[655] Perhaps your Lordship would cho[o]se to see him. I beg pardon for so long & so [condescending?] a letter; & have the honor to be most truly, your Lordships very affec[t] Servt

Rawdon

Earl Cornwallis &c ---

13. Lord Rawdon to Lord Cornwallis, 10 July 1780 (PRO 30/11/2/264–265):

Camden July 10[th] 1780

My Lord

I have the Honor to acknowledge the receipt of your letter of the 6th. Since I wrote by Lieu[t]. Peterson nothing particular has occurred. Mecan continues at Hanging Rock, in which situation I think him well placed on every account. He communicates pretty readily with Rocky Mount; he covers the Country from petty alarms; &, should I have occasion to support McArthur, his Infantry would lose little time by passing along the old path to Linches Creek which I mentioned in my last letter. It was not my design that Mecan's Detachment should have been posted for any length of time at Waxhaw. His business was to disarm such of the Inhabitants as did not enroll in the Militia; to collect grain which I proposed to store at Rugeley's Mills. By the time this service was performed, I designed that Bryan's followers,[656] with the Refugees from Tryon County should have been collected at Waxhaw & left there; with only a small detachment in their rear to have received them in case they should be pressed. Sumpter's Meeting his force on the Catawba Land prevented my scheme from taking place; for I did not think it of consequence enough to carry it through at the expense of any considerable movement. My last letter will show your Lordship that I feel all the necessity of being in force at Camden. And, if I loosened a step from it, it is not without measuring carefully what the Enemy could do in consequence. I think it both right and necessary to inform your Lordship of every minute change of appearance which circumstances wear. Altho' I sometimes fear to perplex you, at a time when I am too conscious of the complicated difficulties under which you labor, I cherish hopes that I may prevail on our friends to remain quiet till they are called upon. If that prospect deceives me, I must endeavor to facilitate their escape; & I will take care to feed them till your Lordship's arrival.

Of this at least, My Lord, be convinced that, doubting my own judgement, I shall not easily be induced to risque any thing which can have extensive consequences. But should I by circumstance find myself necessitated to act, I hope it will be in such a manner as will prove to you that I have well weighed what may happen, & have beforehand considered what steps would be expedient under any probable event. If I can flatter myself that by zealous attention I may relieve your Lordship in any trifling degree under the variety of cares which must arise from your present disjointed Command; & if I can prove to you that I am anxious to fulfil exactly your wishes, it will be a most real satisfaction to

My Lord
Your very faithful
& affect' serv'—
Rawdon

M. *Daniel Huger*[657] *who was under Parole to be on the Islands by the 15th of this Month, having represented that three of his Children are now ill of the Small Pox, I have taken the liberty of extending his term till the First of August.*

Earl Cornwallis
&c &c &c

14. Lord Rawdon to Lord Cornwallis, 12 July 1780 (PRO 30/11/2/280–282):

Camden July 12th 1780

My Lord

I have this day received notice from Capt. Dickson (to whom Governor Martin desired me to pay attention) dated July 8th, signifying that De Kalb with his Army was advanced to Deep River; forming a junction with Caswell.[658] I can see no other object in this, but a move against McArthur; whom I have therefore ordered to fall back to this side of Black Creek. Should the Enemy approach him, I mean to join him with two battalions, the Cavalry, & two Pieces of Cannon. Webster[659] shall be posted with the remainder of my force at Hanging Rock to check the Militia under Sumpter & Rutherford. I am uneasy lest this plan of defence should not meet your Lordships approbation; but I do aver that it proceeds not in any degree from a wish of coming to action, or from a loss of distinguishing myself. It is the result of repeated reflection; & I state it to myself as the safest game I can play. Here, I have no position; & if I am beaten I am gone. If I am routed at one Creek, there is hope of rallying for a stand at another; & ultimately to fight for the town. I am sure you would not have me retire before any force without trying it: In Germany it would have no bad effect; but here, where so much is to be done by opinion as by arms, it would be ruinous. I am fearful of alarming you falsely; but I cannot reconcile it to myself not to give your Lordship immediate notice of every circumstance, stating it in the exact light which I view it in. Having said this, let me add, that having made my disposition, I feel every confidence that an Officer ought to feel. And if I err, it shall be a decided error of judgement. I cannot at present say all I wish, as a violent headache has made me find infinite difficulty in writing the above. I will ease your Lordship upon these points, as nearly as possible. In the mean time, with anxious desire to merit your good opinion as an Officer, I have the Honor to remain

Your Lordship's most faithful
And affect Servt.
Rawdon

I am grieved to enclose
A letter of bad news from
Turnbull.

Earl Cornwallis &c &c &c

Lord Rawdon enclosed the following letter from Turnbull with the above letter to Lord Cornwallis.

15. Lieutenant Colonel Turnbull to Lord Rawdon, 12 July 1780 (PRO 30/11/2/285–286):

Rocky mount July 12th
One o'clock past noon 1780

My Lord,

I have just now rec[d] yours of yesterday. By Intelligence from the other side that Kinlock had pursued the Rebells partly up the Waxhaws on Sunday last and hearing that a Noted Partisan M:Clure[660] *was come home and Reaping his Grain about Twenty Two miles above and that Col. Bratton who Lived about Twelve miles farther was publishing Proclamations and Pardons to who should return to their duty, I proposed to Capt. Huck that I wou[l]d mount twenty of our men*[661] *and give him some militia to the amount of fifty to Beat up those two Quarters.*

The party marched from this [place] *Monday Evening and found only one of the M:Clures and no person at Brattons. My orders to him was not to go farther than Prudence should Direct him. He very unfortunately Encamped about a Quarter of a mile Beyond this and was attackd this morning about Sunrise By a Large Body of Rebells and has been Totally Defeated. Capt. Huck they Inform me is killed. Cornet Hunt*[662] *is wounded and supposed to be prisoner. Lt. Adamson and Lt. McGrigor of the New York Volunteers,*[663] *and all our Twenty* [New York Volunteers] *are Missing. Ens. Cameron of the New York Volunteers, Lt. Lewis of the Militia*[664] *and Twelve Dragoons and Twelve Militia are Returned.*

This is a very Unfortunate affair, my Lord. If Major Ferguson[665] *does not advance from Fair Forest, or some Larger Body of Troops makes head against them I am afraid they will give us Trouble. Their success will no doubt Encourage them to pay us a Visit, and they may Distress us in Provisions.*

I hope your Lordship will be assured that whatever I Plann[e]d I thought could have been Executed without much Danger. Mr. Cameron Says the Ground they were on was not very favourable and they [the rebels] *advanced so Rapidly that the Dragoons had not time to mount.*

Lt. Col. Moore nor Major Walsh is neither of them here nor do I know where they are. I am with Great

Respect
your Lordships
most Obedient and
most Humbl Serv[t].
Geo: Turnbull

16. Lieutenant Colonel Turnbull to Lord Rawdon, 12 July 1780 (PRO 30/11/2/277–278):

Rocky mount July 12th *1780*

Nine oClock in of Evening

My Lord,

I was Unfortunate enough to be obliged to tell you a very Disagreeable story some hours ago—
*   Nine of our missing men have come in, and one Dragoon.*
*   A Negroe Boy who was taken has made his escape and says that Lt. Adamson Fell of[f] his horse Being much bruised is taken prisoner. That seven of ours* [New York Volunteers] *and a sergt. and two* [privates] *of the Dragoons are Likewise wounded and taken Prisoners.*
*   Lt. M⸍Gregor and Cornet Hunt we suppose have made their Escape But have not yet arrived—Capt. Huik is the only Person who was killed Dead on the Spot.*
*   My Militia are so allarmed it will be some days before they Recover their spirits.*
*   There are some wounded Militia I send Down by the Bearer in a wagon to the Care of Doctor Hill.*[666]
*   The Negroe Boy is very Intelligent. He says the Rebels will send Down Lt. Adamson and our wounded men tomorrow.*
*   By what I can Learn the only Bait which Led Huik to Encamp at this cursed unlucky Spot was an Oat Field that was near. But by every account the Position was very unfavourbl.*
*   My Paper and Sealing Wax is almost Expended. In a few days I do not Believe I shall have any material to keep up a Correspondence.*
*   Our Doctor Resigned last week and we have no Body of the Faculty but a mate who is not very Regularly Bred.*[667]
*   I have wrot[e] to Stapleton of the Legion*[668] *and Mr. Gibbs the Surgeons Mate*[669] *of the 33⸍. I Believe the Latter will accept of it if Lord Cornwallis will Permitt him. He writes me He is now going to Charlestown and Expects to join us on his Return. In the mean time if Doctor Hill coud Spare one of his mates with some Medicine it woud oblige us much.*
*   I can Learn nothing of those Dissenters mentioned by Major Carden. The house He mentions which he frequented is on the Waxhaw side. I am with much Esteem your Lordships most faithfull Humbl Serv⸍.*

Geo: Turnbull

Lord Rawdon forwarded the above letter to Lord Cornwallis along with the following letter from himself on 14 July.

17. Lord Rawdon to Lord Cornwallis, 14 July 1780 (PRO 30/11/2/294-295):

Camden July 14ᵗʰ 1780

My Lord

As our Express sets out this morning for McChord's Ferry,[670] *I take that opportunity of informing your Lordship that nothing particular has occurred since I last had the Honor of writing to you. Excepting that I have had notice of the junction being formed between De*

Kalb & Caswell at Coxe's Settlement. From the measures which I have taken, I think every thing in a safe condition; & Doctor Hill has fitted me for any service by dispelling a little fever which had attacked me. The enclosed letter from Turnbull, will shew your Lordship that the misfortune of Huck's Party has not been so bad as it at first appeared. In the course of this day, I hope to learn with certainty something respecting the Enemy Movements; an account of which I should immediately dispatch. I have in the mean time the Honor to remain with equal respect & affection

Your Lordship's
Most faithful & obed. *Serv.*
Rawdon

Earl Cornwallis &c &c --

18. Lord Cornwallis to Lord Rawdon, 15 July 1780 (PRO 30/11/78/18-19):

Charles Town July 15th 1780

My dear Lord

I received early this Morning your Letter of the 12th, I approve very much of your moving Major McArthur to your side of the Black Creek, & should Mr. De Kalbe advance, I would by all means wish you to join him. In regard to the forward position you mention, it is difficult for me having no knowledge of that Country but by a bad map, to give a positive opinion about it, I therefore shall content myself with only saying that if the enemy come within any possibility of reaching you, be compact, & prefer that to any other considerations; every [thing] else I shall leave to your Lordship's judgement, and I am well convinced that I do not misplace my confidence. I forsee that it will be absolutely necessary to act aggressively very soon, to save our friends in N. Carolina, & to preserve the Confidence, in which is included the friendship of the South Carolinians. I am hastening our preparations but we must do it ready or not ready rather than submit to any serious insult. I will come to you as soon as possible, and I think it will be very soon, for altho' everything here is in the most confused state, yet I see no hope that any possible stay of mine could put them into a good Method. There is but one thing would do it. You will easily guess what I mean, if not, Govr. Martin will help you.

Lt. Col. Turnbull's Letter gave me very serious concern, & is indeed a very serious misfortune. Cavalry acts chiefly upon the Nerves, & if ever it loses its terror it loses its greatest force. Tarleton will join us in a few days, in the mean time let me conjure you to take care of the Cavalry & to give the most positive orders against small Detachments; they are always dangerous, especially under ignorant & careless officers. I am sorry to find that you are indisposed, but hope it is now over. Doyle mentions to Ross what you have done about our friends in N. Carolina; I think you perfectly right, & would draw this line for them, that if de Kalbe comes one days march on our side of Charlotte town, that the rising should be general & every possible attack made of the Stores & Convoys in his rear, & then at all events we must go on.

I am &c.
[Cornwallis]
Right Honble. Lord Rawdon

If in consequence of that unlucky officer of the Legion, the Rebels should be troublesome between the Wateree & Broad River, Your Lordship will please to send to Balfour for every Militia assistance he can give you; I have ordered up Innes in a few Days to assemble his Corps; Perhaps Major Graham^{(?)} might move a few miles higher than Friday's Ferry. I shall talk to Innes^{(?)} & write to Balfour about these matters but if you find any pressing unnervancies, you will, to save time, correspond with Balfour yourself, & make what requisitions you think necessary.

Appendix C

How many men were in the battle?

The size of Captain Christian Huck's detachment at the Battle of Williamson's Plantation is difficult to establish with absolute certainty, for the simple fact that the surviving accounts all give different numbers for his men. Sir Henry Clinton's original orders transferring Huck to Lieutenant Colonel Banastre Tarleton's command in 1779 stated that Huck's troop consisted of Captain Huck, Lieutenant Benjamin Hunt, Cornet Nathaniel Swaine, two sergeants, one quartermaster and forty dragoons, and barring any losses this is probably the number that Huck took to Rocky Mount in June. In his first letter to Lord Rawdon on 12 July, Lieutenant Colonel George Turnbull stated that he sent twenty mounted infantry (New York Volunteers) and fifty Tory militia to augment Huck's detachment of British Legion dragoons, but he does not tell us how many dragoons were with Huck.[673] In a letter to Clinton on 15 July, Lord Cornwallis stated that Huck's detachment consisted "of about thirty or forty of [the British Legion], twenty mounted men of the New-York Volunteers, and sixty militia."[674] Tarleton, commander of the British Legion, wrote in his 1787 memoirs that Huck's detachment "consisted of thirty-five dragoons of the legion, twenty mounted infantry of the New-York Volunteers, and about sixty militia."[675] On the other hand, Dr. Uzal Johnson of Major Patrick Ferguson's American Volunteers stated in his diary on 13 July that Huck commanded "one Subaltern and seventeen Privates of the British Legion, two Subalterns and eighteen New York Volunteers and twenty-five Militiamen," while Lieutenant Anthony Allaire of the same corps claimed there were "one subaltern and seventeen dragoons of the Legion, three subalterns and eighteen New York Volunteers, twenty-five militia men."[676] These figures were derived from Lieutenant Hunt, and it is unclear why the numbers of dragoons and militiamen given by Hunt are only half the total given by Turnbull, Cornwallis and Tarleton, or why Johnson and Allaire's figures are not exactly the same, since their diaries are otherwise almost identical.

The numbers given by many of the American sources for Huck's command are much greater. Samuel Killough stated that Huck commanded "two or three hundred Tories."[677] John Craig claimed "four hundred British and Tories" in his published reminiscences, and in his pension application, he gave this breakdown: "about 300 Tories under Colonel Floyd and fifty dragoons under Capt. Hook, and Capt. Adamson with fifty Light Infantry."[678] Colonel William Hill stated in his memoirs that "Hook had about 100 horse & Col. Forguson, at this time commander of the Tory militia, had about 300 men."[679] Dr. Maurice Moore gave an even larger figure, saying

Huck "commanded two hundred British Regulars, one hundred Dragoons, and one hundred mounted Infantry, with about five hundred Tories."[680] Moore seems to have taken the numbers from all of the sources available to him and added them together, producing a total of nine hundred men for Huck's command!

The estimates handed down by most of the Whig veterans of the battle were obviously inflated as the years went by. These statements were not written down until decades after the battle, and it certainly is human nature to magnify the forces of a defeated enemy in order to make the victory seem greater. It would have been almost impossible for Huck to support such a large body of men in the field for any length of time during the summer of 1780, and both American and British officers complained frequently about the scarcity of provisions. It is also difficult to accurately estimate the numbers of a force glimpsed only briefly during the heat of battle, especially when many escaped before the battle was over. Similarly, the figures given by Allaire and Johnson seem too low, and are based on the estimates of a surviving junior officer (Lieutenant Hunt of the Legion) who probably did not know with certainty himself. It is also human nature for the losing side in a battle to downplay its own strength and hence the magnitude of its defeat. Those best in a position to know—Turnbull, Tarleton and Cornwallis— are in general agreement that Huck's detachment consisted of about thirty-five dragoons, twenty New York Volunteers and sixty militia. Huck may have picked up some additional militia along the way, but certainly not the hundreds of men reported by the Whig accounts. Using the best and most reliable information available at this time, it is reasonable to state that Captain Huck's force on 12 July 1780 probably numbered between 115 and 120 men.

As in the case with the British forces, it is also difficult to get an exact number of the patriot troops who actually took part in the battle that day. The numbers run from Dr. John Simpson Bratton's figure of 75 to Dr. Maurice Moore's claim of 260, but the actual number is most likely in between these two extremes. In a letter to Major General Johann DeKalb of the Continental Army written five days after the battle, Brigadier General Thomas Sumter stated, "I had about one hundred and thirty in the action, the enemy twice that number, Seventy of which were Brittesh."[681] General Richard Winn echoed Sumter in his account, written in 1812, in which he said that "about 130 agreed to follow and try the Business."[682] In October 1832, John Craig stated in his Federal pension application that there were about 135 men in the Whig battalion.[683] The specific number "133" first cropped up in *The History of the Revolution of South-Carolina*, published by Dr. David Ramsay in 1785, "The friends of independence having once more taken the field in South-Carolina, a party of the corps, commanded by colonel Sumpter, consisting of one hundred and thirty-three men, on the twelfth of July 1780 engaged at Williams' plantation, in the upper parts of South-Carolina, with a detachment of the British troops and large body of tories, commanded by captain Huck."[684]

Ramsay was a Revolutionary War soldier, having served as a surgeon in the Fourth South Carolina Regiment of Artillery, and his information could easily have been derived from General Sumter, Colonel William Bratton, Colonel William Hill, Colonel Richard Winn or some other veteran of Huck's Defeat. Published only five years after the battle, his account was the earliest reference to Huck's Defeat in published history of the Revolution. William Hill, writing in 1815, stated that "the number of the Americans was 133."[685] This same figure was given by William

McElwee, another York County veteran of the battle, who in 1849 told the historian Benson J. Lossing that the Whig party "numbered only one hundred and thirty-three all told."[686] John Craig's published account, written in 1839, stated that the Whigs numbered 133 men when they first arrived at Old Nation Ford on the evening of 11 July, but that during the march to Bratton's plantation "we lost twenty-three of our number who returned back from whence they came," which would leave only 110 men to attack Huck at Williamson's.[687]

Several accounts mention that the Whig forces started out much larger and shrank during the night of 11 July because of desertions. John Starr Moore told Dr. John Logan that there were originally about 200 men, but during the forced march to Williamson's about 50 dropped out, leaving only about 150 for the attack.[688] Dr. John Simpson Bratton, in the Huck's Defeat celebration of 1839, stated that Colonel Bratton had about 125 men and 50 dropped off before the battle, leaving a total of 75 to attack Huck. This is the figure that the Daughters of the American Revolution placed on its monument at Brattonsville in 1903.[689] Dr. Maurice Moore stated in 1859 that the combined forces of "Lacey, Bratton, McClure, and others" amounted to nearly 400 men, and that the troops under Hill and Colonel Andrew Neal numbered an additional 133 soldiers, a figure which he probably took from Hill's account. Moore also wrote that a large number of men dropped out of the force before it reached Brattonsville and only about 260 were actually in the attack.[690] Taking all these accounts into consideration, it appears that, before rendezvous at Walker's Mill, the original Whig force numbered some two hundred or three hundred men. By the time they reached Williamson's plantation, however, a large group of these men had returned to their homes or their camp, leaving between 130 and 150 men to attack the British. The persistence and precision of the number 133 for the final force tends to confirm Moore's statement that a head count was taken immediately before the battle, and we can consider this to be a reliable figure.

As in the case of the overall numbers, none of the various accounts of the battle agrees on who was in overall command of the rebel forces. In the years after Huck's Defeat, almost every officer above the rank of lieutenant who was present that morning was given credit by someone for commanding the Whig forces. Winn states that "Col. Lacey, Hill and Bratton being present, it was agreed on as Winn had been in the regular service that he should take command and dispose of the men as he thought best."[691] No other source verifies this. Neither Hill nor James Collins says anything about any officer being in overall command, although Collins states that he and his company were under "Colonel Moffitt" at the time.[692] Samuel Killough claimed that his friend Major John Wallace was in command, and during the celebrations at Brattonsville in 1839 and 1903, the Bratton family maintained that Colonel Bratton was in command.[693] Francis Heitman, in his *Historical Register of Continental Officers During the War of the Revolution*, also stated that Bratton was "commander of the forces at the action at Williamson's Plantation."[694] Interestingly, Anthony Allaire and Uzal Johnson of Major Patrick Ferguson's American Volunteers both reported that Colonel Edward Lacey led the rebels, although they also noted that the attack took place at Colonel Bratton's.[695] Hugh Gaston of Chester County, who was in the battle, also stated that "Col. Lacey was highest in command."[696] Joseph Kerr, in his Federal pension application, asserted that Huck was attacked by thirty-one men commanded by "Captain Barnett" (almost certainly Jacob Barnett), but he does not mention any other soldiers as being present.[697] Another veteran, James Kincaid, recalled in his pension application that he was "under Capt. Moffett and Col. Bratton at Hook's Defeat."[698] Thomas McDill stated in a letter to Lyman Draper that Captain John Nixon of Chester County "was in command on the occasion of Houck's Defeat at Bratton's."[699] John Starr Moore reported to Dr. Logan that Captain John McClure and Bratton were in command of the Whig forces, and stated that both Lacey and Winn "acted in the fight as privates."[700]

On the other hand, John Craig's account asserted that the Whig force was "commanded by Colonels Andrew Neal, and Lacy, Bratton, Major Dickson, Capt. McClure, and Capt. Jimeson [Jamieson]," and made no mention of any one officer elected to command all the troops.[701] Dr. Moore similarly maintained that there wasn't a single overall commander "and that on this occasion, the men seemed to act 'more by instinct, than by any order or command.'"[702] His account—based on the reminiscences of his cousin John Adair, his father Alexander Moore and his uncle James Moore—indicated that before any action was decided, a council of the ranking officers was held and a general consensus reached. This was typical militia protocol for the time. It is logical to conclude that with so many independent commands and so many militia officers all combining forces, no one officer could assert supreme authority, although the men could elect an acting commander for the purpose at hand. This is exactly what happened before the Battle of Kings Mountain later that same year. Undoubtedly, each officer maintained command of his own company, battalion or regiment, but the overall command of the Whig forces was a shared authority implemented by repeated officers' councils.

Appendix D

The Huck's Defeat battlefield

For at least two generations following the Battle of Huck's Defeat, the battlefield was well remembered and often visited by residents and local historians, as were the graves of the soldiers killed in the battle. In an 1873 letter to Lyman Draper, William Harbison, the son of Revolutionary War veteran James Harbison, stated that his father was in the battle "at Williamson's where Huck was killed. I have been there myself—saw the graves of the Tories, the place now belongs to Dr. [John Simpson] Bratton."[703] Unfortunately, the last of the Bratton family moved away from Brattonsville in 1915, and with the passing of that generation, the continuity of tradition was broken and the exact location of the battle and graves became uncertain. Before that happened, however, three different maps were drawn by local residents who were the children or grandchildren of Huck's Defeat veterans, and all three show the battlefield and the site of Williamson's plantation to be several hundred yards east or southeast of Colonel William Bratton's home.

The earliest map was drawn about 1857, when the South Carolina historian Dr. John H. Logan was gathering material for a second volume of his book *A History of the Upper Country of South Carolina.* Although he never published this second volume, his notes were copied by Draper and are included in the Thomas Sumter Papers of the Lyman Draper Manuscript Collection.[704] In the course of his research, Dr. Logan interviewed John Starr Moore of York District concerning the Battle of Huck's Defeat. John Starr Moore's father Samuel Moore along with Samuel's brothers John Moore Jr., Nathan Moore and William Moore were all involved in the Battle of Huck's Defeat. Furthermore, John Starr Moore's aunt, Anne Starr, was the wife of Samuel Williamson, who was the son of the James Williamson on whose plantation the battle was fought; Samuel Williamson and three his brothers also fought in the battle. Moore's reminiscences contain important details of the battle not found elsewhere, including a map of the battlefield.[705] This map shows the battlefield located due east of Colonel Bratton's house. Because Moore grew up in the neighborhood, and because his aunt and uncle lived on the plantation where the battle was fought, his information should be considered accurate and reliable.

In 1871, Draper visited Brattonsville to discuss Bratton family history and the battle in detail with two of Bratton's grandsons, John Simpson Bratton Jr. and Dr. James Rufus Bratton. The Brattons informed Draper that the Williamson plantation was located about 60 rods (330 yards) from the Bratton home, down a ridge toward the South Fork of Fishing Creek near

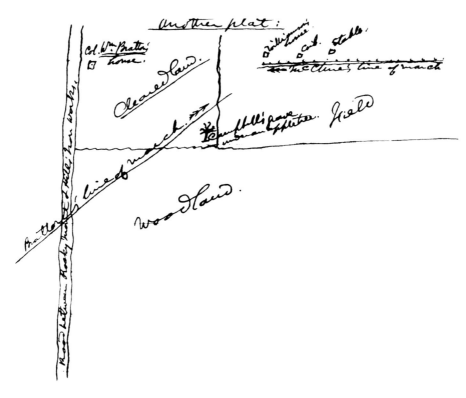

Lyman Draper's hand-drawn copy of a map of James Williamson's plantation and Huck's Defeat battlefield, originally drawn by John Starr Moore for Dr. John H. Logan, circa 1857. *From Thomas Sumter Papers, 16VV277, Draper Manuscript Collection. Image WHi 27324. Courtesy of the Wisconsin Historical Society, Madison, Wisconsin.*

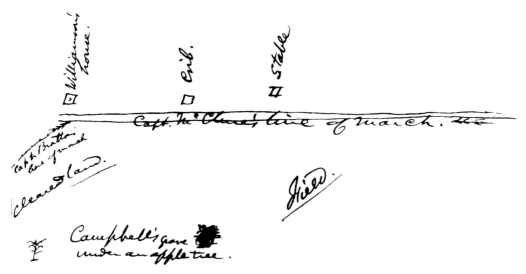

Enlarged plat of the area around the Williamson plantation, showing Colonel William Bratton's and Captain John McClure's lines of march as well as the grave of Campbell, the Whig casualty, near an apple tree. *From Lyman Draper's copy of the John Starr Moore map, Thomas Sumter Papers, 16VV277, Draper Manuscript Collection. Image WHi 27324. Courtesy of the Wisconsin Historical Society, Madison, Wisconsin.*

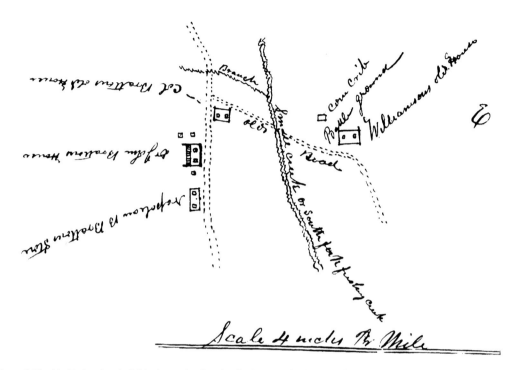

Map of Huck's Defeat battlefield, drawn by Daniel G. Stinson for Lyman C. Draper, 26 March 1876, from a description provided by Napoleon Bonaparte Bratton. *From Thomas Sumter Papers, 15VV278, Draper Manuscript Collection. Image WHi-27323. Courtesy of the Wisconsin Historical Society, Madison, Wisconsin.*

a spring branch.[706] Several years later, Draper sought more details about the actual location of the battle. He urged one of his correspondents, local historian Daniel Green Stinson, to visit Brattonsville and, with the Bratton family's help, draw an accurate map of the battlefield and its relation to the Bratton and Williamson plantations. In February 1876, Stinson visited Brattonsville and discussed the battlefield with Napoleon Bonaparte Bratton, the youngest grandson of Colonel Bratton. Stinson described the visit in a letter to Draper dated 26 March 1876: "Sometime in February I was in the neighborhood of Brattonville, called on N. B. Bratton (grandson of Col. Bratton). The day being very wet I could not go over the ground but got Mr. Bratton to give me a description of locations and course and distances from which the within map is drawn."

This map shows the battlefield, and the Williamson plantation, slightly southeast of Colonel Bratton's house. It also places Williamson's house on the east side of the South Fork of Fishing Creek, which is almost certainly incorrect; but we should bear in mind that the map was drawn from Bratton's memory and not from an actual inspection of the site.[707]

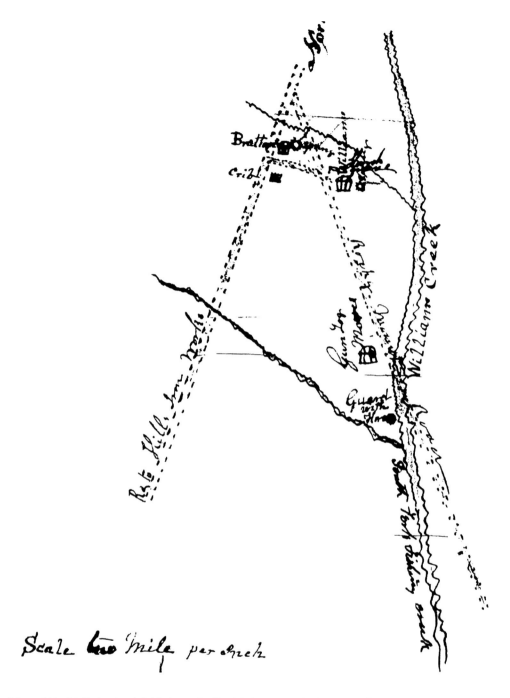

Map of Huck's Defeat battlefield, drawn by Daniel G. Stinson for Lyman C. Draper, 24 August 1876, from a description provided by John Simpson Bratton Jr. *From Thomas Sumter Papers, 5VV54, Draper Manuscript Collection. Image WHi-27322. Courtesy of the Wisconsin Historical Society, Madison, Wisconsin.*

In August 1876, Stinson again visited Brattonsville and this time was able to traverse the Huck's Defeat battlefield with Napoleon's older brother, John Simpson Bratton Jr. The map they produced on that occasion also shows the battlefield and the Williamson plantation to the southeast of the Bratton house, but it shows Williamson's house on the west side of the South Fork of Fishing Creek, which is more likely to be correct than the location shown on the N.B. Bratton map. Stinson forwarded this map to Draper in a letter dated 24 August 1876 that read: "I went over the Battlefield a few weeks ago. Mr. John S. Bratton showed me all the locations as laid down in the above plat. The Bratton house is still the same as it was at that date. The same log house, with the addition of a frame ell added to it. Mrs. Williams, one of the family, lives in it. This house as well as that of Williamson's is down the hill near the spring. The roads are laid down as they run at that date. I have added nothing modern."[708]

In a follow-up letter to Draper dated 15 January 1877, Stinson added: "Last Summer I was on the battle ground of Houycks Defeat. Mr. John Bratton pointed out to me [the] location in general as he recol[l]ected it to be pointed out by the old Soldiers on the day of the celebration the 12 of July 1839. I made a correct plat of the same and forwarded to you from Rock Hill."[709]

This second statement verifies that John Simpson Bratton Jr. was shown the battlefield by the "old soldiers" during the celebration of 12 July 1839. This celebration was arranged by his father, Dr. John Simpson Bratton Sr., and was attended by several veterans of Huck's Defeat. John Simpson Bratton Jr. was 20 years old at the time of the celebration and was one of those who went over the battlefield with the old veterans; therefore, his information should also be considered accurate and reliable.

Samuel Williamson inherited the lower 140 acres of his father's estate, which included his father's original improvements, sometime after 1780, and in turn sold it to Colonel William Bratton in 1787.[710] This lower tract corresponds to the location of the Huck's Defeat battlefield as shown in both the Napoleon Bratton and John S. Bratton maps. Support for the idea that the battlefield lay within Samuel Williamson's 140 acres, the southernmost portion of James Williamson's property, is found in an old manuscript history of Bethesda Presbyterian Church written by Reverend John S. Harris. This document states that "Samuel Williamson's name is recorded in history as having resided on the battle-ground of Houck's defeat, and having killed the first man slain in that battle."[711]

In conclusion, the statements made by John Starr Moore, Napoleon Bonaparte Bratton, John Simpson Bratton Jr. and James Rufus Bratton all indicate that the James Williamson plantation in 1780 was located between three hundred and four hundred yards southeast of Colonel Bratton's house, just west of the South Fork of Fishing Creek.

Appendix E

A biography of Christian Huck

Christian Huck, commander of the Loyalist forces at the Battle of Huck's Defeat, was born about 1748 in one of the German principalities of Europe and immigrated to America sometime before the American Revolution. The information about his birth, such as it is, comes from a British Provincial Army muster roll dated November 1778, wherein Huck stated that he was 30 years old and born in Germany.[712] His surname has been variously spelled as Hauk, Hock, Hook, Houk, Houck, Huck, Huick and Huyck, but the most common spellings are Hook and Huck. So far, I have been unable to locate a birth or baptismal record for a Christian Huck born in Germany in 1748, but there is a record of a "Christian Gottlebe Hauck" born there on 9 October 1747.[713] While Huck's direct ancestry is unknown, the passenger lists for ships arriving in Philadelphia during the colonial period give us the names of several individuals who may have been members of Huck's family. There is, for instance, a man named Christian Hook who arrived in Philadelphia on the brigantine *Pennsylvania Merchant* on 13 September 1733, along with 186 other "Palatines" (immigrants from the Palatinate region of Germany). While it does not seem possible that this man is Huck's father, he could be a relative. The same ship carried another passenger named Hans Georg Hauk.[714] Looking at immigrants named Huck, or some variant thereof, who came into Pennsylvania in 1748 or later (when we might reasonably expect Huck's family to arrive), we find such names as Jacob Hauk and Friedrich Hock (1748), Johann Conradt Hock (1749), Johannes Hock and Andreas Huck (1750), Adam Hauk (1753), Johannes and Michael Hauk (1754), Stephen Hauk (1762), Jacob Houk (1764) and, interestingly enough, a Christian Huck who arrived in Philadelphia in 1772.[715]

We do know that Huck studied law—or "read law"—under Isaac Hunt, a Philadelphia pamphleteer, satirist and lawyer before the outbreak of the Revolution. By 1775, Huck was comfortably settled in a house on Second Street in Philadelphia and was earning a living as an attorney at law.[716] He apparently engaged in buying and selling real estate, with generous terms of payment and credit, as evidenced by the following notice from the *Pennsylvania Gazette* of 12 April 1775, probably written by Huck:

> *CHRISTIAN HUCK, living in Second-street, Philadelphia, has for private sale, Two Thousand Three Hundred Acres of LAND, situate in the county of Berks, and province of Pennsylvania, about 70 miles from the city of Philadelphia, 2 from the river Schuylkill, and*

about 28 from the town of Reading. The land is in general well timbered, and so exceedingly well watered with a great number of springs and creeks, so that it is thought by all that have viewed it, that near ½ of it is fit for meadow; the said creeks all collect themselves on the premises, so as to form a very large stream of water (which is constant throughout the whole year) sufficient to supply several mills; nature has so well calculated the place for all kinds of mills, that she herself has almost made the dams, and it will require very little assistance from art to compleat them....Said Christian Huck will sell all or any parcel of said lands for ready money or short credit, on very low terms, giving security; he is also willing to exchange all or parcel of said lands for other lands or houses in or near Philadelphia; the title to the premises is indisputable, and will be warranted. Whoever desires to view said lands, may be gratified, by applying to John Fisher or Jacob Lutz, Saw-millers, near the premises. Said Christian Huck will also sell by public vendue, on Saturday, the 29th inst., at the Bath tavern, in the Northern Liberties of Philadelphia, the following lots of ground, situate near the said Bath tavern, viz. Four lots of ground, containing in front on the Old Germantown road 20 feet, and in depth 140 feet, one of which has built upon it a small brick tenement, that leases for Six or Seven pounds per annum; also ten other lots joining the aforesaid lots on the east, and fronting on Rose-street, containing each in front 20 feet, and in depth 141 feet; the title to these lots is indisputably clear, and the premises now free from every incumbrance, as will be clearly shewn to any person, who chuses to call at the house of said Christian Huck. The purchase-money is not to be paid until the expiration of one month after sale (perhaps longer credit may be given) in which time the purchaser may make any enquiry into the title, and on his being able to make any legal objection, the same shall be removed, otherwise the sale shall be null and void.[17]

Five days after this notice appeared, British troops fired on American militiamen at Lexington, Massachusetts, and the American Revolution began. Huck seems to have been a Loyalist from the beginning. He was a member of the wealthy upper society of Philadelphia that included prominent Quakers, Anglicans and Germans, many of who supported the royal cause and opposed independence. During this early period of the war, important Philadelphia Loyalists were frequently harassed by the Whigs or "Associators." One of these individuals was Huck's friend and mentor, Isaac Hunt. In July 1776, Hunt accepted a case defending a Philadelphia merchant accused of importing British goods, in defiance of Pennsylvania's boycott on such imports. Although he had not violated any laws, Hunt incurred the wrath of the Associators and became a target for public humiliation. On the morning of 6 September 1776, a group of about thirty Associators removed Hunt from his home and transported him to the London Coffee-house. At the Coffee-house they placed Hunt in a cart and paraded him through the principal streets of the city while a fifer and drummer played "The Rogue's March." The spectacle quickly attracted a large following as it progressed through Philadelphia. At various places the crowd would stop the cart and force Hunt to publicly acknowledge his "misbehavior." Eventually the crowd replaced Hunt with another Tory, Dr. John Kearsley, and paraded him through the streets as well. Kearsley, however, refused to admit any wrongdoing, so the Associators publicly proclaimed him "an enemy of the people and their liberties." The Associators prevented the

¶   HENRY JUNKEN.

CHRISTIAN HUCK, living in Second-street, Philadelphia, has for private sale,

TWO Thousand Three Hundred Acres of LAND, situate in the county of Berks, and province of Pennsylvania, about 70 miles from the city of Philadelphia, 2 from the river Schuylkill, and about 28 from the town of Reading. The land is in general well timbered, and so exceedingly well watered with a great number of springs and creeks, so that it is thought by all that have viewed it, that near ⅓ of it is fit for meadow; the said creeks all collect themselves on the premises, so as to form a very large stream of water (which is constant throughout the whole year) sufficient to supply several mills; nature has so well calculated the place for all kinds of mills, that she herself has almost made the dams, and it will require very little assistance from art to compleat them. From within two miles of the premises, there is in freshes very safe and easy navigation to the aforesaid town of Reading, where there is (particularly for boards and scantling of every kind) as good a price given as at Philadelphia, so that the dealers in these commodities need seldom or never go to Philadelphia market, though from Reading to Philadelphia the navigation is exceeding safe and easy. There is also at Reading a constant market for every kind of country produce, at which, prices are given almost equal to the prices of Philadelphia market. Said *Christian Huck* will sell all or any parcel of said lands for ready money or short credit, on very low terms, giving security; he is also willing to exchange all or parcel of said lands for other lands or houses in or near Philadelphia; the title to the premises is indisputable, and will be warranted. Whoever desires to view said lands, may be gratified, by applying to *John Fisher* or *Jacob Lutz*, Saw-millers, near the premises. Said *Christian Huck* will also sell by public vendue, on Saturday, the 29th inst. at the Bath tavern, in the Northern Liberties of Philadelphia, the following lots of ground, situate near the said Bath tavern, viz. Four lots of ground, containing in front on the Old Germantown road 20 feet, and in depth 140 feet, one of which has built upon it a small brick tenement, that leases for Six or Seven Pounds per annum; also ten other lots joining the aforesaid lots on the east, and fronting on Rose-street, containing each in front 20 feet, and in depth 141 feet; the title to these lots is indisputably clear, and the premises now free from every incumbrance, as will be clearly shewn to any person, who chuses to call at the house of said *Christian Huck*. The purchase-money is not to be paid until the expiration of one month after sale (perhaps longer credit may be given) in which time the purchaser may make any enquiry into the title, and on his being able to make any legal objection, the same shall be removed, otherwise the sale shall be null and void.   **t10s.**

Christian Huck's advertisement of land for sale in Berks County, Pennsylvania, ran in the *Pennsylvania Gazette* on 12 April 1775. *Courtesy of the Dacus Library, Winthrop University, Rock Hill, South Carolina.*

crowd from tarring and feathering the good doctor, but one of his hands was cut by a bayonet, the windows of his house were broken and his property was "abused."[18]

By the summer of 1776, Huck was associating with another well-known group of Philadelphia Loyalists, the four sons of William Allen. The Allens had been early supporters of the Whig cause, but they drew the line at outright rebellion. After the Declaration of Independence was signed on 4 July, the family declared their allegiance to the king. Shortly thereafter, Huck heard a rumor that two hundred Philadelphia Tories, including Allen's sons, were to be seized and sent to North Carolina. He passed the information on the Allens, who then fled Philadelphia. Two of the sons, Andrew and William Jr., joined the British under General Sir William Howe at New York and returned to Philadelphia with Howe when he occupied the city in 1777. Andrew eventually went to England, but William joined the British Provincial Army and raised a battalion of infantry known as the Pennsylvania Loyalists, which he commanded during the Revolution.[19]

Throughout these troubles Huck remained in Philadelphia and continued his real estate ventures. By the fall of 1776, he was living on Front Street near the city vendue house, buying real estate at public auction and reselling it. Huck's interest in city lots suggests that he also derived income from rental properties. He had evidently been unable to sell most of his previously advertised twenty-three hundred acres in Berks County and, in the meantime, had picked up some other property as well. In late November 1776, he ran another advertisement in the *Pennsylvania Gazette*:

> *LANDS TO BE SOLD,*
> *(Or Exchanged for Houses or Lots in the City of Philadelphia)*
> *At a very low price for cash, by CHRISTIAN HOOK, Attorney at Law, dwelling in Front-street, near the City Vendue House, in Philadelphia, one tract of land, consisting of about 2000 acres, lying in the county of Berks, within two miles of the river Schuylkill, and 30 miles from the town of Reading, the soil whereof is middling rich, and the tract in general well timbered; it is most plentifully watered, so that much meadow may be made on the premises, and there is a sufficient stream thereon for a grist or saw-mill; John Myer, or Joseph Fisher, saw millers, living near the premises, will shew them to any body who inclines to see them. Also a tract lying in the county of Northampton, consisting of 3600 acres, is of a very rich soil, plentifully timbered, and about one third thereof with very little pains may be made meadow, and is in the neighbourhood of a very extensive fine country, and distant about ten miles from the river Delaware, which is navigable at least sixty miles above the premises. Also one tract of 300 acres, equal in quality to the last described tract, having a mill seat upon it, and distant but two miles from the aforesaid river.*
> *Also seven lots of ground, lying in the Northern Liberties of Philadelphia.*[20]

On 26 September 1777, the British Army occupied Philadelphia,[21] and Huck probably used the opportunity to assist the British cause in whatever way he could. Whether this involved taking arms against his fellow Pennsylvanians is unclear, but in May 1778, Huck's name appeared on a long list of Loyalists who were "attainted of High Treason" and whose property was to be

November 27, 1776.  Numb. 2501.

The Pennsylvania Gazette.

Containing the Freshest Advices, Foreign and Domestic.

PHILADELPHIA, OCTOBER 29, 1776.

THE Publishers of the several weekly NEWS-PAPERS in this City, are under the disagreeable Necessity of informing their Subscribers, that the extraordinary Advance in the Price of Paper, and other Materials in the Printing Business, has obliged them to raise the Price to FIFTEEN SHILLINGS *per Annum*; and they hope their Customers will not take it amiss to find that Price charged from and after the First Day of *January* next.—Those who should not incline to have the Papers sent after that Time, are desired to call and discharge their Arrears; such as do not, we shall conclude they agree to the advanced Price, and shall continue to send them accordingly.—Persons subscribing for the Papers after this Date to be charged FIFTEEN SHILLINGS *per Annum*, one Half of which to be paid at Entrance.

Wm. and THOMAS BRADFORD.
JOHN DUNLAP.
JAMES HUMPHREYS.
HALL and SELLERS.

To be SOLD at the London Coffee-house, on Wednesday, the 4th day of December next, at 5 o'clock in the afternoon,

THAT large and convenient HOUSE and LOT, situate on the east side of Second-street, between Mulberry and Sassafras-streets; the lot is 36 feet 2 inches front, including part of a ten feet alley, and 220 feet deep, being more or less on said alley, with an adjoining back lot of 34 feet by 30, on which is a new brick stable and coach-house, with a good dry cellar under the whole, paved with brick; the stable is large enough to contain four or more horses; there is a pump of good water in the yard; the house is one of the best stands in Second-street for business, and has been lately repaired; the cellar floor laid with two...

TO BE SOLD,

A VALUABLE plantation, with a suitable proportion of meadow, wood land, and plow land, with good buildings thereon. For further particulars, enquire of BENJAMIN DAVIDS, at the sign of the George, at the corner of Second and Arch-streets.

Nether-Providence, Chester County, Nov. 18, 1776.

To be SOLD by private SALE,

A VALUABLE piece of wood land, well timbered, containing about 25 acres, on which might be erected, at a moderate expence, any kind of water works, situate on Crum-Creek, adjoining a public road leading to divers landing places about 3 miles distance, 14 miles from Philadelphia and 4 from Chester. Any person inclining to purchase, may have an opportunity by applying to ROGER DICKS, near Chester.

LANDS TO BE SOLD,

(Or Exchanged for Houses or Lots in the City of Philadelphia)

AT a very low price for cash, by CHRISTIAN HOOK, Attorney at Law, dwelling in Front-street, near the City Vendue House, in Philadelphia, one tract of land, consisting of about 2000 acres, lying in the county of Berks, within two miles of the river Schuylkill, and 30 miles from the town of Reading, the soil whereof is middling rich, and the tract in general well timbered; it is most plentifully watered, so that much meadow may be made on the premises, and there is a sufficient stream thereon for a grist or saw-mill; John Myer, or Joseph Fisher, saw millers, living near the premises, will shew them to any body who inclines to see them. Also a tract lying in the county of Northampton, consisting of 3600 acres, is of a very rich soil, plentifully timbered, and about one third thereof with very little pains may be made meadow, and is in the neighbourhood of a very extensive fine country, and distant about ten miles from the river Delaware, which is navigable at least forty miles above the premises. Also one tract of 300 acres, equal in quality to the last described tract, having a mill feat upon it, and distant but two miles from the aforesaid river.

Also seven lots of ground, lying in the Northern Liberties of Philadelphia.

To be SOLD by way of public VENDUE, on the 7th day of December next, on the premises,

A PIECE of GROUND, situate in Newtown, Chester

NATHANIEL DEVERELL, from England, living at Mr. Thomas Simmons's, Silk-dyer, in Fifth-street, near the Corner of Arch-street, Philadelphia,

BEGS Leave to inform the Public in general, and his Friends in particular, that he has begun his Trade of making, grinding and steeling of FULLERS SHEARS; where Fullers may be supplied with new Ones, or have their old Ones repaired and fitted up in the best Manner. He will endeavour to give Satisfaction to those who please to favour him with their Commands. Orders from the Country carefully obeyed.

N. B. He likewise makes and sells Nails.

ALL Persons are hereby forewarned from taking an Assignment of a Note or Obligation for Ten Pounds, given by the Subscriber to a certain HENRY EYRAS, who unlawfully detains the said Note, although fully discharged with lawful Interest, and will not be paid again, by MOSES PETERS, of Philadelphia County.

FIVE POUNDS REWARD.

WAS LOST, the 5th day of November, by the subscriber, living in Leacock township, Lancaster county, a Parchment Pocket-Book, with a Bundle of Money, containing about Forty Pounds, on the road leading from Lancaster to Grove's-town. Whoever has found the same, and will deliver it to the owner, shall have the above reward, paid by

CHRISTIAN HAAS.

November 18, 1776.

FOUR DOLLARS REWARD.

STRAYED or STOLEN, on the 15th instant, out of the pasture of the subscriber, living in Germantown, Philadelphia county, a black MARE, about 7 years old, 14 hands high, has lost her left eye, a star in her forehead, some white at her near hind foot, well made, a natural trotter, supposed to be with foal. Whoever secures said Mare, so as the owner may have her again, shall have the above reward, and reasonable charges, paid by JACOB ENGLE.

Robeson Township, Berks County, October 28, 1776.

CAME to the premises of the subscriber, living in Robeson township, a three year old STEER, with a white star in his forehead, and some white on both thighs. The owner is desired to come, prove his property, pay charges, and take him away.

ISAAC WELLS.

Another of Huck's advertisements of land for sale, from the *Pennsylvania Gazette,* 27 November 1776. *Courtesy of the Dacus Library, Winthrop University, Rock Hill, South Carolina.*

forfeited to the state. The Pennsylvania Supreme Council drew up the list on 8 May and printed it in the *Pennsylvania Packet* on 13 May. Titled "A Proclamation, by the Supreme Executive Council of the Common Wealth of Pennsylvania," the notice stated that all the Loyalists on the list, including "Christian Hook, attorney at law," were found to have "severally adhered to, and knowingly and willingly aided and assisted the enemies of this State, and of the United States of America, by having joined their armies at Philadelphia, in the County of Philadelphia, within this State." Acting under the authority of "An Act for the attainder of divers Traitors, if they render not themselves by a certain day, and for vesting their estates in this Common-Wealth and for more effectually discovering the same; and for ascertaining and satisfying the lawful debts and claims thereupon," the Supreme Executive Council ordered that all the men on the list who did not voluntarily relinquish their property by 25 June would "stand and be attainted of High Treason to all intents and purposes, and shall suffer such pains and penalties, and undergo all such pains and penalties, and undergo all such forfeitures as persons attainted of High Treason ought to do. And all the faithful subjects of this State are to take notice of this Proclamation, and govern themselves accordingly."[22]

meet with CONDIGN punifhment, all government here is at an end, and civil fociety no more; for, my Lords, what is civil fociety, but a *public* combination for *private* protection.

My prefent motion therefore, my Lords, is, " That an humble Addrefs be prefented to his Majefty, requefting that be will be pleafed to direct, that all orders and in- ftructions which have been given by the officers, whofe bufinefs it is, to the feveral gaolers, or keepers of other houfes of confinements from time to time, fince the com- mencement of hoftilities, and the bringing of American prifoners into this country, down to the 1ft of the prefent month December, ref, ecting the hiftory and treatment of the faid prifoners may be laid before this Houfe; and that the returns which have been made to office from the faid prifons of their numbers and deaths, together with the accounts of each article of expence, attending their confinement, may likewife be produced."

My Lords, I have made this motion, not only from the feelings of *humanity*, but from motives of POLI- CY. Your Lordfhips will remember, that there is fuch a thing as the law of RETALIATION. Whilft you are making prifoners of the Americans by *fi, ties* and *hundreds*, they are making prifoners of you by WHOLE ARMIES. The fate of General Burgoyne is KNOWN; and if General Howe does not again fhift his pofition, his fate will be the fame. My Lords, I will only add, that I hope this motion will be agreed to, and it will be productive of good; but, my Lords, as it will be fome time before it can have its effect, I muft fignify to your Lordfhips, that it is my intention in the mean while, to promote, as much as lies in me, a fubfcription for the relief of thefe unfortunate pri- foners, in hopes of procuring the contribution of *every* noble Lord of this Houfe; for, my Lords, the majori ty Lords, who have benefited by the American war, can afford it. Thofe who have not (the Bifhops) will remember, that CHARITY COVERETH A MUL- TIFUDE of SINS; and as to the minority Lords, they will be all led to it from PRINCIPLE. Thus, my Lords, I fhall not defpair of there being collected at leaft as much money for thefe HONEST WHIGS, as was procured for thofe *Tory Priefts*, who, for at tempting to undermine the liberties of America, were driven out of THAT country, and are, perhaps for the fame purpofes, now prifoned in THIS.

PENNSYLVANIA, fs.

A PROCLAMATION.

By the SUPREME EXECUTIVE COUNCIL
of the Common Wealth of PENNSYLVANIA.

WHEREAS the following named perfons, late and heretofore inhabitants of this ftate— That is to fay—Enoch Story, late merchant; Samuel Garrigues, the elder, late clerk of the market and trader; James Stevenfon, late baker; Abraham Carlile, houfe carpenter; Peter Defhong, miller; Alexander Bartram, trader; Chriftian Hook, attorney at law; Peter Miller, ferivener; Lodowick Kerker, butcher; Philip Marchinton, trader; Edward Hanlon, cooper; and vintner; Alfred Clifton, gentleman; and Arthur Thomas, breeches maker; all now, or late of the city of

the faid Enoch Story, Samuel Garrigues, James Stevenfon Abraham Carlife, Peter Defhong, Alexan- der Bartram, Chriftian Hook, Peter Miller, Lodowick Kerker, Philip Marchinton, Edward Hanlon, Alfred Clifton, Arthur Thomas, Thomas Livezley, John Roberts, Robert Iredale, Thomas Iredale, Jo- fhua Knight, John Knight, Ifaac Knight, Albin- fon Walton, John Smith, Henry Hugh Fergufon, Samuel Biles, Walter Willet, Richard Hovendon, William Moland, Henry Skyles, Thomas Bulla, Da- vid Dawfon, Jacob James, Jofeph Thomas, Nathaniel Vernon, junior, John Swanwick, John Rankin, Evan Griffith, William Love, John Wilfon, James Brakin, William Thomas, James Pugh, Samuel Kifter, John Kofter, Jofhua Thomas, Hugh Pugh, Jofeph Sutton, John Holder, Henry Ofwalt, Jacob Holder, George Holder, Owen Roberts, Michael Witman, Matthew M'Hugh, George Reine, John Reine, Ingleholt Holtzinger, and Francis Sanderfon, (the faid Francis Sanderfon having a real eftate in this Common- Wealth) to render themfelves refpectively to fome or one of the Juftices of the Supreme Court, or of the Juftices of the Peace of one of the Counties within this State, on or before Thurfday, the twenty-fifth day of June next enfuing, and alfo abide their legal trial for fuch their treafons, on pain that every of them the faid Enoch Story, Samuel Garrigues, James Stevenfon, Abraham Carlifle, Peter Defhong, Alexander Bar- tram, Chriftian Hook, Peter Miller, Lodowick Ker- ker, Philip Marchinton, Edward Hanlon, Alfred Clifton, Arthur Thomas, Thomas Livezley, John Roberts, Robert Iredale, Thomas Iredale, Jo- fhua Knight, John Knight, Ifaac Knight, Al- binfon Walton, John Smith, Henry Hugh Fergu- fon, Samuel Biles, Walter Willet, Richard Hovendon, William Moland, Henry Skyles, Thomas Bulla, Da- vid Dawfon, Jacob James, Jofeph Thomas, Na- thaniel Vernon, John Swanwick, John Rankin, Evan Griffith, William Love, John Wilfon, James Brakin, William Thomas, James Pugh, Samuel Kof- ter, John Kofter, Jofhua Thomas, Hugh Pugh, Jofeph Sutton, John Holder, Henry Ofwalt, Jacob Holder, George Holder, Owen Roberts, Michael Witman, Matthew M Hugh, George Reine, John Reine, In- gleholt Holtzinger, and Francis Sanderfon, not ren- dering himfelf as aforefaid, and abiding the trial aforefaid, fhall, from and after the faid twenty fifth day of June next, ftand and be attainted of High Treafon to all intents and purpofes, and fhall fuf- fer fuch pains and penalties, and undergo all fuch forfeitures as perfons attainted of High Treafon ough to do. And all the faithful fubjects of this State are to take notice of this Proclamation, and govern them- felves accordingly.

GIVEN, by order of the Council, under the Hand of His Excellency the Prefident and the Seal of the State at Lancafter, this eighth day of May, in the year of our Lord One thoufand feven hundred and feventy eight. By order of Council,

THOMAS WHARTON, Junior, Prefident.

GOD SAVE THE COMMONWEALTH.

Attefted by order of the Council,

T. MATLACK, Secretary.

Proclamation from the Supreme Executive Council of the State of Pennsylvania, labeling "Christian Hook, attorney at law," and other prominent Loyalists as guilty of "High Treason." From the *Pennsylvania Packet,* 13 May 1778. *Courtesy of the Culture & Heritage Museums.*

By the time the British withdrew from Philadelphia on 18 June 1778, Huck had abandoned the city and joined the British Army at New York.[23] Huck succeeded in raising a company of thirty men for Provincial duty, and on 7 June 1778, he received a captain's commission in Emmerick's Chasseurs, a Provincial corps of light infantry and dragoons organized in 1777 in New York. The commander of this corps, Major Andreas Emmerick, was of German ancestry, along with Huck and about half the men in the unit; the rest were chiefly of British ancestry, including many born in America. Emmerick's men were recruited primarily from Westchester County, New York, and nearby parts of Connecticut, but one troop of light dragoons was also raised on Long Island. Later, after Philadelphia was occupied, some men—including Christian Huck—were recruited from that area.[24] It was a November 1778 muster roll for "Captain Christian Huck's Company of Chasseurs in his Majesty's Corps of Chasseurs commanded by Lieut. Colonel Emmerick" that provided the meager biographical data that Huck was 30 years old and born in Germany.[25]

The French military term *chasseurs* refers to light troops, either infantry or cavalry, who were trained for rapid action, and that is how Emmerick's men served in the Northern Campaigns of the Revolution. The corps distinguished itself in several battles in 1777 and 1778; the men participated in the Hudson Highland Campaign under Sir Henry Clinton and in numerous skirmishes along the front lines at Kingsbridge. They were also in the Battle of Monmouth.[26] In 1778, Emmerick's corps was augmented with new recruits and expanded to consist of two troops of light dragoons, one infantry company, one rifle company and three chasseur companies, one of which was Huck's company. However, by 1779, internal dissention between the American-born and European-born soldiers undermined the integrity of the corps, and Clinton split the unit up and transferred its companies into other regiments. Huck was given command of one troop of light dragoons and attached to the British Legion to serve under Lieutenant Colonel Banastre Tarleton. One of the rifle companies was assigned to Lieutenant Colonel George Turnbull's New York Volunteers, and these men later served with Huck in South Carolina. Other men transferred to Lord Rawdon's Volunteers of Ireland, the Queen's Rangers and the Third Battalion of DeLancey's Brigade, and also served in the South.[27]

Clinton's original orders assigning Huck's troop to the British Legion specifically stated that it was not to be incorporated into the Legion but rather to be attached to Tarleton's command. Dated 31 August 1779 at British Headquarters, New York, the orders read: "One Troop Consisting of a Quarter Master, Two serjeants, 1 Trumpeter & 40 rank & file, to be form'd out of the Cavalry under the Command of Capt'n Huck, Lt Hunt, and Cornet Twaine [Swaine], to be put under the Orders of Lt Col'l Tarleton but not to be incorporated with the Legion."[28] However, toward the end of 1779, Huck's troop was apparently incorporated into the Legion, and British officers in South Carolina like Lord Cornwallis, Lord Rawdon, Tarleton and Patrick Ferguson always referred to Huck and his troop as "of the Legion." Several of Huck's fellow Loyalists, whose names appeared on the May 1778 list printed in the *Pennsylvania Packet*, also became officers in various Provincial units and eventually commanded dragoons in the British Legion. These men were Captain Richard Hovenden, Captain Jacob James, Captain Nathaniel Vernon Jr. and Lieutenant Walter Willet.[29] No specific information is available as to what military actions Huck may have been involved in during the siege and surrender of Charleston, but General Richard Winn of South Carolina stated in his memoirs that "Huck was one of those that cut Buford to pieces" on 29 May 1780—a reference, of course, to Buford's Defeat at the infamous Battle of the Waxhaws (see chapter 2). Winn made this statement twice, and since he had the opportunity to interrogate several of Huck's officers, his information should be considered reliable.[30]

Meanwhile, back in Pennsylvania, Huck had been branded a traitor and all of his property confiscated by the state, along that of many other Loyalists. In Berks County, the estates of Huck, his old friend Andrew Allen and another Loyalist named Alexander Stedman were all put up for public auction. The *Pennsylvania Gazette* for 6 October 1779 contained a notice dated 27 September 1779, from Reading, Pennsylvania, declaring that the estates of Allen, Stedman and "Christian Hook," all in the county of Berks, "having been in due courts of law forfeited and seized to the use of this State," were to be sold at public vendue at the Reading Courthouse on the first day of November. Huck's property in Berks County consisted of "three tracts of land lying over the Blue Mountains in the said county, two of them containing about 300 acres each, and the other of them containing 280 acres or thereabouts." All persons having claims against these estates were instructed "to exhibit their claims and demands to the justices of the Supreme Court, within the time limited by law, or they will be for ever barred from the recovery thereof."[31] Five days after the fall of Charleston, the *Pennsylvania Gazette* ran another notice mentioning Huck. Dated 13 May 1780, from Philadelphia, this notice included a list of twenty-six men, including Isaac Allen and "Christian Hook," whose estates in Philadelphia County had been "in due course of Law forfeited and seized, to the use of this State." Huck's property in Philadelphia County consisted of "[a] Lot on Germantown Road, about one and a half miles from the city, about 75 feet front, and 150 feet deep, with the remains of a brick kitchen thereof, late of Christian Hook." This property would also be sold at public vendue "for the benefit of the Commonwealth."[32] It is ironic that Huck, who for years had made a living buying forfeited property at public auction and reselling it, was now subject to the same punishment. One is also tempted to wonder how Huck's lot on Germantown Road ended up with nothing but the "remains of a brick kitchen" on it.

In early June 1780, Lord Cornwallis detached at least two troops of dragoons from the British Legion and placed them under the command of Lieutenant Colonel Francis, Lord Rawdon at Camden, South Carolina. One troop under Captain David Kinlock remained based at Camden, while the other troop under Captain Huck was assigned to the command of Lieutenant Colonel Turnbull at Rocky Mount, a British outpost on the Catawba River in northeastern Fairfield County. Working in conjunction with Turnbull's New York Volunteers and the local Tory militia, Huck made several excursions against the rebels in present-day Chester and York Counties during June and early July 1780. In the Backcountry of South Carolina, Huck quickly became notorious for his profanity (ironic in light of his name), which earned him the sobriquet "the swearing captain"; he was especially noted for his dislike of Scotch-Irish Presbyterians.[33] This last character trait may perhaps be traceable to his experiences early in the American Revolution: in Huck's home state of Pennsylvania, as in South Carolina, the Scotch-Irish Presbyterians generally favored the Whig Party and independence, and often employed violence against their Tory neighbors. Certainly Huck had no love for the party that

articles, or any of them, shall have the above reward, and reasonable charges, paid by   ROBERT CANADY.

WHEREAS the estates of Andrew Allen, Alexander Stedman, and Christian Huck, late of the county of Berks, having been in due course of law forfeited and seized to the use of this State, We, the subscribers, agents for the said county, do hereby give notice, that the estates of the said Andrew Allen, A-lexander Stedman and Christian Huck; consisting of the following, viz. one of 850 acres, situated in Heidelberg township, generally known by the name of the Big Spring Tract, late the property of Andrew Allen, two out lots near the town of Reading in the said county, late the property of the said Alexander Stedman, containing five acres each, and three tracts of land lying over the Blue Mountains in the said county, two of them containing about 300 acres each, and the other of them containing 280 acres or thereabouts; late the property of the said Christian Huck: All which will be sold by public vendue, at the Court-House at Reading, on the first day of November. The sales will continue from day to day till the whole be disposed of.

The terms of sale will be according to law, as follows, to wit: One fourth part of the purchase money to be paid in ten days after sale, or the premises again to revert to the State, and the bidder liable to forfeit the said one fourth of the purchase money. The remainder thereof to be paid in one month; and on a certificate being produced from the agents, or either of them, of full payment of the purchase money, a deed will be given, as by law directed.

And we the agents do also, pursuant to law, hereby notify all the claimants of the said premises, or any of them, and creditors of the said Andrew Allen, Alexander Stedman and Christian Huck, or either of them, to exhibit their claims and demands to the justices of the Supreme Court, within the time limited by law, or they will be for ever barred from the recovery thereof.

Reading, Sept. 27, 1779.   DAVID MORGAN,
                             THOMAS PARRY,   } Agents.
                             HENRY HALLER,   }

Confiscation notice for the estates of Andrew Allen, Christian Huck and Alexander Stedman. From the *Pennsylvania Gazette*, 6 October 1779. *Courtesy of the Dacus Library, Winthrop University, Rock Hill, South Carolina.*

Philadelphia, May 13th, 1780.

WHEREAS the Estates of Joseph Galloway, John Roberts, Holton Jones, Joseph Griefwold, Joel Evans, Peter Campbel, Ifaac Allen, Chriftian Hook, John Butcher, Ofwald Eve, Chriftopher Sower, Jonathan Wright, John Wright, Abijah Wright, John Lufburg, Joseph Comely, John Burk, John Robefon, Jofhua Knight, Lawrence Fagan, Richard Swanwick, John Parrock, Samuel Shoemaker, Abraham Paftorious, John Tolley, and William Roden, all late of the county of Philadelphia, having been in due courfe of Law forfeited and feized, to the ufe of this State:

WE the fubfcribers, Agents for the faid county, DO HEREBY GIVE NOTICE, that the Interefts and Eftates of the faid Joseph Galloway, John Roberts, Holton Jones, Joseph Griefwold, Joel Evans, Peter Camphel, Ifaac Allen, Chriftian Hook, John Butcher, Ofwald Eve, Chriftopher Sower, Jonathan Wright, John Wright, Abijah Wright, John Lufburgh, Joseph Comely, John Burk, John Robefon, Jofhua Knight, Lawrence Fagan, Richard Swanwick, John Parrock, Samuel Shoemaker, Abraham Paftorious, John Tolley, and William Roden, in the following Tracts or Parcels of Land, viz. No. 1, A Tract of Land on Schuylkill, in the Northern Liberties, containing about 45 acres, with a good houfe and other valuable improvements thereon; No. 2, A Tract of Land on Hogg Ifland, being 1-3d part of faid Ifland, containing about 105 acres of banked meadow; No. 3, A Tract of Wood Land in Blockly Townfhip, lying on the two branches of Indian Creek, and Haverford Road, late of Joseph Galloway, Efquire:

No. 1, A Tract of Land in Lower Merion Townfhip, containing 300 acres, with a good dwelling houfe, two grift mills, one faw mill, and one paper mill, and divers out houfes, all in good order; No. 2, A Tract of Land adjoining the above, containing 78 acres, with a houfe, &c. No. 3, A Tract of Land on Schuylkill, containing 300 acres, adjoining Frederick Bicking's land, with three dwelling houfes, a powder mill, an oil mill, and a faw mill thereon, with other improvements, late of John Roberts:

A Lot of Ground in Germantown of about 2 acres, with a handfome dwelling houfe, ftore, fhop, and other improvements, late of Holton Jones:

A Tract of Land in the Northern Liberties, containing 88 acres, with a brick houfe and fundry other improvements thereon, late of Joseph Griefwold:

A Tract of Land in Blockley Townfhip, containing about 50 acres, with a dwelling houfes and other improvements thereon, late of Joel Evans:

A Lot of meadow ground in Paffyunk Townfhip, on Greenwich Ifland, near the mouth of Hollanders creek, containing 3 acres, late of Peter Campbel:

No. 1, A Lot of Land on Hickory Lane, of about 5 acres, with the remains of 2 brick houfes thereon; No. 2, A Lot adjoining the above, containing 3 acres, late of Ifaac Allen:

A Lot on Germantown Road, about one and a half miles from the city, about 75 feet front, and 180 feet

Notice of forfeiture and seizure of property belonging to Isaac Allen, "Christian Hook" and other Loyalists in Philadelphia County. From the _Pennsylvania Gazette,_ 17 May 1780. _Courtesy of the Dacus Library, Winthrop University, Rock Hill, South Carolina._

had branded him a traitor, confiscated his property and sold it at public auction. In his 1785 *History of the Revolution of South-Carolina*, Dr. David Ramsay made these remarks concerning Huck, which were frequently repeated by subsequent historians and writers:

> *During his command he had distressed the inhabitants by every species of insult and injury. He had also shocked them with his profanity, having been often heard to say, 'that GOD ALMIGHTY was turned rebel; but that if there were twenty GODS on their side they should all be conquered.' In a very particular man[n]er he displayed his enmity to the Presbyterians, by burning the library and dwellinghouse of their clergyman the rev. mr. Simpson, and all bibles which contained the Scots translations of the psalms. These proceedings, no less impolitick than impious, inspired the numerous devout people of that district with an unusual animation.*[734]

During his brief period of service in the Backcountry, Huck generated so much animosity among the citizens of the upper districts that South Carolina historians have blamed him for atrocities of which he was innocent. One such incident occurred at Camden on 31 May or 1 June 1780, when a party of British Legion dragoons killed a young Whig militiaman named Samuel Wylie (or Wyly or Wiley). The story first appeared in Ramsay's *History of the Revolution of South-Carolina*, and is an example of how Revolutionary War incidents in South Carolina were exaggerated and embellished by nineteenth and early twentieth century historians. As Dr. Ramsay originally told the story:

> *On the nineteenth day after the surrender* [of Charleston], *a quartermaster of lieutenant-colonel Tarleton's legion, of the name of Tuck, with a party of dragoons of that corps, called on mr. Samuel Wyly, an inoffensive private militiaman, and, on his acknowledging that he went as a volunteer to the defence of Charleston, put him to death at his own house near Camden, by cutting him to pieces in a most barbarous manner. Though Mr. Wyly produced a certified copy of his parole as an evidence of his being entitled to the protection due to a prisoner taken by capitulation, yet it availed him nothing. Tuck and his party swore they would not only kill him, but all others who had turned out as volunteers to oppose the British forces.*[735]

The story bears a striking resemblance to the various descriptions of young William Strong's death at the hands of Captain Huck and his party in June 1780. William Dobein James next took up the story of the Samuel Wylie incident in his 1821 book, *A Sketch of the Life of Brig. Gen. Francis Marion, and a History of his Brigade.* James's version is significantly different from Ramsay's. James first relates that "at Camden, a party of [Tarleton's] men cut to pieces Samuel Wyley, whom they mistook for his brother John Wyley, then sheriff of the [Camden] district."[736] He then adds the following footnote:

> *Tarleton dispatched his favourite sergeant Hutt, who always charged by his side, with a sergeant's guard, to perform this deed. The visit was quite unexpected by Wyley. In going up to his house, two men were left concealed, behind two large gate posts, at the entrance of the yard;*

while Hutt, with the rest, broke into the house abruptly; he demanded Wyley's shoe buckles, and while he stooped down to unbuckle them, the wretch Hutt aimed a stroke with his sword at his head. Wyley, seeing the gleam of the descending weapon, parried the blow from his head, by his hand, with the loss of some fingers; then, springing out of the door, he ran for the gate, where the two concealed men despatched him with many blows. The cause of the offence was, that John Wyley, as sheriff, had superintended the execution of some men under the existing state laws, at that time against treason. After the battle of Cowpens Hutt disappeared.[37]

The incident was next taken up in 1905 by Thomas J. Kirkland and Robert M. Kennedy in their *Historic Camden, Part One: Colonial and Revolutionary*, and at this point Christian Huck enters the picture. Kirkland and Kennedy recount Ramsay's and James's versions, inexplicably promoting "Hutt" from sergeant to lieutenant in the process.[38] They then proceed to add the following gruesome details, apparently derived from family tradition:

Samuel Wyly's body is said to have been drawn and quartered and set up on pikes by the roadside, as a warning to others. Family tradition further tells of the pitiful, but vain, appeals made to Lord Rawdon by Mrs. William Lang for the body of her brother. While awaiting an audience with Rawdon at Headquarters, this good lady's feelings were harrowed by the unconscious cruelty of some little Tory boys who were killing flies on the window panes, exclaiming, as each victim fell: 'Ha, there goes another Rebel!'[39]

In a footnote to this shocking story, the authors attempt to reconcile the differences in the names "Tuck" and "Hutt" by stating, "This man was undoubtedly Capt. Christian Huck, who ended his life in the night attack upon Williamson's House about a month later."[40] Thus we can see, in the substance of these three accounts, how the execution of a Whig militiaman at the hands of "Quartermaster Tuck" became exaggerated and distorted into a bloody medieval dismemberment and impaling at the hands of Captain Christian Huck.

The surviving muster rolls for the British Legion in the Southern Campaign, covering the period from October 1780 to April 1782, do not contain a record of a soldier named Hutt.[41] However, Tarleton actually did have a quartermaster named Tuck under his command in 1780. His name was John Tuck, and he served as quartermaster in Captain Richard Hovenden's troop of the British Legion during the Southern Campaign.[42] On 6 June 1780, Tuck was court-martialed in Camden "by Virtue of a Warrant from His Excellency Sir Henry Clinton" for the alleged murder of "Samuel Wiley late Inhabitant of this Province." Lieutenant Colonel Alexander McDonald of the Seventy-first Regiment of Foot presided over the general court-martial, and the judges included Lieutenant Colonel Turnbull of the New York Volunteers and eleven other officers drawn from the British Legion, the Volunteers of Ireland, and the Twenty-third, Thirty-third and Seventy-first Regiments of Foot. During the course of the court-martial, several soldiers from the British Legion and the Seventeenth Light Dragoons testified that on or about 1 June 1780, Tuck and a party of dragoons were feeding and watering their horses when Samuel Wylie emerged from some woods near his house and fired a pistol at Tuck. Wylie's pistol misfired, and as Tuck approached him on horseback, Wylie struck Tuck with the butt of the pistol and fled. The dragoons apprehended Wylie and brought him before Tuck, who then "cut him down" with his sword. After hearing all the evidence, the court acquitted Tuck of the charge of murder.[43] The proceedings of the court-martial make it clear that Christian Huck had nothing to do with Wylie's death, and the claim that Wylie's body was drawn, quartered and placed on a pike just outside of Camden is almost certainly fiction.

There is no doubt, however, that on the morning of Sunday, 11 June 1780, Captain Huck's dragoons and Tory militia visited Upper Fishing Creek Presbyterian Church in Chester County, looking for the Whig militia commanded by Captain John McClure and Colonel William Bratton. This visit resulted in the destruction of Reverend John Simpson's home and library, and possibly the meeting house as well. The raid also resulted in the death of a young Whig militiaman named William Strong, a deed for which Huck and Colonel James Ferguson of the royal militia were held personally responsible.[44] Several days later, Lieutenant Colonel Turnbull sent Huck to destroy the ironworks belonging to Colonel William Hill in the New Acquisition District (modern York County). Hill's Ironworks was, at the time, the headquarters for the Whig militia in the area, and on 17 June, Huck's men dispersed the troops guarding the ironworks, burned Hill's home and all of his outbuildings, destroyed the forge and furnace, and carried off all of Hill's slaves.[45] Huck also reportedly made an excursion into western York County during this period where he "killed a man at the ford on Bullock's Creek, and a mile above killed good old Mr. Fleming, a man of 70."[46]

Huck's final engagement was the Battle of Williamson's Plantation on 12 July 1780, an engagement that has since become well known as Huck's Defeat. Huck set out from Rocky Mount on 10 July with a detachment of British Legion dragoons, New York Volunteers and Tory militia, probably about 120 men in all. He had orders to apprehend McClure and Bratton and disperse the rebel militia in the area. On the evening of 11 July, Huck camped near Bratton's home at the plantation of James Williamson, and early on the morning of 12 July, some 133 Whig militia under the command of McClure, Bratton, Hill, Andrew Neal, Edward Lacey and others surprised Huck and his party. In a very one-sided battle, the local Whigs decimated Huck's command, and Huck was shot from his horse while trying to escape the battlefield.[47] Most of the men who were in the battle gave the credit for killing Huck to John Carroll of Tool's Fork, a branch of upper Fishing Creek. Carroll reportedly loaded two balls in his rifle before firing at Huck, and after the captain fell, Carroll told his comrades, "If you find two rifle balls passed into his head close together, then I killed him, for I loaded with two balls." Two such holes were found, just as Carroll described, and he was given credit for the victory; however, several other men present that day also claimed to have fired the fatal shot, including John Carroll's brother Thomas, Lieutenant Charles Miles of present-day Chester County and Sergeant James Stephenson of present-day York County.[48]

Huck was buried where he fell, in a shallow grave near the Williamson home.[49] Around the year 1796, William Bratton Jr. was studying medicine under his brother-in-law Dr. James Simpson (the son of Reverend John Simpson and husband of Jane Bratton), and the two men disinterred Huck's body "and made a skeleton of it as far as it remained." The two rifle-ball holes were still visible in the skull. Dr. Simpson preserved the skeleton, and members of the family later took the remains to Alabama and then to California.[50]

None of the senior British officers who wrote about Huck's Defeat—Turnbull, Rawdon, Tarleton nor Cornwallis—expressed any real remorse for his death, which might lend credence to the idea that he was not especially popular with his superiors. By contrast, the death of other officers in battle was often lamented by these same commanders. For instance, Tarleton had nothing but praise for Captain Charles Campbell of the British Legion infantry, who was killed by the rebels at Fishing Creek on 18 August. In a classic case of irony, Captain Campbell, who burned Thomas Sumter's home in May 1780, was killed attacking Sumter at Fishing Creek in August. "His death cannot be mentioned without regret," Tarleton noted sadly in his memoirs. "He was a young officer, whose conduct and abilities afforded the most flattering prospect that he would be an honour to his country."[51] Tarleton recorded no such sentiments about Captain Huck; he noted tersely that Huck "neglected his duty," which caused his command to suffer "both disgrace and defeat."[52] In a letter to Lord Rawdon dated 15 July 1780, Lord Cornwallis went even further. While not referring to Huck by name, Cornwallis alluded to "that unlucky officer of the Legion" and called him "ignorant & careless" for allowing his detachment to be ambushed and defeated by the rebels.[53]

Whether Huck had a wife or children is uncertain, but the 1790 census for the city and county of Philadelphia shows several families who may have been his relatives, including John and Elizabeth Hook of Northern Liberties Town in Philadelphia County; John Hauck of the Northern District of Philadelphia County; William Hauck of Spruce Street, Philadelphia; and, even one Christian Hock of Tenth Street, Philadelphia.[54]

It is truly ironic that Huck's memory is preserved today at the scene of his defeat and death, Historic Brattonsville® in York County. This site is the location of the original Bratton and Williamson plantations and the Huck's Defeat battlefield, and also hosts regular reenactments of the Battle of Huck's Defeat. Among the descendants of the Backcountry rebels of South Carolina, Captain Christian Huck is still remembered as "a miscreant who excited universal abhorrence for his cruelty and profanity," to use the words of the nineteenth-century Loyalist biographer Lorenzo Sabine.[55] Any good that Huck did during his life died with him on 12 July 1780 and now only the memory of his belligerence remains. Mark Anthony's comments about Julius Caesar in Shakespeare's famous play are equally applicable to Christian Huck: "The evil that men do lives after them; the good is oft interred with their bones."

Appendix F

Roster of soldiers at the Battle of Huck's Defeat

The number of soldiers involved in the Battle of Huck's Defeat has been a source of local controversy for many years. The most reliable sources—the men who were actually in the battle and their commanding officers—state that there were about 133 Whigs and 115-120 Loyalists in the battle. The names of the Whigs have for the most part been recovered, thanks to the fact that either they or their descendants left statements that placed them in the battle. The names of the Loyalists have presented a more difficult problem, because almost no Loyalist accounts of the battle exist and there are no known rosters of the troops stationed at Rocky Mount in the summer of 1780. All of the men listed in these tables are found in at least one reliable primary or secondary source that either definitively places them in the battle or provides substantial evidence that they were present. The Loyalists listed as "possible participants" are men who are known to have been at the Battle of Beckhamville (Alexander's Old Field, Chester County) on 6 June 1780, or with Huck when he destroyed Fishing Creek Meeting House (Chester County, 11 June 1780) and Hill's Iron Works (York County, 17 June 1780), so it is possible these men were also with Huck at Williamson's Plantation (see key to abbreviations at the end of this appendix).

RANK:

Military ranks were fluid during the American Revolution and varied according to the time and type of service. This is especially true for ranks in the militia, where a soldier might serve as a captain on one tour of duty and as a private on the next tour. The issue is further confused by the tendency of Revolutionary War veterans and their descendants to refer to an officer by the highest rank he attained during (or after) the war, even if his rank was lower at the time of a particular battle or campaign. And sometimes the information given by a particular source is simply wrong; for instance, several nineteenth century sources referred to Captain Christian Huck as "Colonel Huck," although there is no evidence to indicate he ever held such a rank. This list represents as accurately as possible the actual ranks that these soldiers held at the time of Huck's Defeat on 12 July 1780.

UNIT:

The Whigs at Huck's Defeat belonged to several independent militia units that were officially incorporated into Sumter's Brigade either shortly before or shortly after the battle. Based on the Revolutionary War pension applications and reminiscences of men who were in Sumter's Brigade in July 1780, the structure of these regiments appears to have been as follows:

1. Neal's Regiment
    • Colonel: Andrew Neal (Neel, Neil)
    • Lieutenant Colonel: William Hill
    • Major: James Hawthorne
    • Captains: Jacob Barnett, Walter Carson, Joseph Howe, James Jamieson, Andrew Love, Thomas Neal Jr., Robert Thomson
2. Bratton's Regiment
    • Colonel: William Bratton
    • Lieutenant Colonel: None
    • Major: John Wallace
    • Captains: Hugh Bratton, James Martin, John Millar, James Mitchell, John Moffett, James Moore, Benjamin Rainey, James Read
3. Lacey's Regiment
    • Colonel: Edward Lacey
    • Lieutenant Colonel: Patrick McGriff
    • Major: Michael Dickson
    • Captains: John McClure, John McCool, John Nixon, Alexander Pagan, John Steele

There were also a small number of men from North Carolina at Huck's Defeat from the commands of Colonel Martin Armstrong of Surry County and Captain William Alexander of Mecklenburg County.

The British Provincial troops at Huck's Defeat belonged to detachments of two regiments stationed at Rocky Mount in the summer of 1780: the New York Volunteers (mounted infantry) and the British Legion (cavalry). Both regiments were comprised primarily of Loyalists from New York and Pennsylvania who came south in 1779 (Volunteers) or 1780 (Legion). The Loyalist militia for the most part belonged to one of two commands. The Rocky Mount Militia, under Colonel James Ferguson and Major John Owens, was recruited primarily from Chester, Fairfield and Lancaster Counties. The Upper District Militia, under Colonel Matthew Floyd and Lieutenant Colonel John Lisle, was recruited from present-day Spartanburg, Union and Newberry Counties. There also may have been a small detachment of Colonel Henry Rugeley's Camden Militia Regiment stationed at Rocky Mount under the immediate command of Lieutenant John Adamson.

HOME:

As far as we know, all of the soldiers in the Battle of Huck's Defeat were residents of the thirteen American colonies when the Revolution began. Wherever possible, I have identified the area that these men called home, using the modern names of the counties they lived in.

CHURCH (Whigs only):

The Whigs at Huck's Defeat were for the most part members of the eight Presbyterian congregations located in York and Chester Counties in 1780. The names of the congregations to which they belonged during the Revolution have been established using family genealogies, land plats and deeds, pastoral visitation lists, church histories, and cemetery rosters. However, readers should note that following the end of the war, many of these soldiers relocated to other states or transferred to the congregations of churches built after the war was over; for example, William McElwee lived in the area of the Bethel congregation during the Revolution but is actually buried at Bethany ARP Church (established 1797) in York County. The names of the ministers who pastored or supplied these congregations during the Revolution are noted in this list after the name of the churches, which were generally referred to as "meeting houses" in the eighteenth century. "Supply" is a Protestant term for a part-time minister filling in at a church that does not have a full-time pastor.

BEERSHEBA:

Beersheba Presbyterian Church, York County; the Reverend Joseph Alexander, supply.

- Dickson, E. Meek, et al. *Revised Directory of Beersheba Presbyterian Church Cemetery, York County, S.C.* York, SC: Beersheba Memorial Association, 1981.
- ———. *Directory of Beersheba Presbyterian Church Cemetery.* York, SC: Beersheba Memorial Association, 1988.
- Hart, Joseph E. *Beersheba Presbyterian Churchyard, York County, S.C.* York, SC: privately printed, n.d.

BETHEL:

Bethel Presbyterian Church, York County; the Reverend Hezekiah Balch and the Reverend Francis Cummins, supplies.

- Hart, Joseph E. *Bethel Churchyard.* York, SC: privately printed, n.d.
- Webb, R.A. *History of the Presbyterian Church of Bethel.* York, SC: privately printed, 1938.

BETHESDA:

Bethesda Presbyterian Church, York County; the Reverend John Simpson, supply.

- Glover, Roy, ed. *Cemetery Directory of Bethesda Presbyterian Church, 1769–1994.* McConnells, SC: privately printed, 1994.
- Walker, Robert H. *Directory of Bethesda Presbyterian Church Cemetery, December 1776–April 1980.* Rock Hill, SC: privately printed, 1980.

BULLOCKS CREEK:

Bullock's Creek Presbyterian Church, York County; the Reverend Joseph Alexander, pastor.

- Bullock Creek Cemetery Association. *Roster of Cemetery and Historical Sketch of Bullock Creek Church.* York, SC: privately printed, 1976.
- West, Jerry L. *A Historical Sketch of People, Places and Homes of Bullocks Creek, South Carolina.* Richburg, SC: Chester District Genealogical Society, 1986.
- ———. *Bullock's Creek Presbyterian Church Cemetery Roster, Bullock's Creek, York County, South Carolina.* Hickory Grove, SC: Broad River Basin Historical Society, 1993.

CATHOLIC:

Catholic Presbyterian Church, Chester County; the Reverend John Simpson and the Reverend William Martin, supplies.

- Agee, Jean Clawson, et al. *Old Catholic Presbyterian Church Cemetery Inscriptions, Chester County, South Carolina.* Richburg, SC: Chester County Genealogical Society, 1977.
- Strange, Mary Wylie. *The Revolutionary Soldiers of Catholic Presbyterian Church, Chester County, South Carolina.* Richburg, SC: Chester County Historical Committee, 1946.

FISHING CREEK:

Upper and Lower Fishing Creek Presbyterian Churches, Chester County; the Reverend John Simpson, pastor.

- Crowder, Louise K. *Tombstone Records of Chester County, South Carolina and Vicinity.* Chester, SC: privately printed, 1970.
- Hart, Joseph E. *Fishing Creek Presbyterian Churchyard, Chester County, S.C.* York, SC: privately printed, n.d.
- Perry, Max. *List of Visitations beginning December 12, 1774, of Rev. John Simpson while Pastor of Fishing Creek Presbyterian Church, Chester County, S.C.* Richburg, SC: Chester County Genealogical Society, n.d.

ROCKY CREEK:

Rocky Creek Reformed Presbyterian Church, Chester County; the Reverend William Martin, pastor.

- Ellet, Elizabeth F. *The Women of the American Revolution*, vol. 3. New York: Charles Scribner, 1854.

SOURCES:

The names contained in these lists come from a variety of primary and secondary sources, both British and American. At least one reliable documented source stating that the individual was at the battle is listed for each case. Because of space constraints, not all sources could be listed in this table, especially for well-documented individuals such as Christian Huck, William Bratton, Edward Lacey, John McClure, etc. References for prior service by Whig soldiers in the South Carolina Continental regiments are derived primarily from *The Roster of South Carolina Patriots in the American Revolution* by Dr. Bobby G. Moss (see below) and from Revolutionary War pension applications.

AA

South Carolina Revolutionary War Audited Accounts. Microfilm copy at South Carolina Department of Archives and History, Columbia, South Carolina.

Adair

Letter from John Adair Jr., Harodsburg, Kentucky, to Dr. Maurice A. Moore, Glen Springs, South Carolina, dated 17 December 1839. Thomas Sumter Papers, Lyman C. Draper Manuscript Collection, 5VV294–300.

BLW

Revolutionary War Bounty Land Warrants. Microfilm copy at South Carolina Department of Archives and History.

Braisted
> Sir Henry Clinton's orders to disband Emmerick's Chasseurs, dated 31 August 1779, in Todd Braisted, "Emmerick's Chasseurs: Disbanding of Corps." *The On-Line Institute for Advanced Loyalist Studies*, www.royalprovincial.com/military/emmerick/emmords3.htm.

Bratton
> Bratton, William Jr., and John Bratton. "Huck's Defeat: Dr. William Bratton's Story." Manuscript copy at the South Carolina Historical Society, Charleston, South Carolina. Photocopy on file at York County Historical Center, York, South Carolina.

CG
> Bondurant, Mary B. and Sarah F. White. "Tories of Ninety-Six District, S.C. 1783." *Carolina Genealogist*, vol. 2:1–4.

Collins
> Collins, James P. *Autobiography of a Revolutionary Soldier*. Edited by John M. Roberts. New York: Arno Press, 1979.

Cowpens
> Moss, Bobby G. *The Patriots at the Cowpens* (rev. ed.). Blacksburg, SC: Scotia-Hibernia Press, 1983.

CP
> Cornwallis Papers. The National Archives of Great Britain, Public Record Office. Microfilm copy at South Carolina Department of Archives and History.

Craig
> Craig, John. "The War in York and Chester." *Chester Standard*, Chester, SC, 16 March 1854.

Draper
> Thomas Sumter Papers (series VV), Lyman C. Draper Manuscript Collection. State Historical Society of Wisconsin. Microfilm copy at Dacus Library, Winthrop University, Rock Hill, South Carolina.

Ellet
> Ellet, Elizabeth F. *The Women of the American Revolution*, vol. III. New York: Charles Scribner, 1854.

FFGS
> Ferguson Family Group Sheets. Genealogical data compiled by Walter Whatley Brewster. Photocopies on file at York County Historical Center.

FPA
> Revolutionary War Federal Pension Applications, National Archives microfilm series M804. South Carolina Department of Archives and History.

Gaston
> Gaston, Joseph. "A Reminiscence of the Revolution." *The Southern Presbyterian*, Columbia, SC, 22 May 1873.

Hill
> [Hill, William]. *Col. William Hill's Memoirs of the Revolution*. Ed. A.S. Salley Jr. Columbia: Historical Commission of South Carolina, 1921.

Holcomb (1)
> Holcomb, Brent H. *Lancaster County, South Carolina Deed Abstracts 1787–1811*. Easley, SC: Southern Historical Press, 1981.

Holcomb (2)

Holcomb, Brent H. *South Carolina Deed Abstracts 1773–1778, Books F-4 through X-4*. Columbia: SCMAR, 1993.

Howe

Howe, George. *History of the Presbyterian Church in South Carolina. Vol. 1*. Columbia: Duffie & Chapman, 1870.

Lambert

Lambert, Robert S. *South Carolina Loyalists in the American Revolution*. Columbia: USC Press, 1987.

Lathan

Lathan, Robert. *Historical Sketches of the Revolutionary War in the Upcountry of South Carolina*. Transcribed by Jerald L West. Hickory Grove, SC: Broad River Basin Historical Society, 1998.

Logan

Logan, John H., and John Starr Moore. "Hauk's Defeat—Traditions of Starr Moore." Notes from an interview with John Starr Moore. Draper MSS, 16VV272–279.

Lossing

Lossing, Benton J. *Hours Spent with the Living Men and Women of the Revolution*. New York: Funk and Wagnalls, 1889.

Moore

Moore, Maurice A. *The Life of Gen. Edward Lacey*. Spartanburg, SC: Douglas, Evins & Co., 1859.

Moss

Moss, Bobby G. *Roster of South Carolina Patriots in the American Revolution*. Baltimore: Genealogical Publishing, 1983.

PCHD

[Bratton, John S., and W. C. Beatty]. *Proceedings of a Celebration of Huck's Defeat at Brattonsville, York District, S C, July 12, 1839*. Yorkville, SC: Tidings from the Craft, 1895.

Sabine

Sabine, Lorenzo. *Biographical Sketches of Loyalists of the American Revolution*, 2 vols. Baltimore: Genealogical Publishing, 1979.

SP

Charles Lewis deposition 4 June 1785, John Simpson Papers, RG1912. South Caroliniana Library, University of South Carolina, Columbia, SC.

Stinson

Stinson, Daniel Green. "Communication." *Chester Reporter*, Chester, SC, 29 May 1873.

Tarleton

Tarleton, Banastre. *A History of the Campaigns of 1780 and 1781 in the Southern Provinces of North America*. North Stratford, NH: Ayer Company, 1999 (reprint of 1787 edition).

White

White, William Boyce Jr. *Genealogy of Two Early Patton Families of York, Chester and Lancaster Counties, South Carolina*. Roanoke, VA: privately printed, 1996.

Winn

Winn, Richard. "Gen. Winn's Notes, Campaign 1780." Peter Force Papers, series 7E. Reel 3 of 56, microfilm 19,061. Library of Congress, Washington, D.C.

Remarks:

The majority of the Whig militiamen at the Battle of Huck's Defeat were veterans of the Revolution in South Carolina before the fall of Charleston in May 1780. Almost all of them had served in local militia units at some point during the first five years of the war, and many were veterans of the South Carolina regiments assigned to the Continental Line, especially the 3rd South Carolina Regiment of Rangers and the 6th South Carolina Regiment of Riflemen, and were honorably discharged pior to May 1780. Furthermore, many of these men were also veterans of skirmishes with British and Loyalist forces during the spring and early summer of 1780 before Huck's Defeat. Where known, previous Continental service and previous engagements (1780) are indicated in the "Remarks" column using the following abbreviations:

3rd SC
>Third South Carolina Regiment of Rangers

6th SC
>Sixth South Carolina Regiment of Riflemen

B
>Battle of Alexander's Old Field (Beckhamville), Chester County, South Carolina, 6 June 1780.

C
>Siege and capture of Charleston, Charleston County, South Carolina, 29 March–12 May 1780.

CD
>Continental Dragoons (Pulaski's Legion).

M
>Battle of Mobley's Meeting House, Fairfield County, South Carolina, 8 June 1780.

FC
>Skirmish at Fishing Creek Meeting House, Chester County, South Carolina, 11 June 1780.

H
>Battle of Hill's Iron Works, York County, South Carolina, 17 June 1780.

HD
>Battle of Huck's Defeat, York County, South Carolina, 12 July 1780.

R
>Battle of Ramsour's Mill, Lincoln County, North Carolina, 20 June 1780.

KIA
>Killed in action at Huck's Defeat, 12 July 1780.

WIA
>Wounded in action at Huck's Defeat, 12 July 1780.

POW
>Prisoner of war (Loyalist captured by Whigs on 12 July 1780).

Note: An asterisk (*) before the Federal Pension Application number (FPA) indicates that the soldier actually mentioned the Battle of Huck's Defeat in his application. A plus sign (+) after the name of a church indicates that the soldier is buried at that church.

TABLE 1: WHIG MILITIA

NAME	RANK	UNIT	HOME	CONGREGATION	SOURCES	REMARKS
Adair, James	Private	Lacey	Chester	Bethesda	Adair; HD, 10; Lathan, 17; Moore, 8; Howe, 338	
Adair, John	Lieutenant	Lacey	Chester	Bethesda	*FPA W2895; Adair; Logan; Moore, 8, 11n; Howe	3rd SC
Anderson, William	Private	Nixon/Lacey	Chester	Catholic	Ellet, III: 43, 131, 202	3rd SC
Armstrong, William	Private	McClure/Lacey	Chester		*FPA S6534	
Ash[e], Robert	Lieutenant	Bratton	York	Bethesda	HD, 10; Lathan, 17; Howe, 338	
Ball, Isaac	Private	Bratton	York	Bethesda	Logan	
Barber, James	Private	Nixon/Lacey	Chester	Catholic	Ellet, III: 198, 202	
Barber, Joseph	Private	Nixon/Lacey	Chester	Catholic	Ellet, III: 198, 202	
Barnet[t], Jacob	Captain	Barnet/Neal	York	Bethel	*FPA S13967 [Joseph Kerr]	
Barry, John	Private	Neal	York	Bethel	Lathan, 17	
Bishop, Henry	Private	McClure/Lacey	Chester	Fishing Creek	*FPA S9279 [John Bishop]	
Boggs, Thomas	Private	Bratton	York	Bethesda	FPA W27895; HD, 11; Lathan, 17; Howe, 338	3rd SC
Bratton, Hugh	Captain	Bratton/Bratton	York	Bethesda	Craig; Logan; HD, 10; Lathan, 17; Howe, 338	M. H. R
Bratton, Thomas	Private	Bratton/Bratton	York	Bethesda	Logan; HD, 10; Howe, 338	
Bratton, William	Colonel	Bratton	York	Bethesda+	Craig; Logan; Moore, 6, 9; HD, 4-9; Lathan, 17	M. H. R
Brown, Archibald	Private	Nixon/Lacey	Chester		*FPA S39249	6th SC
Brown, Robert	Private	Neal	York	Bethel	FPA R1337; HD, 10; Lathan, 17	
Burris, William	Private	Bratton	York	Bethesda+	HD, 10; Lathan, 17	
Campbell, ------	Private	McClure/Lacey	Chester		Craig; Logan	KIA
Carroll, John	Private	Neal	York	Bethesda	Craig; Logan; HD, 7; Lathan, 17; Moore, 11n	
Carroll, Joseph	Private	Neal	York	Bethel+	*FPA W9778	
Carroll, Thomas	Private	Neal	York	Bethesda	HD, 7, 10; Lathan, 17; Moore, 11n; Howe, 338	
Carson, John	Private	Bratton	York	Bethesda	FPA S35819; HD, 8, 10; Lathan, 17; Howe, 338	3rd SC
Carson, Walter	Captain	Carson/Neal	York	Beersheba	*FPA S32165; Lathan, 17	
Carson, William	Private	Neal	York	Beersheba+	*FPA S9305; HD, 11; Lathan, 17; Howe, 338	M
Chambers, John	Lieutenant	Moffett/Bratton	York	Beersheba+	Bratton; HD, 10; Lathan, 17; Howe, 338	
Clinton, James	Sergeant	Neal	York	Bethel	*FPA S2437	M. S. H
Collins, Daniel	Private	Moffett/Bratton	York	Beersheba	Collins, 25-27	
Collins, James P.	Private	Moffett/Bratton	York	Beersheba	*FPA R2173; Collins, 25-27	
Craig, John	Private	Neal	York	Bethel	*FPA W22864; Craig	B. M. R
Cunningham, George W.	Private	Neal	York		*FPA W2071	
Davis, William	Lieutenant	Neal	York	Bethel+	*FPA S2437 [James Clinton]; FPA W8653	

Name	Rank	Company	County	Church	Sources	Service
Carson, John	Private		York		FPA S35819; PCHD, 8, 10; Lathan, 17; Howe, 338	3rd SC
Carson, Walter	Captain	Carson/Neal	York	Beersheba	*FPA S32165; Lathan, 17	
Carson, William	Private	Neal	York	Beersheba+	*FPA S9305; PCHD, 11; Lathan, 17; Howe, 338	M
Chambers, John	Lieutenant	Moffett/Bratton	York	Beersheba+	Bratton; PCHD, 10; Lathan, 17; Howe, 338	
Clinton, James	Sergeant	Neal	York	Bethel	*FPA S2437	M, H
Collins, Daniel	Private	Moffett/Bratton	York	Beersheba	Collins, 25–27	
Collins, James P.	Private	Moffett/Bratton	York	Beersheba	*FPA R2173; Collins, 25–27	
Craig, John	Private	Neal	York	Bethel	*FPA W22864; Craig	B, M, R
Cunningham, George W.	Private	Neal	York		*FPA W2071	
Davis, William	Lieutenant	Neal	York	Bethel+	*FPA S2437 [James Clinton]; FPA W8653	
David[d]son, William	Private	Bratton	York	Bethesda	*AA 1822; PCHD, 10; Lathan, 17; Howe, 338	
Dickson [Dixon]. [David?]	Private	Moffett/Bratton	York	Beersheba	Collins, 33	
Dickson [Dixon]. [John?]	Private	Moffett/Bratton	York	Beersheba	Collins, 33	
Dickson [Dixon]. Michael	Major	Lacey	Chester	Fishing Creek	Craig; Draper, 16VV156	CD; R
Doyle, Edward	Private	Neal	York	Beersheba (?)	*FPA S32216	
Evans. Owen	Private	Moffett/Bratton (?)	York	Beersheba (?)	*FPA W10965	6th SC; R
Forbes. John	Lieutenant	Moffett/Bratton	York		*FPA R3645	WIA
Gaston. Hugh	Private	McClure/Lacey	Chester	Fishing Creek	*FPA S10729	3rd SC, C, B, M. H
Gaston. William	Private	McClure/Lacey	Chester	Fishing Creek	*FPA S32265	3rd SC, C. B. M. H
Gentry, Clairborne	Private	Armstrong	North Carolina		*FPA W6408 [Samuel Wallace]	
Gill. Arthur	Private	Lacey (?)	Chester	Fishing Creek	PCHD, 11; Lathan, 17–18; Howe. 338	
Gill. James	Private	Lacey (?)	Chester	Fishing Creek	*FPA R4023; PCHD, 11; Lathan, 17; Howe, 338	3rd SC. C
Gill. Robert Jr.	Private	Lacey (?)	Chester	Fishing Creek+	PCHD, 10; Howe. 338	3rd SC
Gill. Thomas	Lieutenant	Lacey (?)	Chester	Fishing Creek	FPA S31061; PCHD, 11; Lathan, 18; Howe, 338	3rd SC
Guy, William	Private	Bratton/Bratton	York	Bethesda+	PCHD, 10; Lathan, 18; Howe, 338	6th SC
Hanna. James	Private	Bratton	York	Bethesda+	PCHD, 10; Lathan, 18; Howe, 338	6th SC
Hanna, William	Private	Bratton	York	Bethesda+	PCHD, 10; Lathan, 18; Howe, 338	
Harbison, James	Private	Nixon/Lacey	Chester	Catholic+	Draper, 4VV36–39	M
Hawthorne, James	Major	Neal	York	Bethel	FPA S21592 [Francis Wylie]	
Hemphill, James	Lieutenant	Bratton	York	Bethesda	*FPA S21277; PCHD, 9; Lathan, 18; Howe, 338	6th SC

Name	Rank	Moffett/Bratton	County	Church	References	Notes
Henderson, John	Lieutenant		York		*FPA R2173 [James Collins]; FPA R4869	H
Hill, William	Lieutenant Colonel	Neal	York	Bethel+	Hill, 8–10; Moore, 7	H
Hillhouse, William	Lieutenant	Jamieson/Neal	York	Bullocks Creek	*FPA S7008: Howe. 338	
Hope, James	Private	Jamieson/Neal	York	Bullocks Creek	Draper, 4VV120	
Houston. Samuel	Private	McClure/Lacey	Chester		*FPA W7810	3rd SC. M. R
Howe, Joseph	Captain	Howe/Neal	York	Bethel+	*FPA S2437 [James Clinton]	
Howie, Robert	Private	Bratton	York	Bethesda+	PCHD, 10: Lathan, 18: Howe. 338	
Hunter. ——	Private	Neal	York		Ellet, III: 279	
Jamieson, James	Captain	Jamieson/Neal	York	Bullocks Creek+	*FPA S21839: PCHD. 11: Lathan. 18	R
Jenkins, Thomas	Captain	Jenkins/Bratton	York		*FPA S31774 [William Jenkins]	
Jenkins. William	Sergeant	Jenkins/Bratton	York		*FPA S31774	
Johns[t]on. James	Lieutenant	McClure/Lacey	Chester	Fishing Creek	*FPA W9088: Moore. 12: Ellet. III: 207	B. M
Johns[t]on. Matthew	Private	McClure/Lacey	Chester	Fishing Creek	Ellet. III: 207	B. M
Jones. Jonathan Jr.	Private	McClure/Lacey (?)	Chester	Fishing Creek+	*AA 4109	
Kelso [Kelsey]. Samuel	Private	McClure/Lacey	Chester	Fishing Creek+	PCHD. 10: Lathan. 18: Howe. 338	
Kidd. John	Private	Bratton	York	Bethesda	PCHD. 10: Lathan. 18: Howe. 338	
Kincaid. James	Private	Moffett/Bratton	York		*FPA R5929	
Knox. William	Lieutenant	McClure/Lacey	Chester	Catholic	*FPA S38900	6th SC
Lacey. Edward	Colonel	Lacey	Chester		Craig; Logan: Lathan. 18: Moore, 6–11: Howe, 338	M
Leech. David	Private	Bratton	York	Bethesda	PCHD. 10: Lathan. 18: Howe. 338	
Lofton. Samuel	Private	Howe/Neal	York		*FPA S17114 [Thomas Lofton]	6th SC
Lofton. Thomas	Lieutenant	Howe/Neal	York		*FPA S17114	6th SC
Love. Andrew	Captain	Bratton or Neal	York	Bethesda	PCHD. 10: Lathan. 18: Howe. 338. 610	
McCaw. James	Private	Pagan/Lacey	Chester		*FPA S18117	
McCaw. John	Private	Moffett/Bratton	York	Beersheba+	PCHD. 11: Lathan. 18	3rd SC. R
McClure. Hugh	Lieutenant	McClure/Lacey	Chester	Fishing Creek+	*FPA W21789: Craig: Gaston: PCHD. 9	3rd SC. C. B. M. H
McClure. John	Captain	McClure/Lacey	Chester	Fishing Creek	Craig: Gaston: PCHD. 4–6: Lathan. 18	3rd SC. C. B. M. H
McConnell. John	Lieutenant	Bratton	York	Bethesda+	PCHD. 8–9: Lathan, 17	M (?)
McCool. John	Captain	McCool/Lacey	Chester		*FPA W10246 [Joseph Robinson]	
McElwee. James	Private	Moffett/Bratton	York	Bethesda (?)	*FPA W9553: Logan; PCHD. 10: Lathan. 18	
McElwee. William	Private	Moffett/Bratton	York	Beersheba (?)	Lossing, 95–104: Logan	
McGarity. William	Private	Nixon/Lacey	Chester	Catholic	*FPA R6713	3rd SC, B, M
McGriff, Patrick "Paddy"	Lieutenant Colonel	Lacey	Chester		FPA W9194 [John Mills]; Draper, 11VV326	

Name	Rank	Commander	County	Church	References	Code
Manahan, William	Sergeant	Bratton	York	Bethesda	PCHD, 11: Howe, 338	
Martin, James	Captain	Bratton or Neal	York	Bethesda+	*FPA S9391; PCHD, 11; Moore, 20; Howe, 338	R
Martin, John	Private	Neal	York	Bethel	FPA W9642: PCHD, 11: Lathan, 18	R
Maxwell, William	Private	Alexander	North Carolina		*FPA W6408 [Samuel Wallace]	
Miles, Charles	Lieutenant	Lacey	Chester		FPA R21890: Craig: Winn, 4: PCHD, 10	
Millar [Miller], John	Captain	Millar/Bratton	York	Bethesda	FPA S1717 [George Ross]: Howe, 338	3rd SC
Miller, "Hopping" John	Sergeant	Lacey	Chester		FPA S38950: PCHD, 10: Lathan, 18	3rd SC. 6th SC
Mills, John	Lieutenant	Lacey	Chester	Fishing Creek+	FPA W9194: Lathan, 17: Moore, 8-9n	3rd SC. 6th SC
Mitchell, James	Captain	Mitchell/Bratton	York	Bethesda+	BLW 2105-300: PCHD, 9: Lathan, 18	3rd SC
Moffett, John	Captain	Moffett/Bratton	York	Beersheba	Collins, 25-27: Craig: PCHD, 4-6, 9: Lathan, 18	
Moore, Alexander	Private	Lacey	York	Bethesda+	PCHD, 10: Moore, 11n: Lathan, 18: Howe, 338	
Moore, James	Captain	Moore/Bratton	York	Bethesda+	PCHD, 9: Lathan, 18: Moore, 9: Howe, 338	3rd SC
Moore, John Jr.	Private	Bratton	York	Bethesda+	Logan: PCHD, 11: Lathan, 18: Howe, 338	3rd SC
Moore, Nathan	Private	Bratton	York	Bethesda+	PCHD, 11: Lathan, 18: Howe, 338	3rd SC
Moore, Samuel	Private	Bratton	York	Bethesda+	PCHD, 11: Lathan, 18: Howe, 338	3rd SC
Moore, William I	Lieutenant	Bratton	York	Bethesda	PCHD, 11: Lathan, 18: Howe, 338	
Moore, William II	Private	Bratton	York	Bethesda	Logan: PCHD, 10: Lathan, 18: Howe, 338	
Morrow, David	Private	McClure/Lacey	Chester	Fishing Creek	*FPA S7253	3rd SC. B. M
Morrow, Joseph	Private	McClure/Lacey	Chester	Fishing Creek+	*FPA S21892	B. M
Neal, Andrew	Colonel	Neal	York	Bethel	Hill, 7-8: Craig: Moore, 7, 9n	
Neal, Thomas Jr.	Captain	Neal/Neal	York	Bethel	FPA R2173 [James Collins]	
Neely, George	Private	McClure/Lacey	Chester	Fishing Creek	*FPA S4613	
Nixon, John	Captain	Nixon/Lacey	Chester	Catholic	Craig: PCHD, 11: Lathan, 18	C
Pagan, Alexander	Captain	Pagan/Lacey	Chester	Fishing Creek	FPA S31061 [Thomas Gill]	R
Pattison [Patterson], Robert	Sergeant	Bratton or Neal	York	Bethel (?)	*FPA S3654	H. R
Patton, John	Private	Thomson/Neal	York		*FPA W162	R
Rainey, Benjamin	Captain	Rainey/Bratton	York	Bethesda	PCHD, 10: Lathan, 18: Howe, 338	
Rainey, Samuel	Private	Bratton	York	Bethesda+	PCHD, 10: Lathan, 18: Howe, 338	
Rainey, Thomas	Private	Bratton	York	Bethesda	PCHD, 10: Lathan, 18: Howe, 338	M
Rea [Ray], Henry	Private	Bratton	York	Bethesda	*FPA W9246: PCHD, 11: Lathan, 18: Howe, 338	R
Read [Reed, Reid], James	Captain	Read/Bratton	York	Bullocks Creek	Winn, 5: Moss, 583, 805, 807	

Name	Rank	McCool/Lacey	Chester	Bullocks Creek	References	Code
Robinson, Joseph	Private	McCool/Lacey	Chester	Bullocks Creek	*FPA W10246	
Robi[n]son, William	Lieutenant	Jamieson/Neal	York	Bullocks Creek	*FPA S21452; FPA W2302 [Robert Wilson]	R
Ross, George	Private	Millar/Bratton	York	Bethesda+	*FPA S1717	
Ross, James	Private	Millar/Bratton	York	Bethesda+	PCHD. 10: Lathan. 18: Howe. 338	
Ross, William	Private	Millar/Bratton	York	Bethesda+	PCHD. 10: Lathan. 18: Howe. 338	
Sad[d]ler. David	Private	Neal	York	Bethesda	*FPA S9471: Logan; PCHD. 11: Lathan. 17: Howe	M
Simpson. the Reverend John	Private	Pagan/Lacey	Chester	Fishing Creek	AA 7019: Craig: Ellet, III: 217–219	B. M
Smith. John	Private	Bratton or Neal	Chester	Fishing Creek	Lathan. 18: White. 2	3rd SC
Smith. Robert	Captain	Winn/Bratton	Fairfield		FPA R9731: PCHD. 10	
Steel[e]. John	Captain	Steel/Lacey	Chester	Catholic	*FPA78810 [Samuel Houston]	3rd SC. C. B. M
Stephenson, James	Private	Lacey or Bratton	York	Bullocks Creek (?)	*FPA W596: Cowpens. 273	
Stephenson. Robert	Private	Neal	York	Bullocks Creek	* AA 7357	
Swann. John	Private	Bratton	York	Bethesda	PCHD. 10: Lathan. 18: Howe. 338	
Thom[p]son. Robert	Captain	Thomson/Neal	York	Bethel	*FPA W162 [John Patton]	
Wallace. James	Captain	Wallace/Bratton	York	Bethesda+	FPA S19145: Lathan. 18: Howe. 338	
Wallace. John	Major	Bratton	York	Bethesda	*FPA S955: PCHD. 11: Lathan. 18: Howe, 338	R
Wallace. Samuel	Private	Wallace/Bratton	York	Bethesda	*FPA W6408	
Watson. Samuel Jr.	Private	Moffett/Bratton	York	Bethel	*FPA S17187	
Williamson. Adam	Private	Bratton	York	Bethesda	PCHD. 11: Lathan. 18: Howe. 338. 610	
Williamson. George	Private	Bratton	York	Bethesda	PCHD. 11: Lathan. 18: Howe. 338. 610	
Williamson. John	Private	Bratton	York	Bethesda	PCHD. 11: Lathan. 18: Howe. 338. 610	
Williamson. Samuel	Private	Bratton	York	Bethesda+	Logan; PCHD. 8. 11: Lathan. 18: Moore. 9n: Howe	
Winn [Wynn]. Richard	Colonel	Bratton	Fairfield		Winn. 4–6: Logan: PCHD. 4	3rd SC. M
Woods. Thomas	Private	Neal	York		*FPA S32614	
Wylie [Wiley]. Francis	Private	McClure/Lacey	Chester	Catholic	*FPA S21592: PCHD. 11	M
Wylie [Wiley]. Peter	Private	McClure/Lacey	Chester	Fishing Creek+	PCHD. 11: Lathan. 18	

TABLE 2: WHIGS CAPTURED BY CAPTAIN HUCK ON 11 JULY 1780

NAME	RANK	UNIT	HOME	CONGREGATION	SOURCES	REMARKS
Bratton, Robert			York	Bethesda	Logan: HD, 5, 12	
Clendennon, Thomas			York	Bethesda+	Logan: HD, 5, 12; Moore, 10; Howe, 338	
Curry, Charles			York	Bethesda'	HD, 10; Moore, 10; Howe, 338	
McClure, James	Private	McClure/Lacey	Chester	Fishing Creek	HD, 10; Ellet, III: 179-80	3rd SC
McRandall, James			York	Bethesda	HD, 5, 12	
Martin, Edward 'Ned'	Private	McClure/Lacey	Chester	Fishing Creek	Ellet, III: 179-80; HD, 12	
Moore, John Sr. 'Gum Log'			York	Bethesda	Logan: HD, 5, 11; Moore, 10	

TABLE 3: PROVINCIAL SOLDIERS AND LOYALIST MILITIA

NAME	RANK	UNIT	HOME	SOURCE	REMARKS
Adamson, John	Lieutenant	Camden militia	Camden, SC	CP 30/11/2/277-278, 285-286; Bratton; Lambert, 298-299	WIA; POW
Burge, Burrel	Private	Rocky Mount militia	Chester County, SC	CCGB	FC [possible HD]
Burge, Jeremiah	Private	Rocky Mount militia	Chester County, SC	CCGB: Holcomb (1), 99	FC [possible HD]
Cameron, Allan	Ensign	New York Volunteers	New York	CP 30/11/2/285-286; Sabine, II: 491	
Dennis, John	Private	Rocky Mount militia	York County, SC	Logan; Howe, 338	H [possible HD]
Featherston, John	Private	Rocky Mount militia	Chester County, SC	Stinson: Ellet, III: 127	B [possible HD]
Featherston, Richard	Private	Rocky Mount militia	Chester County, SC	Ellet, III: 127; Holcomb (1), 20	B [possible HD]
Featherston, William	Private	Rocky Mount militia	Chester County, SC	CG	[possible HD]
Ferguson, Abraham	Private (?)	Rocky Mount militia	Chester County, SC	Ellet, III: 198-202; FFGS	
Ferguson, Adams	Private (?)	Rocky Mount militia	Chester County, SC	Ellet, III: 198-202; FFGS	
Ferguson, James	Colonel	Rocky Mount militia	Chester County, SC	Winn, 5-6; Hill, 10; Craig; HD; Moore, 10; Ellet, III: 199-202	KIA
Ferguson, Robert	Private (?)	Rocky Mount militia	Chester County, SC	Ellet, III: 198-202; FFGS	
Floyd, Abraham	Captain	Upper District militia	Union County, SC	CP 30/11/2/162-163	
Floyd, Matthew	Colonel	Upper District militia	Union County, SC	CP 30/11/2/162-163; Craig; Ellet, III: 179,185; Draper, 9VV13	
Henry, [John ?]	Private (?)	Rocky Mount militia	Fairfield County (?), SC	Draper, 9VV37; Ellet, III: 202	WIA
Houseman, Henry	Captain	Rocky Mount militia	Lancaster County, SC	CP 30/11/2/158-159; HD; Gaston; Holcomb (1 & 2)	B [possible HD]
Huck, Christian	Captain	British Legion	Philadelphia County, PA	CP 30/11/2/285-286; Craig; Winn, 4-6; Hill, 8-10; Bratton	FC, H: KIA
Hunt, Benjamin	Lieutenant	British Legion	Westchester Co., PA	CP 30/11/2/285-286, 277-278: Sabine, II: 534	WIA; POW
Lacey, Reuben	Private	Rocky Mount militia	York County, SC	Moore, 8-9n	
Lewis, [Charles ?]	Lieutenant	Rocky Mount militia	Chester County, SC	CP 30/11/2/285-286; CCGB	FC [possible HD]
Lisle (Lyle), John	Lt. Col.	Upper District militia	Newberry County, SC	Tarleton, 93; Lambert, 119, 128	3rd SC
McGregor, John	Lieutenant	New York Volunteers	Philadelphia, PA	CP 30/11/2/285-286, 277-8: Sabine, II: 553	
Owens, John	Major	Rocky Mount militia	Chester County, SC	Winn, 6-7: Draper, 4VV16-27, 5VV15, 30-31; JHR 1785-6	POW
Robison/Robertson,--	Major	Upper District militia (?)	SC	FPA W22864 [John Craig]; Draper, 4VV86, 11VV416	KIA
Swaine, Nathaniel	Cornet	British Legion		Clinton Papers; Braisted	[possible HD]

Notes

Introduction

1. These counties did not actually exist before 1785. During the Revolution, York County was part of the New Acquisition District, while Chester and Fairfield Counties were part of the District between the Broad and Catawba Rivers. Both the New Acquisition District and the District Between the Broad and Catawba Rivers were electoral districts, which in turn were part of the much larger Camden Judicial District. See David Duncan Wallace, *The History of South Carolina* (New York: American Historical Society, 1934), II:63–65, 336.

2. The term "Scotch-Irish" was employed in Great Britain at least as far back as the sixteenth century to describe persons of Scottish or "Scotch" ancestry who colonized northern Ireland. The term has come under attack in recent decades by individuals who favor the alternate terms "Scots-Irish" or "Ulster Scots." However, "Scotch-Irish" was the historical term used in the North American colonies from the seventeenth century onward to describe Protestant immigrants from the north of Ireland, most of who were of Scottish ancestry. Its use in this book to denote the eighteenth century settlers of the Carolina Backcountry is thus appropriate and historically valid. See James G. Leyburn, *The Scotch-Irish: A Social History* (Chapel Hill, NC: UNC Press, 1962), 215–216, 221.

3. Stephen E. Ambrose, *Band of Brothers* (New York: Simon & Schuster, 1992, 2001), 309, 311.

4. Lawrence E. Babits, *A Devil of a Whipping: The Battle of Cowpens* (Chapel Hill: UNC Press, 1998).

Chapter 1

5. James G. Leyburn, *The Scotch-Irish: A Social History* (Chapel Hill, NC: UNC Press, 1962), 172–173, 215–220, 226–231.

6. Map 1, "South Carolina Counties, 1692," and Map 2, "South Carolina Parishes, 1770," in Walter B. Edgar, Inez Watson et al., eds., *Biographical Directory of the South Carolina House of Representatives, Volume 1, Session Lists 1692–1973* (Columbia, SC: USC Press, 1974), 20, 46; Works Progress Administration (WPA), "Guide Maps to the Development of South Carolina Parishes, Districts and Counties" (Columbia: South Carolina Archives, 1938), 2–3; WPA, "Formation of Counties in South Carolina" (Columbia: South Carolina Archives, 1938), 1.

7. Charles Woodmason, *The Carolina Backcountry on the Eve of the Revolution*, ed. Richard J. Hooker (Chapel Hill: UNC Press, 1953), 166.

8. Brent H. Holcomb, *North Carolina Land Grants in South Carolina* (Baltimore, MD: Genealogical Publishing Company, 1980), iii.

9. Marvin L. Skaggs, *North Carolina Boundary Disputes Involving Her Southern Line* (Chapel Hill: UNC Press, 1941), 46–47, 49–52, 54–55; Hugh T. Lefler and Albert Ray Newsome, *The History of a Southern State: North Carolina* (Chapel Hill: UNC Press, 1973), 163.

10. Skaggs, 38, 50–51, 63, 78, 83; Douglas Summers Brown, *The Catawba Indians: The People of the River* (Columbia: USC Press, 1966), 203–204, 245–246, 255–256.

11. Robert M. Weir, *Colonial South Carolina: A History* (Millwood, NY: KTO Press, 1983), 269–272.

12. Weir, 275.

13. Skaggs, 73, 80; Hugh T. Lefler and William S. Powell, *Colonial North Carolina: A History* (New York: Charles Scribner's Sons, 1973), 96.

14. Skaggs, 74, 76–77, 79–80.

15. Weir, 275; Robert S. Lambert, *South Carolina Loyalists in the American Revolution* (Columbia, SC: USC Press, 1987), 17.

16. Woodmason, 25, 29, 167–169; Skaggs, 77, 89–90; Weir, 275–276, 323.

17. Weir, 275–279; Lefler and Powell, 217–239; Lambert, 17.

18. Weir, 277–278; Lambert, 17–18.

19. Woodmason, 181, 207 n 23–25, 208 n 27, 242 n 50; Lefler and Powell, 277; Lambert, 48, 57 n 40, 76 n 31; Walter Clark, ed. and comp., *The State Records of North Carolina: Volume XIX, 1782–1784* (Goldsboro, NC: Nash Brothers, 1901), 975.

20. David Duncan Wallace, *The History of South Carolina* (New York: The American Historical Society, 1934), II:61; WPA, "Formation of Counties in South Carolina," 1; Lambert, 18.

21. Skaggs, 73, 80.

22. Skaggs, 87–88.

23. Journal of the Second Provincial Congress, 21 November 1775, in William E. Hemphill and Wylma A. Wates, eds., *Extracts from the Journals of the Provincial Congresses of South Carolina, 1775–1776* (Columbia: South Carolina Archives Department, 1960), 142; Lefler and Newsome, 163–164.

24. René Chartrand and David Rickman, *Colonial American Troops 1610–1774*, vol. 3 (Oxford: Osprey Publishing, 2003), 5.

25. Leyburn, 228–231; Chartrand and Rickman, 5–7; Russell F. Weigley, *The Partisan War: the South Carolina Campaign of 1780–1782* (Columbia: USC Press, 1970), 11–14; John W. Gordon, *South Carolina and the American Revolution: A Battlefield History* (Columbia: USC Press, 2003), 13.

26. Hemphill and Wates, xvii.

27. Map 3, "South Carolina Election Districts, 1775, 1776," in Edgar and Watson, 150; list of members, First Provincial Congress, January 1775, in Hemphill and Wates, 7–8; Journal of the First Provincial Congress, 1–2 June and 18 June 1775, in Hemphill and Wates, 33, 34–35, 57; list of members, Second Provincial Congress, November 1775, in Hemphill and Wates, 76; Wallace, II:209 n 16.

28. Journal of the Second Provincial Congress, 9 February 1776, in Hemphill and Wates, 183, 260.

29. Journal of the Second Provincial Congress, 8 November 1775, in Hemphill and Wates, 102–103.

30. Weigley, 13; Weir, 322–323; John S. Pancake, *This Destructive War* (University, AL: University of Alabama Press, 1985), 78–79.

31. Weir, 321–323.

32. Journal of the First Provincial Congress, 3 June 1775, in Hemphill and Wates, 36.

33. Wallace, II:121–122; Weir, 322–323.

34. Journal of the First Provincial Congress, 6 June 1775, in Hemphill and Wates, 39.

35. Journal of the First Provincial Congress, 9–11 June 1775, in Hemphill and Wates, 44–46; Wallace, II:124. William Thomson was also the colonel of the Orangeburg District Militia Regiment, which sometimes caused confusion between "Thomson's militia regiment" and "Thomson's ranger regiment." See A.S. Salley, *The History of Orangeburg County, South Carolina* (Orangeburg: R.L. Berry, 1898), 468.

36. Journal of the First Provincial Congress, 12 June 1775, in Hemphill and Wates, 47–48.

37. Wallace, II:124; Robert D. Bass, *Gamecock* (Orangeburg, SC: Sandlapper Publishing, 2000), 30, 33.

38. Journal of the First Provincial Congress, 14 June 1775, in Hemphill and Wates, 50–51; Henry Laurens, *The Papers of Henry Laurens, Volume 10*, ed. David R. Chesnutt and C. James Taylor (Columbia: USC Press, 1985), 182–183.

39. Journal of the First Provincial Congress, 16 June 1775, in Hemphill and Wates, 55.

40. Journal of the First Provincial Congress, 17 June 1775, in Hemphill and Wates, 55.

41. Laurens, *ibid.*

42. Journal of the Second Provincial Congress, 21 November 1775, in Hemphill and Wates, 143.

43. Lieutenant Governor William Bull to the Earl of Hillsborough, 7 June 1770, quoted in Clyde R. Ferguson, "Functions of the Partisan-Militia in the South during the American Revolution: An Interpretation," in W. Robert Wiggin, ed., *The Revolutionary War in the South: Power, Conflict, and Leadership* (Durham, NC: Duke University Press, 1979), 241; Lambert, 16, 30 n 11.

44. Journal of the Second Provincial Congress, 8 November 1775, in Hemphill and Wates, 104.

45. Ferguson, in Wiggin, 242.

46. Wallace, II:131–137; Weir, 323–325.

47. N. Louise Bailey and Elizabeth Ivey Cooper, *Biographical Directory of the South Carolina House of Representatives, Volume III: 1775–1790* (Columbia: USC Press, 1981), 523–524.

48. William Tennent to Henry Laurens, 20 August 1775, in R.W. Gibbes, ed., *Documentary History of the American Revolution, Volume I: 1764–1776* (Spartanburg: Reprint Company, 1972), 145–146.

49. William Henry Drayton to Council of Safety, 21 August 1775, in John Drayton, ed., *Memoirs of the American Revolution* (Charleston, SC: A.E. Miller, 1821), 376; Wallace, II:136.

50. Drayton to Council of Safety, 30 August 1775, in Drayton, 380.

51. Hemphill and Wates, 8, 33, 77, 87; William Edwin Hemphill, Wylma Anne Wates and R. Nicholas Olsberg, eds., *Journals of the General Assembly and House of Representatives, 1776–1780* (Columbia: USC Press, 1970), 306–307, 311–314, Bailey and Cooper, 523–524.

52. List of justices for Camden District, in Hemphill, Wates and Olsberg, 14; Bailey and Cooper, 88–89.

53. Jerome J. Nadelhaft, *The Disorders of War: The Revolution in South Carolina* (Orono, ME: University of Maine at Orono Press, 1981), 33.

54. John B. O'Neall, "Revolutionary Incidents: Memoir of Joseph McJunkin, of Union," *The Magnolia, or Southern Apalachian*, vol. 2, no. 1 (January 1843): 33; George Howe, *History of the Presbyterian Church in South Carolina*, vol. I (Columbia: Duffie & Chapman, 1870), 332–334, 339, 514–515, 603.

55. Howe, 432–433, 515, 518, 604–605.

56. Muster roll, Turkey Creek Volunteer Militia Company, in A.S. Salley Jr., "Papers of the First Council of Safety of the Revolutionary Party in South Carolina, June–November 1775," *South Carolina Historical and Genealogical Magazine*, vol. III, no. 3 (July 1902): 130–131. A.S. Salley Jr., "Rebel Rolls of 1775," *Charleston Sunday News* (Charleston, SC), 19 March 1899.

57. Maurice A. Moore, *The Life of Gen. Edward Lacey* (Spartanburg, SC: Douglas, Evins & Co., 1859), 3–4; Holcomb, *North Carolina Land Grants*, 79.

58. Salley, "Rebel Rolls."

59. J.D. Bailey, *Reverends Philip Mulkey and James Fowler* (Cowpens: p. p., 1924), 14–15, 17, 20, 23.

60. Elizabeth F. Ellet, *The Women of the American Revolution* (New York: Charles Scribner, 1853–1854), III:216–7; Howe, 424–426, 508–514.

61. Bobby G. Moss, *Roster of South Carolina Patriots in the American Revolution* (Baltimore: Genealogical Publishing Company, 1983), 109 [Joseph Brown], 255 [Michael Dickson], 749 [Alexander Pagan], 961 [Philip Walker]. Philip Walker owned the lower mill on Fishing Creek in present-day Lando, Chester County, until 1784, when he sold it to Hugh White, the owner of White's Mill on upper Fishing Creek in present-day York County. After 1784, Walker's Mill also became known as White's Mill, which created confusion between the two mill sites. In the nineteenth century, many Revolutionary War veterans, including John Craig and John Adair, as well as local historians, such as Maurice Moore and Daniel Stinson, referred to Walker's Mill as "White's Mill in Chester District," forgetting that it was actually Walker's Mill throughout the years of the Revolution. See Elmer O. Parker, note 1, in Maurice Moore, *The Life of General Edward Lacey*, ed. Brent H. Holcomb and Elmer O. Parker (Greenville: A. Press, 1981), 22.

62. Journal of the First Provincial Congress, 2 June 1775, in Hemphill and Wates, 34; list of justices for Camden District and members of the South Carolina General Assembly, 1776–1778, in Hemphill, Wates and Olsberg, 14, 311.

63. Howe, 297–298, 336, 513.

64. Howe, 37–39, 45–48, 427–428, 507, 696–699.

65. Ellet, III:124–126, 164; Howe, 500–501, 697.

66. List of members, Second Provincial Congress, November 1775, in Hemphill and Wates, 76; list of justices for Camden District and members of the South Carolina General Assembly, 1776–1778, in Hemphill, Wates and Olsberg, 14, 306, 313.

67. John Craig, "The War in York and Chester," *Chester Standard* (Chester, SC), 16 March 1854.

68. Journal of the Second Provincial Congress, 7–8 and 13 November 1775, in Hemphill and Wates, 99–105, 137–138; Bass, 29.

69. Journal of the Second Provincial Congress, 7 November 1775, in Hemphill and Wates, 102; A.S. Salley Jr., "Papers of the First Council of Safety of the Revolutionary Party in South

Carolina, June–November 1775," *South Carolina Historical and Genealogical Magazine*, vol. III, no. 1, January 1902, 3; Bass, 30.

70. Georgia Muldrow Gilmer and Elmer O. Parker, *American Revolution Roster, Fort Sullivan (Later Fort Moultrie), 1776–1780, and Battle of Fort Sullivan: Events Leading to First Decisive Victory* (Charleston: Fort Sullivan Chapter Daughters of the American Revolution, 1976), 31–35; James McCaw, Revolutionary War Federal Pension Application (FPA) S18117, National Archives Microfilm Series M804; Bass, 30–31.

71. Journal of the Second Provincial Congress, 13 November 1775, in Hemphill and Wates, 124.

72. Journal of the Second Provincial Congress, 22 February 1776, in Hemphill and Wates, 201–204.

73. Journal of the Second Provincial Congress, 28 February 1776, in Hemphill and Wates, 212–214.

74. Bass, 33–34.

75. William Lewis, FPA R6335; Lawrence E. Babits, *A Devil of a Whipping: The Battle of Cowpens* (Chapel Hill: UNC Press, 1998), 29.

76. Mark M. Boatner, *Encyclopedia of the American Revolution* (Mechanicsburg, PA: Stackpole Books, 1994), 1210.

77. Maurice A. Moore, *Reminiscences of York*, ed. Elmer O. Parker (Greenville, SC: A. Press, 1981), 19–21; Bass, 36.

78. Bass, 38.

79. Bass, 38–39.

80. Daniel G. Stinson, "Mrs. Susannah Smart," *Chester Standard* (Chester, SC), 17 September 1851.

81. Journals of the General Assembly, 20 September 1776, in Hemphill, Wates and Olsberg, 82; Bass, 40.

82. Bass, 40–41.

83. Bass, 41.

84. James Hemphill, FPA S21277.

85. Salley, *Orangeburg County*, 469.

86. Moore, *Lacey*, 4; Craig, "War in York and Chester"; Bailey and Cooper, 524; Bass, 44–45; Boatner, 1033–1034, 1210.

87. Jacob Black, FPA S9281; John Black, FPA W9359; James Fergus, FPA W25573; John Moore, FPA W9205; John C. Dann, ed., *The Revolution Remembered* (Chicago: University of Chicago Press, 1980), 177.

88. Fergus, FPA W25573; Dann, 178; Boatner, 113, 1034.

89. William McGarity, FPA R6713; Boatner, 573–574.

90. Fergus, FPA W25573; George Cunningham, FPA W2071; Dann, 178–181; Boatner, 113.

91. Moore, *Reminiscences*, 16.

92. John Linn to Jennet Linn, 1 April 1779, in Thomas Sumter Papers, Lyman C. Draper Manuscript Collection, 9VV40; Daniel Green Stinson, "Communication," *Chester Reporter* (Chester, SC), 29 May 1873.

93. Fergus, FPA W25573; Dann, 181–182; Moore, *Reminiscences*, 16.

94. Boatner, 1034.

95. James Hemphill, FPA S21277.

96. Boatner, 1034; Craig, "War"; John Knox, FPA W10181; Robert Knox, FPA W26190; Alexander Walker, FPA W8979; Moss, *South Carolina Patriots*, 596 [David McCance], 961

[Philip Walker]; Edward McCrady, *The History of South Carolina in the Revolution, 1775–1780* (New York: Russell and Russell, 1901), 363–364.

97. William Johnston, FPA S18062; Bailey and Cooper, 524.

98. Boatner, 1034–1036, 1062.

99. Bailey and Cooper, 524.

100. William Fleming, FPA S32250.

101. Joseph McJunkin, "Reminiscences of the Revolutionary War," 18 July 1837, in Draper MSS, 23VV168.

102. James Clinton, FPA S2437; George Ross, FPA S1717.

103. Charles P. Borick, *A Gallant Defense: The Siege of Charleston, 1780* (Columbia: USC Press, 2003), 27–28; Boatner, 206–207.

104. Alexander S. Salley, *Records of the Regiments of the South Carolina Line in the Revolutionary War* (Baltimore: Clearfield Company, 1992), 1.

105. Colonel William Thomson's Order Book, in Salley, *Orangeburg County*, 452–453; Darby Erd and Fitzhugh McMasters, "The Third South Carolina Regiment (Rangers), 1775–1780," *Military Uniforms in America*, plate no. 494, Company of Military Historians, Rutland, Maryland.

106. William Moultrie, *Memoirs of the American Revolution* (New York: Arno Press, 1968), II:44, 47; Borick, 57–58.

107. William Wylie, Audited Account (AA) 8822; Hugh Gaston, FPA S10729.

108. Joseph Gaston, FPA W22089.

109. Joseph Gaston, "A Reminiscence of the Revolution," *The Southern Presbyterian* (Columbia, SC), 22 May 1873; Anne Pickens Collins, *A Goodly Heritage: A History of Chester County, South Carolina* (Columbia: Collins Publications, 1986), 33–35.

110. Wylie, AA 8822; Hugh Gaston, FPA S10729; Joseph Johnson, *Traditions and Reminiscences, chiefly of the American Revolution in the South* (Charleston: Walker and James, 1851), 340; Ellet, III:121, 157.

111. Boatner, 114–115, 189–190, 1087.

112. Bobby G. Moss, *Roster of the Loyalists in the Battle of Kings Mountain* (Blacksburg, SC: Scotia-Hibernia Press, 1998), 28–29.

113. Banastre Tarleton, *A History of the Campaigns of 1780 and 1781 in the Southern Provinces of North America* (North Stratford, NH: Ayer Publishing, 1999; reprint of 1787 edition), 15–17; [Uzal Johnson], *Uzal Johnson, Loyalist Surgeon: A Revolutionary War Diary*, ed. Bobby G. Moss (Blacksburg, SC: Scotia-Hibernia Press, 2000), 22–23; Hugh Gaston, FPA S10729; McCrady, 467–469; Boatner, 711.

114. Hugh Gaston, FPA S10729.

115. Samuel Houston, FPA W7810; Joseph Morrow, FPA S21892; Moss, *South Carolina Patriots*, 109 [Joseph Brown].

Chapter 2

116. Charles P. Borick, *A Gallant Defense: The Siege of Charleston, 1780* (Columbia, SC: USC Press, 2003), 35–36, 219–220; Mark M. Boatner, *Encyclopedia of the American Revolution* (Mechanicsburg, PA: Stackpole Books, 1994), 212–213.

117. Banastre Tarleton, *A History of the Campaigns of 1780 and 1781 in the Southern Provinces of North America* (North Stratford, NH: Ayer Publishing, 1999; reprint of 1787 edition), 22.

118. Borick, 234–236.

119. Elizabeth F. Ellet, *The Women of the American Revolution* (New York: Charles Scribner, 1853–1854), III:121, 157; Joseph Johnson, *Traditions and Reminiscences, chiefly of the American Revolution in the South* (Charleston, SC: Walker and James, 1851), 340; Joseph Gaston, "A Reminiscence of the Revolution," *The Southern Presbyterian* (Columbia, SC), 22 May 1873; Hugh Gaston, Revolutionary War Federal Pension Application (FPA) S10729.

120. Borick, 192, 236–237; Boatner, 616, 1173.

121. Tarleton, 26–27; Borick, 236–237; Lyman C. Draper, *King's Mountain and Its Heroes* (Baltimore. MD: Genealogical Publishing, 1971), 68; Boatner, 365, 575.

122. Samuel Houston, FPA W7810; Joseph Morrow, FPA S21892.

123. Sir Henry Clinton, proclamation, 22 May 1780, in Tarleton, 71–72.

124. Draper, *King's Mountain*, 46; Charles Stedman, *The History of the Origin, Progress, and Termination of the American War* (New York: Arno Press, 1969), II:191; Robert S. Lambert, *South Carolina Loyalists in the American Revolution* (Columbia: USC Press, 1987), 97.

125. Tarleton, 27; Robert D. Bass, *Gamecock* (Orangeburg, SC: Sandlapper Publishing, 2000), 51.

126. Bass, 46, 51–52; Boatner, 1077.

127. Brigadier General William Caswell to North Carolina Governor Abner Nash, 3 June 1780, in Walter Clark, ed. and comp., *The State Records of North Carolina, Volume XIV, 1779–1780* (Winston, NC: M.I. & J.C. Stewart, 1896), 832–833.

128. Douglas Summers Brown, *The Catawba Indians: The People of the River* (Columbia: USC Press, 1966), 35–36, 97, 248.

129. Tarleton, 28–30; Boatner, 1173–1174.

130. Tarleton, 30–31.

131. Tarleton, 83–84; Stedman, II:193.

132. Anthony J. Scotti Jr., *Brutal Virtue: The Myth and Reality of Banastre Tarleton* (Bowie, MD: Heritage Books, 2002), 176–177.

133. Tarleton, 30–31, 83–84; Draper, *King's Mountain*, 45; Bass, 53; Boatner, 1174.

134. Tarleton, 31–32; Boatner, 1174–1175.

135. Clark, *The State Records of North Carolina*, XIX: 985n.

136. John Buchanan, *The Road to Guilford Courthouse* (New York: John Wiley & Sons, 1997), 84–85; Draper, *King's Mountain*, 45–46; Borick, 237; Boatner, 1173–1175.

137. Buchanan, 84–85; Scotti, 175–179; Thomas A. Rider, "Massacre or Myth: No Quarter at the Waxhaws, 29 May 1780" (master of arts thesis, University of North Carolina at Chapel Hill, 2002), 25–28; James Piecuch, "Massacre or Myth: Banastre Tarleton at the Waxhaws, May 29, 1780," *Southern Campaigns of the American Revolution*, vol. 1, no. 2, (October 2004): 3–9.

138. Scotti, 173.

139. Rider, 51.

140. Boatner, 1175.

141. Tarleton, 31.

142. Bass, 53; Tarleton, 30.

143. Boatner, 1174–1175; Scotti, 178, 192 n 59, 197 n 78, 197 n 79, 197 n 80; Rider, 1–6, 51–52. The Second College Edition of *Webster's New World Dictionary of the American Language* (New York: World Publishing Company, 1970) notes that "slaughter, as applied to people, suggests extensive and brutal killing, as in battle or by deliberate acts of wanton cruelty; massacre implies the indiscriminate and wholesale slaughter of those who are defenseless or helpless to resist" (1338). The difference would certainly have been lost on Buford's soldiers and the residents of the Backcountry.

144. David Duncan Wallace, *The History of South Carolina* (New York: The American Historical Society, 1934), II:204.

145. Joseph Gaston, "Reminiscence." The Third Regiment of Rangers was a Continental regiment, not militia.

146. Stedman, II:193n, 195; Thomas J. Kirkland and Robert M. Kennedy, *Historic Camden Part One, Colonial and Revolutionary* (Columbia: State Company, 1905), 142–143.

147. Oliver Snoddy, "The Volunteers of Ireland," *The Irish Sword*, vol. 7, no. 27 (1965), 147–149; Boatner, 918–919, 1156–1157.

148. Tarleton, 31–32; Stedman, II:195–196; Boatner, 918–919, 1036; Lambert, 113–119; Daniel G. Stinson to Lyman C. Draper, 20 May 1873, in Draper MSS, 9VV215–216.

149. Sir Henry Clinton and Admiral Marriot Arbuthnot, proclamation, 1 June 1780, in Tarleton, 74–76.

150. Clinton and Arbuthnot, in Tarleton, 74–76; Stedman, 192; Draper, 46; Lambert, 97.

151. Sir Henry Clinton, proclamation, 3 June 1780, in Tarleton, 73–74.

152. Stinson to Draper, 20 May 1873, in Draper MSS, 9VV215–216; Lambert, 113–119.

153. James P. Collins, *Autobiography of a Revolutionary Soldier*, ed. John M. Roberts (New York: Arno Press, 1979), 24.

154. Tarleton, 87, 92–93; Boatner, 58, 941; Lieutenant Colonel George Turnbull to Lord Charles Cornwallis, 12 June 1780, in Cornwallis Papers, PRO 30/11/2/147–148.

155. Lyman C. Draper, research notes on George Turnbull, in Draper MSS, 17VV133–137; Todd Braisted, e-mail to author, 7 January 2005; L. Edward Purcell, *Who was Who in the American Revolution* (New York: Facts on File, 1993), 483; Boatner, 208–209, 243–244, 802, 1129.

156. Muster rolls, Captain Christian Huck's company of chasseurs, Emmerick's Chasseurs, October 1778, November 1778 and 5 January 1779, Public Archives of Canada (PAC), Record Group 8, C series, vol. 1891; Anne M. Ousterhout, *A State Divided* (New York: Greenwood Press, 1987), 158; Lorenzo Sabine, *Biographical Sketches of Loyalists of the American Revolution* (Port Washington, NY: Kennikat Press, 1966), I:552.

157. Sir Henry Clinton, orders transferring Captain Huck's troop of dragoons to the British Legion, 31 August 1779, in Clinton Papers (vol. 67, item 1), William L. Clement Library, University of Michigan, transcribed in Todd Braisted, "Emmerick's Chasseurs: Disbanding of Corps," The On-Line Institute of Loyalist Studies (http:www.royalprovincial.com/military/rhist/emmerick/emmords3.htm).

158. Braisted, e-mail to author, 17 December 2004; Turnbull to Cornwallis, 15 June, 16 June and 19 June 1780, in Cornwallis Papers, PRO 30/11/2/158–159, 162–163, 171–172; Cornwallis to Clinton, 15 July 1780, in Tarleton, 120–121; Tarleton, 93.

159. Richard Winn, "General Richard Winn's Notes—1780," in Peter Force Papers, Library of Congress, Series 7E, 4, 6.

160. David Ramsay, *The History of the Revolution of South-Carolina* (Trenton, NJ: Isaac Collins, 1785), I:135–136; Sabine, I:553.

161. Joseph Gaston, "Reminiscence."

162. McJunkin, "Reminiscences," in Draper MSS, 23VV172.

163. List of members of Second Provincial Congress, November 1775, in William E. Hemphill and Wylma A. Wates, eds., *Extracts from the Journals of the Provincial Congresses of South Carolina, 1775–1776* (Columbia: Archives Department, 1960), 76; list of members, South Carolina General Assembly, 1776–1778, in William Edwin Hemphill, Wylma Anne Wates and R. Nicholas Olsberg, eds., *Journals of the General Assembly and House of Representatives, 1776–1780* (Columbia: USC Press, 1970), 306, 311, 314; N. Louise Bailey and Elizabeth Ivey Cooper, *Biographical Directory of the South Carolina House of Representatives, Volume III: 1775–1790* (Columbia: USC Press, 1981), 86–87, 708–711; John Belton O'Neall, *Annals of Newberry in Two Parts: Part First* (Newberry, SC: Aull and Houseal, 1892), 52–53.

164. Joseph McJunkin, "A Ms. Statement of Maj. McJunkin," undated, in Draper MSS, 23VV204.

165. Samuel McCalla, "Rev. Saml. McCalla's Reminiscences," 2 January 1873, in Draper MSS, 14VV436.

166. Draper interview with Daniel Stinson, 8–18 August 1871, in Draper MSS, 9VV37; Stinson to Draper, 20 May 1873, in Draper MSS, 9VV215; Daniel Stinson, "Communication," *Chester Reporter* (Chester, SC), 29 May 1873; Ellet, III:159.

167. Tarleton, 32; Boatner, 22, 1036.

168. Lambert, 106–107.

169. Joseph Gaston, "Reminiscence"; Ellet, III:99–101, 159–160.

170. Gaston, "Reminiscence."

171. John Craig, "The War in York and Chester," *Chester Standard* (Chester, SC), 16 March 1854; Ellet, III:99–101, 159–160; Draper, interview with Stinson, 8–18 August 1871, in Draper MSS, 9VV12; Samuel McCalla, in Draper MSS, 14VV436–437.

172. Draper, 9VV37.

173. Turnbull to Cornwallis, 15 June 1780.

174. J. Boykin, 1820 survey of Lancaster District, in Robert Mills, *Mills' Atlas of South Carolina* (Lexington, SC: Sandlapper Store, 1979).

175. Brent H. Holcomb, *Lancaster County, South Carolina Deed Abstracts 1787–1811* (Easley, SC: Southern Historical Press, 1981), 25, 95; Brent H. Holcomb, *South Carolina Deed Abstracts 1773–1778, Books F-4 through X-4* (Columbia: South Carolina Magazine of Ancestral Research, 1993), 158, 180, 206, 242.

176. Gaston, "Reminiscence"; Benson J. Lossing, *The Pictorial Field Book of the American Revolution* (Cottonport, LA: Polyanthos, 1972), II: 451 n 1; "Battle of Huck's Defeat," *Yorkville Enquirer* (Yorkville, SC), 2 October 1903.

177. Stinson to Draper, 10 May 1872 and 20 May 1873, in Draper MSS, 9VV72, 9VV215–216; Ellet, III:127.

178. Mary B. Bondurant and Sarah F. White, "Tories of Ninety-Six District, S.C. 1783," *Carolina Genealogist*, vol. 2, 4; Ellet, III:392; Draper, interview with Stinson, 8–18 August 1871, in Draper MSS, 9VV30.

Chapter 3

179. Hugh McClure, Revolutionary War Federal Pension Application (FPA) W21789; William McGarity, FPA R6713; Daniel G. Stinson, "Communication," *Chester Reporter* (Chester, SC), 29 May 1873; John Craig, "The War in York and Chester," *Chester Standard* (Chester, SC), 16 March 1854; Joseph Gaston, "A Reminiscence of the Revolution," *The Southern Presbyterian* (Columbia, SC), 22 May 1873; Lyman C. Draper, interview with Daniel G. Stinson, 8–18 August 1871, in Draper MSS, 9VV12, 15, 19, 37, 177; Stinson to Draper, 20 May 1873, in Draper MSS, 9VV215–217; Elizabeth F. Ellet, *The Women of the American Revolution* (New York: Charles Scribner, 1853–1854), III:132, 159–160, 176–177, 217.

180. [William Hill], *Col. William Hill's Memoirs of the Revolution* , ed. A. S. Salley Jr. (Columbia: State Company, 1921), 6.

181. N. Louise Bailey and Elizabeth Ivey Cooper, *Biographical Directory of the South Carolina House of Representatives, Volume III: 1775–1790* (Columbia: USC Press, 1981), 89, 755; Maurice A. Moore to Lyman C. Draper, 28 July 1870, in Draper MSS, 14VV97–98; Louise Pettus, "Col. Samuel Watson of the Revolution," *York County Genealogical and Historical Society Quarterly*, vol. 8, no. 2 (September 1996): 27.

182. Samuel Gordon, supporting statement for James Clinton, FPA S2437.

183. Laurence K. Wells, *York County, South Carolina, Minutes of the County Court 1786–1797* (Columbia: SCMAR, 1981), 4; Bailey and Cooper, 88–89, 339–341; Emily Bellinger Reynolds and Joan Reynolds Faunt, *Biographical Directory of the Senate of the State of South Carolina 1776–1964* (Columbia: South Carolina Archives Department, 1964), 185, 237.

184. Daniel H. Hill to Lyman C. Draper, 19 August 1869, in Draper MSS, 11VV230–235.

185. Daniel H. Hill, *Col. William Hill and the Campaign of 1780* (p. p., c. 1919), 7; Anne King Gregorie, "William Hill," in *Dictionary of American Biography*, ed. Dumas Malone (New York: Charles Scribner's Sons, 1958), 9:48–49.

186. South Carolina Colonial Plats (1731–1775), 7:257, 8:349, 8:352, 11:124, 17:2; South Carolina Colonial Land Grants (1675–1788), 10:311, 10:511, 11:421, 19:404, 23:684, 32:238, 35:111; South Carolina Auditor General, Memorial Books (1731–1778), 6:269, 10:144, 14:3, 14:17, 14:249; Lyman C. Draper, interview with J.M. Ross, 5 August 1871, in Draper MSS, 11VV329–332.

187. *South Carolina Gazette*, 24 November 1779; Reynolds and Faunt, 237; Journal of the South Carolina General Assembly, 1776, in William Edwin Hemphill, Wylma Anne Wates and R. Nicholas Olsberg, eds., *Journals of the General Assembly and House of Representatives, 1776–1780* (Columbia: USC Press, 1970), 284; Gregorie, 9:48–49; Bailey and Cooper, 339–341; Moore to Draper, 28 July 1870, in Draper MSS, 14VV97–98; Daniel Hill, *Campaign of 1780*, 7.

188. Daniel Hill, *Campaign of 1780*, 8.

189. List of members, South Carolina General Assembly, 1776–1778, and Senate, 1778–1780, in Hemphill, Wates and Olsberg, 312, 323, 326; Gregorie, 9:48–49; Bailey and Cooper, 339–341; Reynolds and Faunt, 237.

190. Lyman C. Draper, interview with James Rufus Bratton and John S. Bratton Jr., July 1871, in Draper MSS, 11VV333–336; John H. Logan, interview with Harriet Rainey Bratton, c. 1857, in Draper MSS, 16VV154; Reynolds and Faunt, 185.

191. Brent H. Holcomb, *Anson County, North Carolina Deed Abstracts 1749–1766, and Abstracts of Wills and Estates 1749–1795* (Baltimore, MD: Genealogical Publishing, 1980), 142; Brent H. Holcomb and Elmer O. Parker, *Mecklenburg County, North Carolina Deed Abstracts 1763–1779* (Greenville, SC: Southern Historical Press, 1979), 17, 71, 107; Brent H. Holcomb, *Tryon County, North Carolina Minutes of the Court of Pleas and Quarter Sessions 1769–1779* (Columbia: SCMAR, 1994), 70, 71; Holcomb, *North Carolina Land Grants*, 50, 77, 79, 128, 133; Brent H. Holcomb, *South Carolina Deed Abstracts 1773–1778, Books F-4 through X-4* (Columbia: SCMAR, 1993), 215; South Carolina Colonial Plats (1731–1775), 8:517.

192. Holcomb, *Tryon County Minutes*, 7, 13, 17.

193. List of justices for Camden District, in Hemphill, Wates and Olsberg, 14; Reynolds and Faunt, 185; Bailey and Cooper, 88–89.

194. Maurice A. Moore to Lyman C. Draper, 28 July 1870, in Draper MSS, 14VV96–97.

195. Lyman C. Draper, interview with James J. Winn, 7–8 June 1871, in Draper MSS, 16VV75; Bailey and Cooper, 777–781; Bobby G. Moss, *Roster of South Carolina Patriots in the American Revolution* (Baltimore: Genealogical Publishing Company, 1983), 1006 [Richard Winn].

196. Bailey and Cooper, 781.

197. The Journal of the Second Provincial Congress referred to this ferry as "Shyra's ferry"; Richard Winn called it "Shiroes ferry" (William E. Hemphill and Wylma A. Wates, eds., *Extracts from the Journals of the Provincial Congresses of South Carolina, 1775–1776* ([Columbia: South Carolina Archives Department, 1960]), 251; Richard Winn, "General Richard Winn's Notes—1780," Peter Force Papers, Library of Congress, Series 7E, 1). Terry Lipscomb has identified it as Shirer's Ferry. See Lipscomb, "South Carolina Revolutionary Battles Part Three," *Names in South Carolina*, vol. XXII, winter 1975, 33, 39 n 2.

198. Winn, "Notes," 1; Draper, interview with Stinson, 8–18 August 1871, in Draper MSS, 9VV12–13; John Craig, FPA W22864; Craig, "War"; Maurice Moore to Draper, 4 January 1870, in Draper MSS, 14VV56; Moore to Draper, 28 July 1870, in Draper MSS, 14VV97–98.

199. Joseph Graham, "Battle of Ramsour's Mill," quoted in David Schenck, *North Carolina 1780–'81* (Bowie, MD: Heritage Books, 2000), 52–53.

200. Winn, "Notes," 1; Ellet, III:177, 291–292.

201. Maurice Moore to Lyman Draper, 31 January 1870, in Draper MSS, 14VV59–60.

202. Winn, "Notes," 1.

203. Hugh Gaston, FPA S10729.

204. Winn, "Notes," 1.

205. Draper, interview with Stinson, 8–18 August 1871, in Draper MSS, 9VV12–13.

206. Winn, "Notes," 1–2.

207. Lieutenant Colonel George Turnbull to Lord Cornwallis, 12 June and 15 June 1780; Robert D. Bass, *Gamecock* (Orangeburg, SC: Sandlapper Publishing, 2000), 55.

208. Walter Whatley Brewster, "Fargeson/Ferguson Family Group Sheets," York County Historical Center; Howard Ferguson, "The Chester County, South Carolina, Fergusons and the British Colonel Ferguson," *Chester County Genealogical Society Bulletin*, vol. 6, no. 3 (September 1983): 77–78.

209. Max Perry, ed., *List of Visitations beginning December 12, 1774 of Rev. John Simpson while Pastor of Fishing Creek Presbyterian Church, Chester County, S.C.* (Richburg: Chester County Genealogical Society, n.d.), 2, 4.

210. South Carolina Colonial Plats, 19:16, 19:20; Mary Lee Barnes, "John Owens of Chester County, South Carolina," *Chester District Genealogical Bulletin*, vol. 18, no. 3 (September 1994): 105.

211. Turnbull to Cornwallis, 15 June 1780.

212. Craig, "War"; Maurice A. Moore, *The Life of Gen. Edward Lacey* (Spartanburg, SC: Douglas, Evins & Co., 1859), 10; Ellet, III:198–201; Winn, "Notes," 5–7; Daniel Hill, *Campaign of 1780*, 9; Robert M. Cooper to Lyman C. Draper, 15 November 1872, in Draper MSS, 14VV17; James Hemphill to Lyman C. Draper, in Draper MSS, 14VV88.

213. Pay Abstract Nr. 159, Colonel W.T. Turner's regiment of Rocky Mount militia, Camden District, SC, from 13 June 1782 to 14 December 1782 (PRO T50, vol. 2), in Murtie June Clark, *Loyalists in the Southern Campaign of the American Revolution* (Baltimore, MD: Genealogical Publishing, 1981), I:152.

214. Turnbull to Cornwallis, 6 July 1780, in Cornwallis Papers, PRO 30/11/2/250–251.

215. Turnbull to Cornwallis, 16 June 1780.

216. Turnbull to Cornwallis, 12 June 1780.

217. Craig, "War."

218. William Hill, *Memoirs*, 4.

219. Holcomb and Parker, *Mecklenburg County*, 116, 187; e-mail, Linda Black Welder to author, 18 January 2005.

220. Lord Rawdon to Lord Cornwallis, 11 June 1780, in Cornwallis Papers, PRO 30/11/2/123–125; Banastre Tarleton, *A History of the Campaigns of 1780 and 1781 in the Southern Provinces of North America* (North Stratford, NH: Ayer Publishing, 1999; reprint of 1787 edition), 86.

221. Charles Stedman, *The History of the Origin, Progress, and Termination of the American War* (New York: Arno Press, 1969), II:198n.

222. Stedman, 225n–226n.

223. Turnbull to Cornwallis, 15 June 1780.

224. Ellet, III:217–218.

225. John Simpson, Audited Account (AA) 7019.

226. Ellet, III:217–218; Winn, "Notes," 28; Stinson to Draper, 5 October 1874, in Draper MSS, 8VV26–27.

227. Craig, "War."

228. Craig, "War"; James Martin, FPA S9391; William Robison, FPA S21452; John Craig, FPA W22864; Henry Rea, FPA W9246.

229. Winn, "Notes," 28.

230. McJunkin, "Reminiscences," in Draper MSS, 23VV168; McJunkin, "Ms. Statement," in Draper MSS, 23VV204; Thomas Young, "Memoir of Major Thomas Young," *Orion*, October 1843, 85; Robert S. Lambert, *South Carolina Loyalists in the American Revolution* (Columbia, SC: USC Press, 1987), 206.

231. Young, 85.

232. McJunkin, "Reminiscences," 23VV204.

233. Tarleton, 85; William Hill, *Memoirs*, 6; Lambert, 106–107.

234. Graham, in Schenck, 52–53.

235. Max Perry, *American Descendants of John "Jean" Gaston* (Greenville, SC: A. Press, 1994), 21, 184; Christopher Strong, FPA W9315; Christopher Strong and William Strong, AA 7484; Moss, *South Carolina Patriots*, 904 [Christopher Strong].

236. Turnbull to Cornwallis, 15 June 1780.

237. Ellet, III:225–226.

238. Ellet, 217.

239. Ellet, 218–219.

240. Charles Lewis deposition, 24 June 1785, in John Simpson Papers, RG 1912, South Caroliniana Library; Elmer O. Parker, "Burning by the British of Reverend Simpson's Home and Hill's Iron Works," *Chester County Genealogical Bulletin,* vol. 3, no. 2, June 1980, 27.

241. Winn, "Notes," 28.

242. William D. James, *A Sketch of the Life of Brig. Gen. Francis Marion* (Charleston: Gould and Riley, 1821), 72.

243. McJunkin, "Ms. Statement," in Draper MSS, 23VV209.

244. Draper, interview with Stinson, 8–18 August 1871, in Draper MSS, 9VV12, 28.

245. Jessie R. Busick, James H. Saye Jr. and Martha H. Sudol, *"Through the Years" 1752–2002, Fishing Creek Presbyterian Church Bicenquinquagenary Celebration* (Chester, SC: p. p., 2002), 1.

246. Ellet, III:124–126.

247. Rawdon to the inhabitants of Charlotte, North Carolina, 11 June 1780, in Cornwallis Papers, PRO 30/11/2/127–128.

248. Rawdon to Cornwallis, 11 June 1780.

249. "At the close of the revolutionary war a number of Whigs went to [Montgomery's] house and killed him. In 1808, his son Green Berry prosecuted four of them for the killing of his father. Having a Lawyer, Matthews, a relative, to prosecute the case, four were indicted viz Capt. John Steele, Benjamin Rowan, John McWaters, & Alexander McKeown. When the case came up in Court neither prosecutor nor lawyer appeared, the case was thrown out of Court," (Daniel G. Stinson to Lyman C. Draper, 25 March 1873, in Draper MSS, 175–176). Stinson also stated that James Boyd's widow employed a man named Norton to kill Montgomery: "Norton after he killed him cut off the fore finger of the right hand and took it to her." Mrs. Boyd later married Norton (Stinson to Draper, 7 May 1873, in Draper MSS, 9VV210). See also Ellet, III:164–165, and George Howe, *History of the Presbyterian Church in South Carolina,* vol. I (Columbia: Duffie & Chapman, 1870), I:500–501.

250. McJunkin, "Reminiscences," in Draper MSS, 23VV168–169.

251. William Hill, *Memoirs,* 6–7.

252. Tarleton, 91–92, 119; Bass, 50, 62; Mark M. Boatner, *Encyclopedia of the American Revolution* (Mechanicsburg, PA: Stackpole Books, 1994), 571, 1036–1037.

253. William Hill, *Memoirs,* 7; Samuel Gordon, supporting statement for James Clinton, FPA S2437.

254. William Hill, *Memoirs,* 7.

255. Turnbull to Cornwallis, 12 June 1780.

256. William Hill, *Memoirs,* 8; Draper, interview with Stinson, 8–18 August 1871, in Draper MSS, 9VV10, 12–13, 28–29.

257. James Hemphill to Lyman C. Draper, 2 October 1874, in Draper MSS, 4VV85; Lambert, 119.

258. Holcomb, *North Carolina Land Grants,* 12, 64; Holcomb and Parker, *Mecklenburg County,* 7, 17, 21, 75.

259. "Claims produced...from the frontiers for services done on the expedition against the Cherokees," in Walter Clark, ed. and comp., *The State Records of North Carolina: Volume XXII, Miscellaneous* (Goldsboro, NC: Nash Brothers, 1907), 820–821.

260. Minutes of the Governor's Council Meeting, Newbern, North Carolina, 31 December 1762, in William L. Saunders, ed. and comp., *The Colonial Records of North Carolina: Volume VI, 1759–1765* (Raleigh, NC: Josephus Daniels, 1888), 799; Holcomb, *Tryon County Minutes*, 18; Lambert, 119.

261. Holcomb, *Mecklenburg County Deed Abstracts*, 109, 111, 116; Holcomb, *Tryon County Minutes*, 56, 69, 81.

262. American Loyalist Claims, Memorial of Matthew Floyd, PRO AO13/128/264–281; Loyalist Transcripts, Memorial of Matthew Floyd, New York Public Library, LT/54/469–478; George Cunningham, FPA W2071; Lambert, 119.

263. William Hill, *Memoirs*, 8.

264. Turnbull to Cornwallis, 15 June 1780; Lambert, 119.

265. Turnbull to Cornwallis, 15 June 1780.

266. Graham, in Schenck, 53–54.

267. Turnbull to Cornwallis, 15 June 1780.

268. Turnbull to Cornwallis, 16 June 1780; Cornwallis to Clinton, 6 August 1780, in Cornwallis Papers, PRO 30/11/72/36; Tarleton, 126–127; Lambert, 119; Ellet, III:179.

269. Turnbull to Cornwallis, 16 June 1780; Abraham Floyd, FPA S32251.

270. Cornwallis to Clinton, 6 August 1780, in Cornwallis Papers, PRO 30/11/72/36; Tarleton, 93, 126–127; Lambert, 128.

271. Journal of the Second Provincial Congress, 24 November 1775, in Hemphill and Wates, 148–149; Journal of the Second Provincial Congress, 8 and 14 February 1776, in Hemphill and Wates, 181, 189; A.S. Salley, *The History of Orangeburg County, South Carolina* (Orangeburg: R.L. Berry, 1898), 387; John Belton O'Neall, *Annals of Newberry in Two Parts: Part First* (Newberry, SC: Aull and Houseal, 1892), 155–157; Moss, *South Carolina Patriots*, 569 [John Liles], 572 [John Lisle].

272. Cornwallis to Clinton, 6 August 1780, in Cornwallis Papers, PRO 30/11/72/36; Tarleton, 93, 126–127; Lambert, 128.

273. Rawdon was camped in the Waxhaws from 10 June until 15 June, at which time he returned to Camden.

274. Turnbull to Cornwallis, 16 June 1780.

275. Rawdon to Cornwallis, 22 June and 24 June 1780, in Cornwallis Papers, PRO 30/11/2/179–182, 189–190; Turnbull to Cornwallis, 6 July 1780.

276. Samuel Houston, FPA W7810; Robert McCreight, FPA S21881; Moss, *South Carolina Patriots*, 109 [Joseph Brown].

277. S.N.D. North et al., *Heads of Families at the First Census of the United States Taken in the Year 1790: South Carolina* (Spartanburg, SC: Reprint Company, 1960), 19; Elmer O. Parker, "Early Surveys West of Lando, S.C.," *Chester County Genealogical Society Bulletin*, vol. V, no. 4 (December 1982): 101; George Neely, FPA S4613. The 1790 census lists Joseph Brown immediately after Nicholas Bishop, and Elmer Parker's map shows Nicholas Bishop's property near the modern intersection of Highways 9 and 901.

278. Moore, *Lacey*, 6; Turnbull to Cornwallis, 16 June 1780; Rawdon to Cornwallis, 22 June 1780.

279. Cornwallis to Turnbull, 16 June 1780, in Cornwallis Papers, PRO 30/11/77/11–12.

280. Bass, 53–54.

281. William Hill, *Memoirs*, 8.

282. John H. Logan and John Starr Moore, "Hauk's Defeat — Traditions of Starr Moore," c. 1857, in Draper MSS, 16VV276.

283. Robert Lathan, *Historical Sketches of the Revolutionary War in the Upcountry of South Carolina*, transcribed by Jerald L. West (Hickory Grove, SC: Broad River Basin Historical Society, 1998), 13; Holcomb, *North Carolina Land Grants*, 118–119; Brent H. Holcomb and Elmer O. Parker, *Camden District, S.C. Wills and Administrations, 1781–1787* (Easley, SC: Southern Historical Press, 1978), 68; Moss, *South Carolina Patriots*, 866 [James Simril], 20 [John Anderson].

284. Lyman C. Draper, interview with General Thomas C. McMackin, 26 May 1871, in Draper MSS, 16VV49; South Carolina Colonial Plats, 38:20; Holcomb, *North Carolina Land Grants*, 135.

285. William Hill, *Memoirs*, 8; James P. Collins, *Autobiography of a Revolutionary Soldier*, ed. John M. Roberts (New York: Arno Press, 1979), 25.

286. John Henderson, AA 3522; Turnbull to Cornwallis, 19 June 1780, in Cornwallis Papers, PRO 30/11/2/171–172.

287. Draper, interview with McMackin, 26 May 1871, in Draper MSS, 16VV49; Daniel Hill, *Campaign of 1780*, 8.

288. William Hill, *Memoirs*, 8; Draper, interview with McMackin, 26 May 1871, in Draper MSS, 16VV49; Turnbull to Cornwallis, 19 June 1780, in Cornwallis Papers, PRO 30/11/2/171–172.

289. Turnbull to Cornwallis, 19 June 1780, in Cornwallis Papers, PRO 30/11/2/171–172; Draper, interview with Stinson, 8–18 August 1871, in Draper MSS, 9VV10, 12–13, 28–29.

290. Draper, interview with McMackin, in Draper MSS, 16VV49–50.

291. Benjamin Rowan, AA 6641; Daniel Hill, *Campaign of 1780*, 8.

292. William Little, "Our Iron Industry of Old," *Rock Hill Weekly Sun* (Rock Hill, SC), 1 January 1897.

293. Joseph Gaston, "A Reminiscence of the Revolution," *The Southern Presbyterian* (Columbia, SC), 22 May 1873.

294. William Hill, *Memoirs*, 8.

295. William Hill, *Memoirs*, 10.

296. General Joseph Graham to Judge Archibald D. Murphey, c. 1820, in Walter Clark, ed., *The State Records of North Carolina*, XIX: 985.

297. Moore, *Lacey*, 6.

298. McJunkin, "Reminiscences," in Draper MSS, 23VV169–171, 205–206; Gaston, "Reminiscence"; Hill, *Memoirs*, 8; Winn, "Notes," 2.

299. Turnbull to Cornwallis, 15 June 1780; Rawdon to Cornwallis, 22 June 1780.

300. Hill, *Memoirs*, 9.

301. Rawdon to Cornwallis, 22 June 1780; Draper, interview with Stinson, 8–18 August 1871, in Draper MSS, 9VV28–29; Logan and Moore, in Draper MSS, 16VV274; Joseph Kerr, FPA S13967; Bass, 55.

302. Winn, "Notes," 2.

303. McJunkin, "Reminiscences," in Draper MSS, 23VV171.

304. John Adair, FPA W2895.

305. Lorenzo Sabine, *Biographical Sketches of Loyalists of the American Revolution* (Port Washington, NY: Kennikat Press, 1966), II:100–103; Robert O. DeMond, *The Loyalists in North Carolina during the American Revolution* (Baltimore: Genealogical Publishing, 1979), 125–126.

306. McJunkin, "Ms. Statement," in Draper MSS, 23VV207.

307. Graham, in Schenck, 54.

308. Graham to Murphey, *c.* 1820, in Clark, *The State Records of North Carolina*, XIX: 984–985.

309. Graham, in Schenck, 54–55.

310. Turnbull to Cornwallis, 19 June 1780.

311. John Henderson, AA 3522, FPA R4869.

312. Graham, in Schenck, 57–62; Hill, *Memoirs*, 8; Winn, "Notes," 2–3; McJunkin, "Reminiscences," in Draper MSS, 23VV171; McJunkin, "Ms. Statement," in Draper MSS, 23VV206–207; Thomas Lofton, FPA S17114; Bass, 57; Boatner, 913–914.

313. James Martin, FPA S9391; William Robison, FPA S21542; John Craig, FPA W22864; Henry Rea, W9246.

314. Hill, *Memoirs*, 8; McJunkin, "Ms. Statement," in Draper MSS, 23VV207; Bass, 57.

315. Stedman, II:196; Sabine, II:100–101; Boatner, 914.

316. Boatner, 1037.

317. Tarleton, 91–92.

318. Clinton, 3 June 1780, in Tarleton, 73–74; Cornwallis to Clinton, 14 July 1780, in Tarleton, 119.

319. Winn, "Notes," 3; James Hemphill, FPA S21277; James Martin, FPA S9391; Henry Rea, FPA W9246.

320. Robert Wilson, FPA W2302.

321. Benjamin Rowan, AA 6641; Ellet, III:178.

322. Samuel E. Belk to Lyman C. Draper, 9 June 1874, in Draper MSS, 6VV312; Ellet, III:178.

323. McJunkin, "Ms. Statement," in Draper MSS, 23VV208.

324. Hill, *Memoirs*, 9.

325. Moore, *Lacey*, 10; Daniel Williams Family Group Sheet, Joe Hart Genealogical Collection (RG-6, Historical Center of York County York, SC).

326. Collins, 24.

327. Holy Bible, King James Version, II Kings 18:33, 35; II Kings 19:10–11.

328. Rawdon to Cornwallis, 22 June and 24 June 1780.

329. Rawdon to Cornwallis, 22 June 1780; Turnbull to Cornwallis, 6 July 1780.

330. Rawdon to Cornwallis, 24 June 1780.

331. Turnbull to Cornwallis, 6 July 1780.

332. J.M. Hope to Lyman C. Draper, 31 August 1874, in Draper MSS, 4VV120.

333. Robert Fleming Family Group Sheet, Joe Hart Genealogical Collection; Moss, *South Carolina Patriots*, 316–318 [Alexander Fleming, Elijah Fleming, Robert Fleming and William Fleming].

334. Charles McClure, AA 4938 ½.

335. Moss, *South Carolina Patriots*, 316–317 [Alexander Fleming].

336. Cornwallis to Rawdon 29 June 1780, in Cornwallis Papers, PRO 30/11/77/18–19.

337. Cornwallis to Clinton, 30 June 1780, in Tarleton, 117–118. Cornwallis's reference to Tryon County is anachronistic. The North Carolina General Assembly abolished Tryon County in 1779 and replaced it with Rutherford and Lincoln Counties. See D.L. Corbitt and L. Polk Denmark, *Chart Showing Origin of North Carolina Counties* (Raleigh: North Carolina Department of Archives and History, 1940).

Chapter 4

338. George C. Rogers Jr., *The History of Georgetown County, South Carolina* (Columbia, SC: USC Press, 1970), 122; Henry Laurens, *The Papers of Henry Laurens, Volume 15*, eds. David R. Chesnutt and C. James Taylor (Columbia: USC Press, 2000), 299 n 4.

339. "Georgetown," *Encyclopedia Americana* (1956), 12:482.

340. McJunkin, "Ms. Statement," in Draper MSS, 23VV208–209; James Hemphill, Revolutionary War Federal Pension Application (FPA) S21277; James Martin, FPA S9391; Henry Rea, FPA W9246.

341. McJunkin, "Reminiscences," in Draper MSS, 23VV172.

342. Robert Wilson, FPA W2302.

343. Peter W. Coldham, *American Migrations 1765–1799* (Baltimore, MD: Genealogical Publishing, 2000), 270.

344. Banastre Tarleton, *A History of the Campaigns of 1780 and 1781 in the Southern Provinces of North America* (North Stratford, NH: Ayer Publishing, 1999; reprint of 1787 edition), 28–29.

345. Coldham, 270.

346. Lieutenant Colonel George Turnbull to Lord Cornwallis, 6 July 1780, in Cornwallis Papers, PRO 30/11/2/250–251.

347. Lord Rawdon to Cornwallis, 7 July 1780, in Cornwallis Papers, PRO 30/11/2/252–255; Maurice A. Moore, *The Life of Gen. Edward Lacey* (Spartanburg, SC: Douglas, Evins & Co., 1859), 2–3.

348. Turnbull to Cornwallis, 6 July 1780; Richard Winn, "General Richard Winn's Notes—1780," Peter Force Papers, Library of Congress, Series 7E, 4; Robert D. Bass, *Gamecock* (Orangeburg: Sandlapper Publishing, 2000), 57.

349. General Joseph Graham to Judge Archibald D. Murphey *c.* 1820, in Walter Clark, ed. and comp., *The State Records of North Carolina: Volume XIX, 1782–1784, with Supplement 1771–1782* (Winston, NC: M.I. & J.C. Stewart, 1896), 985.

350. Colonel James Williams to Mrs. James Williams, 4 July 1780, in R.W. Gibbes, ed., *Documentary History of the American Revolution, Volume II: 1776–1782* (Spartanburg: Reprint Company, 1972), 135.

351. Moss, *South Carolina Patriots*, 429 [Joseph Hayes], 994 [Daniel Williams].

352. John Simpson, Audited Account (AA) 7019.

353. Robert Craighead to Lyman C. Draper, 4 December 1873, in Draper MSS, 15VV46–51; W.H. Craighead, *The Craighead Family* (Paradise, TX: Family Press, 1996), 22–23; Daniel G. Stinson, "Old Waxhaw Church," Part 3, *The Southern Presbyterian* (Columbia, SC), 5 September 1867.

354. Turnbull to Cornwallis, 6 July 1780.

355. Turnbull to Cornwallis, 6 July 1780; Rawdon to Cornwallis, 10 July 1780, in Cornwallis Papers, PRO 30/11/2/264–265; Tarleton, 86.

356. Turnbull to Cornwallis, 6 July 1780.

357. Turnbull to Cornwallis, 6 July 1780.

358. Winn, "Notes," 4; William Hill, *Col. William Hill's Memoirs of the Revolution*, ed. A.S. Salley Jr. (Columbia: The State Company, 1921), 8–9.

359. Winn, "Notes," 4; Bass, 60; Cecil B. Hartley, *The Life of Major General Henry Lee* (New York: Derby & Jackson, 1859), 308–309.

360. Rawdon to Cornwallis, 10 July 1780; Pay Abstract Nr. 159, Colonel W.T. Turner's regiment of Rocky Mount Militia, Camden District, SC, 13 June-13 December 1782 (PRO T50, vol. 2), in Murtie June Clark, *Loyalists in the Southern Campaign of the American Revolution* (Baltimore, MD: Genealogical Publishing, 1981), I:152.

361. Rawdon to Colonel Henry Rugeley, 7 July 1780, in Draper MSS, 4VV267; Bass, 59.

362. Moore, *Lacey*, 2–3.

363. Moore, *Lacey*, 8n–9n; Moss, *South Carolina Patriots*, 547 [Reuben Lacey].

364. Daniel G. Stinson to Lyman C. Draper, 29 April 1873, in Draper MSS, 9VV202.

365. McJunkin, "Ms. Statement," in Draper MSS, 23VV211.

366. Stinson to Draper, 29 May 1873, in Draper MSS, 9VV225–226.

367. Hill, *Memoirs*, 9.

368. [William R. Davie], *The Revolutionary War Sketches of William R. Davie*, ed. Blackwell P. Robinson (Raleigh, NC: North Carolina Department of Cultural Resources, 1976), 8.

369. Davie, *Sketches*, ix; Mark M. Boatner, *Encyclopedia of the American Revolution* (Mechanicsburg, PA: Stackpole Books, 1994), 318–319.

370. Blackwell P. Robinson, *William R. Davie* (Chapel Hill, NC: UNC Press, 1957), 44.

371. Edward M. Boykin to Lyman C. Draper, 7 October 1872, in Draper MSS, 17VV229; Robert S. Lambert, *South Carolina Loyalists in the American Revolution* (Columbia, SC: USC Press, 1987), 298–299.

372. Pay Abstract for Colonel Henry Rugeley's regiment, Camden Militia, from 13 June 1780 to 13 December 1780 (PRO T50, vol. 2), in Clark, *Loyalists*, I:147–148; Lambert, 298–299.

373. Journal of the South Carolina House of Representatives, 28 January 1783, in Theodora Thompson, ed., *Journals of the House of Representatives 1783–1784* (Columbia: USC Press, 1977), 53–54.

374. Boykin to Draper, 7 October 1872, in Draper MSS, 17VV230.

375. Turnbull to Rawdon, 12 July 1780, in Cornwallis Papers, PRO 30/11/2/285–286; Winn, "Notes," 4; Hill, *Memoirs*, 9.

376. Lambert, 128.

377. [John S. Bratton and W. C. Beatty], *Proceedings of a Celebration of Huck's Defeat* (Yorkville, SC: Tidings from the Craft, 1895), 4; Joseph Johnson, *Traditions and Reminiscences, chiefly of the American Revolution in the South* (Charleston, SC: Walker and James, 1851), 336; Elizabeth F. Ellet, *The Women of the American Revolution* (New York: Charles Scribner, 1853–1854), I:240.

378. Turnbull to Rawdon, 12 July 1780, in Cornwallis Papers, PRO 30/11/2/285–286; Lorenzo Sabine, *Biographical Sketches of Loyalists of the American Revolution* (Port Washington, NY: Kennikat Press, 1966), II:534; muster rolls, Captain John Althause's rifle company, Emmerick's Chasseurs, November 1778, 5 January 1779, and 24 April 1779, PAC/RG8/"C"/1891; e-mail, Todd Braisted to author, 12 December 2003; Sir Henry Clinton, orders disbanding Emmerick's Chasseurs, 31

August 1779, in Todd Braisted, "Emmerick's Chasseurs: Disbanding of Corps," The On-Line Institute for Advanced Loyalist Studies (http://www.royalprovincial.com/military/emmerick/emmords3.htm).

379. Turnbull to Rawdon, 12 July 1780, in Cornwallis Papers, PRO 30/11/2/285–286.

380. Coldham, 286; muster roll, Captain Bernard Kane's company, New York Volunteers, Savannah, GA, 29 November 1779 (PAC/RG81/"C"/1874), in Clark, *Loyalists*, III:202; list of British-American officers in North America, in Clark, *Loyalists*, III:353; Sabine, II:553; e-mail, Braisted to author, 12 December 2003. Sabine states that McGregor was a native of Philadelphia, but he has probably confused John McGregor of the New York Volunteers with another John McGregor who served in the Pennsylvania Loyalists in 1777 and 1778.

381. Muster roll, Captain William Johnston's company, New York Volunteers, Savannah, GA, 29 November 1779 (PAC/RG81/ "C"/1874), in Clark, *Loyalists*, III:198; e-mail, Braisted to author, 12 December 2003.

382. James Hemphill to Lyman C. Draper, 29 July 1874, in Draper MSS, 4VV76; Draper, interview with Stinson, 8–18 August 1871, in Draper MSS, 9VV13–14; Tarleton, 92–93, 126–127; Ellet, III:195.

383. John Craig, FPA W22864.

384. John Adair, W2895; Winn, "Notes," 5–6; Hill, *Memoirs*, 9; John Craig, "The War in York and Chester," *Chester Standard* (Chester, SC), 16 March 1854; Ellet, III:198–202; Robert M. Cooper to Lyman C. Draper, 15 November 1872, in Draper MSS, 14VV16–17; Moore, *Lacey*, 10.

385. Turnbull to Rawdon, 12 July 1780, in Cornwallis Papers, PRO 30/11/2/285–286; John Craig, "War"; John Adair, FPA W2895; Thomas Lofton, FPA S17114; John Adair Jr. to Maurice A. Moore, 17 December 1839, in Draper MSS, 5VV294–300.

386. Turnbull to Rawdon, 12 July 1780; Elmer O. Parker, "Early Surveys West of Lando, S.C.," *Chester County Genealogical Society Bulletin*, vol. V, no. 4 (December 1982): 101

387. Daniel G. Stinson, "A Sketch of John Bishop," *Chester Reporter* (Chester, SC), 18 June 1874; Parker, "Early Summers."

388. Stinson to Draper, 25 November 1872, in Draper MSS, 9VV118–119, and 19 February 1876, in Draper MSS, 15VV280–281.

389. Stinson to Draper, 25 November 1872, in Draper MSS, 9VV118–119, and 19 February 1876, in Draper MSS, 15VV280–281.

390. Ellet, III:179, 182–183; Max Perry, *American Descendants of John "Jean" Gaston* (Greenville: A. Press, 1994), 140–141, 150.

391. Ellet, III:179–180.

392. Ellet, III:180–183.

393. John H. Logan and John Starr Moore, "Hauk's Defeat — Traditions of Starr Moore," c. 1857, in Draper MSS, 16VV274.

394. Winn, "Notes," 4.

395. John Adair Jr. to Maurice A. Moore, 17 December 1839, in Draper MSS, 5VV294; Moore, *Lacey*, 7; Thomas Mayhugh, "Early Surveys, Lewis Turnout, Chester Co., S.C.," *Chester District Genealogical Society Bulletin*, vol. XIV, no. 3 (September 1991): 92.

396. Moore, *Lacey*, 3.

397. Moore, *Lacey*, 8; Mayhugh, 92; Adair to Moore, 17 December 1839, in Draper MSS, 5VV294; James Hemphill to Lyman C. Draper, 29 July 1874, in Draper MSS, 4VV74.

398. Adair to Moore, 17 December 1839, in Draper MSS, 5VV294; Moore, *Lacey*, 8.

399. Ellet, III:270–271.

400. Moore, *Lacey*, 8; Lyman C. Draper, interview with Rebecca Lacey, 1 June 1871, in Draper MSS, 16VV62.

401. Thomas Mayhugh, "Land Grants and Early Surveys on the Headwaters of the South Fork of Fishing Creek, York County, S.C.," unpublished map, 1993.

402. Bratton and Beatty, 5; Logan and Moore, in Draper MSS, 16VV276; John Moore Family Group Sheet, Joe Hart Genealogical Collection.

403. Bratton and Beatty, 5, 12; Moore, *Lacey*, 10; Logan and Moore, in Draper MSS, 16VV275.

404. Ellet, III: 276–277.

405. William Bratton Jr. and John Bratton, "Huck's Defeat: Dr. William Bratton's Story," (Winnsboro, SC: unpublished manuscript, n. d.), 1.

406. Ernest Jackson, "Battle of Huck's Defeat Important Engagement," *Charlotte Observer* (Charlotte, NC), 28 September 1930; Samuel B. Mendenhall, *Tales of York County* (Rock Hill, SC: Reynolds and Reynolds, 1989), 12.

407. Bratton and Bratton, 1.

408. Bratton and Bratton, 1–4; Ellet, I:241–242; Ellet, III:202; Draper, interview with Stinson, 8–18 August 1871, in Draper MSS, 9VV37.

409. Bratton and Bratton, 4–5.

410. Bratton and Bratton, 5–6.

411. Ellet, I:241–242.

412. Johnson, *Traditions*, 342.

413. Bratton and Bratton, 6. Richard Winn, Maurice Moore and Daniel Stinson thought that Martha Bratton and her family spent the night at the Williamson plantation, but William Bratton Jr. and Rufus Bratton both stated that the family was locked in the Bratton house (Draper, interview with Rufus Bratton, July 1871, in Draper MSS, 11VV333–334; General Richard Winn to Captain Hugh McCall, 31 May 1812, in Draper MSS, 5VV89; Maurice A. Moore to Lyman C. Draper, 4 January 1870, in Draper MSS, 14VV57; Stinson to Draper, 22 April 1873, in Draper MSS, 9VV205).

414. Draper, interview with Rufus Bratton, in Draper MSS, 11VV335; William Bratton Family Group Sheet, Joe Hart Genealogical Collection.

415. Bratton and Beatty, 5, 12; Moore, *Lacey*, 10; Logan and Moore, in Draper MSS, 16VV275.

416. Turnbull to Rawdon, 12 July 1780.

417. Winn, "Notes," 5.

418. Draper, interview with John S. Bratton, in Draper MSS, 11VV335; Logan and Moore, in Draper MSS, 16VV273, 277; Daniel G. Stinson and Napoleon B. Bratton, "Map of Hook's Defeat," 26 March 1876, in Draper MSS, 15VV278; Daniel G. Stinson and John S. Bratton Jr., "Plan of the Battleground of Huyck's Defeat," 24 August 1876, in Draper MSS, 5VV54.

419. Hill, *Memoirs*, 9; Moore, *Lacey*, 9.

420. Winn, "Notes," 5; Logan and Moore, in Draper MSS, 16VV277.

421. Winn, "Notes," 5; Hill, *Memoirs*, 9.

422. James P. Collins, *Autobiography of a Revolutionary Soldier*, ed. John M. Roberts (New York: Arno Press, 1979), 26.

423. Logan and Moore, in Draper MSS, 16VV273, 277.

424. Logan and Moore, in Draper MSS, 16VV272–273; Bratton and Beatty, 5, 12; Moore, *Lacey*, 10.

425. Hill, *Memoirs*, 9; Logan and Moore, in Draper MSS, 16VV272–273; Bratton and Beatty, 11; James Williamson Family Group Sheet, Joe Hart Genealogical Collection; Donald K. Campbell, *A Williamson Saga* (Little Rock, AK: p. p., 2002), 7, 9.

Chapter 5

426. Daniel G. Stinson to Lyman C. Draper, 25 November 1872, in Lyman C. Draper MSS, 9VV118–119, and 19 February 1876, in Lyman C. Draper MSS, 15VV280–281.

427. John Craig, "The War in York and Chester," *Chester Standard* (Chester, SC), 16 March 1854.

428. Daniel G. Stinson, "Old Waxhaw Church," Part 3, *The Southern Presbyterian* (Columbia, SC), 5 September 1867; Elizabeth F. Ellet, *The Women of the American Revolution* (New York: Charles Scribner, 1853–1854), III:183.

429. Richard Winn, "General Richard Winn's Notes—1780," in Peter Force Papers, Library of Congress, Series 7E, 4; William Hill, *Col. William Hill's Memoirs of the Revolution*, ed. A.S. Salley Jr. (Columbia: The State Company, 1921), 9; James P. Collins, *Autobiography of a Revolutionary Soldier*, ed. John M. Roberts (New York: Arno Press, 1979), 25–26; Maurice A. Moore, *The Life of Gen. Edward Lacey* (Spartanburg, SC: Douglas, Evins & Co., 1859), 6–7; Joseph Kerr, Federal Pension Application (FPA) S13967.

430. Ellet, III:182–183; John H. Logan and John Starr Moore, "Hauk's Defeat — Traditions of Starr Moore," c. 1857, in Draper MSS, 16VV274.

431. Sun and moon data for 11 July 1780, York County, SC, from U.S. Naval Observatory Web site (http://mach.usno.navy.mil).

432. [William Bratton Jr. and John Bratton], "Huck's Defeat: Dr. William Bratton's Story," (Winnsboro, SC: unpublished manuscript, n. d.), 6.

433. Craig, "War"; John Adair Jr. to Maurice A. Moore, 17 December 1839, in Draper MSS, 5VV295; Moore, *Lacey*, 7; Ellet, III:183–184.

434. Ellet, III:183–184.

435. Logan and Moore, in Draper MSS, 16VV274.

436. Adair to Moore, 17 December 1839, in Draper MSS, 5VV295; Ellet, III:184.

437. Adair to Moore, 17 December 1839, in Draper MSS, 5VV295.

438. Adair to Moore, 17 December 1839, in Draper MSS, 5VV295; Craig, "War"; Logan and Moore, in Draper MSS, 16VV274; Moore, *Lacey*, 7.

439. Winn, "Notes," 4.

440. Adair to Moore, 17 December 1839, in Draper MSS, 5VV295; Moore, *Lacey*, 8.

441. Draper, interview with Stinson, 8–18 August 1871, in Draper MSS, 9VV16; Ellet, III:184.

442. Winn, "Notes," 6.

443. Thomas Mayhugh, "Early Surveys, Lewis Turnout, Chester Co., S.C.," *Chester District Genealogical Society Bulletin*, vol. XIV, no. 3 (September 1991): 92.

444. Logan and Moore, in Draper MSS, 16VV276.

445. Moore, *Lacey*, 8.

446. Logan and Moore, in Draper MSS, 16VV272, 276; Adair to Moore, in Draper MSS, 5VV297; Moore, *Lacey*, 8.

447. Adair to Moore, in Draper MSS, 5VV297–298; Stinson to Draper, 22 April 1873, in Draper MSS, 9VV207; Draper, interview with A.P. Wylie, July 1871, in Draper MSS, 11VV326; Moore to Draper, 4 January 1870, in Draper MSS, 14VV57; Draper, interview with Moore, in Draper MSS, 23VV232.

448. Moore, *Lacey*, 8n; Bobby G. Moss, *Roster of South Carolina Patriots in the American Revolution* (Baltimore, MD: Genealogical Publishing Company, 1983), 547 [Reuben Lacey].

449. Moore, *Lacey*, 8n–9n.

450. Robert Wilson, Revolutionary War Federal Pension Application (FPA) W2302; Moss, *South Carolina Patriots*, 805 [James Reed], 807 [James Reid].

451. Winn, "Notes," 5.

452. Logan and Moore, in Draper MSS, 16VV276.

453. Winn, "Notes," 5.

454. Winn, "Notes," 4–5; Hill, *Memoirs*, 9; Craig, "War"; Moore, *Lacey*, 8–9; [John S. Bratton and W.C. Beatty], *Proceedings of a Celebration of Huck's Defeat* (Yorkville, SC: Tidings from the Craft, 1895), 6; Logan and Moore, in Draper MSS, 16VV272.

455. Logan and Moore, in Draper MSS, 16VV276.

456. Moore, *Lacey*, 9–10.

457. Hill, *Memoirs*, 10; Logan and Moore, in Draper MSS, 16VV272, 273; Moore, *Lacey*, 9.

458. Sun and moon data for 12 July 1780, York County, SC, U.S. Naval Observatory Web site (http://mach.usno.navy.mil); Draper, interview with Stinson, 8–18 August 1871, in Draper MSS, 9VV20; Logan and Moore, in Draper MSS, 16VV272, 273; Craig, "War"; Moore, *Lacey*, 9; Collins, 26.

459. David Ramsay, *The History of the Revolution of South-Carolina* (Trenton, NJ: Isaac Collins, 1785), I:135; Joseph McJunkin, "Reminiscences," in Draper MSS, 23VV174.

460. Hill, *Memoirs*, 9.

461. General Richard Winn to Captain Hugh McCall, 31 May 1812, in Draper MSS, 5VV89.

462. Logan and Moore, in Draper MSS, 16VV272; Craig, "War"; Moore, *Lacey*, 9–10; Collins, 26; Winn, "Notes," 5.

463. Draper, interview with Stinson, 8–18 August 1871, in Draper MSS, 9VV13–14; Stinson to Draper, 22 April 1873, in Draper MSS, 9VV206; Thomas McDill to Draper, 2 September 1874, in Draper MSS, 15VV355; Ellet, III:185.

464. Winn, "Notes," 5; Winn to McCall, in Draper MSS, 5VV89; Bratton and Bratton, 13–14; Collins, 26.

465. Johnson, *Diary*, 44; Craig, "War"; Draper, interview with Lemuel Carroll, June 1871, in Draper MSS, 16VV72–73.

466. Collins, 26.

467. Winn, "Notes," 6; Hill, *Memoirs*, 10; Bratton and Bratton, 9–10, 13–14; Thomas J. Kirkland and Robert M. Kennedy, *Historic Camden Part One, Colonial and Revolutionary* (Columbia, SC: State Company, 1905), 284–285.

468. Logan and Moore, in Draper MSS, 16VV273; Draper, interview with Rufus Bratton, in Draper MSS, 11VV333; Craig, "War"; Collins, 26; Moore, *Lacey*, 11n; James Stephenson, FPA W596; McJunkin, "Reminiscences," in Draper MSS, 23VV174.

469. Logan and Moore, in Draper MSS, 16VV273; Draper, interview with Rufus Bratton, in Draper MSS, 11VV333.

470. Winn, "Notes," 5–6; Logan and Moore, in Draper MSS, 16VV272–273; Bratton and Beatty, 5; Moore, *Lacey*, 9, 10n.

471. Hill, *Memoirs*, 10.

472. Draper MSS, 9VV104; Moore, *Lacey*, 7; Ellet, III:286.

473. Winn, "Notes," 5.

474. Craig, "War"; Bratton and Beatty, 6.

475. Logan and Moore, in Draper MSS, 16VV273–274.

476. Stinson to Draper, 22 April 1873, in Draper MSS, 9VV205–206; Winn, "Notes," 5–6.

477. John Forbes, FPA R3645.

478. Francis Heitman, *Historical Register of Officers of the Continental Army during the War of the Revolution* (Baltimore: Genealogical Publishing, 1982), 118.

479. George Neely, FPA S4613.

480. Bratton and Bratton, 8–12.

481. Bratton and Bratton, 8–12; Joseph Johnson, *Traditions and Reminiscences, chiefly of the American Revolution in the South* (Charleston: Walker and James, 1851), 342; Draper, interview with Rufus Bratton, in Draper MSS, 11VV333–334; Stinson to Draper, 22 April 1783.

482. Bratton and Bratton, 6–9; Winn, "Notes," 6.

483. Bratton and Bratton, 6–9.

484. U.S. Naval Observatory Web site.

485. Winn, "Notes," 6.

486. Winn, "Notes," 9–13; Kirkland and Kennedy, 28–284.

487. Winn, "Notes," 6.

488. Hill, *Memoirs*, 10–11.

489. Winn, "Notes," 6–7, 8.

490. Winn, "Notes," 6.

491. 4 Craig, "War."

492. McDill to Draper, in Draper MSS, 15VV355.

493. Moore, *Lacey*, 11 n 2.

494. Collins, 27.

495. Craig, "War."

496. Adair to Moore, in Draper MSS, 5VV300.

497. McJunkin, "Ms. Statement," in Draper MSS, 23VV210.

498. See I Samuel 17:54: "And David took the head of the Philistine, and brought it to Jerusalem, but he put his armour in his tent."

499. Draper, interview with Lemuel Carroll, in Draper MSS, 16VV72–73.

500. Draper, interview with Rufus Bratton, in Draper MSS, 11VV334.

501. Bratton and Beatty, 4; Ellet, I:240.

502. Ellet, III:185.

503. Moore, *Lacey*, 10.

504. Johnson, *Traditions*, 341.

505. Samuel Killough, supporting statement for Mrs. John Wallace, FPA W955.

506. Bratton and Bratton, 12–13; Moore, *Lacey*, 10.

507. Adair to Moore, in Draper MSS, 5VV300; Moore, *Lacey*, II n 1.

508. Winn, "Notes," 6; Craig, "War"; Collins, 27.

509. Winn, "Notes," 6.

510. Hill, *Memoirs*, 10.

511. Daniel G. Stinson, interview with Judge Peter Wylie on William Wylie's military service, 1872, in Draper MSS, 9VV104; Ellet, III:286.

512. Lieutenant Colonel George Turnbull to Lord Rawdon, 12 July 1780, in Cornwallis Papers, PRO 30/11/2/285–286.

513. Johnson, *Diary*, 44.

514. Lyman C. Draper, *King's Mountain and Its Heroes* (Baltimore: Genealogical Publishing, 1971), 73–75; Wes Hope, *The Spartanburg Area in the American Revolution* (Spartanburg: p.p., 2002), 16.

515. Turnbull to Rawdon, 12 July 1780.

516. Turnbull to Rawdon, 12 July 1780; Murtie June Clark, *Loyalists in the Southern Campaign of the American Revolution* (Baltimore: Genealogical Publishing, 1981), III:177, 181, 212, 345, 353; e-mail from Todd Braisted to author, 19 January 2005.

517. Brigadier General Thomas Sumter to Major General Johann DeKalb, 17 July 1780, in Walter Clark, ed. and comp., *The State Records of North Carolina: Volume XIV, 1779–1780* (Winston, NC: M.I. & J.C. Stewart, 1896), 505.

518. Hill, *Memoirs*, 10.

519. Moore, *Lacey*, 10.

520. Hill, *Memoirs*, 10–11.

521. Johnson, *Diary*, 44; Anthony Allaire, "Diary of Lieut. Anthony Allaire of Ferguson's Corps," in Draper, *King's Mountain*, 500.

522. Johnson, *Diary*, xxiii, 115.

523. Johnson, *Diary*, 44.

524. Allaire, 500.

525. Johnson, *Diary*, 44.

526. Allaire, 500.

527. Lord Cornwallis to Sir Henry Clinton, 15 July 1780, in Banastre Tarleton, *A History of the Campaigns of 1780 and 1781 in the Southern Provinces of North America* (North Stratford, NH: Ayer Publishing, 1999; reprint of 1787 edition), 121.

528. Tarleton, 93.

529. Cornwallis to Rawdon, 13 July 1780, in Cornwallis Papers, PRO 30/11/78/12–13.

530. Draper, *King's Mountain*, 78–80; Hope, 16–17.

531. Mark M. Boatner, *Encyclopedia of the American Revolution* (Mechanicsburg, PA: Stackpole Books, 1994), 159.

532. George Neely, FPA S4613; Samuel Gordon, in FPA S2437; Bratton and Beatty, 6; Johnson, *Traditions*, 343; Ellet, III:185.

533. Cornwallis to Clinton, 6 August 1780; Tarleton, 126–127; Robert S. Lambert, *South Carolina Loyalists in the American Revolution* (Columbia: USC Press, 1987), 128.

534. Tarleton, 93.

535. Walter B. Edgar, Inez Watson et al., eds., *Biographical Directory of the South Carolina House of Representatives, Vol. 1, Session Lists 1692–1973* (Columbia: USC Press, 1974), 164; N. Louise Bailey and Elizabeth Ivey Cooper, *Biographical Directory of the South Carolina House of Representatives, Volume III: 1775–1790* (Columbia: USC Press, 1981), 523.

536. Johnson, *Diary*, 46; Draper, *King's Mountain*, 80–82, 474–475; Hope, *Spartanaburg*, 18.

537. Rawdon to Cornwallis, 14 July 1780, in Cornwallis Papers, PRO 30/11/2/294–295.

538. Cornwallis to Clinton, 14 July 1780, in Tarleton, 118–119.

539. Cornwallis to Clinton, 14 July 1780, in Tarleton, 119–120.

540. Cornwallis to Rawdon, 15 July 1780, in Cornwallis Papers, PRO 30/11/78/18–19.

541. Ellet, III:185–186.

542. Sumter to DeKalb, 17 July 1780, in Walter Clark, *The State Records of North Carolina*, XIV:507.

543. Draper, *King's Mountain*, 82; Hope, 19.

544. Cornwallis to Clinton, 15 July 1780, in Tarleton, 120–121.

545. Boatner, 1211.

546. Tarleton, 93.

547. Sumter to DeKalb, 17 July 1780, in Clark, *The State Records of North Carolina*, XIV:505–507; also transcribed by Lyman C. Draper in Draper MSS, 7VV16–19, from the Horatio Gates Papers, New-York Historical Society.

548. Winn, "Notes," 6, 8.

549. Hill, *Memoirs*, 11.

550. [William R. Davie], *The Revolutionary War Sketches of William R. Davie*, ed. Blackwell P. Robinson (Raleigh, NC: North Carolina Department of Cultural Resources, 1976), 8–9.

551. DeKalb to Sumter, 21 July 1780, in Draper MSS, 17VV19; Robert D. Bass, *Gamecock* (Orangeburg: Sandlapper Publishing, 2000), 63.

552. Davie, 9–10.

553. Davie, 10.

554. Major Thomas Blount to North Carolina Governor Abner Nash, 23 July 1780, in Walter Clark, ed. and comp., *The State Records of North Carolina: Volume XV, 1780–1781* (Goldsboro: Nash Brothers, 1898), 6–7.

555. Winn, "Notes," 7–8.

556. John Simpson, Audited Account (AA) 4019; pay schedule for Third South Carolina Regiment, in Journal of the First Provincial Congress, 9 June 1775, in William E. Hemphill and Wylma A. Wates, eds., *Extracts from the Journals of the Provincial Congresses of South Carolina, 1775–1776* (Columbia: South Carolina Archives Department, 1960), 43.

557. Tarleton, 120; Bass, 63; Boatner, 159–161.

558. Cornwallis to Rawdon, 26 July 1780, in Cornwallis Papers, PRO 30/11/78/48–49.

559. Hill, *Memoirs*, 12; Draper, interview with Stinson, 8–18 August 1871, in Draper MSS, 9VV14; Johnson, *Traditions*, 344; Bass, 63.

560. Winn, "Notes," 8–10; Hill, *Memoirs*, 11–12; Johnson, *Diary*, 50–51; Johnson, *Traditions*, 344; Bass, 63–64.

561. Johnson, *Diary*, 51; Draper, *King's Mountain*, 87–88; Hope, 20–12.

Chapter 6

562. Richard Winn, "General Richard Winn's Notes—1780," in Peter Force Papers, Library of Congress, Series 7E, 11–14; William Hill, *Col. William Hill's Memoirs of the Revolution*, ed. A.S. Salley Jr. (Columbia: The State Company, 1921), 12–13.

563. Lord Cornwallis to Sir Henry Clinton, 6 August 1780; Banastre Tarleton, *A History of the Campaigns of 1780 and 1781 in the Southern Provinces of North America* (North Stratford, NH: Ayer Publishing, 1999; reprint of 1787 edition), 126–127.

564. Wes Hope, *The Spartanburg Area in the American Revolution* (Spartanburg: p. p., 2002), 21–23.

565. Mark M. Boatner, *Encyclopedia of the American Revolution* (Mechanicsburg, PA: Stackpole Books, 1994), 1171.

566. Boatner, 159–170.

567. Boatner, 368–369. Boatner incorrectly states that this battle happened at "Catawba Ford, N.C.," when in fact it happened on the Catawba River in what is now Chester County, South Carolina.

568. Lyman C. Draper, *King's Mountain and Its Heroes* (Baltimore. MD: Genealogical Publishing, 1971), 104–115; Boatner, 756.

569. *Virginia Gazette* (Richmond, VA), 23 August 1780.

570. *Pennsylvania Gazette and Weekly Advertiser* (Philadelphia PA), 30 August 1780.

571. *Maryland Journal and Baltimore Advertiser* (Baltimore, MD), 5 September 1780.

572. *New-Jersey Journal* (Newark, NJ), 6 September 1780.

573. Boatner, 189.

574. Benson J. Lossing, *The Pictorial Field Book of the American Revolution* (Cottonport, LA: Polyanthos, 1972), II:453.

575. Edward McCrady, *The History of South Carolina in the Revolution, 1775–1780* (New York: Russell and Russell, 1901), 599.

576. David Ramsay, *The History of the Revolution of South-Carolina* (Trenton, NJ: Isaac Collins, 1785), I:135; Maurice A. Moore, *The Life of Gen. Edward Lacey* (Spartanburg, SC: Douglas, Evins & Co., 1859), 11; McCrady, 599.

577. Boatner, 575–583.

578. Bobby G. Moss, *Roster of South Carolina Patriots in the American Revolution* (Baltimore: Genealogical Publishing Company, 1983), 70 [Henry Bishop], 604 [John McClure], 719 [Andrew Neel, Thomas Neel Jr.], 730 [John Nixon]; Daniel G. Stinson to Lyman C. Draper, 19 October 1871, in Draper MSS, 9VV59; John H. Logan's notes, in Draper MSS, 16VV148.

579. Draper, interview with Lemuel Carroll, in Draper MSS, 16VV72–73; Moore, *Lacey*, 11n.

580. George Howe, *History of the Presbyterian Church in South Carolina*, vol. I (Columbia, SC: Duffie & Chapman, 1870), 610, 614.

581. Howe, 426, 513–514, 523.

582. Howe, 514, 559, 635–636.

583. John Craig, "The War in York and Chester," *Chester Standard* (Chester, SC), 16 March 1854; John Craig, Revolutionary War Federal Pension Application (FPA) W22864; Silas Emmett Lucas Jr., *Marriage and Death Notices from Pendleton (S.C.) Messenger 1807–1851*(Easley, SC: Southern Historical Press, 1977), 69.

584. Samuel B. Mendenhall, *Tales of York County* (Rock Hill, SC: Reynolds and Reynolds, 1989), 23–24; tombstone inscriptions for David Sadler and Elsy Bratton Sadler, Roberts Presbyterian Church, Anderson County, SC.

585. Mendenhall, 12; Ernest Jackson, "Battle of Huck's Defeat Important Engagement," *Charlotte Observer* (Charlotte, NC), 28 September 1930; tombstone inscription for Watt and Polly, Historic Brattonsville, York County, SC.

586. Stinson to Lyman Draper, 8–18 August 1871, in Draper MSS, 9VV13–14; Thomas McDill to Draper, 2 September 1873, in Draper MSS, 15VV355; Elizabeth F. Ellet, *The Women of the American Revolution* (New York: Charles Scribner, 1853–1854), III: 185.

587. James P. Collins, *Autobiography of a Revolutionary Soldier*, ed. John M. Roberts (New York: Arno Press, 1979), 49–59, 68–72, 79–89, 149, 162–168, 171–176; James Collins, FPA R2173.

588. Brent H. Holcomb and Elmer O. Parker, *Chester County, South Carolina Minutes of the County Court 1785–1799* (Greenville, SC: Southern Historical Press, 1997), 1–5; N. Louise Bailey and Elizabeth Ivey Cooper, *Biographical Directory of the South Carolina House of Representatives, Volume III: 1775–1790* (Columbia: USC Press, 1981), 410–411; Moore, *Lacey*, 26–27.

589. Holcomb and Parker, 7; Bailey and Cooper, 29–30; John Adair, FPA W2895.

590. Bailey and Cooper, 88–89; Emily Bellinger Reynolds and Joan Reynolds Faunt, *Biographical Directory of the Senate of the State of South Carolina 1776–1964* (Columbia: South Carolina Archives Department, 1964), 185.

591. Bailey and Cooper, 339–340; Anne King Gregorie, "William Hill," in *Dictionary of American Biography*, ed. Dumas Malone (New York: Charles Scribner's Sons, 1958), IX: 48; Daniel H. Hill, *Col. William Hill and the Campaign of 1780* (p. p., c. 1919), 1; Douglas Southall Freeman, *Lee's Lieutenants* (New York: Charles Scribner's Sons, 1942), I:19–20.

592. Bailey and Cooper, 779–781; Gregorie, "Richard Winn," in Malone, ed., *Dictionary of American Biography*, XX: 390.

593. Bailey and Cooper, 693–697; Boatner, 1078–1079.

594. Lorenzo Sabine, *Biographical Sketches of Loyalists of the American Revolution* (Port Washington, NY: Kennikat Press, 1966), I:553.

595. David Duncan Wallace, *The History of South Carolina* (New York: The American Historical Society, 1934), II: 302–304.

596. American Loyalist Claims, Memorial of Matthew Floyd, PRO AO13/128/264–281; Loyalist Transcripts, Memorial of Matthew Floyd, New York Public Library, LT/54/469–478; Coldham, 683–684; Damon M. Floyd, Damon Floyd's Web Page: My Genealogy Page, "Descendants of Col. Matthew Floyd and Sarah," http://damonfloyd.com/genealogy/floyd-p/p3.htm#i2031.

597. Laurence K. Wells, *York County, South Carolina, Minutes of the County Court 1786–1797* (Columbia: SCMAR, 1981), 6, 10; Abraham Floyd, FPA S32251; Damon Floyd, http://damonfloyd.com/genealogy/floyd-p/p3.htm#i2031.

598. Robert S. Lambert, *South Carolina Loyalists in the American Revolution* (Columbia: USC Press, 1987), 298–299.

599. Journal of the House of Representatives, 28 January 1783, in Theodora Thompson, ed., *Journals of the House of Representatives 1783–1784* (Columbia: USC Press, 1977), 53–54.

600. Journal of the House of Representatives, 14 March 1784, in Thompson, 552.

601. Lambert, 298.

602. Robert Raymond, "Fanciful Tale Hangs Around Adamson's Life," *Columbia State* (Columbia, SC), 14 December 1955; Glinda Price-Coleman, "Granddaughter of the Revolution," *Chester News and Reporter* (Chester, SC), 18 March 1992; Thomas J. Kirkland and Robert M. Kennedy, *Historic Camden Part One, Colonial and Revolutionary* (Columbia: State Company, 1905), 289–290; Mendenhall, 14.

603. Pay Abstract Nr. 159, Colonel W.T. Turner's regiment of Rocky Mount Militia, Camden District, SC, 13 June-13 December 1782 (PRO T50, vol. 2), in Murtie June Clark, *Loyalists in the Southern Campaign of the Revolutionary War* (Baltimore: Genealogical Publishing, 1981), I:152.

604. Journal of the House of Representatives, 4 March 1785, in Lark E. Adams and Rosa S. Lumpkin, eds., *Journals of the House of Representatives 1785–1786* (Columbia: USC Press, 1979), 186–187.

605. Journal of the House of Representatives, 14 March 1785, in Adams and Lumpkin, 230–231.

606. Mary Lee Barnes, "John Owens of Chester County, South Carolina," *Chester District Genealogical Bulletin*, vol. 18, no. 3 (September 1994): 105–108; Robert M. Cooper to Draper, 23 September 1874, in Draper MSS, 4VV26–27.

607. Muster roll, Captain David Ogilvy's company, British Legion cavalry, 25 October 1780–24 December 1780 (PAC/RG81/"C"/1883), in Clark, *Loyalists*, II:227; muster roll, Captain Thomas Sandford's troop of light dragoons, British Legion, 25 October 1781–24 December 1781 and 25 December 1781–23 February 1782 (PAC/G81/"C"/1884), in Clark, *Loyalists*, II:238, 240; abstract, sixty-one days' pay, officers and enlisted men of British Legion cavalry, 25 October 1782–25 December 1782 (PRO 30/55, Doc. 6493), in Clark, *Loyalists*, III:408; e-mail, Todd Braisted to author, 12 December 2003.

608. List of British-American officers in North America, in Clark, *Loyalists*, III:353; Draper, biographical notes on Lieutenant Colonel George Turnbull, in Draper MSS, 17VV135–138; *Boston Centinel*, 17 October 1810, quoted in Draper MSS, 17VV135.

609. Muster roll, Major John Coffin's troop of mounted infantry, New York Volunteers, 14 September 1780–24 June 1781 (PAC/RG81/"C"/1874), in Clark, *Loyalists*, III:183; muster rolls, Captain Bernard Kane's company of light infantry, New York Volunteers, 24 February 1781–24 December 1781 (PAC/RG81/"C"/1874), Clark, *Loyalists*, III:203–205; muster roll, Captain Archibald McLean's company of light infantry, New York Volunteers, 16 January 1783 (PAC/RG81/"C"/1874), Clark, *Loyalists*, III:209; pay abstract, New York Volunteers, 25 August 1783–24 October 1783 (PAC/RG81/"C"/1875), Clark, *Loyalists*, III:211; list of New York Volunteers serving on half-pay, Clark, *Loyalists*, III:345; list of British officers serving in North America, Clark, *Loyalists*, III:353; Sabine, II:553; e-mail, Braisted to author, 12 December 2003; John Adair, FPA W2895.

610. Muster roll, Captain Nathaniel Vernon's troop, British Legion, 25 December 1781–23 February 1782 (PAC/G81/"C"/1884), in Clark, *Loyalists*, II:245; pay abstract, British Legion cavalry

officers, 25 October 1782–25 December 1782 (PRO 30/55, Doc. 6493), Clark, *Loyalists*, III:408; Marion Gilroy, comp., "Queen's County Grants," in *Loyalists and Land Settlement in Nova Scotia* (Baltimore: Genealogical Publishing, 1990, 1995), 72; Milton Rubincam, *The Old United Empire Loyalist List* (Baltimore: Genealogical Publishing Company, 1969), appendix B, 149.

Epilogue

611. Mark M. Boatner, *Encyclopedia of the American Revolution* (Mechanicsburg, PA: Stackpole Books, 1994), 706–707.

612. Boatner, 707.

613. Quoted in John Buchanan, *The Road to Guilford Courthouse* (New York: John Wiley & Sons, 1997), 328.

614. Buchanan, 366.

615. Michael A. Bellesiles, *Arming America* (New York: Alfred A. Knopf, 2000), 193, 196, 197.

616. Boatner, 167; North Carolina Daughters of the American Revolution, *Roster of Soldiers from North Carolina in the American Revolution* (Baltimore: Genealogical Publishing Company, 2003).

617. Bellesiles, 193, 196, 197; Boatner, 167; Buchanan, 318, 320; Lawrence E. Babits, *A Devil of a Whipping* (Chapel Hill: UNC Press, 1998), 55, 76–78, 81–95.

618. "Battlefield Detectives: Cowpens," Grenada Productions, The History Channel, 17 December 2004.

619. Maurice A. Moore, *The Life of Gen. Edward Lacey* (Spartanburg, SC: Douglas, Evins & Co., 1859), 8.

620. David Sadler, FPA S9471.

621. Elizabeth F. Ellet, *The Women of the American Revolution* (New York: Charles Scribner, 1853–1854), III:394–395; George Howe, *History of the Presbyterian Church in South Carolina,* vol. I (Columbia, SC: Duffie & Chapman, 1870), 510; Lyman C. Draper, *King's Mountain and Its Heroes* (Baltimore. MD: Genealogical Publishing, 1971), 465; Robert D. Bass, *Gamecock* (Orangeburg, SC: Sandlapper Publishing, 2000), 83–84.

622. Russell F. Weigley, *The Partisan War: the South Carolina Campaign of 1780–1782* (Columbia: USC Press, 1970), 1–3.

Appendix A

623. The Battle of Monck's Corner actually occurred 14 April 1780, almost two months before the Battle of Mobley's Meeting House.

624. This is in reference to the Florida expedition of 1778.

625. South Carolina fielded only six numbered regiments during the Revolution, of which Thomas Sumter's rifle regiment was the Sixth; there was no "Fortieth Regiment." The "No. 40" may indicate that Samuel Wallace's musket formerly belonged to the British Fortieth Regiment of Foot.

626. Since Stokes County was created from Surry County, North Carolina, in 1789, Clairborne Gentry and Colonel Martin Armstrong would have been residents of Surry County in 1780. See

D.L. Corbitt and L. Polk Denmark, *Chart Showing Origin of North Carolina Counties* (Raleigh, NC: North Carolina Department of Archives and History, 1940).

Appendix B

627. Probably the home of Samuel Leslie, a prominent citizen of the Waxhaw community. See Brent H. Holcomb and Elmer O. Parker, *Mecklenburg County, North Carolina Deed Abstracts 1763–1779* (Greenville, SC: Southern Historical Press, 1979), 116, 187.

628. Colonel Henry Rugeley was a wealthy Camden merchant who organized a regiment of Loyalist militia in June 1780. See L. Edward Purcell, *Who was Who in the American Revolution* (New York: Facts on File, 1993), 418–419; Murtie June Clark, *Loyalists in the Southern Campaign of the American Revolution* (Baltimore, MD: Genealogical Publishing, 1981), I:147–148.

629. Captain Alexander Ross was Lord Cornwallis's aide-de-camp (Purcell, 417).

630. The exact nature of this incident, and the identity of the individuals involved, is still unknown to the author.

631. Turnbull is referring to the Whig militia officers Robert Patton, William Bratton and Richard Winn.

632. Lord Rawdon was camped in the Waxhaws from 10 June until 15 June; he then returned to Camden (Rawdon to Lord Cornwallis, 11 June 1780).

633. Captain John Henderson of the New Acquisition Regiment was captured at Hill's Ironworks on 17 June 1780. See John Henderson, Audited Account (AA) 3522.

634. Colonel John Twigg (or Twiggs) commanded a regiment of mounted Georgia militia that operated in the Carolina Backcountry in 1780 and 1781. See Robert D. Bass, *Gamecock* (Orangeburg, SC: Sandlapper Publishing, 2000), 102.

635. Lieutenant Colonel John Moore was nominally an officer in Colonel John Hamilton's Royal North Carolina Regiment. Moore commanded the battalion of North Carolina Loyalist militia at the Battle of Ramsour's Mill in present-day Lincoln County, North Carolina, on 20 June 1780. See David Schenck, *North Carolina 1780–'81* (Bowie, MD: Heritage Books, 2000), 52–53.

636. Brigadier General Griffith Rutherford of Rowan County, North Carolina, commanded the Whig militia in Salisbury District (Schenck, 35, 51–52; Purcell, 421).

637. Major (or Lieutenant Colonel) Joseph Brown served in Colonel Edward Lacey's Militia Regiment during 1779 and 1780. See Bobby G. Moss, *Roster of South Carolina Patriots in the American Revolution* (Baltimore: Genealogical Publishing Company, 1983), 109; Samuel Houston, FPA W7810; Joseph Morrow, FPA S21892.

638. Captain David Kinlock of Long Island, New York, commanded a troop of dragoons in the British Legion (Clark, *Loyalists*, II: 211–213).

639. Major John Carden, a Provincial officer of the Prince of Wales regiment, commanded the British post at Hanging Rock in what is now Lancaster County, South Carolina, from June to August 1780 (Clark, Loyalists, III: 221–223; Bass, 68; Purcell, 81).

640. Major Archibald McArthur, a Scottish officer, commanded the First Battalion of the Seventy-first Highland Regiment of Foot in the Cheraw District (Bass, 48, 54).

641. Colonel Joseph Kershaw was a prominent Whig merchant and militia officer who lived in Camden. See Moss, *South Carolina Patriots*, 531; Robert S. Lambert, *South Carolina Loyalists in the American Revolution* (Columbia: USC Press, 1985), 4, 38, 298.

642. Major Nicholas Welsh (aka Walsh or Welch) commanded a company in the Royal North Carolina Regiment under Colonel John Hamilton (Schenck, 52–53; Clark, Loyalists, I: 377–378).

643. Lieutenant Colonel John Hamilton commanded the Royal North Carolina Regiment, a Provincial regiment comprised of North Carolina Loyalists (Clark, *Loyalists*, I: 370–376).

644. Captain Daniel McNeil (or McNeal) commanded a company in the Royal North Carolina Regiment (Clark, *Loyalists*, I: 395–397).

645. Probably Lieutenant Colonel Wellbore Ellis Doyle of Lord Rowdon's regiment, the Volunteers of Ireland (Clark, *Loyalists*, III: 273–278).

646. Turnbull always referred to the New York Volunteers as "our regiment" or "our men." He never referred to the Legion dragoons or the militia in those terms.

647. Major Thomas Mecan of the Twenty-third Regiment of Foot (Royal Welsh Fusiliers), a regiment of British regulars, was posted at Rugeley's Mill near Camden (e-mail, Todd Braisted to author, 29 May 2003).

648. Mecklenburg and Rowan Counties, North Carolina—like the New Acquisition District and the District between the Broad and Catawba Rivers in South Carolina—were settled predominantly by Scotch-Irish Presbyterians from the north of Ireland, the "Irish Skum" referred to by Turnbull.

649. Lieutenant Robert Peterson of the First Battalion, New Jersey Volunteers, was reassigned to Major Henry Sheridan, second-in-command of the New York Volunteers. Sheridan's company was not formed until 1781 (e-mail, Braisted to author, 30 May 2003).

650. Major General Johann DeKalb arrived in Hillsborough, North Carolina, with two brigades of Maryland and Delaware Continental troops on 22 June 1780. He camped at Buffalo Ford for two weeks and then moved to Coxe's Mill, where he turned command over to Major General Horatio Gates on 25 July. See Mark M. Boatner, *Encyclopedia of the American Revolution* (Mechanicsburg, PA: Stackpole Books, 1994), 159.

651. This is a reference to Edward Lacey Sr., a dedicated Loyalist and the father of Colonel Edward Lacey Jr., a dedicated Whig, and Reuben Lacey, a Whig-turned-Loyalist.

652. Lord Rawdon is referring to his countrymen, the Scotch-Irish from northern Ireland.

653. Colonel William T. Turner commanded a regiment of Loyalist militia in Camden District, South Carolina (Clark, *Loyalists*, I: 152).

654. Lieutenant Colonel Nisbet Balfour of the Twenty-third Regiment of Foot was commandant of Fort Ninety Six at the time (Boatner, 56).

655. Ethan Allen was a well-known officer from Vermont who served in both the militia and the Continental Army. He is best known as the commander of the Green Mountain Boys who captured the British Fort Ticonderoga in May 1775 (Purcell, 11–12).

656. Colonel Samuel Bryan commanded a regiment of Loyalist militia from the upper Yadkin River in North Carolina.

657. Daniel Huger was the eldest of the five Huger brothers of Charleston and the brother of Brigadier General Isaac Huger. Daniel was a planer and member of the colonial assembly before the war, and served on the executive council in 1780 (Purcell, 241).

658. Major General Richard Caswell was senior commandant of North Carolina Whig militia. Josiah Martin was royal governor of North Carolina from 1771 to 1775. The identity of Captain Dickson is uncertain (Boatner, 189, 681–682).

659. Lieutenant Colonel James Webster commanded the Thirty-third Regiment of Foot and was an acting brigade commander in Cornwallis's army during the Southern Campaign (Boatner, 1178–1179).

660. Captain John McClure.

661. New York Volunteers.

662. Lieutenant Benjamin Hunt of the British Legion was second-in-command of Captain Christian Huck's dragoon troop during this period. Turnbull was mistaken in referring to Hunt as a "cornet," when he was in fact a full lieutenant (Clinton, orders disbanding Emmerick's Chasseurs, 31 August 1779; e-mail, Braisted to author, 30 May 2003; Clark, *Loyalists*, II: 227, 238, 240).

663. Lieutenant John Adamson of Camden, South Carolina, commanded a company of Loyalist militia in Colonel Henry Rugeley's Camden Militia Regiment (Clark, *Loyalists*, I: 147–148); Lieutenant John McGregor of the New York Volunteers commanded the twenty men of that regiment who accompanied Huck to Williamson's Plantation (Clark, *Loyalists*, II: 183, 202–211).

664. Ensign Allen Cameron of the New York Volunteers was second-in-command of the detachment that accompanied Huck to Williamson's Plantation (Clark, *Loyalists*, II: 190–191). "Lt. Lewis" may have been Charles Lewis, who is known to have accompanied Huck on his expedition to Fishing Creek Church on 11 June 1780 (Charles Lewis deposition 24 June 1785, John Simpson Papers, South Caroliniana Library).

665. Major Patrick Ferguson of the Seventy-first Highland Regiment of Foot was the inspector of Loyalist militia in the Southern provinces. He was killed at the Battle of Kings Mountain on 7 October 1780 (Boatner, 364–365).

666. Surgeon's Mate Hugh Hill was senior medical officer of Lord Rawdon's Volunteers of Ireland at Camden while the chief surgeon, George Armstrong, was on leave in Europe (Clark, *Loyalists*, III: 267–268).

667. The surgeon who resigned from the New York Volunteers was probably Dr. James Murdoch; the surgeon's mate was most likely Nicholas Humphreys (Clark, *Loyalists*, III:177, 181, 212, 345, 353; e-mail, Braisted to author, 19 January 2005).

668. Dr. Wynne Stapleton was chief surgeon for the British Legion; he died later that year (e-mail, Braisted to author, 29 May 2003).

669. Dr. Thomas Gibbs was chief surgeon for the New York Volunteers (Clark, *Loyalists*, 178; e-mail, Braisted to author, 29 May 2003).

670. McCord's Ferry was located on the Congaree River between the modern counties of Richland and Calhoun. In the 1825 *Mills' Atlas of South Carolina*, McCord's Ferry connects Richland District and Orangeburg District (Orangeburg and Richland District maps, 1820, in *Mills' Atlas of South Carolina*).

671. Major Colin Graham of the British Sixteenth Regiment of foot commanded a light infantry company stationed at Friday's Ferry on the Conganee River (e-mail, Todd Braisted to author, 3 May 2005).

672. Lieutenant Colonel Alexander Innes was a veteran of the British Sixty-third Regiment of the Foot before the war, and commanded a provincial regiment called the South Carolina Royalists during the Revolution (Clark, Loyalists, I: 1–7, III: 368)

Appendix C

673. Lieutenant Colonel George Turnbull to Lord Rawdon, 12 July 1780 in Cornwallis Papers, PRO 30/11/2/285–286.

674. Lord Cornwallis to Sir Henry Clinton, 15 July 1780, in Banastre Tarleton, *A History of the Campaigns of 1780 and 1781 in the Southern Provinces of North America* (North Stratford, NH: Ayer Publishing, 1999; reprint of 1787 edition), 121.

675. Tarleton, 93.

676. [Uzal Johnson], *Uzal Johnson, Loyalist Surgeon: A Revolutionary War Diary*, ed. Bobby G. Moss (Blacksburg, SC: Scotia-Hibernia Press, 2000), 44; Anthony Allaire, "Diary," Lyman C. Draper, *King's Mountain and Its Heroes* (Baltimore. MD: Genealogical Publishing, 1971), 500.

677. Samuel Killough, supporting statement for Mrs. John Wallace, Revolutionary War Federal Pension Application (FPA) W955.

678. John Craig, "The War in York and Chester," *Chester Standard* (Chester, SC), 16 March 1854; John Craig, FPA W22864.

679. William Hill, *Col. William Hill's Memoirs of the Revolution*, ed. A.S. Salley Jr. (Columbia: The State Company, 1921), 8–9.

680. Maurice A. Moore *The Life of Gen. Edward Lacey* (Spartanburg, SC: Douglas, Evins & Co., 1859), 6.

681. Brigadier General Thomas Sumter to Major General Johann DeKalb, 17 July 1780, in Walter Clark, ed. and comp., *The State Records of North Carolina: Volume XIV, 1779–1780* (Winston, NC: M.I. & J.C. Stewart, 1896), 507.

682. Richard Winn, "General Richard Winn's Notes—1780," in Peter Force Papers, Library of Congress, Series 7E, 4.

683. John Craig, FPA W22864.

684. David Ramsay, *The History of the Revolution of South-Carolina* (Trenton, NJ: Isaac Collins, 1785), I:135.

685. Hill, *Memoirs*, 9.

686. Benson J. Lossing, *Hours Spent with the Living Men and Women of the Revolution* (New York: Funk and Wagnalls, 1889), 97.

687. Craig, "War."

688. John H. Logan and John Starr Moore, "Hauk's Defeat — Traditions of Starr Moore," c. 1857, in Draper MSS, 16VV272.

689. [John S. Bratton and W.C. Beatty], *Proceedings of a Celebration of Huck's Defeat* (Yorkville, SC: Tidings from the Craft, 1895), 5; *Yorkville Enquirer* (Yorkville, SC), 2 October 1903.

690. Moore, *Lacey*, 7.

691. Winn, "Notes," 4.

692. Hill, *Memoirs*, 9; James P. Collins, *Autobiography of a Revolutionary Soldier*, ed. John M. Roberts (New York: Arno Press, 1979), 25.

693. Killough, supporting statement for Mrs. John Wallace, Revolutionary War Federal Pension Application (FPA) W955; Bratton and Beatty, 5; *Yorkville Enquirer*, 2 October 1903.

694. Francis Heitman, *Historical Register of Officers of the Continental Army during the War of the Revolution* (Baltimore: Genealogical Publishing, 1982), 118.

695. Allaire, "Diary," in Draper, *King's Mountain*, 500; Johnson, *Diary*, 44.

696. Hugh Gaston, FPA S10729.

697. Joseph Kerr, FPA S13967.

698. James Kincaid, FPA R5929.

699. Thomas McDill to Draper, in Draper MSS, 15VV355.

700. Logan and Moore, in Draper MSS, 16VV272–279.

701. Craig, "War."

702. Moore, *Lacey*, 4.

Appendix D

703. William Harbison to Lyman C. Draper, 5 March 1873, in Draper MSS, 4VV36.

704. Logan and Moore, in Draper MSS, 16VV272–279.

705. Logan and Moore, in Draper MSS, 16VV277.

706. Draper, interview with Rufus Bratton and John S. Bratton, July 1871, in Draper MSS, 11VV336.

707. Daniel G. Stinson and Napoleon B. Bratton, "Map of Hook's Defeat," 26 March 1876, in Draper MSS, 15VV277–278.

708. Daniel G. Stinson and John S. Bratton Jr., "Plan of the Battleground of Huyck's Defeat," 24 August 1876, in Draper MSS, 5VV54.

709. Stinson to Draper, 15 January 1877, in Draper MSS, 15VV292.

710. York County Deed Book A, 286; Thomas Mayhugh, "James Williamson's Plantation," *Chester District Genealogical Society Bulletin*, Vol. XVI, No. 4 (December 1992), 111–118.

711. Quoted in George Howe, *History of the Presbyterian Church in South Carolina*, Vol. 1 (Columbia: Duffie and Chapman, 1870), 610.

Appendix E

712. Muster roll, Captain Christian Huck's company of chasseurs, Emmerick's Chasseurs, November 1778, PAC/RG8/"C"/1891.

713. Church of Jesus Christ of Latter-Day Saints, "International Genealogical Index," www.familysearch.org.

714. State of Pennsylvania, *Minutes of the Provincial Council of Pennsylvania*, vol. III (Philadelphia: Jo. Severns, 1852), 518–519.

715. Gale Research Inc., *Passenger and Immigration Lists Index 1538–1940*, Family Tree Maker Family Archives CD No. 354.

716. Marge Baskin, "Friends, Comrades and Enemies: Christian Huck (c. 1748 – 1780)," Oatmeal for the Foxhounds: Banastre Tarleton and the British Legion, www.banastretarleton.org; Anne M. Ousterhout, *A State Divided* (New York: Greenwood Press, 1987), 117, 158.

717. *Pennsylvania Gazette* (Philadelphia), 12 April 1775.

718. Ousterhout, 117; Philip Katcher and Michael Youens, *The American Provincial Corps 1775–1784* (Reading, Berkshire: Osprey Publishing Limited, 1973), 13.

719. Katcher and Youens, 158.

720. *Pennsylvania Gazette*, 27 November 1776.

721. Mark M. Boatner, *Encyclopedia of the American Revolution* (Mechanicsburg, PA: Stackpole Books, 1994), 856.

722. *Pennsylvania Packet* (Philadelphia), 13 May 1778.

723. Boatner, 856; Lorenzo Sabine, *Biographical Sketches of Loyalists of the American Revolution* (Port Washington, NY: Kennikat Press, 1966), I: 553.

724. Todd Braisted, "A History of Emmerick's Chasseurs," The On-Line Institute for Advanced Loyalist Studies (http://www.royalprovincial.com/military/rhist/emmerick/emmhist.htm).

725. Muster roll, Captain Huck's company of chasseurs, November 1778.

726. Braisted, "History of Emmerick's Chasseurs."

727. Braisted, "History of Emmerick's Chasseurs."

728. Sir Henry Clinton, orders disbanding Emmerick's Chasseurs, 31 August 1779, in Todd Braisted, "Emmerick's Chasseurs: Disbanding of Corps," The On-Line Institute for Advanced Loyalist Studies (http://www.royalprovincial.com/military/emmerick/emmords3.htm).

729. Murtie June Clark, *Loyalists in the Southern Campaign of the American Revolution* (Baltimore, MD: Genealogical Publishing, 1981), II:202–210; Katcher and Youens, 13; Donald J. Gara, "Biographical Sketches on Cavalry Officers of the British Legion, 1778–1782," The On-Line Institute for Advanced Loyalist Studies (www.royalprovincial.com/military/rhist/britlegn/blcav1.htm).

730. Richard Winn, "General Richard Winn's Notes—1780," in Peter Force Papers, Library of Congress, Series 7E, 4, 6.

731. *Pennsylvania Gazette*, 6 October 1779.

732. *Pennsylvania Gazette*, 17 May 1780.

733. Sabine, I: 553.

734. David Ramsay, *The History of the Revolution of South-Carolina* (Trenton, NJ: Isaac Collins, 1785), I:136.

735. Ramsay, I:141–142.

736. William D. James, *A Sketch of the Life of Brig. Gen. Francis Marion* (Charleston, SC: Gould and Riley, 1821), 40–41.

737. James, 40n–41n.

738. Thomas J. Kirkland and Robert M. Kennedy, *Historic Camden Part One, Colonial and Revolutionary* (Columbia, SC: State Company, 1905), 139–140.

739. Kirkland and Kennedy, 140–141.

740. Kirkland and Kennedy, 139n–140n.

741. Muster rolls, British Legion, October 1780–April 1782, in Clark, *Loyalists*, II:197–251.

742. Muster rolls, Captain Richard Hovenden's troop, British Legion, 25 October 1780–23 February 1782 (PAC/RG81/"C"/1883, 1884), in Clark, *Loyalists*, 202–206.

743. Proceedings of a general court-martial of Quartermaster John Tuck of the British Legion, 6 June 1780, Camden, South Carolina (PRO, War Office/Class 71/Vol. 92/111–114), transcribed in Todd Braisted, "General Court Martial of John Tuck," The On-Line Institute for Advanced Loyalist Studies (www.royalprovincial.com/military/courts/cmtuck.htm).

744. Winn, "Notes," 28; Joseph McJunkin, "Ms. Statement," in Draper MSS, 23VV209; Lyman C. Draper, interview with Daniel G. Stinson, in Draper MSS, 9VV12, 28; Elizabeth F. Ellet, *The Women of the American Revolution* (New York: Charles Scribner, 1853–1854), III: 216–220, 225–228.

745. Lieutenant Colonel George Turnbull to Lord Cornwallis, 16 June and 19 June 1780; [William Hill], *Col. William Hill's Memoirs of the Revolution*, ed. A.S. Salley Jr. (Columbia: The State Company, 1921), 8; Maurice A. Moore, *The Life of Gen. Edward Lacey* (Spartanburg, SC: Douglas, Evins & Co., 1859), 6; Robert S. Lambert, *South Carolina Loyalists in the American Revolution* (Columbia: USC Press, 1987), 127.

746. J.M. Hope to Draper, 31 August 1874, in Draper MSS, 4VV120.

747. Turnbull to Lord Rawdon, 12 July 1780; Banastre Tarleton, *A History of the Campaigns of 1780 and 1781 in the Southern Provinces of North America* (North Stratford, NH: Ayer Publishing, 1999; reprint of 1787 edition), 92–93; Lambert, 128.

748. Moore, *Lacey*, 11n; John Craig, "The War in York and Chester," *Chester Standard* (Chester, SC), 16 March 1854; James Stephenson, FPA W596; Draper, interview with Rufus Bratton, in Draper MSS, 11VV333.

749. Daniel G. Stinson and John S. Bratton Jr., "Plan of the Battleground of Huyck's Defeat," in Draper MSS, 5VV54.

750. Draper, interview with Rufus Bratton, Draper MSS, 11VV333; John H. Logan's notes, in Draper MSS, 16VV155.

751. Tarleton, 114–115.

752. Tarleton, 93.

753. Cornwallis to Rawdon, 15 July 1780, in Cornwallis Papers, PRO 30/11/78/18–19.

754. S.N.D. North et al., *Heads of Families at the First Census of the United States Taken in the Year 1790: Pennsylvania* (Baltimore: Genealogical Publishing, 1970), 200, 216, 230, 240.

755. Sabine, I: 553.

Bibliography

An overview of sources

The primary sources for the Battle of Huck's Defeat may be divided into two broad categories, British and American. Unfortunately, no eyewitness accounts of the battle from British or Loyalist sources are known to exist. The earliest and most important British sources are the letters written by Lieutenant Colonel George Turnbull to Lord Rawdon and Lord Cornwallis during the summer of 1780. These letters are part of the Cornwallis Papers in The National Archives (Public Record Office) of Great Britain, and those relevant to the events described in this book are fully transcribed in appendix B with the permission of The National Archives. These letters not only give us the first after-action reports of the battle, but also provide the British perspective on the events leading up to and following the battle. There are also entries in the diaries kept by two Provincial officers, Lieutenant Anthony Allaire and Dr. Uzal Johnson of Major Patrick Ferguson's command. Allaire's diary was transcribed and published by historian Dr. Lyman C. Draper in the appendix of his book *King's Mountain and Its Heroes* (1881). Johnson's diary, which is in the collection of the Public Record Office in Northern Ireland, has been transcribed, edited and annotated by Dr. Bobby G. Moss as *Uzal Johnson, Loyalist Surgeon: A Revolutionary War Diary* (2000). Johnson and Allaire were close friends, and their diaries are almost identical up through the Battle of Kings Mountain (7 October 1780), following which the men were taken prisoner and separated.

The memoirs of Lieutenant Colonel Banastre Tarleton, *A History of the Campaigns of 1780 and 1781 in the Southern Provinces of North America*, were first published in 1787, and they are indispensable for any study of the Revolution in the South. Tarleton's comments on Huck's Defeat are brief but important, and his memoirs have the bonus of reproducing many important documents from the Southern Campaign, including all of Sir Henry Clinton's proclamations and Cornwallis's letters mentioning Captain Christian Huck. Another important British source for the Southern Campaign was written by Lord Cornwallis's commissary, Charles Stedman, who provides a Loyalist perspective on the war in both the Northern and Southern theaters. Titled *The History of the Origin, Progress, and Termination of the American War*, Stedman's memoirs were published in two volumes in London in 1794. Although Stedman's account does not contain any additional details on Huck's Defeat, it provides a great deal of information on the war in the Carolina Backcountry and the logistical problems the British Army faced there.

None of these British accounts goes into much detail on Huck's Defeat, although the statements do give us some important information such as the numbers of men in Huck's detachment and the names of some of the officers present in the battle. Nonetheless, this information is derived from the reports of Provincial officers who survived Huck's Defeat and can be considered fairly reliable, although that does not mean the accounts are always in agreement with each other on some important points, such as the number of men in Huck's command.

The American (Whig) accounts are more numerous. First, we have several manuscript accounts written or dictated by soldiers who fought in the battle or who served under Thomas Sumter during the summer of 1780. The reminiscences of Richard Winn (1812), William Hill (1815), John Craig (1839), John Adair (1839) and James P. Collins (1859) all contain firsthand accounts of Huck's Defeat. Unfortunately for historians, most of these accounts were written long after the battle took place, when the veterans were quite old, and none agrees in every detail. As a consequence, almost all contain some factual errors, especially regarding details such as the chronological sequence of events as well as the dates of battles and skirmishes. The veterans sometimes forget the names of their commanding officers or recall them incorrectly. In addition, the authors sometimes embellish their own roles in the conflict while reducing or ignoring the contributions of others. None of these accounts can stand alone as a definitive record of Huck's Defeat or any other battle of the Revolution, but used together and in conjunction with other sources, they can be a valuable asset.

General Richard Winn's account of Huck's Defeat is contained in a memoir that he sent to his friend Captain Hugh McCall of Savannah, Georgia, who was writing a history of the state of Georgia. General Winn set down these reminiscences while serving as a U.S. congressman from South Carolina. Dated Washington, D.C., 10 April 1812, and titled "General Richard Winn's Notes—1780," Winn's account is now part of the Peter Force Papers (Series 7E, Library of Congress, microfilm 19,061, reel 3 of 6). These notes were first transcribed and published by Samuel C. Williams of the Tennessee Historical Commission in *The South Carolina Genealogical and Historical Magazine* in October 1942 and January 1943. However, Williams's transcription was not verbatim, and it omitted the final pages of Winn's text and some important maps for the battle sites of Huck's Defeat, Fishdam Ford and Blackstock's Plantation. A little more than a month after penning the above treatise, Winn sent another letter to Hugh McCall that included additional details of Huck's Defeat, including the Huck quote about "raining militia" from which the title of this book is derived. This letter is found in the Thomas Sumter Papers of the Lyman C. Draper Manuscript Collection, 5VV89. Winn has been frequently criticized because he overstates his role in the events of that period and places himself at the center of almost every action. Nonetheless, his account remains one of the most detailed and accurate of the surviving memoirs.

Colonel William Hill's memoirs were written in February 1815, but like Winn's notes, they were not published until the twentieth century. By Hill's admission, his goal was to set the record straight among historians about the overlooked battles in South Carolina, in particular the Battle of Kings Mountain. Hill emphasized his role and that of Colonel Edward Lacey in the success of that operation, and deplored the fact that the only South Carolina commander mentioned by historians was Colonel James Williams, who was mortally wounded in the battle.

Hill and Lacey, in particular, did not get along well with Williams, and Hill blamed Williams for the fact that General Sumter was not present at the Battle of Kings Mountain. According to Hill, it was Williams's two attempts to take over command of Sumter's Brigade in the summer and fall of 1780 that forced Sumter to go to Hillsborough, North Carolina, in order to obtain a brigadier's commission from South Carolina Governor John Rutledge, thus causing him to be absent when Major Patrick Ferguson was defeated at Kings Mountain in October 1780. Hill's criticism of William Bratton and other officers is also implicit in the manuscript, and his own children kept him from publishing it during his lifetime. However, Hill did send the entire manuscript to General Sumter for his review, and Sumter made some minor grammatical changes but did not alter the content of the manuscript, thus adding his own support to Hill's comments. Like Winn's memoirs, Hill's reminiscences contain some obvious lapses of memory and factual mistakes, as well as a tendency to overemphasize his role in the events he describes. Hill's memoirs were edited by A.S. Salley Jr. as *Col. William Hill's Memoirs of the Revolution* and published by The South Carolina Historical Commission in 1921.

John Craig served in the New Acquisition Militia Regiment, McClure's Rangers and Sumter's Brigade during the Revolution, and provided one of the most coherent and accurate accounts of the battles of 1780. Following the Bratton family's celebration of Huck's Defeat in July 1839, which played up the Bratton involvement in the battle and was widely publicized by local newspapers, Craig wrote an account of his own services in the war, including a detailed account of "the Battle of Williamson's Lane." Titled "The War in York and Chester," Craig's reminiscence was originally printed in the *Pendleton Messenger* in November 1839 and subsequently was reprinted in the *Chester Standard* of 16 March 1854 and in some other newspapers. Craig also left a very detailed Federal pension application, and both of his accounts contain a wealth of information concerning the New Acquisition Militia Regiment's role in winning the war in the Backcountry.

John Adair served in the Third South Carolina Regiment of Rangers under Colonel William Thomson during the early phase of the Revolution, and after the fall of Charleston, Adair was an officer in Colonel Edward Lacey's militia regiment. Like Craig, Adair was prompted to set down his own version of Huck's Defeat after the "Bratton glorification" of 1839. He dictated his account of the battle to his son John Adair Jr., who enclosed it in a letter to his second cousin Dr. Maurice Moore of York District. Dated Harodsburg, Kentucky, 17 December 1839, the letter is found in the Thomas Sumter Papers of the Lyman C. Draper Manuscript Collection, 5VV294–300. Adair also filed a detailed Federal pension application, which provides additional details of his service in the Revolution.

Several soldiers who were not actually in the Battle of Huck's Defeat but who served under Sumter in the summer and fall of 1780 also left important accounts that fill in many of the details of that critical period. One of these soldiers was Joseph Gaston of Chester District, the youngest of Justice John Gaston's nine sons, all of whom served in the American Revolution. Although Gaston was only sixteen years old when Charleston surrendered to the British in May 1780, he immediately joined the militia company commanded by his cousin Captain John McClure, and he served faithfully for the duration of the war. At a reunion of Revolutionary War veterans in Chester District on the Fourth of July in 1835, the attendees appointed a committee to obtain reminiscences of the war from surviving veterans in the area. Joseph Gaston was one of the few who was able to comply with this request. His memoir, dated 28 June 1836, was printed in *The Columbia Hive* newspaper on 6 August 1836 and later appeared in another Columbia newspaper called *The Southern Presbyterian* on 22 May 1873.

Joseph McJunkin of Union District was not at Huck's Defeat either, but his memoirs (which exist in several versions) provide important details about the events before and after the battle. McJunkin served in Colonel Thomas Brandon's Fair Forest Militia Regiment and kept a journal of his experiences. In addition to a detailed Federal pension application, McJunkin left several other manuscripts describing his adventures in the war. The first printed version of McJunkin's reminiscences was published by Judge John Belton O'Neill of Newberry District as "Revolutionary Incidents: Memoir of Joseph McJunkin, of Union" and appeared in a periodical called *The Magnolia, or Southern Apalachian* in January 1843. In 1847, McJunkin's son-in-law, the Reverend James Hodge Saye, published a highly edited and annotated version of McJunkin's reminiscences in the Richmond, Virginia, *Watchman and Observer*. Many modern historians have mistakenly assumed that Saye's manuscript is a verbatim transcription of McJunkin's notes, but this is not the case. Saye combined McJunkin's unpublished memoirs with O'Neill's published version and injected liberal doses of his own opinions, commentary and local color, thus creating a hodgepodge of McJunkin's statements and his own views. Fortunately for modern historians, Draper transcribed McJunkin's original manuscripts while they were in the Reverend Saye's possession (they were subsequently lost in a shipwreck) and included them in the Draper Manuscript Collection. One of these manuscripts is titled "Reminiscences of the Revolutionary War related by Major Joseph McJunkin, of the militia of South Carolina, written July 18th 1837" and is found on pages 23VV168–174 of the Thomas Sumter Papers. The other account is titled "A Ms. Statement of Maj. McJunkin as noted in his own handwriting, without date or address, but which Mr. Saye supposes was written for Prof. Nott, as he furnished him a statement—also got his Diary or Journal kept in the war" and is found in 23VV204–212 of the Sumter Papers.

Both of Colonel William Bratton's sons also left descriptions of the battle. One of the earliest local accounts of Huck's Defeat was prepared in 1839 under the direction of Dr. John Simpson Bratton, the youngest son of William and Martha Bratton. On 12 July of that year, Dr. Bratton hosted a celebration at Brattonsville commemorating the patriot victory over Captain Huck. Colonel W.C. Beatty gave a colorful and somewhat romanticized speech about the battle, which nonetheless contained many details handed down from the Brattons. Following the speech, the hosts read a list containing the names of about eighty Whigs who fought in the battle, and the celebrants drank toasts to their memory. Much of the information was provided by Dr. Bratton, but since he was not born until 1789, his knowledge of the battle could only have been derived from stories he heard from his parents, older siblings and neighbors. Bratton's wife Harriet was the daughter of Samuel Rainey, another veteran of the battle, and the Rainey family's traditions were undoubtedly incorporated into the account as well. Additional information came from local veterans such as Samuel Williamson and Alexander Moore, and from a manuscript history of the conflict in York and Chester written by the Reverend Samuel McCreary, which unfortunately has not survived. The proceedings of the Bratton celebration were carried in local York and Chester newspapers and were used as a source by many subsequent writers. The entire proceedings were published in York in 1895 in a booklet titled *Proceedings of a Celebration of the Battle of Huck's Defeat at Brattonsville, York District, S.C., July 12th, 1839.* This booklet has been widely circulated in South Carolina and continues to be a valuable source on the battle.

Colonel Bratton's oldest son, Dr. William Bratton Jr. of Winnsboro, South Carolina, also left an important account of Huck's Defeat. William Bratton Jr. was almost seven years old at the time of Huck's Defeat, and sometime before his death in December 1850, he dictated his recollection of the battle to his son John Bratton (later Brigadier General John Bratton of the Confederate Army), who faithfully transcribed his father's words. William Bratton Jr.'s account is different from most other reminiscences in that it gives us a child's memories and a child's viewpoint; it is more concerned with Huck's interaction with Martha and the family's experiences, than with the battle and the soldiers. A handwritten copy of Bratton's document, titled *Huck's Defeat: Dr. William Bratton's Story*, survives in the archives of the South Carolina Historical Society in Charleston. Thomas Kirkland and Robert Kennedy published excerpts of Dr. Bratton's story in their book *Historic Camden, Part One: Colonial and Revolutionary* (1905), although their transcription does not exactly match the document at the South Carolina Historical Society.

The largest number of firsthand accounts for Huck's Defeat, or any other battle of the Revolution, is the state and Federal pension applications filed by Revolutionary War veterans in the 1820s and 1830s. The South Carolina state pension applications, along with audited accounts for Revolutionary War militia service and indents for payments on these accounts, are available on microfilm at the South Carolina Department of Archives and History at its main branch in Columbia. The Federal pension applications are preserved by the National Archives and Records Administration in Washington, D.C., and are available on microfilm at the South Carolina Archives and other institutions. Both the state and Federal pension applications are detailed depositions describing Revolutionary War service, sworn before local magistrates in the presence of witnesses, and often accompanied by supporting testimony from fellow veterans, wives, children or other legal heirs. The original documents were recorded at the veterans' local county or district courthouses, and copies were forwarded to the state and Federal government to process their claims. Excerpts from many of the pension applications and audited accounts describing Huck's Defeat as well as other relevant events are transcribed here in appendix A. While some of these accounts are detailed and coherent, others are not. Most of the veterans were in their seventies or eighties when they filed for their pensions, and it clear that in many cases their memories were failing them. Very few veterans had any documentation to back up their stories, and there were only a few published histories available at the time for use as references. However, there are enough of these pension claims to enable us to compare and cross-check the information in them, and to come up with a consensus view based on the sum total of the evidence.

Historians and scholars of the Revolution in South Carolina first took up the story of Huck's Defeat in print in 1785, when Dr. David Ramsay published *The History of the Revolution of South-Carolina: from a British province to an independent state.* Ramsay was a Revolutionary War veteran, having served as a surgeon in the Fourth South Carolina Regiment of Artillery, and he undoubtedly had contacts among the Whig officers in the Upcountry who provided him with firsthand details of Huck's Defeat. His history contains a brief but important account of the battle, along with some comments on Huck's personality and his "enmity" to the Backcountry Presbyterians. Ramsay's account of Huck's Defeat was repeated almost verbatim three years later by the British historian William Gordon in *The History of the Rise, Progress, and Establishment of the Independence of the United States of America*, published in four volumes in London in 1788. Ramsay's and Gordon's histories were widely read in their day, and many nineteenth century historians used them as sources.

These early accounts were incorporated into subsequent histories of the Revolution in South Carolina, such as William Dobein James's *A Sketch of the Life of Brig. Gen. Francis Marion* (1821), Dr. Joseph Johnson's *Traditions and Reminiscences, chiefly of the American Revolution in the South* (1851), Dr. John H. Logan's *A History of the Upper Country of South Carolina, from the Earliest Periods to the Close of the War of Independence* (1859) and Cecil B. Hartley's *Life of Major General Henry Lee, Commander of Lee's Legion in the Revolutionary War, and Subsequently Governor of Virginia; to which is added the Life of General Thomas Sumter of South Carolina*, also published in 1859. Benson J. Lossing's monumental *Pictorial Field-Book of the American Revolution*, published in two volumes between 1850 and 1852, contained historical information on Huck's Defeat and many other South Carolina battles, and featured Lossing's wonderful engravings of the scenes and battlefields of the Revolution as they appeared in 1849, when he traveled through the area.

On the heels of Lossing's opus on the Revolution, Elizabeth F. Ellet brought the female perspective to the forefront in her immensely popular three-volume series, *The Women of the Revolution*, originally published in 1853 and 1854. Each volume contains biographies of women who lived through the Revolution and were noted for their courage and bravery. The first volume contains Martha Bratton's story, but it is the third volume that really highlights the war in the South Carolina Backcountry. Volume III contains many of the stories from the Fishing Creek and Rocky Creek families involved the events of 1780, and it relies heavily on the research of a Chester County native named Daniel Green Stinson. Stinson was the son of a Revolutionary War veteran and was a Chester County magistrate. As magistrate, he assisted many veterans in filing the paperwork for their Revolutionary War pensions. In addition, he collected the traditions of his family members, friends and neighbors concerning the war. Although he contributed many articles to local newspapers and periodicals, Stinson apparently did not have the desire to write a book about the Revolution in York and Chester himself. Instead, he provided his notes to Ellet in manuscript form, and she incorporated them, almost verbatim, into her stories.

In addition to Stinson's notes, Ellet also made use of Dr. John Bratton's 1839 proceedings, Dr. William Bratton's reminiscences, Dr. Joseph Johnson's *Traditions and Reminiscences* and the Reverend Samuel McCreary's unpublished Revolutionary War manuscript. Ellet's volumes are filled with details taken from all these sources, but like most of the other histories of that period, they are also embellished and exaggerated. Her heavy reliance on other peoples' research led her to commit significant factual errors, such as her confusion between Colonel William Bratton and his son John Bratton in her first volume, and her confusion between William Bratton Jr. and his brother John in her third volume. In 1859, Ellet followed her successful trilogy with a single volume called *Domestic History of the American Revolution*, a condensed version of her original trilogy that contained many of the same stories.

The most detailed and widely read nineteenth century account of Huck's Defeat was written by Dr. Maurice A. Moore, a native of York County. Moore's version of the battle appeared in *The Life of Gen. Edward Lacey*, a biography of the South Carolina militia leader Colonel (later General) Edward Lacey published in 1859. Moore provided additional information about Huck's Defeat and the war in the Backcountry in a series of anonymous articles titled "Reminiscences of a Septugenarian," which he wrote for the *Yorkville Enquirer* newspaper in the 1870s. These articles were later collected by South Carolina historian Elmer O. Parker and published in book form as *Reminiscences of York* (1981). Moore's father, Alexander Moore, was a close friend of Colonel Lacey's and served with him during the Revolution. In compiling his history, Dr. Moore drew on the personal reminiscences of his father, his uncle James Moore, his grandfather William Ervin, his second cousin John Adair as well as the depositions and memoirs of John Craig, Robert Wilson and other local Revolutionary War veterans. Some of Moore's most important sources were the reminiscences of Major (later General) John Adair, who also served under Lacey and was in the battle of Huck's Defeat. In 1839, John Adair Jr. collected his father's memories of the battle and sent them in a letter to Moore, who incorporated them into his biography of Lacey. Moore's detailed sketch of Huck's Defeat was utilized by innumerable subsequent historians, including General Edward McCrady, whose two-volume *History of South Carolina in the Revolution* (1901) has become one of the standard references on the war in South Carolina. Most of the twentieth century accounts of Huck's Defeat relied heavily on Moore and McCrady. Unfortunately, Moore's book also contains some serious historical errors that were picked up by subsequent writers and propagated without verification. His comments should be used with discretion and only after careful comparison with other, more accurate primary sources.

The same year that Moore wrote his biography of Lacey, Dr. John H. Logan published *A History of the Upper Country of South Carolina*. As part of his research for a projected second volume of this history, Logan visited many families in the South Carolina Upcountry and recorded their Revolutionary War traditions. One of the people Logan interviewed was John Starr Moore of York District, who provided Logan with a great deal of information on Huck's Defeat. John Starr Moore's father, Samuel Moore, along with Samuel's brothers John Moore Jr., Nathan Moore and William Moore were all veterans of the battle. His grandfather, John "Gum Log" Moore Sr., was one of the prisoners locked in the corncrib the night before Huck's Defeat. Furthermore, Moore's aunt, Anne Starr, was the wife of Samuel Williamson, the son of James Williamson on whose plantation the battle was fought; Samuel Williamson and three of his brothers were also in the battle. Samuel supposedly fired the first shot of the battle, and he inherited his father's old home and the battle site. Starr Moore's reminiscences contain important details of the battle not found elsewhere, including a map of the Williamson plantation and the Huck's Defeat battlefield.

Outside of the state and Federal pension applications, the greatest single source of information on Huck's Defeat and the other battles in the Southern Campaign of the Revolution is the manuscript collection of the Wisconsin historian Dr. Lyman Copeland Draper, secretary of the State Historical Society of Wisconsin. Draper spent years researching the early settlement of the Ohio and Appalachian frontiers, the French and Indian War and the Revolution in the South. On these subjects, he amassed a great deal of primary and secondary source material, including books, journals, diaries, newspaper clippings and magazine articles. He copied manuscripts and letters from the Library of Congress, the New-York Historical Society and other institutions, and corresponded with and interviewed dozens of local historians and descendants of Revolutionary War soldiers. Draper wrote several books on the Revolution, including *King's Mountain and Its Heroes* (1881), an exhaustive study that is still the standard history of that battle. He also planned to write a biography of Thomas Sumter, spending years gathering information on Sumter's life, his officers and men, and their campaigns. As part of this research, Draper conducted extensive correspondence with local historians who were personally acquainted with or related to South Carolina's Revolutionary War veterans. Among his most prolific correspondents were Dr. Maurice Moore and Daniel G. Stinson, both of who provided Draper with an enormous amount of information on the soldiers from York and Chester as well as on the battles in the South Carolina Backcountry. In the spring of 1871, Draper visited Brattonsville and interviewed two of Colonel William Bratton's grandsons, Dr. John Simpson Bratton Jr. and Dr. James Rufus Bratton. He also corresponded with and interviewed other local antiquarians, including the Reverend James Hodge Saye and Dr. A.P. Wylie.

Although Draper never published this Sumter biography, his notes and correspondence on the Revolutionary War in the Carolinas survive in the Kings Mountain Papers (Series DD), the South Carolina Papers (Series TT), the South Carolina in the Revolution Papers (Series UU), the Frontier Wars Papers (Series U) and the Thomas Sumter Papers (Series VV). These collections make up five of the fifty series of manuscripts contained in the Lyman C. Draper Manuscript Collection at the Wisconsin Historical Society. These 50 series in turn contain 486 volumes and include hundreds of thousands of pages of Draper's voluminous research and correspondence. Available on microfilm, the Draper Manuscript Collection is an invaluable resource for researching the Revolution in the South Carolina Backcountry.

Most of the twentieth century histories of the Revolution in South Carolina say something about Huck's Defeat, although few of them go beyond the information in Maurice Moore's account and the memoirs of Richard Winn and William Hill. John Buchanan's *The Road to Guilford Courthouse: The American Revolution in the Carolinas* (1997) and Walter Edgar's *Partisans and Redcoats: The Southern Conflict that Turned the Tide of the American Revolution* (2001) contain the most detailed accounts of Huck's Defeat, although both rely heavily on Moore.

PRIMARY SOURCES

A. South Carolina Audited Accounts (AA) for Revolutionary War service

(South Carolina Department of Archives and History, Columbia, South Carolina, microfilm reels RW 2685–RW 2848)

Brown, Alexander. AA 792, 20 January 1785.

Davidson, William. AA 1822, 28 April 1785.

Fleming, Elijah. AA 2422, 13 September 1784.

Henderson, John. AA 3522, 19 January 1793, 25 November 1795.

Jones, Jonathan Jr. AA 4109, 15 August 1826.

McClure (McCluer), Charles. AA 4938 ½, 29 November 1819

McClure (McCluer), James. AA 4936, 12 December 1783, 6 December 1820.

McClure (McCluer), John. AA 4939, 8 May 1786.

Ramsey, James. AA 6233, 16 June 1785.

Rowan, Benjamin. AA 6641, 13 May 1785.

Simpson, Reverend John. AA7019, 18 March 1781, 12 March 1785.

Steel (Steele), John. AA 7342, 15 February 1784.

Stephenson, James. AA 7354, 8 September 1840.

Stephenson, Robert. AA 7357, 27 October 1784.

Strong, Christopher and Strong, William. AA 7484, 17 May 1785.

Wylie, William. AA 8822, 1 October 1784.

B. Federal Pension Applications (FPA) for Revolutionary War service
(South Carolina Department of Archives and History, Columbia, South Carolina, microfilm reels RW 1–RW 2669)

Dates are for initial pension application by soldier, widow or heirs. Most files contain supporting depositions and subsequent documentation with later dates

Adair, John. W2895, 12 July 1832, Harrodsburg, Kentucky.

Armstrong, William. S6534, 6 March 1833, Anderson District, South Carolina.

Bishop, John. S9279, 24 November 1832, Chester District, South Carolina.

Bishop, Nicholas. S17847, March 1836, Anderson District, South Carolina.

Bishop, William. S30275, 8 December 1834, Hopkins County, Kentucky.

Black, Jacob. S9281, 15 October 1832, York District, South Carolina.

Black, John. W9359, 16 October 1832, York District, South Carolina.

Boggs, Thomas. W27895, 11 April 1846, York District, South Carolina.

Brown, Archibald. S39249, 28 March 1822, Chester District, South Carolina.

Brown, Robert. R1337, 18 April 1854, Westmoreland County, Pennsylvania.

Carroll, Joseph. W9778, 26 January 1846, York District, South Carolina.

Carson, John. S35819, 7 September 1818, Hardin County, Kentucky.

Carson, Walter. S32165, 13 May 1833, Jennings County, Indiana.

Carson, William. S9305, 22 May 1821, York District, South Carolina.

Clinton, James. S2437, 20 May 1833, Caldwell County, Kentucky.

Collins, James P. R2173, 8 April 1834, East Feliciana Parish, Louisiana.

Craig, John. W22864, 3 October 1832, Pickens District, South Carolina.

Cunningham, George W. W2071, 13 August 1832, Bedford County, Tennessee.

Darwin, John. S21155, October 1834, York District, South Carolina.

Doyle, Edward. S32216, 18 September 1832, Blount County, Alabama.

Evans, Owen. W10965, 28 October 1832, Morgan County, Alabama.

Fergus, James. W25573, 1 September 1832, Carroll County, Tennessee.

Fleming, William. S32250, 3 September 1832, Hall County, Georgia.

Floyd, Abraham. S32251, 9 May 1834, Decatur County, Indiana.

Forbes, John. R3645, 16 June 1846, York District, South Carolina.

Gaston, Hugh. S10729, 25 April 1834, Wilcox County, Alabama.

Gaston, James. W23082, 6 August 1832, Wayne County, Illinois.

Gaston, John Jr. W30007, 12 September 1836, Jefferson County, Illinois

Gaston, Joseph. W22089, 22 June 1833, Chester District, South Carolina.

Gaston, William. S32265, 24 September 1832, Marion County, Illinois.

Gill, George. S21229, 2 October 1832, Chester District, South Carolina.

Gill, Thomas. S31061, 3 September 1832, Crawford County, Illinois.

Graham, Joseph. 30 October 1832, Lincoln County, North Carolina.

Goyne, James. S30442, Kemper County, Mississippi.

Hemphill, James. S21277, 16 October 1832, Lincoln County, Tennessee.

Henderson, John. R4869, 28 June 1833, McNairy County, Tennessee.

Hillhouse, William. S7008, 3 February 1834, Marengo County, Alabama.

Houston, Samuel. W7810, 6 May 1833, Fayette County, Georgia.

Jamieson, James. S21839, 16 October 1832, Chester District, South Carolina.

Jenkins, William. S31774, 4 August 1832, Jackson County, Alabama.

Johnson (Johnston), James. W9088, 23 July 1846, Chester District, South Carolina.

Kerr, Joseph. S13967, 4 September 1832, White County, Tennessee.

Kincaid, James. R5929, 1 July 1833, Buncombe County, North Carolina.

Knox, John. W10181, 15 July 1842, Owen County, Indiana.

Knox, Robert. W26190, 13 August 1832, Switzerland County, Indiana.

Knox, William. S38900, 20 July 1818, Chester District, South Carolina.

Lewis, William. R6335, 22 April 1835, Fairfield District, South Carolina.

Lofton, Thomas. S17114, 10 December 1832, Pickens County, Alabama.

Martin, James. S9391, 16 October 1832, York District, South Carolina.

McCaw, James. S18117, 21 September 1833, Chester District, South Carolina.

McClure, Hugh. W21789, 26 November 1846, Chester District, South Carolina.

McCreight, Robert. S21881, 19 July 1832, Fairfield District, South Carolina.

McElwee, James. W9553, 26 September 1832, Pike County, Missouri.

McGarity, William. R6713, 11 November 1826, Chester District, South Carolina.

Martin, James. S9391, 16 October 1832, York District, South Carolina.

Martin, John. W9642, 11 April 1846, York District, South Carolina.

Miles, Charles. R21890, 5 September 1826, Robertson County, Tennessee.

Miller, John. S38950, 20 July 1818, Chester District, South Carolina.

Mills, John. W9194, 30 June 1846, Chester District, South Carolina.

Moore, John. W9205, 11 April 1849, York District, South Carolina.

Morrow, David. S7253, 22 September 1833, Lawrence County, Alabama.

Morrow, Joseph. S21892, 19 December 1832, Chester District, South Carolina.

Neely, George. S4613, 21 September 1832, Williamson County, Tennessee.

Pattison (Patterson), Robert. S3654, 27 August 1832, Giles County, Tennessee.

Patton, John. W162, 10 August 1832, Bedford County, Tennessee.

Rea, Henry. W9246, 16 October 1832, York District, South Carolina.

Robinson, Joseph. W10246. 24 December 1846, York District, South Carolina.

Robison, William. S21452, 25 March 1833, York District, South Carolina.

Ross, George. W8979, 14 November 1832, Harden County, Tennessee.

Sadler, David. S9471, 6 March 1833, Anderson District, South Carolina.

Smith, Robert. R9731, 17 February 1857, Butts County, Georgia.

Stephenson, James. W596, 26 August 1839, Maury County, Tennessee.

Sterling, Silas C. R101020, 8 July 1832, Blount County, Alabama.

Walker, Alexander. W8979, 1848, Chester District, South Carolina.

Wallace, James. S19145, 20 October 1832, York District, South Carolina.

Wallace, John. R11064, 18 August 1855, York District, South Carolina.

Wallace, John. W955, 24 November 1838, Rutherford County, Tennessee.

Wallace, John. S17178, 5 August 1833, Ray County, Missouri.

Wallace (Wallis), Samuel. W6408, 13 February 1834, Jackson County, Tennessee.

Walker, Alexander. W8979, 19 January 1848, Chester District, South Carolina.

Watson, Samuel Jr. S17187, 27 September 1832, Pike County, Illinois.

Wilson, Robert. W2302, 16 October 1832, York District, South Carolina.

Woods, Thomas. S32614, 22 October 1832, Dallas County, Alabama.

Wylie, Francis. S21592, 8 October 1834, Chester District, South Carolina.

C. Unpublished manuscripts and records

1. Dacus Library, Winthrop University, Rock Hill, South Carolina:
   - Lyman C. Draper Manuscript Collection. State Historical Society of Wisconsin.
2. Historical Center of York County, York, South Carolina:
   - Brewster, Walter Whatley. "Col. James Ferguson, Jr., of Rocky & Fishing Creeks." Ferguson family group sheets, 29 December 1981.
   - Hart, Joseph. Joe Hart Genealogical Collection. RG6.
   - Moore, Maurice A., letter to Mrs. C.L. Williams, 2 February 1856 (copy).
3. Library of Congress, Washington, D.C.:
   - Winn, Richard. "General Richard Winn's Notes—1780." Peter Force Papers, series 7E. Reel 3 of 56. Library of Congress microfilm reel 19,061.
4. Public Archives of Canada, Ontario:
   - Muster Roll of Captain Christian Huck's Company of Chasseurs in his Majesty's Corps of Chasseurs commanded by Lieutenant Colonel Emmerick. October 1778, November 1778 and 5 January 1779. RG8, "C" series, vol. 1891.
   - Muster Roll of Captain John Althause's Company Rifle Men of His Majesty's Battalion of Chasseurs Commanded by Lieutenant Colonel Emmerick, Kingsbridge. November 1778, 5 January 1779 and 24 April 1779. RG8, "C" series, vol. 1891.
5. South Carolina Department of Archives and History, Columbia, South Carolina:
   - Great Britain Exchequer and Audit Office. Public Records of Great Britain: American Loyalist Claims. Series 11, reel 135. AO13/127–128, 1775–1835. Public Record Office, Kew, Surrey, England. SCDAH microfilm reel RW 3158.

- Transcripts of Examinations and Decisions on Loyalist Claims (American Loyalist Transcripts), 1783–1790. Vol. 52–54 (Claims: 1899–1901). New York Public Library, New York, New York. SCDAH microfilm reel RW 3169.
- Charles Cornwallis Papers (CP), Public Record Office, Kew, Surrey, England. Series 30/11/2, SCDAH microfilm reel RW 3145A; series 30/11/77–78, RW 3149; series 30/11/78–89, RW 3150.
- Revolutionary War Federal Pension Applications (FPA). Microfilm Series M804. National Archives and Records Administration, Washington, D.C. SCDAH microfilm reels RW 1–RW 2669.
- South Carolina Audited Accounts for Revolutionary War Service Claims. SCDAH microfilm reels RW 2685–RW 2848.
- South Carolina Auditor General. Memorial Books, 1731–1778. SCDAH microfilm reels ST 0088–ST 0094.
- South Carolina Colonial Plat Books, 1731–1775. SCDAH microfilm reels ST 0038–ST 0052.
- South Carolina Colonial Land Grants, 1675–1788. SCDAH microfilm reels ST 0059–ST 0085.
- Works Progress Administration. "Formation of Counties in South Carolina." Columbia: South Carolina Archives, 1938.
- ———. "Guide Maps to the Development of South Carolina Parishes, Districts and Counties." Columbia: South Carolina Archives, 1938.

6. South Carolina Historical Society, Charleston, South Carolina:
- Bratton, William Jr., and Bratton, John. "Huck's Defeat: Dr. William Bratton's Story." Winnsboro, SC: unpublished manuscript, n.d. (before December 1850). File No. 43/1018: John Bratton (1831–1898).

7. South Caroliniana Library, University of South Carolina, Columbia, South Carolina:
- Faden, William, royal geographer. "The Marches of Lord Cornwallis in the Southern Provinces Now States of North America Comprehending the Two Carolinas, with Virginia and Maryland, and the Delaware Counties." Map contained in *A History of the Campaigns of 1780 and 1781 in the Southern Provinces of North America,* by Banastre Tarleton. 2nd ed. London: T. Cadell & W. Davies, 1796.
- Lewis, Charles. Deposition regarding Loyalist services of Jeremiah and Burrel Burge. Camden District Court, 24 June 1785. John Simpson Family Papers. RG1912.

D. Colonial and state record series

1. State Records of South Carolina:
- Hemphill, William Edwin, and Wylma Anne Wates, eds. *Extracts from the Journals of the Provincial Congresses of South Carolina, 1775-1776.* Columbia: South Carolina Archives Department, 1960.
- Hemphill, William Edwin, Wylma Anne Wates and R. Nicholas Olsberg, eds. *Journals of the General Assembly and House of Representatives, 1776-1780.* Columbia: University of South Carolina Press, 1970.

- Thompson, Theodora J., ed. *Journals of the South Carolina House of Representatives 1783-1784*. Columbia: University of South Carolina Press, 1977.
- Adams, Lark Emerson, and Rosa Stoney Lumpkin, eds. *Journals of the South Carolina House of Representatives 1785-1786*. Columbia: University of South Carolina Press, 1979.

2. Colonial Records of North Carolina:
- Saunders, William L., ed. and comp. *The Colonial Records of North Carolina: Volume VI, 1759-1765*. Raleigh, NC: Josephus Daniels, 1888.
- ———. *The Colonial Records of North Carolina: Volume IX, 1771 to 1775*. Raleigh: Josephus Daniels, 1890.

3. State Records of North Carolina:
- Clark, Walter, ed. and comp. *The State Records of North Carolina: Volume XI, 1776, and Supplement, 1730 to 1776*. Winston, NC: M.I. & J.C. Stewart, 1895.
- ———. *The State Records of North Carolina: Volume XIV, 1779-1780*. Winston, NC: M.I. & J.C. Stewart, 1896.
- ———. *The State Records of North Carolina: Volume XV, 1780-1781*. Goldsboro, NC: Nash Brothers, 1898.
- ———. *The State Records of North Carolina: Volume XIX, 1782-1784, with Supplement 1771-1782*. Goldsboro, NC: Nash Brothers, 1901.
- ———. *The State Records of North Carolina: Volume XXII, Miscellaneous*. Goldsboro, NC: Nash Brothers, 1907.

4. Colonial Records of Pennsylvania:
- State of Pennsylvania. *Minutes of the Provincial Council of Pennsylvania, from the Organization to the Termination of the Proprietary Government*. Pennsylvania Archives, Colonial Records Series, vol. III. Philadelphia: Jo. Severns, 1852.

E. Newspapers

Charlotte Observer (Charlotte, North Carolina). 28 September 1930.

Chester News and Reporter (Chester, South Carolina). 18 March 1992.

Chester Reporter (Chester, South Carolina). 29 May 1873; 18 June 1874.

Chester Standard (Chester, South Carolina). 17 September 1871; 16 March 1854.

Maryland Journal and Baltimore Advertiser (Baltimore, Maryland). 5 September 1780.

New-Jersey Journal (Newark, New Jersey). 6 September 1780.

Pennsylvania Gazette and Weekly Advertiser (Philadelphia, Pennsylvania). 12 April 1775, 27 November 1776, 6 October 1779, 17 May 1780, 30 August 1780.

Pennsylvania Packet or the General Advertiser (Philadelphia, Pennsylvania). 13 May 1778.

Rock Hill Weekly Sun (Rock Hill, South Carolina). 1 January 1897.

South Carolina Gazette (Charleston, South Carolina), 24 November 1774.

Southern Home (Charlotte, North Carolina). 29 November 1875.

Southern Presbyterian (Columbia, South Carolina). 15 August 1867, 22 August 1867, 5 September 1867, 12 September 1867, 19 September 1867, 22 May 1873.

The State (Columbia, South Carolina). 14 December 1955.

The Sunday News (Charleston, South Carolina). 19 March 1899.

Virginia Gazette (Purdie and Dixon, Richmond, Virginia). 23 August 1780.

Yorkville Enquirer (York, South Carolina). 2 October 1903.

F. Articles, journals and memoirs

- Allaire, Anthony. "Diary of Lieut. Anthony Allaire of Ferguson's Corps." In *King's Mountain and Its Heroes*, by Lyman C. Draper. Baltimore: Genealogical Publishing Company, 1967 (originally published Cincinnati: P. G. Thompson, 1881). 484-515.
- Bondurant, Mary B., and Sarah F. White. "Tories of Ninety-Six District, S.C. 1783." *Carolina Genealogist*, vol. 2, 1-4.
- Craig, John. "The War in York and Chester." *Chester Standard* (Chester, SC), 16 March 1854: 1.
- Gaston, Joseph. "A Reminiscence of the Revolution." *Southern Presbyterian*, 22 May 1873.
- Little, William. "Our Iron Industry of Old." *Rock Hill Weekly Sun*, 1 January 1897.
- Logan, John H., and John Starr Moore. "Hauk's Defeat—Traditions of Starr Moore." Circa 1857. Thomas Sumter Papers, Lyman C. Draper Manuscript Collection, 16VV272-279.
- McJunkin, Joseph. "Reminiscences of the Revolutionary War related by Major Joseph McJunkin, of the militia of South Carolina, written July 18th 1837." Thomas Sumter Papers, Lyman C. Draper Manuscript Collection, 23VV168-174.
- McJunkin, Joseph. "A Ms. Statement of Maj. McJunkin as noted in his own handwriting, without date or address, but which Mr. Saye supposes was written for Prof. Nott, as he furnished him a statement—also got his Diary or Journal kept in the war." Undated. Thomas Sumter Papers, Lyman C. Draper Manuscript Collection, 23VV204-212.
- O'Neall, John Belton. "Revolutionary Incidents: Memoir of Joseph McJunkin, of Union." *The Magnolia, or Southern Apalachian*, vol. 2, no. 1 (January 1843): 30-40.
- Salley, A.S. Jr. "Papers of the First Council of Safety of the Revolutionary Party in South Carolina, June–November 1775." *South Carolina Historical and Genealogical Magazine*, vol. III, no. 1 (January 1902): 3-15.
  - ———. "Papers of the First Council of Safety of the Revolutionary Party in South Carolina, June–November 1775." *South Carolina Historical and Genealogical Magazine*, vol. III, no. 3 (July 1902): 123-138.
  - ———. "Rebel Rolls of 1775." Charleston *Sunday News*, 19 March 1899.
- Williams, Samuel C., ed. "General Richard Winn's Notes—1780, Part 1." *South Carolina Historical and Genealogical Magazine*, vol. XLIII (October 1942): 201-212.
  - ———. "General Richard Winn's Notes—1780, Part 2." *South Carolina Historical and Genealogical Magazine*, vol. XLIV (November 1942): 1-10.
- Young, Thomas. "Memoir of Major Thomas Young, A Revolutionary Patriot of South Carolina, Part 1." *Orion* (October 1843): 84-88.

———. "Memoir of Major Thomas Young, A Revolutionary Patriot of South Carolina, Part 2." *Orion*, November 1843: 100–105.

G. Books

- [Bratton, John S., and W. C. Beatty]. *Proceedings of a Celebration of Huck's Defeat at Brattonsville, York District, S.C., July 12ᵗʰ, 1839.* Yorkville, SC: Tidings from the Craft, 1895.
- [Chesney, Alexander]. *Journal of Capt. Alexander Chesney, Adjutant to Maj. Patrick Ferguson.* Edited by Bobby G. Moss. Blacksburg, SC: Scotia-Hibernia Press, 2002.
- Clark, Murtie June. *Loyalists in the Southern Campaign of the American Revolution.* 3 vols. Baltimore, MD: Genealogical Publishing, 1981.
- [Collins, James P.] *Autobiography of a Revolutionary Soldier.* Edited by John M. Roberts. New York: Arno Press, 1979 (originally published Clinton, LA: The Feliciana Democrat, 1859).
- Dann, John C., ed. *The Revolution Remembered: Eyewitness Accounts of the War for Independence.* Chicago: University of Chicago Press, 1980.
- [Davie, William Richardson]. *The Revolutionary War Sketches of William R. Davie.* Edited by Blackwell P. Robinson. Raleigh: North Carolina Department of Cultural Resources, Division of Archives and History, 1976.
- Drayton, John, ed. *Memoirs of the American Revolution from its Commencement to the Year 1776, inclusive as Relating to the State of South-Carolina and Occasionally Refering [sic] to the States of North-Carolina and Georgia.* 2 vols. Charleston, SC: A.E. Miller, 1821.
- Gibbes, R.W., ed. *Documentary History of the American Revolution.* 3 vols. Spartanburg: Reprint Company, 1972 (originally published New York: D. Appleton & Company, 1853–1857).
- Gilroy, Marion, comp. *Loyalists and Land Settlement in Nova Scotia.* Public Archives of Nova Scotia Publication No. 4. Baltimore: Genealogical Publishing, 1990, 1995.
- Hill, Daniel H. *Col. William Hill and the Campaign of 1780.* Edited by Daniel H. Hill Jr. Privately printed, c. 1919.
- [Hill, William]. *Col. William Hill's Memoirs of the Revolution.* Edited by A.S. Salley Jr. Columbia: The State Company, 1921.
- Holcomb, Brent H. *Anson County, North Carolina Deed Abstracts 1749-1766; Abstracts of Wills & Estates 1749–1795.* Baltimore: Genealogical Publishing, 1980.
- ———. *Lancaster County, South Carolina Deed Abstracts 1787–1811.* Easley, SC: Southern Historical Press, 1981.
- ———. *North Carolina Land Grants in South Carolina.* Baltimore: Genealogical Publishing, 1980.
- ———. *South Carolina Deed Abstracts 1773–1778, Books F–4 through X–4.* Columbia: South Carolina Magazine of Ancestral Research, 1993.
- ———. *Tryon County, North Carolina Minutes of the Court of Pleas and Quarter Sessions 1769–1779.* Columbia: South Carolina Magazine of Ancestral Research, 1994.

- Holcomb, Brent H., and Elmer O. Parker. *Camden District, S.C. Wills and Administrations 1781-1787*. Easley, SC: Southern Historical Press, 1978.
- ———. *Chester County, South Carolina Minutes of the County Court 1785–1799*. Greenville, SC: Southern Historical Press, 1997 (originally published Easley, SC: Southern Historical Press, 1979).
- ———. *Mecklenburg County, North Carolina Deed Abstracts 1763–1779*. Easley, SC: Southern Historical Press, 1979.
- [Johnson, Uzal]. *Uzal Johnson, Loyalist Surgeon*. Edited by Bobby G. Moss. Blacksburg, SC: Scotia-Hibernia Press, 2000.
- Laurens, Henry. *The Papers of Henry Laurens*. 16 vols. Edited by Philip M. Hamer, George C. Rogers Jr., David R. Chesnutt and C. James Taylor. Columbia: University of South Carolina Press, 1985.
- Lossing, Benson J. *Hours with the Living Men and Women of the Revolution: A Pilgrimage*. New York: Funk and Wagnalls, 1889.
- ———. *The Pictorial Field Book of the American Revolution*. 2 vols. Cottonport, LA: Polyanthos, 1972 (originally published New York: Harper and Brothers, 1850, 1852).
- Lucas, Silas Emmett Jr. *Marriage and Death Notices from Pendleton (SC) Messenger 1807–1851*. Easley, SC: Southern Historical Press, 1977.
- Moultrie, William. *Memoirs of the American Revolution*. 2 vols. New York: Arno Press, 1968 (originally published New York: D. Longworth, 1802).
- North Carolina Daughters of the American Revolution. *Roster of Soldiers from North Carolina in the American Revolution*. Baltimore: Genealogical Publishing Company, 2003 (originally published Durham: Clearfield Company, 1932).
- North, S.N.D. et al. *Heads of Families at the First Census of the United States Taken in the Year 1790: Pennsylvania*. Baltimore: Genealogical Publishing, 1970 (originally published Washington, DC: U.S. Government Printing Office, 1908).
- ———. *Heads of Families at the First Census of the United States Taken in the Year 1790: South Carolina*. Spartanburg, SC: Reprint Company, 1960 (originally published Washington, DC: U.S. Government Printing Office, 1908).
- Reese, George H., comp. *The Cornwallis Papers: Abstracts of Americana*. Charlottesville, VA: University Press of Virginia, for the Virginia Independence Bicentennial Commission, 1970.
- Rubincam, Milton. *The Old United Empire Loyalists List*. Baltimore: Genealogical Publishing, 1969 (originally published as *The Centennial of the Settlement of Upper Canada by the United Empire Loyalists 1784–1884*. Toronto: Rose Publishing, 1885).
- [Simpson, John]. *List of visitations beginning December 12, 1774 of Rev. John Simpson while Pastor of Fishing Creek Presbyterian Church, Chester County, S.C.* Edited by Max Perry. Richburg, SC: Chester County Genealogical Society, n.d.
- Stedman, Charles. *The History of the Origin, Progress, and Termination of the American War*. 2 vols. New York: Arno Press, 1969 (originally published London: privately printed, 1794).

- Tarleton, Banastre. *A History of the Campaigns of 1780 and 1781 in the Southern Provinces of North America*. North Stratford, NH: Ayer Company, 1999 (originally published London: T. Cadell, 1787).
- Wells, Laurence K. *York County, South Carolina Minutes of the County Court 1786–1797*. Columbia: South Carolina Magazine of Ancestral Research, 1981.
- Woodmason, Charles. *The Carolina Backcountry on the Eve of the Revolution*. Edited by Richard J. Hooker. Chapel Hill: University of North Carolina Press, 1953.

SECONDARY SOURCES

A. Unpublished theses and papers

- Jarrell, Hampton. "Huck's Defeat, A Turning of the Tide." Unpublished manuscript, 1976. Copy at Historical Center of York County, York, SC.
- Metzloff, Paul W. "A Window of Motivation in the War for American Independence: The Battle of Williamson's Plantation, 12 July 1780." Master of arts thesis, University of North Carolina at Chapel Hill, 1999.
- Rider, Thomas A. "Massacre or Myth: No Quarter at the Waxhaws, 29 May 1780." Master of arts thesis, University of North Carolina at Chapel Hill, 2002.
- Scoggins, Michael C. "Huck's Defeat: The Battle of Williamson's Plantation." Undergraduate research paper, Winthrop University, 2000.
- ———. "The Revolution in the South Carolina Backcountry, May, June and July 1780." Graduate research paper, Winthrop University, 2003.

B. Maps and charts

- Corbitt, D.L., and L. Polk Denmark. *Chart Showing Origin of North Carolina Counties*. Raleigh, NC: North Carolina Department of Archives and History, 1940.
- Mayhugh, Thomas. "Land Grants and Early Surveys on the Headwaters of the South Fork of Fishing Creek, York County, S.C." Unpublished map, 1993. Copy at Historical Center of York County, York, South Carolina.
- Mills, Robert. *Mills' Atlas of South Carolina*. Lexington, SC: Sandlapper Store, 1979 (originally published 1825).

C. Articles

- "An Account of the Unveiling of a Monument, October 1st, 1903, Erected by the King's Mountain Chapter, Daughters of the American Revolution on the Battlefield of Huck's Defeat at Brattonsville, South Carolina." *Yorkville Enquirer* (York, SC), 2 October 1903.
- Barnes, Mary Lee. "John Owen of Chester County, South Carolina." *Chester District Genealogical Bulletin*, vol. 18, no. 3 (September 1994): 105–110.

- Baskin, Marge. "Friends, Comrades and Enemies: Christian Huck (c. 1748–1780)." Oatmeal for the Foxhounds: Banastre Tarleton and the British Legion, http://www.banastretarleton.org (accessed 20 December 2004).
- Braisted, Todd. "A History of Emmerick's Chasseurs." The On-Line Institute for Advanced Loyalist Studies, http://www.royalprovincial.com/military/rhist/emmerick/emmhist.htm (accessed 24 May 2002).
- ———. "Emmerick's Chasseurs: Disbanding of Corps." The On-Line Institute for Advanced Loyalist Studies, http://www.royalprovincial.com/military/emmerick/emmords3.htm (accessed 17 October 2002).
- ———. "General Court Martial of John Tuck." The On-Line Institute for Advanced Loyalist Studies, http://www.royalprovincial.com/military/courts/cmtuck.htm (accessed 20 December 2004).
- Erd, Darby, and Fitzhugh McMasters. "The Third South Carolina Regiment (Rangers), 1775–1780." *Military Uniforms in America*, plate no. 494. Company of Military Historians, Rutland, Maryland.
- Ferguson, Clyde R. "Functions of the Partisan-Militia in the South During the American Revolution: An Interpretation," in *The Revolutionary War in the South: Power, Conflict, and Leadership.* Edited by W. Robert Wiggin. Durham, NC: Duke University Press, 1979, 239–258.
- Ferguson, Howard. "The Chester County, South Carolina, Fergusons and the British Colonel Ferguson." *Chester County Genealogical Society Bulletin*, vol. 6, no. 3 (September 1983): 77–78.
- Floyd, Damon M. "Descendants of Col. Matthew Floyd and Sarah." Damon Floyd's Web Page, http://damonfloyd.com/genealogy/floyd-p/p3.htm#i2031 (accessed 1 June 2004).
- Gara, Donald J. "Biographical Sketches on Cavalry Officers of the British Legion, 1778–1782." The On-Line Institute for Advanced Loyalist Studies, http://www.royalprovincial.com/military/rhist/britlegn/blcav1.htm (accessed 24 May 2002).
- Gregorie, Anne King. "William Hill." In *Dictionary of American Biography*, vol. IX, edited by Dumas Malone. New York: Charles Scribner's Sons, 1932.
- ———. "William Thomson." In *Dictionary of American Biography*, vol. IX, edited by Dumas Malone. New York: Charles Scribner's Sons, 1932.
- ———. "Richard Winn." In *Dictionary of American Biography*, vol. XX, edited by Dumas Malone. New York: Charles Scribner's Sons, 1936.
- Jackson, Ernest. "Battle of Huck's Defeat Important Engagement." *Charlotte Observer* (Charlotte, NC), 28 September 1930.
- Lipscomb, Terry W. "South Carolina Revolutionary Battles, Part One." *Names in South Carolina*, vol. XX (Winter 1973): 18–23.
- ———. "South Carolina Revolutionary Battles, Part Two." *Names in South Carolina.* vol. XI (Winter 1974): 23–27.
- ———. "South Carolina Revolutionary Battles, Part Three." *Names in South Carolina*, vol. XXII (Winter 1975): 33–39.

- Mayhugh, Thomas M. "Early Surveys, Lewis Turnout, Chester Co., S.C." *Chester District Genealogical Society Bulletin*, vol. XIV, no. 3 (September 1991): 92.
- ———. "James Williamson's Plantation." *Chester District Genealogical Society Bulletin*, vol. XVI, no. 4 (December 1992): 111–118.
- Parker, Elmer O. "Burning by the British of Reverend Simpson's Home and Hill's Iron Works." *Chester County Genealogical Society Bulletin*, vol. 3, no. 2 (June 1980): 27–28.
- ———. "Early Survey's West of Lando, S.C." *Chester County Genealogical Society Bulletin*, vol. 5, no. 4 (Deccember 1982): 100.
- ———. "White's Mill." *Chester County Genealogical Society Bulletin*, vol. 4, no. 2 (June 1981): 33–35.
- Pettus, Louise. "Col. Samuel Watson of the Revolution." *York County Genealogical and Historical Society Quarterly*, vol. 8, no. 2 (September 1996): 27-28.
- Piecuch, James. "Massacre or Myth: Banastre Tarleton at the Waxhaws, May 29, 1780." *Southern Campaigns of the American Revolution*, vol. 1, no. 2 (October 2004): 3–9.
- Price-Coleman, Glinda. "Granddaughter of the Revolution." *Chester News and Reporter* (Chester, SC), 18 March 1992.
- Raymond, Robert. "Fanciful Tale Hangs Around Adamson's Life." *The State* (Columbia, SC), 14 December 1955.
- Scoggins, Michael C. "Huck's Defeat: The Battle of Williamson's Plantation." *York County Genealogical and Historical Society Quarterly*, part 1: vol. 14, no. 3 (September 2001); part 2: vol. 14, no. 4 (December 2001); part 3: vol. 15, no. 1 (March 2002); part 4: vol. 15, no. 2 (June 2002); part 5: vol. 15, no. 3 (September 2002); part 6: vol. 15, no. 4 (December 2002); part 7: vol. 16, no. 1 (March 2003).
- Snoddy, Oliver. "The Volunteers of Ireland." *The Irish Sword*, vol. 7, no. 27 (1965): 147–159.
- Stinson, Daniel Green. "A Sketch of John Bishop." *Chester Reporter* (Chester, SC), 18 June 1874.
- ———. "Communication." *Chester Reporter* (Chester, SC), 29 May 1873.
- ———. "Mrs. Susannah Smart." *Chester Standard* (Chester, SC), 17 September 1851.
- ———. "The Old Waxhaw Church." *Southern Presbyterian* (Columbia, SC), part 1, 15 August 1867; part 2, 22 August 1867; part 3, 5 September 1867; part 4, 12 September 1867; part 5, 19 September 1867.

D. Books

- Ambrose, Stephen E. *Band of Brothers: E Company, 506th Regiment, 101st Airborne from Normandy to Hitler's Eagle's Nest.* New York: Simon & Schuster, 1992, 2001.
- Babits, Lawrence E. *A Devil of a Whipping: The Battle of Cowpens.* Chapel Hill, NC: University of North Carolina Press, 1998.
- Bailey, J.D. *Commanders at Kings Mountain.* Gaffney, SC: E.H. DeCamp, 1926.
- ———. *Reverends Philip Mulkey and James Fowler.* Cowpens, SC: Privately printed, 1924.

- Bailey, N. Louise, and Elizabeth Ivey Cooper, eds. *Biographical Directory of the South Carolina House of Representatives, Volume III: 1775–1790*. Columbia, SC: University of South Carolina Press, 1981.
- Bass, Robert D. *Gamecock: The Life and Campaigns of General Thomas Sumter*. Orangeburg: Sandlapper Publishing, 2000 (originally published New York: Holt, Rinehart & Winston, 1961).
- Bellesiles, Michael A. *Arming America: The Origins of a National Gun Culture*. New York: Alfred A. Knopf, 2000.
- Boatner, Mark Mayo III. *Encyclopedia of the American Revolution*. Mechanicsburg, PA: Stackpole Books, 1994 (originally published New York: David McKay Company, 1966, 1974).
- Borick, Carl P. *A Gallant Defense: The Siege of Charleston, 1780*. Columbia: University of South Carolina Press, 2003.
- Brown, Douglas Summers. *The Catawba Indians: The People of the River*. Columbia: University of South Carolina Press, 1966.
- Buchanan, John. *The Road to Guilford Courthouse: The American Revolution in the Carolinas*. New York: John Wiley & Sons, 1997.
- Busick, Jessie R., James H. Saye Jr. and Martha H. Sudol. *"Through the Years" 1752–2002, Fishing Creek Presbyterian Church Bicenquinquagenary Celebration September 22, 2002*. Chester, SC: privately printed, 2002.
- Campbell, Donald K. *A Williamson Saga: Samuel and John*. Little Rock, AK: privately printed, 2002.
- Chartrand, René, and David Rickman. *Colonial American Troops, 1610–1774*. Vol. 3. Osprey Men-at-Arms Series No. 383. Oxford, England: Osprey Publishing, 2003.
- Carroll, Robert, and Stephen Prickett, eds. *The Bible: Authorized King James Version*. Oxford: Oxford University Press, 1997.
- Coldham, Peter Wilson. *American Migrations 1765–1799*. Baltimore: Genealogical Publishing, 2000.
- Collins, Anne Pickens. *A Goodly Heritage: A History of Chester County, South Carolina*. Columbia: Collins Publications, 1986.
- Craighead, W.H. *The Craighead Family: A Genealogical Memoir of Rev. Robert and Agnes Hart Craighead's Descendants*. Paradise, TX: Family Press, 1996.
- Crow, Jeffrey J., and Larry E. Tise. *The Southern Experience in the American Revolution*. Chapel Hill: University of North Carolina Press, 1978.
- DeMond, Robert O. *The Loyalists in North Carolina during the Revolution*. Baltimore: Genealogical Publishing, 1979 (originally published Durham, NC: Duke University Press, 1940).
- Draper, Lyman C. *King's Mountain and Its Heroes*. Baltimore: Genealogical Publishing, 1967 (originally published Cincinnati: P.G. Thomson, 1881).
- Edgar, Walter B. *Partisans and Redcoats: The Southern Conflict that Turned the Tide of the American Revolution*. New York: William Morrow, 2001.

- Edgar, Walter B., Inez Watson et al., eds. *Biographical Directory of the South Carolina House of Representatives, Volume I: Session Lists 1692–1973.* Columbia: University of South Carolina Press, 1974.
- Edgar, Walter B., and N. Louise Bailey, eds. *Biographical Directory of the South Carolina House of Representatives, Volume II: The Commons House of Assembly, 1682–1775.* Columbia: University of South Carolina Press, 1977.
- Ellet, Elizabeth F. *Domestic History of the American Revolution.* New York: Charles Scribner, 1859.
- ———. *The Women of the American Revolution.* 3 vols. New York: Charles Scribner, 1853–1854.
- Freeman, Douglas Southall. *Lee's Lieutenants: A Study in Command.* 3 vols. New York: Charles Scribner's Sons, 1942.
- Gordon, John. *South Carolina and the American Revolution: A Battlefield History.* Columbia: University of South Carolina Press, 2003.
- Gordon, William. *The History of the Rise, Progress, and Establishment of the Independence of the United States of America: Including an Account of the Late War; and of the Thirteen Colonies, from their Origin to that Period.* 4 vols. New York: Books for Libraries Press, 1969 (originally published London: privately printed, 1788).
- Hartley, Cecil B. *Life of Major General Henry Lee, Commander of Lee's Legion in the Revolutionary War, and Subsequently Governor of Virginia; to which is added the Life of General Thomas Sumter of South Carolina.* New York: Derby & Jackson, 1859.
- Heitman, Francis B. *Historical Register of Officers of the Continental Army During the War of the Revolution April, 1775, to December, 1783.* Baltimore: Genealogical Publishing, 1982 (originally published Washington, DC: U.S. Government Printing Office, 1903).
- Higgin, W. Robert, ed. *The Revolutionary War in the South: Power, Conflict, and Leadership.* Durham, NC: Duke University Press, 1979.
- Hope, Wes. *The Spartanburg Area in the American Revolution.* Spartanburg: privately printed, 2002.
- Howe, George. *History of the Presbyterian Church in South Carolina*, vol. I. Columbia, SC: Duffie and Chapman, 1870.
- James, William D. *A Sketch of the Life of Brig. Gen. Francis Marion, and a History of his Brigade: from its rise in June, 1780, until disbanded in December, 1782, with descriptions of characters and scenes, not heretofore published.* Charleston: Gould and Riley, printers, 1821.
- Johnson, Joseph. *Traditions and Reminiscences, Chiefly of the American Revolution in the South.* Charleston: Walker and James, 1851.
- Katcher, Philip, and Michael Youens. *The American Provincial Corps 1775–1784.* Reading, Berkshire, England: Osprey Publishing Limited, 1973.
- Kirkland, Thomas J., and Robert M. Kennedy. *Historic Camden Part One, Colonial and Revolutionary.* Columbia: The State Company, 1905.
- Lambert, Robert Stansbury. *South Carolina Loyalists in the American Revolution.* Columbia: University of South Carolina Press, 1987.

- Lathan, Robert. *Historical Sketches of the Revolutionary War in the Upcountry of South Carolina.* Transcribed by Jerald L. West. Hickory Grove, SC: Broad River Basin Historical Society, 1998.
- Lefler, Hugh T., and Albert Ray Newsome. *The History of a Southern State: North Carolina.* Chapel Hill: University of North Carolina Press, 1973.
- Lefler, Hugh T., and William S. Powell. *Colonial North Carolina: A History.* New York: Charles Scribner's Sons, 1973.
- Logan, John H. *A History of the Upper Country of South Carolina, from the Earliest Periods to the Close of the War of Independence*, vol. I. Charleston, SC: Courtenay, 1859.
- Lossing, Benson J. *The Pictorial Field Book of the American Revolution.* 2 vols. Cottonport, LA: Polyanthos, 1972 (originally published New York: Harper & Brothers, 1850–1852).
- McCrady, Edward. *The History of South Carolina in the Revolution 1775–1780.* New York: Russell and Russell, 1910 (originally published New York: Macmillan, 1901).
- McCrady, Edward. *The History of South Carolina in the Revolution 1780–1783.* New York: Russell and Russell, 1910 (originally published New York: Macmillan, 1902).
- Mendenhall, Samuel Brooks. *Tales of York County.* Rock Hill, SC: Reynolds and Reynolds Printing, 1989.
- Moore, Maurice A. *The Life of Gen. Edward Lacey.* Spartanburg, SC: Douglas, Evins & Co., 1859.
- ———. *Life of General Edward Lacey.* Edited by Brent H. Holcomb and Elmer O. Parker. Greenville, SC: A. Press, 1981.
- ———. *Reminiscences of York.* Edited by Elmer O. Parker. Greenville: A. Press, 1981.
- Moss, Bobby Gilmer. *Roster of the Loyalists in the Battle of Kings Mountain.* Blacksburg, SC: Scotia-Hibernia Press, 1998.
- ———. *South Carolina Patriots in the American Revolution.* Baltimore: Genealogical Publishing, 1983.
- Nadelhaft, Jerome J. *The Disorders of War: The Revolution in South Carolina.* Orono, ME: University of Maine at Orono Press, 1981.
- O'Neall, John Belton. *Annals of Newberry in Two Parts: Part First.* Newberry, SC: Aull and Houseal, 1892.
- Ousterhout, Anne M. *A State Divided: Opposition in Pennsylvania to the American Revolution.* Contributions in American History, no. 123. New York: Greenwood Press, 1987.
- Pancake, John S. *This Destructive War: The British Campaign in the Carolinas 1780–1782.* University, AL: University of Alabama Press, 1985.
- Purcell, L. Edward. *Who was Who in the American Revolution.* New York: Facts on File, 1993.
- Perry, Max. *American Descendants of John "Jean" Gaston.* Greenville: A. Press, 1994.
- Ramsay, David. *The History of the Revolution of South-Carolina: from a British Province to an Independent State*, 2 vols. Trenton, NJ: Isaac Collins, printer, 1785.

- Reynolds, Emily Bellinger, and Joan Reynolds Faunt. *Biographical Directory of the Senate of the State of South Carolina 1776–1964*. Columbia: South Carolina Archives Department, 1964.
- Robinson, Blackwell P. *William R. Davie*. Chapel Hill: University of North Carolina Press, 1957.
- Sabine, Lorenzo. *Biographical Sketches of Loyalists of the American Revolution with an Historical Essay*, 2 vols. Baltimore: Genealogical Publishing, 1979 (originally published Boston: Little, Brown, & Co., 1864).
- Schenck, David. *North Carolina 1780–'81, Being a History of the Invasion of the Carolinas by the British Army Under Lord Cornwallis in 1780–'81*. Bowie, MD: Heritage Books, 2000 (originally published Raleigh: Edwards & Broughton, 1889).
- Scoggins, Michael C. *A Brief History of Historic Brattonsville*. Rock Hill, SC: York County Culture and Heritage Commission, 2004.
- Scotti, Anthony J. *Brutal Virtue: The Myth and Reality of Banastre Tarleton*. Bowie, MD: Heritage Books, 2002.
- Skaggs, Marvin Lucien. *North Carolina Boundary Disputes Involving her Southern Line*. Chapel Hill: University of North Carolina Press, 1941.
- Strong, Esther. *Strong and Allied Families*. Edited by Theresa M. Hicks. Privately printed, December 1980.
- Thomas, Samuel N. *The Dye Is Cast: The Scots-Irish and the Revolution in the Carolina Backcountry*. Columbia: Palmetto Conservation Foundation, 1997.
- Wallace, David Duncan. *The History of South Carolina*, 2 vols. New York: The American Historical Society, 1934.
- Weigley, Russell F. *The Partisan War: The South Carolina Campaign of 1780–1782*. Columbia: USC Press, 1970.
- Weir, Robert M. *Colonial South Carolina: A History*. Millwood, NY: KTO Press, 1983.
- White, William Boyce Jr. *Genealogy of Two Early Patton Families of York, Chester and Lancaster Counties, South Carolina*. Roanoke, VA: privately printed, 1996.

E. Church histories and cemetery directories

- Agee, Jean Clawson et al. *Old Catholic Presbyterian Church Cemetery Inscriptions, Chester County, South Carolina*. Richburg, SC: Chester County Genealogical Society, 1977.
- Bullock Creek Cemetery Association. *Roster of Cemetery and Historical Sketch of Bullock Creek Church*. York, SC: privately printed, 1976.
- Crowder, Louise K. *Tombstone Records of Chester County, South Carolina and Vicinity*. Chester, SC: privately printed, 1970.
- Dickson, E. Meek et al. *Revised Directory of Beersheba Presbyterian Church Cemetery, York County, S.C.* York: Beersheba Memorial Association, 1981.
- ———. *Directory of Beersheba Presbyterian Church Cemetery*. York: Beersheba Memorial Association, 1988.

- Glover, Roy, ed. *Cemetery Directory of Bethesda Presbyterian Church, 1769–1994.* McConnells, SC: privately printed, 1994.
- Hart, Joseph E. *Beersheba Presbyterian Churchyard, York County, S.C.* York: privately printed, n.d.
- ———. *Bethel Churchyard.* York: privately printed, n.d.
- ———. *Fishing Creek Presbyterian Churchyard, Chester County, S.C.* York: privately printed, n.d.
- Strange, Mary Wylie. *The Revolutionary Soldiers of Catholic Presbyterian Church, Chester County, South Carolina.* Richburg: Chester County Historical Committee, 1946.
- Walker, Robert H. *Directory of Bethesda Presbyterian Church Cemetery, December 1776–April 1980.* Rock Hill, SC: privately printed, 1980.
- Webb, R.A. *History of the Presbyterian Church of Bethel.* York: privately printed, 1938.
- West, Jerry L. *A Historical Sketch of People, Places and Homes of Bullocks Creek, South Carolina.* Richburg: Chester District Genealogical Society, 1986.
- ———. *Bullock's Creek Presbyterian Church Cemetery Roster, Bullock's Creek, York County, South Carolina.* Hickory Grove, SC: Broad River Basin Historical Society, 1993.

F. Electronic sources

- Broderbund. *Genealogical Records: Loyalists in the American Revolution.* Family Tree Maker's Family Archives CD no. 144.
- Gale Research Inc. *Passenger and Immigration Lists Index 1538–1940.* Family Tree Maker's Family Archives CD no. 354.

G. Web sites

- Baskin, Marge. Oatmeal for the Foxhounds: Banastre Tarleton and the British Legion. Historical information on Banastre Tarleton, Lord Rawdon, Christian Huck and other important figures in the Southern Campaign of the Revolutionary War. http://www.banastretarleton.org
- Braisted, Todd, and Nan Cole. The On-Line Institute for Advanced Loyalist Studies. Historical background, muster rolls and a tremendous amount of other information on the British Legion, New York Volunteers, Volunteers of Ireland, and other Provincial and Loyalist regiments in the Revolutionary War. http://www.royalprovincial.com
- Floyd, Damon M. Damon Floyd's Web Page: My Genealogy Page. Family history Web site providing genealogical information on Matthew Floyd and his descendants. http://damonfloyd.com
- Church of Jesus Christ of Latter-Day Saints. International Genealogical Index. A database of birth, baptismal and marriage records from all over the world, including members of the Huck family. http://www.familysearch.org

- Culture & Heritage Museums. Historic Brattonsville® Web site for Historic Brattonsville®, York County, South Carolina, an eighteenth and nineteenth century plantation that includes Colonel William Bratton's home place and the site of the Battle of Huck's Defeat. http://www.chmuseums.org/Brattonsville.htm
- U.S. Naval Observatory, Astronomical Applications Department. Data Services: Sun and moon rise and set times, moon phases, eclipses, seasons, positions of solar system objects and other data. Used in determining astronomical data for 11 and 12 July 1780, York County, South Carolina. http://mach.usno.navy.mil

Index

Symbols

17th Light Dragoons 44, 95, 226
1st Battalion of DeLancey's Brigade 144
1st South Carolina Regiment of Riflemen 32
23rd Regiment of Foot 97, 98, 226
2nd South Carolina Regiment of Foot 26, 38
2nd South Carolina Regiment of Riflemen 32, 33
3rd Battalion of DeLancey's Brigade 221
3rd Battalion of the New Jersey Volunteers 144
3rd South Carolina Regiment of Rangers 26, 31, 33, 38, 47, 61, 78, 157
4th South Carolina Regiment of Artillery 32, 206, 283
60th Regiment of Foot 51
6th South Carolina Regiment of Riflemen 34, 35, 38, 44, 80, 82, 83, 93, 157
71st Highland Regiment of Foot 43, 131, 226

A

Adair, James 104
Adair, John 84, 104, 110, 111, 118, 119, 120, 121, 161, 175, 285
Adair, John Jr. 121, 285
Adair, Mary 104, 121
Adair, William Jr. 104, 121
Adair, William Sr. 29, 104, 111, 121

Adamson, John 100, 102, 106, 109, 116, 118, 121, 122, 126, 162, 165, 169, 171
Alexander, Joseph 28, 31, 73
Alexander, William 180
Alexander's Old Field 52, 54, 55, 57, 74
Alexander's Old Field, Battle of 112, 146, 158, 165, 174, 183
Allaire, Anthony 126, 127
Allen, Andrew 218, 222
Allen, William 218
Allen, William Jr. 218
Allison Creek 59
American Volunteers 39, 43, 130, 205, 207
Anderson, Robert 176
Anderson County 34, 148
Anson County, NC 76
Arbuthnot, Marriot 38, 49, 53
Ardesoif, John Plumer 93
Armstrong, Martin 180
Armstrong Ford Road 59, 107, 108
Ashe, John 35, 36
Augusta, GA 34, 35, 36, 37
aurora borealis 110, 118

B

backcountry militia 23, 26, 32, 33, 34, 38, 83, 146, 159
Bacon's Bridge, Battle of 178
Balch, Hezekiah 29

Ball, Isaac 105, 113

banditti 21, 23

Barnett, Jacob "Jack" 110, 176

Beaver Creek 136

Beckhamville 52, 158, 183

Beersheba Presbyterian Church 28, 110

Bella 172, 173

Bethel Presbyterian Church 28, 29, 37, 59, 75

Bethesda Presbyterian Church 28, 29, 30, 59, 61, 67, 68, 148

Bigger's Ferry 84

Biggin's Bridge 39

Bishop, Henry 102, 147, 162

Bishop, James 102

Bishop, John 162, 173

Bishop, Nicholas 79, 102, 175

Bishop, Nicholas Jr. 102

Bishop, William 102

Blackstock's Plantation, Battle of 147, 155, 162, 166, 170, 177

Blackstock Road 132

Black Creek (Black River) 133

Black Hole, Battle of 34

Black Riders 100

Black Swamp 37, 121, 165

bounty Irish 63, 89, 91, 97

Boyd, James 73

Boyd, James (Loyalist) 35

Boykin, Edward M. 100

Braddock, Edward 19, 29

Brandon, Thomas 52, 67, 83, 130, 144

Brandywine, PA, Battle of 178

Bratton, Christina Winn 151

Bratton, Elizabeth 107

Bratton, Hugh 59, 110, 126

Bratton, James Rufus 116, 120, 209, 213

Bratton, Jane 107

Bratton, John 59

Bratton, John S. (General) 150

Bratton, John Simpson Jr. 209, 213

Bratton, John Simpson Sr. 206, 207, 213

Bratton, Martha 107

Bratton, Martha Robertson 59, 105, 107, 118, 121

Bratton, Napoleon Bonaparte 211, 213

Bratton, Robert 59, 105, 108

Bratton, Thomas 59

Bratton, William 28, 37, 57, 58, 59, 60, 61, 62, 63, 67, 68, 70, 75, 77, 83, 87, 101, 104, 105, 106, 107, 109, 110, 111, 112, 113, 114, 117, 118, 119, 120, 122, 140, 150, 152, 165, 168, 170, 171, 176, 177, 178, 181, 183, 207, 208, 211, 213, 227

Bratton, William Jr. 105, 106, 110, 118, 119, 150, 151, 227

Bratton's Plantation, Battle of 13, 162, 164, 165, 166, 169, 170, 174, 175, 176, 177, 178

Bratton's Regiment 140, 163

Brattonsville 150, 207, 209, 213, 228

Brevard, Hugh 77

Briar Creek, GA, Battle of 36, 76, 78, 159, 177, 179

British Legion 13, 39, 44, 51, 52, 63, 89, 90, 95, 101, 110, 121, 122, 124, 126, 127, 143, 146, 153, 154, 205, 221, 222, 225, 226, 227, 228

Broad River 22, 23, 25, 27, 35, 52, 57, 61, 67, 68, 73, 75, 76, 78, 81, 90, 91, 130, 132, 141, 151, 164, 171

Brown, Archibald 162

Brown, Joseph 30, 40, 79, 169

Brown, Thomas 180

Brown's Crossroads 79, 80, 83, 89, 90, 95, 96, 97, 102, 175

Browne, Thomas 27

Bryan, Samuel 131, 165

Buford, Abraham 41, 44, 45, 46, 47, 95

Buford's Defeat 52, 57, 96, 146, 183, 222

Buford's Massacre 46

Bull, Stephen 34

Bull, William 26

Bullock's Creek 27, 58, 60, 76, 77, 90, 91, 116, 227

Bullock's Creek Presbyterian Church 28, 29, 57, 68, 71, 73

Burge, Burrell 70

Burge, Jeremiah 70

Burke County, NC 68, 128

Byers, William 28, 182

C

Calhoun, _____ 82

Calhoun, Patrick 82

Camden 44, 45, 64, 73, 90, 100, 122, 124, 136, 139, 169, 222

Camden, Battle of 143, 146, 179

Camden District 22, 27, 28, 30, 38, 48, 55, 59, 61, 70, 100, 172, 174

Camden Militia Regiment (Loyalist) 100

Cameron, _____ 117

Cameron, Allan 102, 122, 124

Campbell, _____ 117

Campbell, Archibald 35, 36

Campbell, Charles 44, 228

Camp Catawba 95, 134

Carden, John 89

Carroll, John 116, 120, 147, 227

Carroll, Lemuel 120, 147

Carroll, Thomas 147, 227

Caswell, Richard 87, 96, 130, 144

Catawba Indians 19, 33, 64, 72, 77, 93, 100, 164

Catawba Old Town 93

Catawba River 14, 21, 22, 27, 44, 48, 54, 65, 80, 84, 95, 97, 98, 109, 150, 162, 167, 169, 171, 172, 175, 176, 177, 180, 181, 222, 268

Cathcart, Sir William 39

Catholic Presbyterian Church 30, 38, 110

Cedar Creek 54, 63

Cedar Springs, Battle of 124, 129

Chambers, John 118, 119

Charleston 13, 19, 20, 21, 27, 31, 32, 33, 34, 37, 38, 39, 40, 41, 43, 45, 47, 49, 50, 51, 52, 53, 54, 55, 57, 59, 63, 64, 71, 74, 75, 76, 78, 79, 87, 90, 92, 97, 125, 130, 146, 149, 151, 152, 153, 155, 157, 158, 161, 162, 163, 164, 165, 166, 167, 168, 169, 171, 173, 174, 177, 180, 182, 221

Charlotte, NC 64, 72, 74, 77, 78, 87, 111, 162, 165, 166, 169

Cheraw District 22, 48, 131

Cheraw Hill 48

Cherokee County 22, 141

Cherokee Expedition 52, 78, 79, 93, 113, 121

Cherokee Ford 141

Cherokee Indians 19, 20, 31, 33, 34, 64, 76, 157, 165

Cherokee Line 22, 129

Cherokee War 20, 21, 23, 76

Chester County 23, 29, 30, 36, 47, 53, 63, 79, 103, 113, 149, 150, 153, 207, 227

Chester District 31, 109, 117, 169, 172

Christian, William 33

Clarke, Elijah 141, 143

Clem's Branch of Sugar Creek 93, 121, 162, 167, 169, 170, 181

Clendennon, Thomas 105, 108

Clinton, James 58, 163

Clinton, Sir Henry 33, 38, 41, 43, 48, 49, 51, 52, 53, 87, 92, 127, 129, 130, 132, 143, 205, 221, 226

Cochrane, Charles 39

Coffell, Joseph 21

Coleman, Charles 61

Coleman, Christopher 35

Collins, Daniel 88, 158

Collins, James P. 50, 88, 115, 116, 120, 149, 158, 164, 207

Congaree Fort, Battle of 170

Cooper River 39

Coosawhatchie Bridge, Battle of 37, 38, 165

Cornwallis, Charles, Earl 43, 44, 46, 47, 48, 49, 51, 53, 54, 61, 63, 65, 68, 69, 72, 75, 76, 77, 78, 79, 85, 86, 89, 90, 92, 97, 98, 125, 127, 129, 130, 132, 143, 151, 153, 205, 206, 221, 222

Council of Safety 26, 27

Covenanters 30, 31, 71, 73

cowboys 65, 100

Cowpens, Battle of 13, 15, 147, 149, 150, 155, 156, 157, 178, 179, 226

Coxe's Mill, NC 139

Coxe's settlement, NC 130, 132

Craig, John 30, 63, 64, 67, 109, 110, 111, 115, 116, 120, 165, 205, 206, 207, 208, 246, 251, 252, 253, 254, 258, 261, 263, 269, 275, 278, 280, 285

Craighead, Alexander 29, 96

Craighead, Robert 96

Craighead, Thomas B. 96

Craven County 20, 59, 63

Crawford, Robert 100

Creek Indians 34

Cross Creek, NC 144

Crowder's Creek 27

Cummins, Francis 29

Cunningham, Moses 27

Cunningham, Patrick 31

Cunningham, Robert 27

Cunningham, William 67, 73, 132

Curry, Charles 105, 108

D

Davidson, William Lee 169

Davie, William Richardson 100, 136, 140

Davis, William 164

Deep River, NC 131, 132

De Kalb, Johann 74, 86, 98, 125, 130, 132, 133, 136, 139

Dickson, Michael 30, 110, 165, 208

District between the Broad and Catawba Rivers 23, 26, 29, 30, 35, 38, 43, 60, 63, 88, 140

District between the Broad and Saludy Rivers 23

District in the Upper Part of the New Acquisition 23

Doyle, Edward 166

Drake, _____ 37

Draper, Lyman C. 54, 71, 91, 120, 127, 132, 147, 208, 209

Drayton, William Henry 27, 28

Dunlap, James 130, 132, 143

Dutch Fork District 25, 26, 61, 74, 78, 130, 147

Dutch Fork Militia Regiment 52, 73, 78

E

Earle's Ford 128, 130, 132

Elbert, Samuel 35, 36

Ellet, Elizabeth 69, 71, 103, 105, 110, 284

Elliot, _____ 137

Emmerick, Andreas 51, 221

Emmerick's Chasseurs 51, 101, 221

Enoree River 78, 130, 144

Eutaw Springs, Battle of 177, 178, 179

F

Fairfield County 23, 60, 222

Fair Forest Creek 35, 52, 67, 122

Fair Forest Militia Regiment 38, 52, 67, 83

Falls, Gilbraith 169

Featherstone, John 55, 57

Featherstone, Richard 55

Featherstone, Sarah 55

Featherstone, William 55

Fergus, James 36

Ferguson, James 63, 65, 68, 89, 91, 102, 113, 114, 125, 146, 159, 161, 169, 175, 182

Ferguson, Moses 81

Ferguson, Patrick 39, 43, 122, 123, 126, 128, 143, 205, 221

Fergus Crossroads 82

Fishdam Ford, Battle of 130, 155, 171, 177

Fishing Creek 29, 52, 53, 54, 59, 63, 65, 68, 69, 70, 72, 77, 88, 91, 102, 110, 116, 121, 124, 126, 127, 164, 170, 175, 176, 179, 180, 181, 227

Fishing Creek, Battle of 130, 143, 146, 155, 159, 162, 168, 171, 228
Fitzpatrick, Thomas 28
Flat Rock Meeting House 29
Fleming, Alexander 91
Fleming, Elijah 91
Fleming, Robert 91, 227
Fleming, Robert Jr. 91
Fleming, William 37, 91
Fletchall, Thomas 27
Florida Expedition 34, 52, 158
Floyd, Abraham 78, 79, 102, 125
Floyd, Matthew 75, 78, 89, 90, 102, 109, 115, 120, 125, 129, 165
flying camp 174
Forbes, John 117, 166
Fort McIntosh, GA, Battle of 61
Fort Moultrie 50
Fort Ninety Six 31, 33, 43, 124
Fort Prince 130, 132
Fowler, James 29
Fraser, James 144
French and Indian War 19, 29, 51
Frost, James 40, 169

G

Gadsden, Christopher 26
Gaston, Alexander 38
Gaston, David 38, 147
Gaston, Ebenezer 38, 147
Gaston, Hugh 38, 62, 167, 207
Gaston, James 38
Gaston, John 38, 47, 54, 55, 68, 69, 103
Gaston, John Jr. 38
Gaston, Joseph 38, 47, 52, 54
Gaston, Robert 38
Gaston, William 29, 36, 38, 167
Gates, Horatio 74, 129, 136, 139, 143
General Assembly 28, 30, 34, 52, 61
Gentry, Clairborne 180
George, Weaver 88, 120

Georgetown 93
Georgia Campaign 37, 38, 52, 79
Georgia Militia 35, 129, 130
Georgia Refugees 73, 83, 87, 141, 181
Gibbs, Thomas 124
Gillespie brothers 98
Gordon, Samuel 58, 74, 164
Gore, Michael 169
Gowen's Old Fort 129
Graham, Joseph 68, 84, 95, 143
Great Canebrake, Battle of 31
Greene, Nathanael 74, 129, 146, 176, 181
Greenville 300
Greenville County 34
Guy, Jean Bratton 59
Guy, Samuel 59
Guyan Moore Creek 76

H

Haggins, William 100
Hagler's Branch of Sugar Creek 87, 93, 168, 172, 176, 177
Halifax County, NC 62
Hamilton, John 62, 91
Hammond, LeRoy 33, 34, 36
Hampton, Andrew 130, 141
Hampton, Edward 132
Hampton, Henry 61, 62
Hampton, John 61, 62
Hanging Rock 48, 99, 136, 140, 147, 162
Hanging Rock, Battle of 143, 150, 155, 162, 164, 165, 166, 168, 171, 172, 174, 176, 177, 178, 182, 183
Hanging Rock Creek 48, 133
Harbison, James 209
Harbison, William 209
Harris, George 73
Hart, Oliver 27, 289
Hawthorne, James 177, 183
Hayes, Joseph 96
Hayne, Isaac 59

Hemphill, James 168, 178

Henderson, John 81, 85, 164, 168

Henderson, William 32

Henry, _____ 106

Hill, Daniel Harvey 58

Hill, Hugh 124, 130

Hill, Jane "Nanny" McCall 59

Hill, William 58, 59, 63, 64, 74, 79, 81, 83, 87,
    88, 99, 101, 111, 117, 119, 121, 124, 126,
    136, 140, 150, 152, 158, 167, 168, 205,
    206, 207, 227

Hill, William Jr. 82

Hill's Iron Works 59, 67, 73, 75, 76, 77, 78, 79,
    80, 84, 158, 227

Hill's Iron Works, Battle of 82, 101, 164, 175

Hillhouse, William 166, 168

Hillsborough, NC 43, 86, 131, 144

Hope, J. M. 91

Hope, James 91

Houseman, Henry 54, 55, 57, 63, 102

Houston, John 35

Houston, Samuel 169

Hovenden, Richard 221, 226

Howe, Joseph 164, 171

Howe, Robert 34, 35

Howe, Sir William 218

Huck, Christian 13, 15, 51, 52, 64, 65, 68,
    79, 80, 83, 85, 88, 89, 101, 102, 105,
    108, 109, 112, 113, 114, 115, 120, 121,
    122, 125, 127, 130, 133, 147, 151, 215, 221,
    226, 228

Huck's Defeat 13, 14, 15, 111, 119, 121, 122, 123,
    126, 129, 130, 133, 134, 140, 143, 144, 146,
    147, 150, 151, 155, 157, 158, 159, 207, 209,
    213, 215, 227, 228

Huger, Benjamin 32

Huger, Isaac 32, 39, 41

Humphreys, Nicholas 124

Hunt, Benjamin 52, 101, 116, 119, 122, 124, 127,
    128, 153, 205, 206

Hunt, Isaac 215, 216

Hutt, _____ 225, 226

I

Indian Creek, NC 62, 68

Indian Wars 23, 45, 150

Innes, Alexander 130, 132, 144

J

Jackson, Andrew 100

Jackson, Robert 100

James, Jacob 221

James, William Dobein 70, 225, 284

Jamieson, James 67, 86, 91, 166, 168, 176, 177,
    208

Jefferson, Thomas 131

Jenkins, Thomas 170

Jenkins, William 170

Johnson, Uzal 126, 127

Johnston, James 85, 169

Jones, John 129, 130

Jones, Jonathan 69

Jones, Jonathan Jr. 170

Jones, William 40, 174

K

Kennedy, Robert M. 226

Kershaw, Eli 26, 38, 47

Kershaw, Joseph 152

Kershaw County 136, 143

Kettle Creek, GA, Battle of 35

Killough, Samuel 120, 179

Kings Mountain 155, 181

Kings Mountain, Battle of 13, 149, 150, 168,
    208

Kinlock, David 89, 90, 95, 97, 99, 101, 122,
    222

Kirkland, Moses 27

Kirkland, Thomas J. 226

Kirkpatrick, James 29

Kirkpatrick, Thomas 35

Knox, James 70, 132

L

Lacey, Edward Jr. 29, 35, 37, 61, 62, 79, 95, 99, 104, 110, 111, 112, 113, 116, 121, 139, 149, 150, 159, 165, 166, 167, 169, 173, 174, 175, 178, 182, 207, 208

Lacey, Edward Sr. 29, 95, 98, 112

Lacey, Reuben 99, 112

Lacey's Regiment 35, 40, 43, 67, 84, 104, 110, 150, 162, 169, 171, 173, 175

Lancaster County 44, 97, 100, 136, 176

Lancaster District 54, 170

Land, Ben 72, 73

Land's Ford 140

Land's Ford Road 79

Lando 30, 79

Laurens, John 165

Lawson's Fork 27

Leaper (Leeper), Robert 37, 181

Lenud's Ferry 41

Leonard, David 55

Leslie, Samuel 64

Lewis, Charles 70, 102, 122, 125

Lewisville 30

Lewis Turnout 104

Lincoln, Benjamin 35, 41, 49, 161, 180

Lincoln County, NC 61, 164, 169, 176

Lisle (Lyle), James 52, 67, 73, 83, 130

Lisle (Lyle), John 78, 102, 125, 129, 158

Little River 61, 67

Little River District 25, 144

Little River Militia Regiment 96

Locke, Francis 84, 85, 86, 165, 171, 172, 176, 177

Locke, Sarah Wallace 179

Lofton, Thomas 171

Logan, John H. 207, 209, 284

Long Cane Creek 33, 68

Lossing, Benson J. 146, 207, 284

Love, Alexander 28

Love, Andrew 35

Lower Fishing Creek Presbyterian Church 30, 63, 148

Lower Ninety Six Militia Regiment 33, 36

Loyalist militia 13, 43, 48, 51, 55, 57, 63, 64, 65, 75, 76, 77, 78, 82, 89, 90, 95, 99, 100, 101, 105, 114, 115, 122, 124, 125, 126, 127, 130, 141, 155, 158, 222, 227

Loyal American Regiment 51

Lynches River 49

M

Maitland, John 37

Martin, Edward 103, 105, 108, 117

Martin, James 67, 86, 172

Martin, Olive McClure 103

Martin, William 30, 31, 71, 73

Maxwell, William 180

Mayson, James 26

McAfee, Robert 28

McArthur, Archibald 131, 133

McCalla, David 53

McCalla, Samuel 53

McCaw, James 171

McClure, Charles 91

McClure, Hugh 38, 54, 57, 103, 165, 169, 174, 178

McClure, James 103, 105, 108, 117

McClure, John 38, 41, 47, 52, 54, 61, 62, 63, 67, 68, 70, 79, 83, 101, 102, 103, 104, 109, 110, 111, 112, 113, 116, 121, 122, 132, 140, 147, 149, 165, 167, 169, 174, 182, 183, 208, 227

McClure, Mary 110

McClure, Mary Gaston 103, 109

McClure's Rangers 38, 39, 41, 47, 57, 62, 64, 175, 281

McCool, John 177

McCrady, Edward 146

McDaniels, Thomas 55

McDonald, Alexander 226

McDonald's Ford, Catawba River 168

McDowell, Charles 128, 130, 132, 141

McDowell, Joseph 68, 77, 130, 144

McElwee, James 171, 182

McElwee, William 207

McGarity, William 57

McGirt, Daniel 38

McGregor, John 102, 122, 124, 128

McGriff, Patrick 29, 173

McIntosh, Alexander 32

McJunkin, Joseph 38, 52, 70, 73, 83, 87, 93, 99,
    120, 132

McKeown, Alexander 54

McKeown, Samuel 54

McMullen, John 175

McRandall, James 108

McRandall, Robert 105

McRee, James 29

Mecan, Thomas 97, 98

Mecklenburg County, NC 28, 59, 64, 72, 73,
    76, 84, 96, 97, 100, 144, 164, 168, 169,
    175, 179, 180

Mecklenburg County Militia Regiment 90,
    96, 140

Miles, Charles 29, 109, 116, 173, 227

Millar, John 177

Miller, John 162

Mills, Ambrose 130

Mills, John 67, 96, 112, 157, 172, 173

Mills, Mary 173

Mobley's Meeting House 61

Mobley's Meeting House, Battle of 61, 62, 67,
    112, 146, 158, 164, 165, 167, 169, 174, 178,
    182, 183

Moderators 21, 23, 25

Moffett, John 110, 120, 149, 150, 159, 164, 167,
    170, 171, 175, 177, 181, 182, 207, 208

Monck's Corner, Battle of 39, 47, 121, 167

Montgomery, ___ 73

Moore, Alexander 120, 208, 285

Moore, Isaac 113

Moore, James 114, 208, 285

Moore, John (Loyalist) 68, 76, 85, 89, 90, 92,
    97, 123, 171

Moore, John Jr. 105, 110, 117, 209, 285

Moore, John Sr. 105, 108, 113, 117

Moore, John Starr 111, 116, 117, 207, 208, 209,
    213, 285

Moore, Maurice 60, 62, 83, 99, 112, 114, 121,
    126, 147, 205, 206, 207

Moore, Nathan 105, 209, 285

Moore, Patrick 141

Moore, Samuel 105, 209, 285

Moore, William 105, 209, 285

Morrow, David 173, 174

Morrow, Mary 173

Moultrie, William 26, 33, 37, 121, 165

mounted militia 26, 29, 36, 38, 61, 65, 67, 100,
    101, 139, 161, 164, 169, 172, 173, 181, 182

mounted state troops 167, 172, 173

Murdoch, James 124

Musgrove's Mill, Battle of 144, 147, 150, 155

N

Neal (Neel, Neil), Andrew 27, 61, 62, 75, 81,
    83, 104, 109, 110, 113, 114, 130, 140, 147,
    164, 165, 166, 168, 171, 175, 177, 178, 181,
    182, 183, 208

Neal (Neel, Neil), Thomas Jr. 27, 147, 165

Neal (Neel, Neil), Thomas Sr. 27, 28, 29, 30, 31,
    34, 35, 37, 75, 78, 113, 130, 164, 165, 168,
    175

Neely, George 117

Newbern, NC 173

Newberry County 147

Newriver, General 100

New Acquisition District 22, 23, 26, 27, 29, 35,
    36, 37, 38, 57, 59, 61, 63, 67, 68, 69, 73, 76,
    84, 86, 87, 90, 97, 116, 124, 132, 227

New Acquisition Militia Regiment 27, 28, 30,
    31, 33, 34, 35, 36, 37, 57, 58, 59, 60, 63, 75,
    76, 78, 81, 113, 140, 152

New District Regiment 22, 130

New York Volunteers 13, 51, 63, 75, 77, 89, 101,
    102, 107, 114, 115, 122, 124, 125, 126, 127,
    146, 153, 154, 205, 206, 221, 222, 226, 227

Ninety Six District 22, 23, 25, 27, 31, 34, 54, 68, 74
Ninety Six Militia Regiment 31
Nixon, John 30, 36, 38, 104, 110, 120, 140, 147, 162, 208
Nixon, Mary Adair 104
North Carolina Militia 34, 35, 36, 39, 67, 74, 76, 84, 86, 87, 100, 128, 131, 169
North Fork of the Tyger River 130
North Pacolet River 128

O

Oconee County 33, 34
Oconee River 180
Old Nation Ford 95, 96, 98, 111, 129, 140, 162, 207
Orangeburg 37, 165
Orangeburg District 27
Owens, John 63, 102, 112, 119, 125, 135

P

Pacolet River 32, 141
Padget's Creek 123, 126
Pagan, Alexander 30, 38, 67, 96, 110, 171
Pagan, Mary Mills 172
Parker, Sir Peter 33
Pattison, Robert 175
Patton, John 176
Patton, Robert 77, 83
Pearis, Richard 54, 68, 74, 92
Pendleton District 148
Peters, John 177
Petit, ____ 137
Pickens, Andrew 33, 35, 54, 58, 68
Pickens County 34
Pickens District 31, 165
Polk, Ezekiel 26, 31
Poor Hill 93, 181
Porterfield, Charles 87, 131
Port Royal Island 37

Prevost, Augustine 34, 35, 37
Prevost, Mark 36
Price, Isaac 87
Price, John 104, 111, 112
Prince 172, 173
Prince of Wales Regiment 89
Provincial Congress 23, 26, 28, 30, 31, 33, 52
Purysburg 35

Q

Queen's Rangers 221
Quinn's Road 90

R

Rainey, Samuel 105
Rainey, Thomas 59
Ramsay, David 206, 225, 283
Ramsour's Mill, NC 61, 68, 76, 80, 84, 85
Ramsour's Mill, NC, Battle of 86, 87, 89, 90, 92, 97, 144, 147, 164, 165, 169, 171, 172, 176, 177, 179
ranger 245
rangers 26, 27, 31, 38, 76, 122, 139, 172, 173
Rawdon, Francis, Lord 48, 50, 58, 63, 64, 65, 72, 74, 77, 89, 90, 95, 97, 98, 122, 124, 127, 130, 133, 140, 143, 153, 154, 161, 205, 221, 222, 226
Rea, Henry 67, 176
Read, James 113, 114, 115
Reedy River 31, 33, 175
Regulators 21, 23, 25
Regulator War 27, 45
Richardson, Richard 25, 27, 28, 31, 32, 34
Richardson, William 100
Richburg 79
Richland County 23
Robertson, ____ 102, 166
Robertson, Charles 141
Roberts Presbyterian Church 148
Robins, Thomas 29

Robinson, Joseph 27, 177

Robison, ____ 102, 165

Robison, William 67, 177

Rocky Allison Creek 81

Rocky Comfort Creek, GA 36

Rocky Creek 30, 48, 53, 54, 55, 57, 63, 71, 72, 102, 104

Rocky Creek Presbyterian Church 30, 148

Rocky Mount 48, 51, 54, 55, 62, 63, 65, 67, 70, 73, 75, 76, 78, 79, 81, 85, 89, 95, 96, 97, 98, 99, 102, 104, 117, 119, 120, 122, 124, 126, 128, 136, 140, 147, 174, 205, 222, 227

Rocky Mount, Battle of 141, 143, 155, 162, 164, 166, 167, 168, 169, 170, 171, 172, 174, 175, 176, 177, 181, 182, 183

Rocky Mount Militia Regiment (Loyalist) 63, 99, 100, 102

Rocky Mount Road 59, 102, 111, 112, 121

Rodman 103

Ross, Alexander 72, 95, 98

Ross, Francis 28, 33, 35, 36, 37, 78

Ross, George 177

Rowan, Benjamin 82, 87

Rowan County, NC 59, 84, 96, 97, 100, 180

Rowan County Militia Regiment 90, 100, 140, 171

Royal American Regiment 51

Royal North Carolina Regiment 62, 76, 91

Rugeley, Henry 99, 100

Rugeley's Mill 97

Rutherford, Griffith 33, 34, 80, 83, 84, 85, 86, 87, 92, 96, 131, 171, 180

Rutherford County, NC 164

Rutledge, John 38, 43, 44, 85, 169

S

Sadler, David 114, 117, 178

Sadler, Elisa 107, 158

Sadler, Richard 165

Salisbury, NC 67, 72, 74, 77, 78, 80, 85, 86, 100, 131, 165

Salisbury District Militia Brigade 80

Saluda River 31, 67

Sam, Miller 115, 120

Sandy River 29, 54, 99, 153

Sandy River Baptist Church 29, 30

Santee River 32, 39, 41, 44, 167

Savage, John 31

Savannah, GA 35, 37, 54, 78, 102

Savannah River 20, 25, 34, 35, 36, 37

Scoffelites 21, 25

Scotch-Irish 14, 19, 25, 27, 28, 29, 30, 38, 44, 45, 53, 59, 63, 71, 97, 104, 222

Seneca Fort 165, 173

Seneca Old Town 33

Seneca River 33

Shelby, Isaac 141, 143, 144, 150

Shiloh Methodist Church 132

Shirer's Ferry 61, 74

Siege of Fort Ninety Six 176

Simpson, John 29, 30, 31, 65, 70, 71, 96, 139, 148, 158, 227

Simpson, Mary Remer 69

Simpson's Meeting House 30, 63, 64

Snow Campaign 32, 38, 52, 61, 75, 93

South Carolina Militia 35, 41, 80, 86, 87, 90, 96, 150, 169, 171, 172

South Carolina Royalists 144

South Fork of Fishing Creek 29, 30, 59, 101, 105, 107, 114, 148, 209, 211, 213

South Fork of the Catawba River 85

South Pacolet River 129

Spartanburg (city) 124

Spartanburg County 22, 130, 132

Spartanburg District 164

Spartan District 25, 27, 35, 52, 122, 124, 126, 128, 130, 132, 141, 143, 144

Spartan Militia Regiment 52, 73, 83

St. Augustine, FL 34, 151

Stallions (Stallings) Plantation, Battle of 164, 179

Stapleton, Wynne 124

Starved Valley 93

state troops 173

Stedman, Alexander 222

Stedman, Charles 65

Steedham. Adam 67

Steele Creek, NC/SC 84, 87, 129, 175

Steele Creek Presbyterian Church, NC 84

Steel (Steele), John 38, 47, 54, 91, 110, 120, 165, 169, 174

Stephenson, James 116, 178, 227

Stephenson, Rossanna 178

Stinson, Daniel Green 69, 71, 99, 103, 105, 111, 117, 211, 213, 284

Stokes County, NC 180

Stono Ferry, Battle of 37, 38, 61, 100, 157, 158, 159, 165, 178

Strong, Christopher 68

Strong, Janet "Jenney" 68, 69

Strong, William 69, 115, 227

Stroud, William Jr. 57

Sugar Creek, NC/SC 87, 96

Sullivan's Island 37

Sullivan's Island, Battle of 33, 38, 61

Sumter, Thomas 13, 30, 32, 33, 34, 44, 79, 83, 85, 86, 87, 98, 130, 133, 139, 140, 143, 150, 151, 161, 162, 164, 165, 166, 167, 168, 169, 170, 171, 172, 173, 175, 176, 178, 181, 182, 206, 209

Sumter, Tom 44

Sumter's Brigade 30, 85, 95, 99, 101, 121, 129, 140, 143, 146, 149, 150, 151, 168, 172, 173, 176, 177, 180

Susy Bole's Branch of Turkey Creek 29

Swaine, Nathaniel 52

T

Tarleton, Banastre 39, 44, 45, 46, 48, 52, 87, 127, 129, 133, 143, 205, 221

Tarleton's Quarter 46

Taylor, Thomas 152

Tennent, William 27, 28

Thicketty Creek 35, 141

Thicketty Fort, Battle of 141

Thomas, Jane Black 124

Thomas, John Jr. 73, 83, 124, 128, 130

Thomas, John Sr. 27, 31, 52, 67, 73, 124

Thompson, Robert 176

Thomson, William 26, 31, 38, 47, 61

Thomson's Rangers 26, 31, 33, 61

Tool's Fork of Fishing Creek 227

Tryon County, NC 27, 59, 76, 92

Tryon County Militia Regiment 27, 130

Tuck, John 225, 226

Tuckasegee Ford, NC 73, 80, 83

Tugaloo River 33

Turkey Creek 29, 76, 77, 88, 90

Turkey Creek Volunteer Militia Company 29

Turnbull, George 50, 51, 62, 70, 75, 77, 78, 79, 83, 85, 89, 90, 95, 96, 97, 107, 122, 124, 127, 153, 154, 169, 172, 175, 176, 177, 221, 222, 226

Turner, Dr. 121

Turner, William T. 63, 99

Twiggs, John 85

Tyger River 78, 123, 130

U

Union (city) 67

Union County 22, 52, 76, 123

Union District 164

Upper District Militia Regiment (Loyalist) 78, 102, 129

Upper Fishing Creek Presbyterian Church 29, 30, 38, 62, 63, 64, 68, 69, 71, 102, 115, 148, 227

V

Vernon, Nathaniel Jr. 221

Volunteers of Ireland 48, 124, 221, 226

W

Wade, George 55, 97

Wade, Joe 57

Wade's Mill 97
Walker, Philip 30
Walker's Crossroads 104
Walker's Mill 30, 65, 79, 102, 103, 110, 207
Wallace, D. W. 173
Wallace, John 121, 179
Wallace, Samuel 180
Washington, George 74, 129, 178
Washington, William 41, 121
Wateree Ferry, Battle of 143
Watson, Samuel 26, 35, 37, 57, 58, 60, 75, 164, 167, 168
Watson, Samuel Jr. 181, 182
Watt 105
Waxhaws, Battle of the 44, 46, 64, 71, 76, 95, 222
Waxhaw Creek 64, 100, 136
Waxhaw Presbyterian Church 44, 45, 96, 154
Waxhaw settlement 44, 58, 64, 72, 77, 78, 80, 96, 98, 99, 100, 101, 109, 122, 140, 176
Webster, James 133
Welsh, Nicholas 76, 90, 123
White's Mill 30, 181
Willet, Walter 221
Williams, Daniel 88, 96, 120
Williams, James 96, 144
Williamson, Adam 108
Williamson, Andrew 31, 33, 34, 35, 36, 37, 54, 58, 68, 92, 121, 165, 178
Williamson, Anne Starr 209, 285
Williamson, George 108
Williamson, James 13, 107, 108, 114, 158, 209, 213, 227
Williamson, James Jr. 108
Williamson, James Sr. 285
Williamson, John 108
Williamson, Samuel 108, 113, 114, 148, 209, 213, 285
Williamson's Brigade 33
Williamson's Lane 13, 107, 113, 165, 176, 182
Williamson's Plantation, Battle of 13, 114, 119, 124, 162, 167, 168, 171, 172, 174, 175, 177, 183, 205, 227

Wilson, Robert 87, 172, 285
Winn, John 61, 79
Winn, Richard 26, 61, 62, 63, 67, 70, 77, 83, 107, 109, 111, 112, 113, 115, 116, 117, 119, 121, 136, 138, 150, 151, 164, 174, 206, 207, 208, 222
Winnsboro 61, 164
Wofford's Iron Works, Battle of 143
Woods, Thomas 182
Wylie, Francis 182
Wylie, James 57
Wylie, John 225
Wylie, Samuel 225, 226
Wylie, William 121

Y

Yadkin River, NC 86, 131, 176, 177
Yager (rifle) 174
York County 13, 22, 23, 28, 29, 58, 59, 76, 113, 150, 152, 165, 168, 170, 175, 178, 179, 180, 207, 227, 295
York District 31, 109, 117, 164, 165, 168, 169, 170, 176, 177
Young, John 67
Young, Thomas 67

About the Author

Michael C. Scoggins is a research historian and curatorial assistant for the Culture & Heritage Museums of York County, South Carolina. He has degrees in science, engineering technology and history from the University of South Carolina, York Technical College and Winthrop University, and was employed as an electronics engineer for twenty years before changing careers to pursue his lifelong interest in military history and Southern history. In addition to *The Day It Rained Militia*, he also wrote the introduction and bibliography for The History Press re-edition of Benson J. Lossing's 1889 classic *Hours with the Living Men and Women of the Revolution* (May 2005) and is co-author, along with Dr. Bobby G. Moss, of the highly acclaimed *African-American Patriots in the Southern Campaign of the American Revolution* and the forthcoming *African-American Loyalists in the Southern Campaign of the American Revolution*.

Scoggins has contributed articles to the *South Carolina Encyclopedia* and numerous historical and genealogical journals, and is a frequent lecturer and speaker on topics of local and regional history, the Revolutionary War in the Carolinas and the War between the States. In addition to being a military historian, he is also an amateur radio operator, electronics technician, musician and aviation enthusiast, and repairs and restores antique electronics gear as a hobby. He is a member of the Company of Military Historians, the Brigade of the American Revolution, the Scotch-Irish Society of the USA, the Amateur Radio Relay League and is district representative for the Confederation of South Carolina Local Historical Societies. Scoggins lives near McConnells, South Carolina, the site of Historic Brattonsville and the Battle of Huck's Defeat, and he is a direct descendant of the Scotch-Irish, English and German pioneers who settled in the Southern Piedmont area during the late eighteenth and early nineteenth centuries.